Mountain Voices

I believe that man will not merely endure: he will prevail.

—William Faulkner
Nobel Prize Acceptance Speech,
December 10, 1950

Mountain Voices

A Legacy of the Blue Ridge and Great Smokies

by Warren Moore

foreword by Sam Ervin

JOHN F. BLAIR, PUBLISHER

1406 Plaza Drive

Winston-Salem, North Carolina 27103

Library of Congress Cataloging-in-Publication Data

Moore, Irene Warren.
      Mountain Voices: a legacy of the Blue Ridge and Great Smokies/compiled,
      photographed, and edited by Warren Moore.—3rd edition.
         p.   cm.
      ISBN 0-9654911-0-2 hardcover.
      ISBN 0-9654911-1-0 paperback.
1. Appalachian Mountains, Southern—Social life and customs. 2. North Carolina—Social life and customs. 3. Mountain whites (Southern states)—Appalachian Mountains, Southern-—Social life and customs. 4. Mountain whites (Southern states)—North Carolina-—Social life and customs. 5. Oral history I. Title

F217.A65M66 1988   88-11261
975-dc19   CIP

Manufactured in the United States of America by R. R. Donnelley & S
Third Edition/First Printing

Dedicated to my parents,
Irene and Beverly Moore,
and the people of the
Southern Appalachian Mountains.

Contents

Foreword

Warren Moore has compiled a fascinating story in her book, *Mountain Voices*.

Her story reveals the ways of life of the people who made their homes in the Appalachian Mountains of North Carolina after the first persons of British and European ancestry invaded this area and erected cabins in it.

This area cannot be defined with exactness. It may be deemed, however, to embrace virtually all the rural portions of the present counties of Alleghany, Ashe, Watauga, Avery, Mitchell, Yancey, Buncombe, Madison, Henderson, Transylvania, Haywood, Jackson, Macon, Swain, Graham, Clay, and Cherokee and parts of the adjacent counties of Surry, Wilkes, Alexander, Caldwell, Burke, McDowell, Rutherford, and Polk.

Grandfather, Table Rock, Mount Mitchell, Chimney Rock, Clingman's Dome, and many other distinctive peaks, most of which are higher than any mountains in the United States east of the Rockies, and the New River, the Estatoe, the Linville, the French Broad, the Pigeon, and the Tuckasegee, and their tributaries which once teemed with fish, and the coves, forests, and fields which once swarmed with wildlife, have always made the Appalachian Mountains of North Carolina a place of unsurpassed charm and beauty.

Early settlers traveling westward in quest of new homesites were often enthralled by their charm and beauty, and built their cabins among them instead of journeying further to more accessible and arable lands in the West.

They and their descendants paid severe penalties for their so doing. They lived in a state of comparative isolation and suffered many privations for several successive gen-

erations. Owing to the inadequacy of roads and other means of communication, the people of the mountains had little contact with the outside world during these generations.

Despite their charm and beauty, winters in the Appalachian Mountains were harsh. The economic opportunities afforded at any time to those who dwelt among them were limited, and few of them were able to accumulate any wealth.

Their farms were small, and usually rocky and lacking in fertility. They had to rely on their personal exertions and the simple things around them for the means of maintaining life.

They kept a few horses and mules for heavy labor, transportation, and travel. They kept a few sheep for woolen clothing, and raised a small amount of flax for thread and woven fabrics. They kept a few cows, pigs, chickens, guineas, and beehives, and maintained a few apple, peach, and plum trees to supplement the produce of their small gardens. They depended in large measure on domestic herbs and roots for remedies for their ailments. As a consequence of necessity and their own ingenuity, they became independent of the outside world for everything except such items as coffee and tools.

The schools their children attended were woefully inadequate, and few of them were able to send their sons to the University of North Carolina, Wake Forest College, and other outside institutions of higher learning.

Virtually all of them were members of Protestant churches, and habitually heard texts from the King James version of the Bible expounded by preachers whose education and training, if any, for their divine tasks were rather scanty.

In seasons of relaxation, they made merry with song, the fiddle, the harp, the dulcimer, and other musical instruments; log-rollings, corn-shuckings, quilting parties, athletic contests; and country and clog dancing. Their love of music inspired Scotty Wiseman and his wife, Lula Belle, natives of Avery County, to give us their beautiful love song: "Have I Told You Lately That I Love You?"

As a result of their privations and isolation, North Carolina mountaineers became ingenious, self-reliant, and individualistic in the highest degree.

Although they were fiercely independent, they would faithfully heed the advice of those who enjoyed their confidence. The eloquent Zeb Vance, a product of Buncombe County, was their outstanding hero.

Since they lacked the large bodies of fertile land of other parts of the South, slavery was of little concern to most of the mountainous counties.

When the war clouds were gathering just before the Civil War, Vance, a lover of the old Union, spoke against secession in some of the mountainous counties. While he was speaking in Madison County in opposition to secession, someone dashed up and handed him a copy of Lincoln's call for North Carolina to furnish troops to help the Union subjugate the then seceded states.

As Vance was later accustomed to remark his right arm had gone up in a gesture for the Union, but came down for the Confederacy. As a result of Lincoln's call, he saw no alternative to secession.

After that occasion, Vance spoke in other mountain counties for secession, but was unable to return to those in which he had advocated the preservation of the Union.

Old-timers cited these events to explain why a few mountain counties favored the Union, but the others fought gallantly for the Confederacy.

As a child in Morganton, I became acquainted with some mountaineers who brought their legal problems to my father. As a youth, I got to know others when I fished for trout in mountain streams. As a young lawyer, I met multitudes of them while helping my father try cases in mountain courts. Over the years, I formed enduring friendships with men of the mountains whose strength matched their beautiful mountains.

As a result of these personal experiences, I have long understood and loved the people of the Appalachian Mountains of North Carolina.

Consequently, I have resented the writers from outside areas who neither knew nor understood the mountaineers, and who wrote books characterizing them as stereotyped identical beings whose vices vastly outweighed their virtues.

These outsiders ignored the truth that the North Carolina mountaineers, like other people, were the products of their heredity, their environment, and their own exertions, and that they inherited the virtues of their English, Scotch-Irish, German, and Huguenot ancestors, and that their privations and isolation converted them into as ingenious, self-reliant, and individualistic beings as the earth has ever known.

Although a native North Carolinian, Warren was born, reared, and educated outside the mountainous area. She has not repeated the errors of other outside writers. In gathering materials for her book, she visited men and women of the mountains who were the product of generations of privation and isolation in their homes and places of work, acquired an understanding, affection, and admiration for them, and interviewed them respecting their own experiences and what their ancestors told them about theirs. Her book is based on revealing and captivating excerpts from these interviews.

Many changes have occurred in the Appalachian Mountains of North Carolina during the recent past. State Superintendents of Public Instruction James Y. Joyner, Arch T. Allen, and other enlightened educators have supervised the conversion of their public schools into institutions adequate for the instruction of the children of the mountainous region.

Appalachian State University, Western Carolina University, Mars Hill College, The University of North Carolina at Asheville, and Brevard College are offering the young men and women of the area the benefits of higher education.

Dependable highways make the region accessible to all, and industry has invaded the mountainous counties and is opening many economic doors to the mountaineers.

It is devoutly to be wished, however that despite these beneficial changes, the descendants of the people of the Appalachian Mountains of North Carolina of the era of privation and isolation will retain throughout the future the self-reliant and individualistic spirits of their ancestors.

SAM J. ERVIN, JR.
former United States senator

Preface

Warren Moore with mountain cougar cub.

Photo credit: Jim Morton

The mountains of North Carolina have always been special to me. I am from North Carolina originally and have visited the mountains all my life. Many of my years growing up were spent in these mountains as a "summer person." Later, while working at a ski resort during a winter there, I came to know many of the native people. Over the years, I have developed a deep appreciation for the people in the area, as well as the natural beauty that lures in most outsiders.

About six years ago, the idea for this book began to take shape. While living and teaching in New York City, I began interviewing the people and photographing their mountains during vacations and my occasional trips back to the region. At the time, I felt fairly familiar with this area, but soon found out how little I really did know about it. The realization came that a move back to North Carolina would be essential if I were going to cover this vast territory to any viable extent. I also came to understand how unique the area was. The physical attributes of the land here are magnificent; but it is the people, as in most places, who make the area rich.

Since then, I have traveled extensively throughout the North Carolina mountains, meeting people and gathering both oral histories and taped interviews over the course of five years. I have photographed the people, their farms, towns, scenic spots, and visual details of their daily living situations. *Mountain Voices* is a combination of these photographs and portions of the oral histories. It is an attempt to help preserve the rich flavor and culture of this area in a realistic way.

The people here are fiercely independent. The rugged individualistic nature of these mountaineers has helped them survive in an area of great hardship. Most have a lively sense of humor and have developed a great deal of patience in coping with the harsh aspects of life and human nature. It is difficult to generalize about the people in this area because they are quite different from one another from place to place, but a few common character traits do surface. Most of them are, by nature, very hard workers, both men and women. They are proud of their heritage and deeply love their part of the country. I found tremendous strength in these individuals, even the frailest ones.

I concentrated on the North Carolina section of the Appalachian Mountains because limits had to be set somewhere. This section can be used as a window through which a view of the culture prevalent throughout the extended area may be seen. The territory includes large parts of the Blue Ridge, Balsams, Black Mountains, Brushy Mountains, the Great Smokies, and other ranges. Although there are differences among all of these areas, many similarities exist here as well as in the mountainous parts of Virginia, Tennessee, and northern Georgia. Because of the geography and terrain, most of the people in the Southern Appalachians have lived a more isolated life than people in other rural areas, which has resulted in a kind of self-preservation of their culture.

Many elements of this culture have been taken out of context in the past, which has often resulted in a distorted view of the area. My hope is that this book will put many of these elements back into their proper perspective and help dispel some of the erroneous notions often connected with the people in this part of the Southern Appalachian Mountains.

As I traveled through the mountains, my views of the area and the people began to change, enhanced by both the accounts that I heard and from actually experiencing the scenes of daily life. I came to understand the comforts of sitting by a wood-burning stove waiting for the cornbread to come out and savoring the aromas that came from the pots on top. Even going to an outhouse became less and less of a bother, as I came to understand how people could become used to this inconvenience. While most people had normal bathrooms in the house, some people, particularly older ones in remote places, just didn't see the need to change things that worked well enough already. Their homes were very comfortable. Their running water often came from a spring, and much of the food came from their own gardens. There was a feeling of contentment and self-sufficiency.

I spent many hours driving alone through the mountains. It took a long time to get to various places, and much of the territory was unfamiliar to me. In spending so much time alone, either hiking or driving on back roads that were sparsely populated, I found it easy to go back in time and imagine what life here must have been like.

I often stayed in motels in unfamiliar places. At these times, I could readily identify with the traveling salesman. At other times, however, I was fortunate enough to stay with friends whom I had known from years past, with wonderful mountain families whom I had interviewed, or in many of the lovely inns sprinkled throughout the mountains. In all of these places, the people involved were encouraging and helped to spur me on in this endeavor. Any task such as this is bound to take a long time to carry out and put together properly. Loneliness and discouragement would take their toll from time to time. But always during those low periods, I would interview some-one who imparted such wisdom or displayed a terrific sense of humor, or I would look out over such an inspiring view of mountain ranges, that I would find myself again driven to continue with the project.

There was only enough room in this volume to include a small part of the material gathered during the research. I hope, however, that the voices and pictures presented here will come together to provide a verbal and visual portrait of this very special sec-tion of rural America. Some of the photographs do not always belong to the people whose comments surround or accompany them, as they have been arranged to per-tain to the content of what is being discussed and to carry the story over in a visual way. (A photographic index of people is provided at the end of the book, in order that you might identify more fully with the particular speakers during the course of your reading.) The text is compiled from interviews and the speaker is identified at the end of the paragraph. The smaller italic text is my own commentary.

I will always be thankful that I was able to carry out this project. My own life has been thoroughly enriched by the experience. I have met so many wonderful people and seen such beautiful sights. I have learned a great deal about the mountains, the culture, and rural philosophy in general. Most important, however, are the wonderful friends I have made in the process. The people interviewed made great efforts in guid-ing me through this area. They have been supportive, and they have cared. This is their book. I hope it reflects their warmth, sincerity, intelligence, and vitality.

The North Carolina of *Mountain Voices*

Damascus

Volney

Galax

VIRGINIA

NORTH CAROLINA

ASHE

Piney Creek

Cumberland Knob

Low Gap

Mount Airy

Mountain City

Shatley Springs

ALLEGHANY

Sparta

SURRY

Ashland

Jefferson

Roaring Gap

Mountain Park

Glendale Springs

McGrady

Traphill

Zionville

Halls Mill

WATAUGA

Boone

BLUE RIDGE PARKWAY

WILKES

Ronda

Valle Crucis

Deep Gap

Aho

Millers Creek

Banner Elk

Seven Devils

Blowing Rock

Wilkesboro

Erwin

Roan Mountain

Elk Park

Cranberry

Grandfather Mountain

Ferguson

Brushy Mountains

Buladean

Minneapolis

Globe

Boomer

MITCHELL

Newland

Linville

Patterson

Kings Creek

ALEXANDER

Sioux

AVERY

Plumtree

Crossnore

YANCEY

Bakersville

Brown Mountain

CALDWELL

Taylorsville

Bald Creek

Burnsville

Ledger

Penland

BLUE RIDGE PARKWAY

Lenoir

iss

Spruce Pine

Table Rock

s Hill

Celo

Little Switzerland

Table Rock

Woodlawn

BURKE

arnardsville

Mount Mitchell

Lake Tahoma

Lake Nebo

erville

MBE

McDOWELL

Marion

Morganton

Black Mountain

Old Fort

Sugar Hill

airview

MOUNTAINS

Gerton

Chimney Rock

Bat Cave

Lake Lure

Lake Lure

RUTHERFORD

her

RIDGE

Lake Lure

RSON

Rutherfordton

POLK

Flat Rock

Mill Spring

Tuxedo

Lake Summit

Tyron

Area of North Carolina shown on map

A Cove is
Larger Than a Hollow

The Terrain and the Elements

THE LAND LOOMS UP OVER EVERYTHING HERE. As I drive through these mountains, I am constantly confronted with the land: soaring mountain peaks; sharp blind curves in the road; deep valleys separating the ridges; smaller recessions or hollows with houses tucked in them; winding streams and larger creeks with dangerous, protruding boulders. At other times a wide, flowing river suddenly appears or a sheer wall of rock with trees growing up all along the top. There are waterfalls and magical summer wildflowers everywhere. In the fall the peaks and valleys seem on fire with the glorious colors of the leaves, particularly in the light of late afternoon. Later, after many of the leaves have fallen, rime ice (frozen frost) covers the tree limbs as if an omen of the coming winter. And when winter finally arrives, the snows are so beautiful. Roads are hazardous, but one gets used to getting around in ice and snow here. It has always been that way. In winter streams of rock ice form on the cliffs and craggy protrusions along roads and trails where water has seeped down, giving the impression of frozen waterfalls.

It's no wonder that these people have always been so attached to the land. It has been their main source of sustenance, and different facets of it just dramatically appear in front of them all the time.

The land here can't be avoided. It becomes part of you. There is a haunting, yet somehow comforting, feeling that comes when looking out over vast expanses of rolling layers of mountain ridges, as in the Blue Ridge, or the craggier and steeper sections of the Smokies where the mountains seem closer together.

When clouds roll in over the mountains, they sometimes hang heavily among the ridges, creating thick mists. A cloud will run into a mountain and either ooze into it or have its bottom ripped off by a peak. When the winds are high, massive cloud formations swirl over the cliffs. Thunder and lightning crash all around, and the violence of the terrain becomes overwhelming. I once watched such a storm from Mount Mitchell and felt the turbulence rumble through me. But my feelings of awe and excitement

(Opposite) Frosted ridge in early spring, Smoky Mountains

were soon overshadowed by the realization that I had better head for shelter before the storm reached me.

At other times the clouds create fog that blankets everything, especially in the morning. The effect can be ominous or mystical. Driving at night along winding roads, the black masses of mountains come up all around. They look like solid shadows, dark against the sky. Then above that, bright stars appear and most times the moon in one of its stages. Sometimes clouds move across. At these times mysterious feelings and unspoken, exhilarating thoughts flow in and out.

The beauty encountered in daily life here has obviously contributed to the tolerance with which these people have dealt with the harsh and isolated conditions. It also added a mysticism to much of their folklore and enriched their lives. Their feeling of being a part of the land has helped many of them understand what is really important in life and what is not. Because of this, many of these people have stayed instead of moving on to places where making a living might have been easier—or they have gone away only to come home again.

I remember walking along beside Raymond Presnell and hearing him describe the feel and taste of the air on Beech Mountain when he was a child. The gleam in his eyes and the tone of his voice carried me back to a time that I had never even known. He was showing me his multitude of beehives, and we were surrounded by mountains. Grandfather Mountain was off in the distance. I thought it was wonderful here, but somehow his description made me feel that the air on his mountain years ago was cleaner and fresher than the air around us now, and I had been able to breathe in a little bit of it, too.

In the late spring, pale green colors begin to appear as the snow melts. Around April, light green leaves start to unfold, giving a freshness to everything, and this is beautifully contrasted with the magical frozen frost that still covers the highest elevations. One spring day, a Cherokee friend guided some of us over roads through the reservation. He pointed out hedgehogs and places where wild boars had been rooting near the roadside. As we ascended to the higher peaks in the Smoky Mountain National Park, we became spellbound by the frost that soon covered the rocks and coated the trees. We were amazed—we had just left a spring day and entered an icy fairyland. He explained to us that the Indians describe this as "where the clouds froze on the trees." By late April or May, spring would be in full force with dogwood flowers, mountain laurel blooms, and apple blossoms. All of this would then make way for the lush green of summer, when the days are warm and the nights are chilly.

One summer day, I had gone for a hike in the woods. The trail led deep into the forest. Hazy, warm light filtered in through the trees above. I couldn't help noticing the light green glow of new moss growing along the trail and clumps of luscious ferns along the banks and under trees. Patches of yellow or sometimes orange blossoms of jewel weed would light up different sections way out in the woods. A squirrel scampered by and stopped to linger on a log for a while. He wasn't bothered by me at first. After he left, I walked over and kicked away the moist log. Water was bubbling up from

(Opposite) Outbuildings at Shular farm, Caney Fork, Jackson County

underneath the ground. Here was a fresh mountain spring, and he had discovered it! The trail kept winding up toward the top of the mountain. I saw signs of a path curving away from the trail through a hedge of rhododendron bushes and decided to make a detour. After wedging my way through the leaves and branches, I suddenly found myself on the side of a mountain overlooking blue-green layers of ridges folding over one another out to the end of the horizon.

The ever-changing land is present everywhere here.

Lake Glenville, Jackson County

THE LAND

Sometimes I think about how peaceful it was and about one of those beautiful mountain streams unspoiled. We used to fish right along with the Indians—no sign of contamination or pollution. You could just drink out of most of the streams without any fear. And the beauty of the mountains when you got really out in the mountains away from so-called civilization, I just wish sometimes we could go back to that. But, we can't; I really would like to build a fence around Western North Carolina. *(Dan Moore)*

Now you take people that've never seen these mountains, they couldn't believe it. You can start here and walk about all day and never get to the top of one. And you take people that have been on level ground all their lives and never been away and in the mountains, they can't believe what these mountains are like. *(Walter Winebarger)*

I think it's real nice here. Last year we went to the Caribbean. Have you been down there? I thought that was kind of level in general. Why, then the next thing we knew, we were on a mountain 5,000 feet high, with coconuts and bananas, sugar cane. Beat all I ever seen! *(Tom Oates)*

It's where I grew up. If you grew up in the city, you probably like it. But I would die. They'd just have to take me somewhere. I couldn't stay in the city. There wouldn't be any way. You'll find more common people in the mountains than anywhere you go. You could be an outright stranger, never been in this country, and come into the mountains; and the bigger part of them are going to treat you just like you would your own. That's one reason that I like the mountains better than I do the cities. You can go into these cities and ask about somebody that stayed in it if you want to find them. They don't know who stayed there. They don't know their next door neighbor. You come into these mountains and you can ask about anybody you want and they'll tell you where he is.

Another reason I like the mountains is it isn't crowded. It's getting crowded and it's going to get worse. You know, the tourists are coming in and it's going to get a lot worse; but it'll never be as bad as the city. I worked up in Buffalo, New York, and I wouldn't go back to New York if they gave me all of the state. Even if they said, "You come back; you can have the whole thing," I'd just say, "You keep it."

Another thing in the mountains is you can go out and enjoy. If you like to go out here and take your dog and let him run, you can hear him. You can go out here and hunt. If you are in town, right there you sit. That's one thing now that I've always regretted—where people raised children in town. The poor little younguns haven't got anywhere to enjoy themselves except shut up in a little lot, a little pen. *(Stanley Hicks)*

I really enjoy the different seasons in the mountains because they come more unique here. As springtime comes, it brings an abundance of flowers and it brings very moderate weather, not too extreme either way. We may have some, but it makes it the best when the bad does go away and we do have some sunshine. It makes everything more beautiful.

5

When autumn comes, the leaves color and the air is nice and balmy, just nice to be out there. It's no doubt the most beautiful place to enjoy yourself in the world. The streams generally trickle down over the rocks and look refreshing. And then, the rocks on the hills and the cliffs that you see, and people up on them rambling about, like on the Beech [Mountain] where I was raised. *(Raymond Presnell)*

My dad and I have been places in the Smoky Mountains; we've been up the left-hand prong of the Deep Creek which has the only other section of virgin timber in the mountains, besides the Joyce Kilmer Memorial Forest, which is in the Blue Ridge. You can't see the sunshine at twelve o'clock (noon). It gets dark; it gets dark, dark. I mean it's beautiful back in there. Another place, Slick Rock, is on the Tennessee-North Carolina border near Chattanooga. That's how far south and west you have to

go. It's below Lake Chilhowee, and it takes you roughly three hours to walk back in there. Now that's hard walking. But, we used to take off and try to get to a certain point in there where a spring bubbled up. That's where we'd stop and drink water, by daylight every morning, or every time we'd go in there. And that's the only place that I've ever seen when the sun rose over that particular peak and shone through, it made a perfect cross. I mean it was perfect, and it hung right there in the air, and it would float. Of course, as the sun moved, it moved. It'd make you feel kind of funny. *(Mike Hensley)*

When I was growing up, it seemed to me that the fern on the mountain was there just for that purpose; and the fern was beautiful. And it was there through the woods, beautiful woods, big timber over it and undergrowth, big trees everywhere, and this beautiful fern just grew like a paradise, almost, you know, naturally without any help. You couldn't raise anything like that; you couldn't raise anything that beautiful if you undertook it, to save your life you couldn't. *(Raymond Presnell)*

I live on the mountain. There are trees and everything, and all you can see is mountains. When the leaves start turning, they fall off. After the wood's rotted a whole lot, it glows after it gets dark. I found one piece one night. It was a real big 'un . . . about that long and that wide, a real big 'un. That was foxfire. But, it ain't really a-burning. It's glowing. (You can find all kinds of things coming up the trail at nighttime.) My parents leave pieces just everywhere coming up the trail; so, if we come up the trail at nighttime, we can see each side of the trail and won't go off the edge of it. You can't see nobody. *(Child)*

I was born right here in this old house. My father and my grandfather and my great grandfather built it. It's seventy-some years old, this house is, except the roof. Now the roof was re-covered. You see,

Blue Ridge Mountains, Transylvania County

Mountain lion

back then it was covered with those chestnut shingles. There was a steam engine came in and they sawed shingles. The log cabin before that was covered with boards that you split out with a fro. And in the mountains at that time, the panther they called it, which they call a mountain cougar or mountain lion anymore, they said they'd come of a night and dig boards off the roof, scratch and dig. And catty meows. A catty meow is a cat between a bobcat and the panther. The catty meow is a cat, a pretty cat, a mountain cat. The bobcat, they were kind of slouchy, ran kind of slouchy when they ran. And the mountains now, at one time, were called "God's Country."

Well, now a haint, the way they used to teach it in the mountains, what's called a haint, is when you're out at night—now this was back when you couldn't ride. You were always on foot, walking, and in the dark at night, no light. And you'd learn to walk of the durandum, they called it, of your body; of keeping on your bearings; the bearing that would grow in your body from walking. The gravity was on the planet, but people didn't know then

what was doing it. Bearing, they called it. It's in your body, grows in it to follow those paths. It'd get dark as a dungeon.

Well now, a lot of times when the moon is partly shining, with the clouds running over it and hiding it and shaping it out and it'll go off. Well you'll be walking along what they call a hang, and you will see a rock or an old stump of a tree, or stuff like that; and if you're scary, now, scary of seeing something, you'll get to looking at that, and you'll imagine there's a pair of eyes. There's a head, and then when you see the head, there's a pair of eyes. Then you'll study a little more, and there's a nose with it. Then you'll study a little more and there's a mouth; then a little more and there's the body, hands. And then, you're running; most people run. And then, go off and tell they've seen a ghost. That's what they call a haint.

But, now a ghost is different. That's a spirit from where somebody that'd hidden their treasure, and God wanted somebody, poor people or somebody of the poor people to take it from God and not be skittish too much and not run, and stay there and

7

talk with it and ask it what it appeared to them for, and it would tell them where it was hidden; and then they could go dig it out. That's a ghost. Now a haint like I told you is something you imagine. You imagine it. But a ghost is a real thing. *(Ray Hicks)*

Once I went off the trail at nighttime, but I don't want to run into that creature up there. You can't see nobody. I almost saw it one time. Saw its one eye. All you see is one big eye—that big around. That's all you can see. There ain't no body. If you kick at it, you just go right down the road. I tried to throw a rock at it. The rock hit his eye, but I don't know what it done to its eye. Just turned around and went on. Turned back around and went on. *(Child)*

Yes, the North Carolina mountains were once a secluded, witch-haunted region. We were in these mountains for many years, and the roads were bad, little more than what we'd call log roads now. *(Horton Cooper)*

To me the mountains are very beautiful. I just love to climb mountains, just to climb a mountain and get up there and see the facing, and go over and over again, and every time see something different. It's got a different look, and it's all beautiful except where man has destroyed it. *(Piercy Carter)*

Jean and Landon Roberts took me on long drives through the countryside to show me spectacular views and special, remote places which they particularly loved. One day we went for a picnic at their farm on the top of a mountain in Madison County. On the way, we picked up Jr. Wilde and his grandson, Jacky. Jr. helped tend Landon's cattle and some of the crops on the farm. The end of the summer had come, and Jr. had planned to gather some other helpers later that afternoon to round up the cattle that were pastured on top of the

Landon Roberts

mountain and drive them down to lower ground. We invited Jr. and Jacky to join our picnic before beginning their work. When we stopped at a country store to pick up some cold drinks, Jacky enthusiastically offered to run in and get them. Landon chuckled as the young boy raced into the store and mentioned that we should check to see what Jacky came back with. He was only twelve years old but had a much greater fondness for chewing tobacco than for chewing gum. Soon we had turned into the road that led up through the Roberts' property and found ourselves bounced and jostled as the Jeep was maneuvered over the rugged terrain. We began to notice thick clouds moving in, and Jacky launched into a dramatic description of a lightning storm over the mountain that he had watched just a few days earlier. Thunder had boomed, lightning bolts had crashed all around, and wild black clouds had darkened the sky. This made us a little uneasy about the picnic. When it began to rain, we decided to stop for lunch in a little hollow before moving on to the top of the mountain. Soon the clouds began to clear and other local people arrived to help with gathering in the cows. It was time to make the steep trek up to Mike's Knob.

When we had nearly reached the mountain-top, we came upon a wide, bright green meadow with cows lazily grazing all about. Everyone joined in to help gather the cattle. We would form circles around some of them to aim them toward the proper path. Sometimes the cows would be enticed out of the woods with salt or mooing sounds and rounded up. Eventually, we reached the very top of the mountain, and one of the most luxurious views I've ever seen spread out before us. The air was cool and fresh after the recent rain. The clouds had cleared around us, but other billowing formations could be seen moving into nearby peaks. We looked to the west out over Spring Creek and into the mountain ranges of Tennessee. Toward the southwest, Sandy Mush Bald seemed to jut right up beside us. Asheville and Leicester lay to the southeast, and the green hues of Max Patch that capped a nearby mountain were visible in the northwest. The lush green of the summer foliage gave a softness to the steep and craggy peaks that surrounded us. Varying shades of blues and greens clothed the mountain-sides, and dark shadows could be seen moving along the land as clouds passed over. Small clumps of dark purple thistle sprinkled the area where we stood. It was magical. (W. M.)

We drive out here sometimes for no other purpose than to see the sun go down. You can look for fifty miles right back in yonder and see the sun go down. You can almost see Knoxville in there. It's the prettiest sunset I've ever seen anywhere. Right in there the horizon is out of this world. *(Bob Phillips)*

I've got this vine growing on it. It's a kudzu, and can't nothing put up with it but groundhogs and copperhead snakes. You can't get rid of it. My wife said, "Let's get some goats." I said, "No. They'd skin every tree; they wouldn't eat that." *(Tom Oates)*

That was the greatest thrill on earth when the time of year came to pull your shoes off. My mother never would let us go barefooted until we saw a catbird. She said, "When catbirds come, spring is here." So we'd look for that. We thought it was plenty warm enough to go barefooted, but we had to produce a catbird or let her see one. (Quay Smathers)

One time I called Delia Reed to ask about something. They had just had a big snow, and she was telling me about it. She said that they had gotten "a lot more than an apron full." About two feet of snow had fallen, and they had already started planting their garden before the snow came. She said, "We thought spring was here, but it fooled us. Didn't it?" (W.M.)

I've been on the farm all my life. If I had to be in town, I don't know if I could survive or not. I wonder sometimes. Honey, a woman who used to live over there in the field, her and her husband wanted me to go with them to her cousin's in Spartanburg, South Carolina. And at four-thirty Sunday afternoon, the thermometer was still standing at ninety degrees. Honey, I thought I'd smother to death! And that's the last time I've been down in the lowlands.

I started collecting four-leaf clovers about 1930 when I found the first one. I started up here the other day to get the paper, and I found two. I found them weeding my garden. They're not too hard for me to find. Just seems like four-leaf clovers grow where I can find them. I went over there to the other side of the house in the field one evening to see if I could find me a clover and, honey, I found ninety-three in just a few minutes, just as fast as I could pick them.

9

Ruth Settles with four-leaf clovers

I like to get out and walk. I'd prefer walking and going to the mountains. I've been studying strong of goin' back up there on the mountain to Face Rock again; I haven't been up there in years. I really like the mountains myself. And the further back in the mountain I can get to live, the better I like it.

Honey, I like to walk yet. I take a notion to walk every once in a while. I have a brother that lives up on Bear Wallow Road beside the Gerton Post Office. I take out up through the pasture, go over and see him. But it was about '43, one Monday afternoon, honey, I kinda wished I'd stayed at home. Just a short distance below the head of the road, down in Mr. McClure's pasture, honey, I took me a stick and made a fox club. I've never been so scared in all my born days. What made it really worse; I think, than it would've been, I had my baby with me. He was about two and a half years old and I had him on my back, and he thought it was my brother-in-law's cat. He said, "Mama, there's a cat following us." And I didn't pay any attention to it. He said again, "This cat's a-followin' us." I slid him down off my back and I looked around and, honey, it was that fox still a-comin' toward me. And I grabbed me a stick. It come on down to where I was, rubbed in agin' me, looked up at me and growled and started walkin' off. And I hit it right between the ears, and, honey, I permed it a-flat; killed it and took it on down to my brother's. *(Ruth Settles)*

Now the first settlers in this country settled in the hollows close to the water, and their wood could come downhill for their fuel 'cause [without roads] they weren't going anywhere. It didn't matter whether you could get down or not. After they got to building roads and got to going somewhere, they moved out of the hollows up on the ridges. Then they had to carry water from way down in the hollows or dig a well, one. *(Jonah Parker)*

I love fall! Those first days when you feel fall in the air. It's my favorite time of year. I get this feeling of urgency. I think I inherited that from my ancestors who lived in these mountains all these years, because when winter was coming on, they had to get the crops in, everything stored away, and get prepared to survive the winter. It was urgent, really. And I still get that feeling in the fall. **(Jonah Parker)**

A hollow is a depression between two hills just big enough for a little house to be perched in. A cove is a bigger territory. It is a large recess in the mountains. For example, Steven's Cove has 640 acres. So a cove covers a pretty good-sized area, but it is not as big as a valley. *(Landon Roberts)*

I was up there on the mountain one day and went to a spring, but couldn't find it. It's a big spring, but the flood came in 1916 and just covered it up. I went up there two or three times trying to get in there, but I couldn't do it. I sold the timber off the mountain to a man, and he went across there and said, "I hit two oceans up there. Did you know it was there?" I said, "Yeah, but I didn't know where it was." And we went up there with another bulldozer to go on in there to get that water at the head. Bob Willis happened to be up there above it and got a cool breeze and opened it up, and there was a cave in there. That's where the water comes from, and you get eighteen to twenty gallons a minute. It fills a 1,000-gallon tank in forty-six minutes. Now we've got 1,000 gallons of water right up there when we need it. *(Tom Oates)*

HARSH CONDITIONS

It's cold in the wintertime. Over there where I was born and raised there on the hill, honey, when that cold wind blowed, I'm telling you it felt like you didn't have on any clothes at all. *(Ruth Settles)*

Well, I just want to say that I don't know whether I can think of anything but my wood for winter and the winter coming and not enough wood in yet to keep us from freezing, but I'll try. Our grandsons, three of them, have promised to come when they get a day off. But, when that'll be, I don't know. Winter may be done here. Anyway, it keeps me worried. *(Lyda Coffey)*

The river used to stay iced over six weeks at a time. It was so cold back then, and you could take a wagon and horses and go from here to Spruce Pine on the river without ever getting off. They used to go down after freight.

And the boys at the Presbyterian School would build a fire out here at night and they would skate. That was one of their activities. And they would ride us on their shoulders, you know, and they'd push us on chairs, just a regular chair we'd turn upside down. You'd sit on the rails and they'd push us with the chair. And I couldn't wait 'til I grew up so I could date these boys, you know. But, after I grew up, we didn't have them. [The school had burned down.] **(Kay Wilkins)**

When there were blizzards in the wintertime, people didn't get snowed in like they do now because they had horses and steers and they could just go. No, it didn't bother them back then half like it does now because they had the horses and steers and they'd just wade, you know, waist deep and go right on through it. And people would go from here to Lenoir and Wilkesboro in a wagon and a team of horses or mules. I never happened to be in any of that. By the time I got big enough to really go around like that, why there were vehicles, you know, cars. *(Walter Winebarger)*

We've got a Ford car we bought. He keeps it penned up. He won't put it out on the salt road. *(Pearl Marshall)*

I ain't going to put it out on these salty roads and let the salt eat it up. They cost too much money nowadays, I tell you. *(Gayton Marshall)*

That salt eats them up. *(Pearl Marshall)*

The first snow that fell, I measured it here in the yard sixteen and a half inches. Then the next week it come twelve inches, and I measured that out there on top of the first. The first was still out there. It hadn't hardly melted a bit. It was hitting right on twenty-two inches. But, now, the deepest snow that ever came in this country was 1936. It came the seventeenth day of March and it struck me at my navel. Right there. Forty-one inches deep. And there were drifts in places around here; in the hollows, sixty feet deep or deeper. That was when the kids got caught in the schoolhouse and had to stay in the schoolhouse for a week. They carried food to them. *(Gayton Marshall)*

The train was blocked. If they were riding Tweetsie they couldn't get home. Some of them stayed in the schoolhouse, some of them stayed up here, and they didn't get home for two or three days. *(Pearl Marshall)*

Fresh snow on split–rail fence overlooking MacRae Meadows, Grandfather Mountain

There was a motor grader and two automobiles up here at the graveyard snowed plumb over, covered plumb over. And straight down through here was deep as my head. It was over a week before they ever got it opened up. They had to take 'dozers, I mean big 'dozers. That's the deepest snow that's ever come in this country that anybody remembers. *(Gayton Marshall)*

We had one in 1960 that was pretty big, though. *(Pearl Marshall)*

I think it was twenty-two inches. I was helping build that road up above Boone on Highway 421, running a shovel. I took a big 'dozer and went up in there and opened the road where they could get out. All the way across that mountain and back. It took me one whole day to make one trip up and go to the other end and turn around and come back. It took me a day. And I reckon if part of my tractor had slipped off, I'd been going yet. I tell you, it was dangerous. *(Gayton Marshall)*

We had a boy last weekend from Rutherfordton on the Parkway that froze to death. Two high school students. They were eighteen years old and the Parkway ranger wondered how they got through. Said they usually put up a barricade. But, it was down, and they went through going up in there seeing about rock climbing. And their car got stalled in a snow drift and they couldn't get it out. They had started walking and it was twenty miles to Asheville. They were at the Craggy Gardens, and they started walking. One of them was dressed more to suit the cold. He got tired, and the other one said he couldn't get him to go on with him. So that one just stopped and said he would take shelter under a rock. He sheltered under a rock, and the other one went walking on back to Mount Mitchell, and the Parkway ranger ran into him and picked him up. They had to put him in the hospital because he was cold. And he went back about nine miles to where they found the other one, and he was dead. *(Pearl Marshall)*

It gets cold up there on those Craggy Mountains, up there next to Mount Mitchell. It gets cold up there. *(Gayton Marshall)*

All the trees are one-sided. *(Pearl Marshall)*

13

My, I appreciated rainy days back then. I could wash. I had my wood stove in here and would get my water hot and go out there and catch rainwater, fill up tubs. *(Delia Reed)*

There was a spout—they didn't have gutters all the way around, but they had a gutter which ran above and across the front steps and then the spout ran down at the end, and she [Mama] always kept a tub setting under that spout. I remember running out and catching water in a bucket 'cause it'd rain hard, and you'd get a lot of water off that roof in that spout. *(Wanda Moss)*

I took advantage of that. Well, rainwater's good wash water—soft. *(Delia Reed)*

Well, now, you washed over at the creek in the warm weather. *(Wanda Moss)*

I had a big ol' pot out yonder, and I'd build a fire around that big ol' iron pot and boil my clothes in that. I had water right there, you see. I never did beat them on the rocks. A lot of people did, but I had a rub board that I used. And we had our cows and we churned, had our butter; and it all had to be carried out there to what we called a spring box and kept in there. *(Delia Reed)*

So after supper, we had to go back to the spring box to put the milk back in the thing. *(Wanda Moss)*

And then, when you go through with that, you think, "My, wasn't it great to have electricity." A refrigerator was the first thing I wanted when we got electricity. *(Delia Reed)*

And it was inconvenient taking baths. There was just a big ol' washtub. We just had one of those round galvanized tubs, and my mother used to pop us in there and give us a bath. Heat the water in a kettle and pour it in there, put in some cold and add some hot water from the stove. She would wash our hair and pour water over our heads. I had long hair up through the second grade, and my

mother used to curl my hair with brown paper strips cut from brown paper bags, folded and then you catch the ends of it and turn it up and then twist it. Well, just twist it around and if it was thin paper, it would stay. Used to do my hair like that, and every morning I had these long curls. My mother must have gone to a lot of trouble to send us to school. *(Wanda Moss)*

I grew up in Haywood County, in Cherokee. I still remember a woman I knew doing her washing in the winter. I will always remember those blue claws. You know she didn't want to do the washing in the winter, but she had to. So she went to the stream and did the wash. The water was so cold that it turned her hands blue, but she still did the wash because it had to be done. **(Lewis Green)**

Well, youngun, I want you to know one thing, I've been here on this creek many years, faced many a storm, cold, rain, used to work away from home all the time. And this road wasn't here then. The old road ran up over there. And all the feed stuff that we fed our cattle and hogs, we carried it on our back. I picked up many a one-hundred-pound bag of cotton meal or whatever it was to feed the cows and carried it here and never laid it down. I was little, but I was tough as they made them. I walked from here four miles down this creek and pulled a cross-cut saw for twenty-five cents an hour—two dollars and fifty cents a day. How many young men would take that now? They wouldn't take it. I stayed in that one job there eight months flat. But, them good ol' days is gone and worse a-coming and nobody knows exactly what's going to happen. *(Willard Watson)*

I've crossed on the ice many times, ride a horse across it on the ice and never break through and drove a wagon across it time after time and not break through. See, a wagon sets on four wheels. If you had your horses ice shod—that is, to stand up on ice—why they'd pull your wagon right on across that ice without any trouble. You take the corks on the back of the shoe and heat them in a forge and hammer them down to a keen point. Well, then across the toe up here you'll weld a piece across there and hammer it down to a small inch. That way a horse can hold its feet on the ice, but without that, they'd just fall. And a horse when it falls and catches on those front knees, they don't have to fall but two or three times until they're crippled. Then they can't stand up, and they can't pull anything.

And my daddy always had logging jobs as a usual thing in the wintertime, and we would have to go to work regardless of the weather. I worked many a day when my dinner would freeze so hard that you couldn't eat a bit of it without building a fire and setting the bucket on the fire. Why you could have killed a bull from here across the road with a biscuit, that's how hard they'd freeze in half a day. And we worked in a hollow one winter where the first snow fell the first of November and was there the first of May. We logged that entire winter up there, and there were places that I believe the ground froze eighteen inches deep up there in that north hollow. And we just had a small team of horses. Well, we kept them ice shod all the time, so they could stand up. That's one thing that we did. Marsh Greer was the blacksmith that kept my daddy's horseshoes fixed. Well, we'd take that little

Winter farm scene, Watauga County

nine-hundred-pound team. They weighed about nine hundred to 1000 pounds each. And we'd put logs on a skid way up there. Four head wouldn't have been able to pull them if the ground were dry, but they could on that frozen ground and on that snow. Why any log that we could get broke loose, we could put it on a skid with that little team. And we always used a J-grab, so that we could get the team loose from the log in case we needed to, if the log started to run. *(Myron Houston)*

all of two months before that ever thawed enough, so the ice would break down. And it never thawed 'til April—spring.

That day, the thirtieth of December, it was twenty below zero because he went by Tom Critchard's store and the thermometer was hanging out there—twenty below zero. But, we were used to waiting it out. We'd walk to school at Boone (two miles at that time, you know) in the snow and all and in the cold weather. We thought nothing about

Rime ice on ridge in Great Smoky Mountain National Park

It was 1917, and in November it started snowing. I don't remember what time in November, but it started and that didn't melt off; and, in a few days some more came on, froze fast. And in a few days more came on, and it never did melt off from the time it started sometime in November 'til it packed up all winter and everything froze over.
(Marion Coffey)

When Marion would come down home—and he did the day we got married—he lived down here two miles below at his mother's. And he just came down through the field, a narrow way cut off, in place of going around the bridge. The river was froze over, you know, and he just came across that river on the ice and snow right up to the near road to my home, in a buggy, driving two horses. It was

getting cold, getting out in that snow, riding on a plank. We didn't have a sled. And that's the only year it's ever started snowing in November and never melted off the first one, and more came on, all winter that I ever remember. *(Lyda Coffey)*

It was late January, and I had driven up to the mountains to spend four days interviewing people and taking photographs. A new snow had just fallen, and more was supposed to be on the way. I was staying at a friend's house outside of Sylva beside the Tuckasegee River. I had been so impressed during the first two days of my visit to walk outside and see the river's water speeding by surrounded by white-covered mountains. The drives through the mountains to visit people were

Meat Camp Creek, Watauga County

Picnic tables in winter, along the Tuckasegee River, Jackson County

spectacular, and long walks through trails in the forest where no human tracks had been made were silent and beautiful. The serenity made the cold seem unimportant. People talked about the fact that it was mighty cold, but nobody paid much attention to it. Things went on as usual.

On that second night, I had gone to bed wearing my flannel pajamas, two pairs of socks, and a sweater. The bed had blankets and a quilt. I remember waking up in the middle of the night and thinking that it was so cold that I would never get up out of that bed for anything. The next morning I was awakened by my friend standing at the door with a parka. He was screaming at me to get up and stand by the fire in the living room. This was a recently rebuilt cabin. We were supposed to have heat, but it didn't seem to be very effective at that point.

When I walked out on the porch, I was amazed at what I saw. The river was steaming, and mists were rising up from it. We found out later that it was twenty-one degrees below zero. The old swing that hung out over the river swept back and forth, and the only audible sounds were those of the water churning by. Chunks of ice had begun to form along the bank, and occasionally one would break loose in the strong current only to get caught up again at the river's edge.

As the day progressed, our time was consumed with efforts to further insulate the house from the cold. My friend's car was dead, but mine worked.

We spent hours driving around Jackson County, looking for insulation material of various sorts at different hardware stores. We had to keep the car running all the time, and we raced across parking lots because the cold hurt our feet so much.

Then more hours were spent with my portable hair dryer trying to get plastic to pull tight into frames we had tacked onto the insides of windows. Doorsills had to be caulked too. We were lucky. One of the water lines had not frozen, so we did have some water. The electricity was on, and the stove worked, so we could have baths using water heated on the stove. Another friend called whose pipes had frozen. We told her to come over and stay with us. At least we had water, and she could have a bath if she wanted.

Heat, food, water, and companionship— basic necessities that we had all taken for granted—had quickly become luxuries. Here we were in a cabin out in the country, and it was cold. We took water to Lilly and Hester who lived nearby. There was not much to think about that day except for keeping warm and making sure that we could all get through this. During this ordeal, flashes of recognition would come in and out, and I gradually realized that I now had a truer understanding of the stories of harsh conditions that I had been listening to for years. They had come to life for me.
(W. M.)

RIVERS AND FLOODS

The year of the flood was 1916. Well, we lived up there on that mountain, and at the back of our house (that's where the chimney was for the fireplace) Mommy had the prettiest flower bed there I've ever seen in my life. I can see it now. It was every kind of a flower that you could think of, she had in that flower bed. And it was a long thing, might near as long as the house. You know, it'd come up on each side of the chimney and across. So that day I told Mommy, "I want to cut some of them." She said, "No, don't cut my flowers; just leave them there." Well, we used to carry them in the house because the yard was full, so I didn't cut them. But that night when the flood started, I was coming above the house, and there was two little streams of water running on each side of our house and barn. That night when the flood hit, them branches got up and you could have buried our house in the one that went down beside that chimney, and it cut off that flower bed, and there's a straight bank down 'til you could have put our little house in it, in the hole, and the other side was about as bad.

After they seen it was raining and the water was getting up, Poppy went up to see about the cows. He had about four or five cows up there, a combination of his and ours, and a horse. He went up to see about them. He said the water was up there a little bit, but he believed it'd be all right. They came back to the house, and they talked about us leaving the house for a while and said, "No, we'd just better stay here." But, if we'd started out, we couldn't have got out for either branch on each side of us. You know, we'd have walked right into a branch. And there was a huge mountain above our house. We lived kind of down low. And it cut that mountain. You never seen nothing. . .the boys would run and jump over the opening of it, but it was deep.

But, over on Middle Fork, that's in Henderson County, back up in the mountains where all my mother's people lived, her half-brother, he lived on the upper end of the creek, it washed his house away and wife and two kids. And they couldn't never find them. And they said they'd have to wait 'til the water went down and they'd find them. But when they got to hunting, they found Aunt Belle, and she'd got caught in a barbed wire, and she was way up in a tree where it'd carried her up in it, you know; and the two kids, they were kind of beat up, and they found them by dogs way down the creek. He left home the next day, and he was knocked pretty bad in the water, but he finally got out. And the next day, why Grandma told him, "Edgar, I want you to go see about Junie and her family up on that mountain." That was my mommy. And he walked from Middle Fork, way back across that mountain, and come in at that mountain yonder to see about us. We were all right, but if we'd got out of the house and started, it would have been too bad. Our house wasn't hurt. Through Asheville and Canton it was horrible—drowned people and washed them away, 'cause the French Broad got up bad. *(Nanny Suttles)*

But, after the 1916 washout, there was no more eels. I don't know why; reckon it washed them away, killed them or something; great big boulders of dirt, of rock, I guess it killed them.

Our house was not ruined in the flood. The creek was on the back side of it, but in front the highway ran right down the front, almost by the front porch. And in that 1916 washout, I was there by myself. I was scared to death. And my husband had gone down to his daddy and mother's to see about them, and it kept raining, so he didn't start home; but I was there with the two boys, and I was afraid to get up the next morning and look out. But I got up, and it had washed that highway away, maybe, oh I guess, a gully as deep as this house, and it stayed that way, and they had to make the road around it.

Linville Gorge, Avery County

The Tuckasegee River

The waters run down fast in the mountains, and my husband said he was afraid to look out where he was. And he come through the mountains home to see about us. Well, he said he saw us and he never was so glad of anything in his life that nothing had washed away. But it just like to got us. Now it washed a big bridge away, and up above us there was another big bridge, and it washed it away. So we had to ford the creek awhile. And they finally came; the convicts built that first, and they came back and rebuilt it. They had to—[it was a] state highway.

It was awful. It washed one family's house plumb away. They left it sometime during the night and they had a wagon frame with a cover on it; they set under that wagon frame while it was raining, and their house washed away. And over in another community, a slide came down, hit a man's porch, knocked it in the creek with his wife on it. She drowned and one of the daughters. Why, it was the worst time anybody ever saw. *(Sue Oates)*

Oh, the 1916. Well, it started raining. It rained for several days and on Sunday morning it just finally kept building up. Sunday morning, the water flooded all around the Southern Depot. The water was nine feet deep in the depot down there. It was summertime, August, and I was working at the grocery store. We rode in the boat into the grocery store on Monday morning. The first flood that got in there, I reckon, was Saturday sometime. Monday morning it was still three or four feet deep. And there was one bridge left in I don't know how many miles up and down the river. The only bridge that survived was the West Asheville bridge, which was built in 1911 and was way above the water. And the Southern Railway bridge right below it. The water and the big lumber sticks would go down the river and the river bridge was low, close to the water, and the water just went over the top of the railroad bridge, but it was stout enough, so it withstood the flood. But, they couldn't get trains out of there. It washed away all the lumber plants and everything down there.

At that time, we belonged to the church over on this side of the river. So we came across about eight-thirty and after, when church was out, they closed the bridge, the bridge you crossed back over. The

lumber was coming down and hitting. You could feel it tremble—you could see the bridge tremble when it hit the columns—but the bridge stayed. Now it's torn down, and a new one's built.
(Piercy Carter)

***Out at Biltmore, they had a lot of people who drowned out there, and a lot of people didn't get out. They climbed trees. I've seen pictures of people in those trees, way up in the trees. The river was way up in Swannanoa. It just rained and rained, days and days of rain. The Toxaway went out, but that doesn't come this way. It's on the other side of the Blue Ridge, so it went down into South Carolina and flooded down through there a whole lot.*
(Piercy Carter)

That flood was 1940. It came the fourteenth of August, and I was scared to death. It washed away everything in the world we had but one cow, just left us one cow; that's all we had. We didn't have a house, a shelter, a change of shoes, nothin'. Everything in the world—just had the cow, that's all we had. And she followed us all night. We were walking around through the woods trying to find a dry place, and that ol' cow followed right along after us all the time. I had an organ that went all the way to Elkin, I guess, in the flood.

I made stack cake, made everything. My husband would sit down at the table and tell me what he wanted, and I'd just fix it if I could. He got me a big cookbook. It washed away in the flood. The only warning was that it was pouring down rain. My husband would tell me, "Why, it'll never come up here; the water'll never come up here. It never has been this high." And he wasn't afraid of it, but I was scared of it. And when I started out of the house, I didn't know that the kitchen steps were just two steps, and I thought I'd just step down. And I stepped down and I run under the house,

everything but my head. And if he hadn't've caught me, I'd have gone right off with the house. Mr. Hall got hold of me somehow and pulled me back. I would have just been washed down the mountain over mud and rocks and everything.

There were lots of people killed in that flood. There was a little girl up here. They never found her for a week or so. And there were some little boys down at the river fishing, and they saw a hand sticking up out of the sand and they went to see what it was; and they found the little girl's hand. They went home and told her folks about it, and they went down there and dug her up. It was Bill Todd's little girl. They came from Boone. They'd had a store there, lived there and had a store, and she'd gone home to visit her grandparents and went to the revival, and it washed them away. Said she was standing with her uncle on the porch and [it] just come a-sloshing and everything and just took them up. *(Mamie Hall)*

Mamie was a widow three times. Her father was the first policeman in North Wilkesboro. The sheriff, Mitch Vannoy, helped teach her how to read and write. She later married him. He was the first Democratic sheriff in Wilkes County. Her second husband was Grant Hendren, the county agent. Her third husband was Jim Hall. He was a farmer and a sawmiller. During the Depression, she worked for the New Deal, teaching people how to make their own mattresses. In her later years, she always said that she had three hats behind her cookstove, one for each husband. (W. M.)

I was living on the mountain then, during the flood of 1940. A store back up here above Dillsboro store, and the mill house and the iron bridge, that whole thing, the store and the mill house and iron bridge all washed away. Down below here, below Dillsboro, two or three houses close to the river washed away. They claim that a cloud busted at the head of the river and then the dam broke loose, too. *(Lilly Wykle)*

23

BEYOND THE HARDTOP

Everybody here, when I was growing up, everybody that went to town, they walked or rode a horse or something, had wagons. But, everybody walked faster than the wagon. Didn't even look back to see if somebody was going to pick them up 'cause wasn't no car to pick them up. *(Grady Reed)*

Somebody wrote, "The roads are not" —now don't blush —" the roads are not passable, not even jack-assable." And they were bad, sister. They were very narrow. This road that goes from Cranberry on into Plumtree and to Spruce Pine, I remember it distinctly because I lived in Minneapolis and walked it every day during the four months of school, and then I'd have to go to the mill and the store and the post office, borrow meal and flour. (Usually neighbors borrowed meal and flour and everything else when they'd run out.) It wasn't a good sled road. I remember when this [Highway] 19 wasn't a good sled road. It had chuck holes in it and rocks, and the wagons would rattle over it like a freight train. This road was just a path then. And I know a lot of the highways now in Avery County that were just paths, and some were blazed trails. I remember we had a lot of blazed trails here in Avery County when I was a young boy. They were bad.

Most everybody had work horses, at least two of them, some several. And they had sleds. They used big sleds, medium-sized sleds, too, of course, depending on whether one horse or two horses or three horses would pull it, through the snow. Yeah, I was out in snow all the time nearly every day when I was a boy. I was the only son of the family. My father had eleven children. *(Horton Cooper)*

It was the inability not of communication, but of transportation, landlock that kept everyone isolated. *(Landon Roberts)*

That was one reason that area was backward, as far as industrial development was concerned because the transportation was not available. There were no decent roads really up to recent years, and the rail services were just from Asheville west on the little Branch Railroad. Southern Railway didn't merge with Branch. The freight rates were high, and it was hard to ship anything into there and ship it out. *(Dan Moore)*

To make a sled, well, you'd go out in the woods, and we generally hunted a sourwood tree that had a crook on the end of it. Get you two of them. You know, they grow up and crook out just like that on the end. Pelt them down flat and put you a beam across them, put you some standards in them. Put six standards generally, three on each side. Put a cross-stitch on it and call it a bench. You just bored a two-inch hole and put it down over your standard; that's what you put all your stuff on. Build you a box on that and make you a place to haul whatever you wanted to haul. If you wanted to haul corn, you'd have to put a box on it. If you hauled wood, you just used standards. Used a lot of them to haul fertilizer to the field on, haul your plow from one place to another. Carried it around on that. Used to make little ones to play on. Get out on a hill and ride it down the hill. *(Nelson Cabe)*

That's the way the roads were kept and built then— by working. I know Mr. Newt Harrison had a team of mules, and he pulled the road scraper with mules and my daddy operated the road scraper. They didn't clear snow. They just filled the ruts up with it, scraped the roads to make them smooth. That's all they did. When the snow got so bad, they just rode their horses. There weren't many cars when I grew up. *(Frank Norris)*

The WPA [Works Progress Administration] jobs were road work, country roads, you know. And we didn't have any machinery. Hand tools, wheelbarrows, mattock, pick, shovel; we didn't have any trucks either, any machinery. But we dug it out, worked these roads, beat rock with a rock hammer on these roads. Then after I moved here, we worked on this road up through here, all this, we worked this. They did use dynamite to shoot the cliffside, and then we went in there and worked this rock out here, beat them up with sledgehammers. *(Raymond Presnell)*

light. People generally started before daylight and would be down halfway between here and the store time it got daylight—I mean the mouth of this creek. And then they put the rest of the day in going there, and it'd be black dark, time they got back. And the people'd camp out along there at the mouth of this creek. They'd get down that far, and they'd camp out the night and go on into town.

Sunset, clouds, and silouettes, Lewis farm, Little Savannah, Jackson County

Yeah. It's a fact. Used to be between here and town you'd see a string of wagons with steers, and horses too, just bumper to bumper from here to Dillsboro. They'd haul acid wood, tanbark, telephone poles, and crossties. It was every day, six days a week. If you got up and started before daylight, why you'd get back in the summertime about four o'clock. But in the wintertime, it'd take you all day long to go to town and back, if you started a little before day-

Then they'd head back and they'd camp out the next night before they got back. It lasted up 'til about 1925 'til they concreted the main road. It was 1925 when they finished it, part of them coming from Dillsboro this way and part from Macon County, and they met. *(Grady Reed)*

The only way you could get to Green Park Hotel was to go out the road here. And the road was new,

Mountain road, Cherokee County

and in the wintertime when it thawed through, it just went down to where the brakes would drag; as far as that goes—knee deep, the mud was. And we'd hit the grade of the hill out there. Well, we didn't have to pull one wagon off the road 'cause couldn't anybody pass anyway. We'd just unhook one team and hook it in front of the other team and drag that one to the top. Come right back; bring them both back and get the other wagon and get it up. Did that fifty times. It was the only way to get up there. To pull a two-horse load, you had to hitch four horses to it to get it up there.

If you were hauling produce, you'd go south. Oh, I've hauled to Statesville. I know one time we were at Statesville and it was Saturday evening and we wanted to get shed of our loads on Saturday, so we didn't stop for supper at all; we just kept going 'til we got sold out. And it was after dark when we came into the lot where we were camped. They slept in the wagons. And it was just pouring rain; it was just coming down in sheets. It wasn't but just a little step across there to the restaurant, but it was raining, so you couldn't get there without getting drowned. I said, "What about just going to bed? We're both give out and we'll just go to bed and get up in the morning and go over there and have them set the table." He said, "Okay." Well, we went to bed and got up the next morning hungry as bears. We went and fed our horses and beat it over to the restaurant and went in there. The waitress came and asked us what we wanted. I said, "Bring it all out here. We haven't had any supper, just set the table and we'll eat." They just set it out there, and we ate about twice as much as we would any other time, you know. I told Howard before we were out there, "I'm going to make them set the table; I don't care what they charge. We've got to have something to eat for breakfast." When we got ready to go, he threw the ticket out there—one dollar apiece for us. I said, "That isn't too bad!"

We had covered wagons. My wagon bed was twelve feet long and the bows were almost as high as from this floor to the ceiling, to where the bows came over. That's all we had. And you had big ol' heavy quilts, three or four; and they took them

along. And while the wagon was loaded with the stuff, when you had to camp out; it took a long time to drive, so you'd sleep under the wagon, lay on one quilt and put the rest over you. And they had a provision box, and we always had baked bread and put meat and whatever in the box. I forgot what all we cooked. And we'd get out there with our frying pan. And there was always a jar of grease; we had plenty of hogs and lard. And we'd get out there and build a little fire in the campground and cook a pan of apples or a pan of potatoes or a pan of whatever we had or wanted to go with whatever we had in our provision box. And after we got the wagon empty, we'd sleep in the wagon. Before that, we had to sleep under the wagon. *(Marion Coffey)*

We were married in 1917, but he'd done that all his life. I guess you wagoned on 'til you got a truck. When did you get a truck? *(Lyda Coffey)*

Oh, I don't remember. It was an A-Model Ford was the first I had. It had to be in the early twenties. *(Marion Coffey)*

I went with him a couple of times and slept under the wagon and then in the wagon after it was emptied. You know, we'd have to camp out coming back; it was gravel road then, no hardtop; it was just muddy roads that the horses had to pull.
(Lyda Coffey)

It was a place where people could walk and ride horseback. And buggies and a few wagons would come across from Bryson City going to Whittier, to Sylva, going east to west, west to east. This was the stopping place. And they'd spend the night here. So often it would be after dark and we'd be inside, and we'd hear a "Hello" from the front of the house. They always called. It was just something you didn't do was go up and knock on a man's door after dark. They would stay at night. They were charged fifty cents for supper and breakfast and bed. But their horses were charged a dollar apiece because it cost more to feed the horses. So we had several travelers,

(Right) Haystacks near the New River, Ashe County (Opposite) Cows in pasture-land, Madison County

and we never knew how many would come for the night. There was no telephone, so they couldn't make reservations. *(Annie Dee Leatherman Smith)*

I was born in 1908, and that's when there weren't any roads much. They had the old cabbage road, they called it, down to Marion. It wound round and round down through McDowell [County] into Marion. And that was about the only road. We just had paths, and some of them you had to go under the rhododendron and mountain laurel. There were worlds of chestnuts, and we picked up chestnuts, and they sold them and made money. When the railroad company finished the railroad through here, then they began to sell acid wood and tanbark and the products from the forest, and they made more money. *(Carrie Burnette)*

It took two days to go out there and back with a wagon and team. Had to haul all our merchandise from that little post office there at Elk Park for several years. When the salesman would come along and you gave him an order, it'd be shipped to Elk Park. Tweetsie Railroad would bring it up that far, and we'd have to go over there and get it. And horse teams, that was the only way to get it. That was before trucks and cars came along. Then the Tweetsie Railroad, they took it over to Boone, Shulls

Mills first. The lumber company there had a commissary store and a hardware store and the depot. Then it went on to Boone. Shulls Mills was the closest—five miles. *(Howard Mast, Sr.)*

The roads were bad. They weren't as good as sled roads would be now, dusty and rocky in dry weather. In going to school, why we would stir up the dust. Some of us would run ahead and the others would run ahead of us. Sometimes you'd come to a dusty place in the road where it was drifted up like snow. And people used sleds then to go to the mill and some to the store. I've seen some people riding their milk cow to the mill, the grist mill, and carry corn to get it ground. But there are two or three things that could be said about the people here. They were ambitious. Most of them were terribly poor. They were hard-working. Most of them were intelligent. They were eager to learn about the outside world. (Horton Cooper)

Well, you know Granny Moody died at about ninety-two or ninety-three, and she never would ride with anybody. She was a real little, feisty woman, and she'd literally get out—and her in her nineties—and walk from one family to another, three, four, or five miles. She would head out early in the morning and walk to visit Grandfather. She'd walk all day long and never would ride with anybody. People would stop and offer her a ride, and she'd say, "Ain't got time for such automobiles." And she'd walk off. But, one day they said Henry Ford and Thomas Edison came through. (You know they came through this country touring and were probably in one of the first cars ever seen around here.) When they came along and stopped, she rode with them. I guess she figured that was a time in history, so she got in and rode with them.
(Jimmy Moss)

***Mountain road,
Haywood County***

SUBSISTENCE FARMING

I worked right out in the cornfield hoeing corn and setting cabbage and digging taters or picking up. And on stacks of hay—back then we stacked them out in the field, you know. And we had long poles, and we raked the hay with the horses. We'd go over it with a fork and make shocks, make big hay shocks, round shocks, you know. And then, we'd go back and run the poles over the shocks, and we'd carry them around the stack poles and then we'd get all that carried in around the stack poles—the shocks. And then, I'd get on the stack and he'd throw up to me to make a stack clear on as high as this room, and slide down it. Then we'd start another one. The children were out making shocks. We never did keep them out of school, though. We never did do that. And all but Bill went through college, and they're teachers now. So they'd work when at home. Oh, the younguns could work; but we never kept them out of school. I was raised up just like them, right out in the cornfield. And before I was even big enough to hoe any, I was down pulling the weeds around the corn, so the ones that come on hoeing (the bigger children) could get the weeds and come on quicker. We've never known anything but work. *(Lyda Coffey)*

There were three girls first. We'd get up on the mountain and Daddy'd cut wood to haul out on the wagon. We'd be up on the mountainside and we'd help him saw up that wood. Called it acid wood at that time, and we had to help him saw with a cross-cut saw. And we'd pitch it down, you know. We ball-hooted the logs down off the mountain. That's rolling and rolling, pitching down a hill. That's how we got it down. And my daddy split shingles to go on top of the house, and I helped him. Had to saw that, you know. He'd made them to cover our house. He mostly made a living at home. He'd sell that wood I was telling about. The first time I ever went to Dillsboro was on top of a load of that wood. I guess I was about twelve or thirteen. *(Delia Reed)*

My older brothers, I've heard them talk about going from here to Lenoir. It'd take two days to go from here to Lenoir. Well, they'd take a load of chestnuts, potatoes, and cabbage, and whatever would sell, and go down there and maybe stay a day or two and then they'd start back up. Coming back, I think they would make it a little quicker than they would coming down because they always had a

"Old Sam", a Charolais bull, Madison County

load and there wasn't any road, and mud and snow and everything was knee-deep to the horses and axle-deep to the wagon. And it would take about a week for them to go to Lenoir and get rid of their load and then come back. I don't know how many times they'd go. They'd have to go down there maybe to peddle out something that way to get their coffee and sugar and salt and anything that they had to have. And more than that, why they raised it, canned, and put away everything they had to have. *(Walter Winebarger)*

We had cracklin' cornbread, mush, spoon bread, and grated bread. My daddy had a big old piece of tin and he drove nails in it, and he'd hold it over a plank and he'd rub that corn up and down over that and grate it. That's how you made the bread.

My mother set out two orchards—the paying orchard and the pleasure orchard—and we dried fruit. We dried apples and my daddy had tin and we'd just cover it over at night, cover it with another piece of tin and put pieces on two-by-fours—that dried it. She was a hard-working woman and she had twelve children. And there were two of them that were dead at an early age, and she raised the other ten. I remember how she would go bring in tomatoes with baskets, and we had lots of company, and we cooked on an old wood stove. We had a fireplace; we cooked a lot on the fireplace. We did finally get a stove. She sold a wagon load of chickens to buy her a stove. It was drawn by horses and they had beds on the wagons and they covered it over. There was a wagon full of chickens to get a stove.

We raised corn and would gather it in, and my daddy would help shuck it. He could sit and shuck corn, and then we had to sell it. We sold it for thirty-three and a third cents a bushel. We sold three hundred bushels for one hundred dollars. We had a hard time. I made soap, lye soap. The soap was soft, and sometimes I'd lay it out on a plank with paper under it, and it would dry. We washed with it. We had big old pots, and we'd boil our clothes in them near the spring. We'd boil the clothes and punch them with a punching stick. I washed for other people. My younger sister was going to quit school. I

had some washing then, and I had her to help me wash. She never wanted to quit another day. She went on to school. She graduated. She was having a good time compared to what I had. *(Lillian Hooper)*

I've got a lot of rough miles on me. A man I know was raised on the Biltmore Estate near Asheville. There's 13,000 acres and they milked 2,000 head of purebred Jerseys twice a day. They farmed that land, didn't have a tractor on the farm, had mules and hand hoes. And you hand hoed and cut corn by hand with a machete. That's hard on a man's back. We took horses and mules and plowed these fields and took a hoe and laid the corn and never sprayed it. But now all you do is just plant it, spray it, and forget it. *(Walter Winebarger)*

There's a lot of times you had all you wanted to eat, but sometimes it wasn't what you wanted to eat. **(Edd Presnell)**

Top of wood-burning stove at Ray Hick's house

Tobacco farm, near Fines Creek, Haywood County

This is another sermon that came from my heritage. You know we never considered the chores work; that was just the chores. You got up in the morning, and you fed the hogs and turned out the chickens and fed the cow and milked her and fed the mule, and then you'd go to the spring. You went and did your ten hours' work in the fields. You came back in the evening, you brought in your eggs and shut up the chickens, and you milked the cow and fed her and put her up, you watered the mule and fed him and put him up, and you carried in the water, and then you carried in the stove wood for the next day. And all of this was the chores. It wasn't considered work. *(Jonah Parker)*

You raised your living. Dug it out of the ground. (Walter Winebarger)

Like I say, just what little sugar and coffee and salt that you couldn't raise, that's all they had to buy.

They didn't go to buy everything to eat, and they canned enough stuff and raised it to do them 'til the next season. It was pretty rough going. I tell my boys that I wish they had to go a month like I was brought up all through my young days. They would wake up. But now they've got to have pay every week. If they go out and help me, why they have to have pay for it. I give them more than I got all of my growing up. I'd work a lot of days or weeks at a sawmill, all week saw or log or cut timber, whatever there was to do, and Dad would give me fifty cents. Well that would buy about as much as ten dollars now. It'd buy me a pack of smoking tobacco and go to the show. *(Walter Winebarger)*

It was a lot different than it is now. There wasn't but just a few houses. There wasn't but five houses on the creek here back in this settlement and everybody just farmed a little bit, got out crossties and pulpwood to make a living. Wouldn't have nothing like a tractor, no automobiles. We farmed with horses and mules and steers. Did you ever see the ol' steers? I've broke several of them. These were big

33

cattle, oxen. You could train them and work them and not even have a line on them. All you had to do was talk to them. They minded you, what you'd tell them to do. I've plowed with them, logged with them. I've hooked them to a wagon, everything. I finally traded them and got me a pair of horses. Use them better than steers—little faster, little easier to handle. Steers are pretty slow, most of them. Oxen, that's what we call steers, oxen; that's the same thing. *(Nelson Cabe)*

Well, now you put anything up there, and that mule will remember that. A horse will just walk in a hole or anything. If that mule ever steps in a hole, you can't ever get him back there. He'll remember that same place. And a horse will just go along and fall into it again. They don't watch where they're going. And a mule will just watch anything strange around. *(Boyd Payne)*

Plowing with a tractor on these hills, they get away from you. If they turn over, you're gone because you can't get out of that seat and out from between those wheels. Yeah, I know a boy up here that got killed. I think mules are smarter than horses. I think they've got more sense than horses have when you go to plowing. You can talk to a mule and control him, but you can't a horse. I'd rather have a mule than a horse. I like to plow with them. And a mule can stand the hot weather; he can stand to get out there and plow all day, and it won't hurt him. A horse can't stand it. And if there's a hole out there and it's not covered up, he's not going to step in it. That's one thing about a mule; you're not going to drive him off over a bluff or ride him off into a hole. You'll not get him to go across bridges with cracks in it. You'll just not get him to do those things. Then a mule can get out of a barn and get loose, get in a cornfield, eat what corn he wants, what it takes to do him, and he won't eat any more. A horse will eat enough to kill

him if a horse gets out. You've never seen a mule foundered in your life. And a mule don't ever get colic. A horse will get colic. He'll get too hot and climb into the water and just drink all the water he can get. A mule won't do that. A mule to stay cool if he's hot, well, he may drink a little water, but he won't drink enough to make him sick. *(Clifford Casey)*

My daddy made molasses. He took molasses, and he had corn on the cob and beans. Now, honey, the same way that produce is brought into Watauga County we took it out into Lenoir, Newton, Caldwell, all those small towns, and North Wilkesboro and all. He'd make as high as four or five trips in the fall of the year. Now as far as food that he bought, he would buy flour for breadmaking and he'd get a hundred pounds of sugar. Back then you couldn't get coffee except in a grain [bean], and I don't know how many pounds that was, but it was quite a few pounds. And my mother had two little coffee mills, poured it in and ground it, you know.

And Mama made all our clothes, and he'd usually get a bolt of cotton flannel for our gowns. We pretty well lived on the farm. About all that Mama ever went out for was coffee and sugar and flour and rice. We had the local general store, and Mama would churn two or three times a week. They usually milked two cows. Mama would send eggs and butter to Mr. Critcher's little country store. Anything that didn't have to be for our table, she sold. Mama made our (she called them aprons) but they were buttoned up behind a Peter Pan collar and a sash that tied like a pinafore. We always had two bonnets, one to be in the laundry.

And the last time that me and Nell Hayes had bonnets, we were out in the orchard; and Nell Hayes hung her bonnet up in an apple tree, and a cow ate the strings off it. She would make our bonnets like our little aprons. Part of them was yellow,

(Opposite) Typical Appalachian cabin with footbridge crossing creek

pink, and blue, a little baby check. About all the little girls wore pigtails. Have you ever worn pigtails? Some of the children do now, but we wore our hair long. I had my hair cut the first time when I graduated from the seventh grade. And that cow ate off Nell's strings; and, oh, she cried her heart out. *(Lottie Greene)*

We had an open fireplace and our cook stove. And my fireplace in my home where I was raised, honey, I do believe that's the best fireplace in McDowell County. (Ruth Settles)

When you made a good fire in that fireplace, you had to either open a door or crack the window, one. It was really a good fireplace. We cooked some on the fire and on the cook stove, too. We had a spring house, and we had a place dug out under the hill in the sand rock where we kept our potatoes and our canned stuff. Didn't any of it freeze in the wintertime. We had a door to it. We kept it closed in the wintertime. We left it open in the summer most of the time. Back then, when I was home, nothing was ever bothered; but, boy, now you sure can't leave yourself and go back and it all be together. *(Ruth Settles)*

People have been really hard workers up here, and they didn't know it really. They thought they were playing it out, and they didn't really realize what they were doing, just to survive. And yet they felt in a way that they weren't doing all they could in that sense. They felt sort of the reason they didn't have more was their fault. (Raymond Presnell)

Papa had thirty or forty cows, and he'd take a whole truck load, wagon load, of butter to town and sell it, and he drove cattle in through Charlotte and all down through there. He raised hogs every year to pay his taxes, and he drove those hogs through plumb to Charlotte and sold them for three cents a pound. And they'd take two hundred maybe at one trip, and there wasn't a bridge across up here. The horses had to swim across, and the wagon was turned way down this a-way and would swim around and go down if you didn't have it loaded awfully heavy, and the hogs had to swim across the river. And it took them about three weeks to get from here to Charlotte. They'd just leave the hogs out at night. They were so tired and give out they'd just pile down. They'd throw the corn in. They [the hogs] wouldn't wander off; they were too tired. They didn't try to go. They stayed around pretty close and watched them, the work hands would. And they'd go through the state. That's where Papa met Mama down there. And Grandpa Carr had a big farm, and he had a big barn. And he had lots fenced in for people to put their cattle in when they'd come along. They'd get there in three days. They'd stay there and rest one day and then get on. And he'd come back with droves of horses. He'd swap cattle. He'd bring back everything nearly. *(Carrie Johnson)*

You'd sell your cattle in October, and they had to be walked out of here to Shouns Crossroads in Tennessee to be loaded on a rail car and be shipped to Lancaster, Pennsylvania. It was fifteen miles or more, maybe twenty. Oh, I've seen the road full of sheep—lambs done the same way. They walked the lambs to sheds, loaded the boxcar, and shipped them.

Well, I'll tell you, after the first few miles they [the cows and sheep] sort of learned what the road was, and they'd stay in it pretty well. But the first few miles were rough. They'd go most anywhere. They were still feeling good and were running, you know. But they'd get tired, and they'd get to where they'd stay in the road. Them collie dogs was pretty well trained. *(Alfred Adams)*

I picked a many a gallon of strawberries and toted them off the mountain. Get a dollar a gallon. Four or five dollars would buy me a whole outfit. Five dollars now won't get you a pair of shoes. You could get a whole outfit, cloth to make your dress, nice little ready-made then, cheaper than you can now. Twenty-five or thirty dollars will get you a dress now. (Lilly Wykle)

But the women really have worked side by side with their men. They don't mind going to the field, pulling corn and doing things like that. It's a lot better than it used to be. My husband's grandmother was kind of a small woman. They were hoeing corn, and there were a bunch of sprouts there, and she was pulling those sprouts. Her husband said, "Don't do that. There might be a snake in there." She said, "There ain't no snake in there." And she hit another thing, and a copperhead was there, and it bit her on the hand, and it made her hand crippled. *(Carrie Burnette)*

You had to walk or go in a wagon, and you were going faster walking than you were in a wagon. I know my father one time had an old horse, and he started to ride him to Canton to town on Saturday or sometime. So he just tied him up to a tree up here and walked on down there. He said he'd rather walk, could get along faster than he could riding a horse. That's just the way they were. Your transportation was a wagon. My daddy carpentered a lot. Every now and then he'd get carpentry work. Outside of that it was farming. It was raising apples. We had an apple orchard on the mountain. We'd sell them, peddle them out in a wagon down here. And they had an apple house up a way on the mountain. So they'd go up there and pick those

apples and haul them off on a sled, put them in the apple house. When they got ready to go sell the apples, they'd go take the sled, not a wagon, get a load of apples, bring them off, and load them on a wagon.

And then, if you had a good milk cow or butter cow that would make plenty of milk and butter, that cow would set your table. You'd sell that butter. We never did sell any milk or buttermilk. We always gave it away to people who were poorer than we were. Mother would churn the butter. We didn't have a refrigerator. We had a spring box, and she'd wrap that butter in cheesecloth and put it in a little split basket, wet grape leaves and put around it in the summertime when it was hot, and I'd carry that butter to Canton. And never in my lifetime did I ever spend one penny of that money. I always carried the money back to her. Like I said, a good milk cow would furnish the table.

Your apple money and stuff like that would pay the taxes and other expenses that you had. You had to have a little sugar. You didn't have to have any lard because you used hog lard. You'd have plenty of butter. You had plenty of good sweet milk to drink. You had to buy salt, soda, sugar, coffee, baking powder, and flour. And you needed to buy shoes and clothing. I clothed myself ever since I was twelve years old. I raised chickens. A man pulled a little rubber-tire wagon buying up chickens. He had a little set of scales, and he'd weigh them and he'd pay me for the chickens. Of course, you had your own corn there to feed them, so you weren't out on anything like that. *(Quay Smathers)*

There were seven of us children, and we gathered bark and roots and fern. We gathered fern, and my daddy hauled it with mules out to Elk Park and Banner Elk. And that was our main money crop. We didn't get too much money, but we raised most of our food and did without most of the clothing. We were pretty poorly dressed most of the time, a lot of us were. I know I was. *(Raymond Presnell)*

PART TWO

Roots and Yarbs

The People and Their History

THE COURTHOUSE IN SYLVA SITS MAJESTICALLY ON A STEEP HILL and towers up over the town. It can be seen from a long way off, framed by surrounding mountain peaks. The sight of it is striking from the highway on the approach to Sylva. Its prominence makes a statement somehow. Beautiful courthouses dominate other county seats throughout the mountains and seem to stand as symbols of the sense of democracy and debate that still pervades the area.

I remember walking by the courthouse in North Wilkesboro. I had to stop and admire it for a while. It was a very commanding white building and seemed to send out signals that law and justice could be found within its walls. The cannon that stood in front stirred up thoughts about the rich history of this area. Visions of Civil War battles and raids on mountain homes by deserters or conflicting forces came to mind. I also thought of the Over the Mountain March during the American Revolution. Bill Wilkins' eyes had been full of fire as he described the scene of mountaineers gathering forces and marching to Kings Mountain to protect their families and homesteads from threatened occupation by the British.

One time, I was out at Green's Creek visiting Delia and Grady Reed. Grady was showing me his beautiful hunting dogs, and suddenly a political joke came to mind. This led him on to other stories and political comments, all laced with a little humor that naturally goes along with most of Grady's descriptions through those raised eyebrows, the twinkle in his eyes, and the upward lilt in his voice. A good bit of basic wisdom comes through, too.

People in the Southern Appalachians, from all walks of life, have a strong sense of history, and the main method for transmitting and savoring important events from the past has been through their oral tradition. Stories have been handed down over the years and still are. Illuminating descriptions of the Civil War or comments on political issues come just as easily to a backwoods farmer as to a college professor.

The Clarke family was very helpful in educating me about their area near Asheville. They invited me to family dinners and introduced me to local people, such as Nanny Suttles, Ruth and Clinard Settles, the Owenby family, the Bradleys and Merrells. They invited me to a square dance held in celebration of Mr. Clarke's running

(Opposite) "Slick", Ray Hicks's beagle hound on the front porch, Watauga County

for Congress. Elspie Clarke took me on a horseback ride over mountain trails and told me of her father's (James G.K. McClure) love for the area and efforts to set up the Farmers' Federation. Their son-in-law, John Ager, has just finished a book on Mr. McClure's life. The love of this area that this family inspired had a tremendously energizing effect on me. One day I had driven over to visit with Modeen and Roscoe Bradley. The trip was picturesque, and their farm was immaculately kept. I had expected to visit with some good down-to-earth country people. That they were, but they were much more articulate in their speech and thinking than I was. This was another lesson I learned during this journey. Phelps Merrell was visiting them and begins this chapter. You will soon see why I really think it needs no introduction.

Ashe County scene

40

ORIGINS

There's adequate reason for the lateness of this settlement in the region west of the crest of the Blue Ridge Mountains. On October 7, 1763, George III, King of England, issued a proclamation in which he prohibited any settlement west of the source of the rivers which flowed into the Atlantic Ocean. Then, after the Revolution, they were free to move into the western section.

One of the first settlers in the territory across the crest of the Blue Ridge was Samuel Davidson, who came across Swannanoa Gap in the latter part of 1784. He was killed by the Indians, and his family was forced to flee to Old Fort east of the crest of the Blue Ridge. A few months later, in 1785, a group of his relatives and friends came from Catawba across the Swannanoa Gap and formed a colony around the mouth of the Bee Tree Creek. These were the first white settlers west of the Blue Ridge Mountains. *(Phelps Merrell)*

Lilly and Hester Wykle

Have you heard about the Over the Mountain March, the Battle of Kings Mountain? We consider it the turning point of the Revolution. There was a Colonel Ferguson who was a British colonel. He was coming from Charleston up through Morganton and that area, and he sent word into the mountains up our way that if the mountain men didn't come down and join the king's forces and help the king's army, he was coming up and would burn their homes. Well, you don't tell a mountain man you're going to burn his home. Anyway, the word got around, and from over near Abingdon, Virginia,

and Johnson City [Tennessee], some former Indian scouts decided they'd go find Ferguson. They came through Plumtree and picked up men as they came along. They finally caught up with Ferguson at Kings Mountain. He had heard they were coming, and he got up on what is now known as Kings Mountain and thought he was safe. These mountain men surrounded that mountain and went up on all sides at the same time. They hid behind trees. It was a complete victory and the battle didn't last but about an hour and twenty minutes. They killed or captured everybody on that hill. Ferguson was killed, and he's buried there. From then on, Cornwallis started making his retreat, and that was the turning point of the Revolutionary War. We re-enact this over the mountain march. That's what it was called, "The Over the Mountain March." *(Bill Wilkins)*

Ben Cleveland is the man who blew that horn from Rendezvous [Mountain] to call the 340 men from Wilkes County to Kings Mountain in the Revolutionary War. Remember, there wasn't any law, there were some people who took advantage of houses where the menfolk had gone into the war. They would rob them, particularly to get the meat and the horses. If you robbed a man of his horse, that was his life. You had to have a horse to go anywhere, so it was a very serious thing.

Most of the people that migrated to the United States were the Scotch-Irish. They came with their Greek books under their arms, and most of them served in indenture as teachers. By this time the Catholics had got Delaware, the Dutch had New York, and the Quakers had Pennsylvania; and there wasn't any land up there, so they came down as soon as they served indenture, down to the Appalachian Mountains, and settled in the coves and the hollows. Of course, they lost the chance of education, but they handed down the stories, the "Jack Tales" and the "Grandfather Tales," and they sang

Sam Ervin

their songs. They're the ones that loved their "R's." They said "Har" and "Far," and they said "Winder" for window. They rolled that "R" every time. That's between Chaucer and Elizabethan, and it's the original English. Today it's all but disappeared from the British Isles, and people come with their tape recorders to hear the ballads and to hear the language that's still, in some cases, spoken by the Scotch-Irish. They are a good-looking people, and you'll see them all up and down the mountains, and you can recognize them. We look alike up in the mountains. The people have that kind of look. I've been privileged to travel all around the United States, and people out in Oregon look a certain way, the people in California, and you ought to see those beauties down in Mississippi where it's moist. We do look like a certain area. And that taxi driver up on Washington Square who can tell you what state you come from has a point. *(Annie Winkler)*

I called Mary McBryde, Sam Ervin's secretary and trusted assistant, to set up an interview with him. She was very helpful and arranged things quickly. Sam Ervin had been a friend of my father for years. He was interested in what I was doing as I had described it to Mrs. McBryde.

On the day of the interview, I drove through the rolling hills of the Piedmont from Greensboro up to Morganton, and I saw Table Rock as I approached. The directions to the house in town were faultless and led me there on time. I was a little bit nervous. I had seen "Senator Sam" on television during the Watergate hearings and had been proud of him. I had watched those eyebrows raise up and seen the spark in his eyes when he commented on human nature and the merits of conducting life in an honest fashion. But what

I think the worst thing that people ever do to the mountain people is to try to stereotype them because they're, if anything, more individualistic than any other group of people I know. Most of my people were Scotch-Irish. The Scotch-Irish have got a Presbyterian conscience. It won't keep you from sinning, but it'll keep you from enjoying your sin, and it will smite you unmercifully if you don't do what it tells you is right. The Scotch-Irish were Scots and not Irish at all, and the English induced them to move from Scotland over to Ireland when they confiscated the lands of the Irish rebels in about 1600. Some of them over there now are feuding and fussing with the Irish Republican Army. (Sam Ervin)

would he be like in person now, years later? The sparkle was still there. We sat in his office surrounded by books of all sorts. He immediately put me at ease, and after hearing about my purposes in pursuing this book and some of my experiences, he launched into wonderful accounts of his own recollections and ideas about mountain people. He also gave me other sources to contact for a fuller view of the area and its history, which were very dear to him.

Later on, I asked him if he would write a foreword to my book. He accepted, and I sent him the transcript of his own interview for review along with excerpts from many other interviews, so that he could get a feel for the material that eventually would come out in this book. He painstakingly went through his own transcript, making corrections and clarifications where necessary in his own hand, and studied the other material that I

had sent him. After a good deal of work, he sent me a beautiful foreword with best wishes for a successful book that he believed in. Soon after this, he was taken ill, and I was pained to find that my thank-you letter probably had reached him after his death.

When my father and I drove up for the funeral, we used the same directions from my notes to get to the house. We talked to Sam's daughter and decided to wander around the town for a while before going to the church. When we later arrived, the church was jam-packed. We rationalized that we had done our best and that Sam would know we had tried. Then we saw a good number of old friends from all over the state among the many politicians. They let me slip into the funeral as an honorary pallbearer with my father and other lawyers. Afterward, I was able to visit with Sam's lovely wife, Miss Margaret, his son, and other family members. I talked with Mary McBryde who recently had worked with him on the foreword to my book and heard of his feelings about it. There were lots of mountain people there too.

As we drove away from the church, the streets of Morganton were lined with people. These were mostly local people, and the church had not been large enough to hold them. They loved this man and were a testament to him. (W. M.)

Lily pads on Bass Lake, Moses H. Cone Estate, near Blowing Rock

The Scotch-Irish came in overwhelming numbers, so rapidly that when the American Revolution came, they were new in the colonies in which they lived and isolated from other cultural influences. The Scotch-Irish and the Germans filled up the great wasteland of the Piedmont which, contrary to popular notion, was unpopulated when they arrived. They had no direct contact with the English who lived far to the east. When the war came, they had no loyalty to the colonial government because the colonial government had already begun to send tax gatherers among them. The Battle of Alamance in 1771, before the Revolution ever came, was the Scotch-Irish rebelling against tax gatherers who came in from the east—the English. Constituted authority had been their problem. After we won the Revolutionary War, in payment for our service, the young government gave us land in the mountains. So we went into the mountains, not yet integrated into American society and having nothing whatever to share with the plantation South, and became the same kind of farmer our ancestors had been for hundreds of years, keeping elbow room, developing our own elaborate homesteads, with a house with a chimney outside. If we got pretentious, we'd build one just like it, turn it the other way and put a chimney on the other end. Then, if we got overcrowded, we'd take the roof off and raise it up with our oblong rooms with doors opposite each other and a window beside a chimney to throw daylight on the hearth where the women worked. We kept our animals around us, so we had sheep barns and pig pens and stables for the cows, stables for the horses. We had corncribs and all these things close by, root cellars, just right out there, a place for everything. These elaborate Appalachian homesteads were duplications of what we'd had in the old country. *(Cratis Williams)*

Well, Harold's mother grew up in a house that had a separate kitchen. And she said many a morning when it snowed, they'd wake up and their blanket was covered in snow. Snow had come in through the cracks. On one end of the house there was a kitchen and dining room with a big fireplace in it.

Then they had the living quarters on the other end, and you had to go out on the porch and come around. That was for fire purposes. They had a loft; had a little thing that went up to a loft, but that had just one big room. There was a fireplace in it and two beds in that room. Then there was another room just back of that. They slept in it too, but the fireplace was the only heat they had. You had to go across the porch, and had to wash on the porch which went across to the kitchen. On the way to the kitchen, you broke the ice and washed your face. See, they had a bench built along the porch. If

Outbuildings at Letha Hicks's farm, Haywood County

it was real, real cold, they'd bring a bucket and set it in the house. And they'd bank the fire back at night, and they kept a fire going all the time. *(Rachel Sutton)*

The spring was always down the hill from the house. It was always right off in a hole. The spring was down a pair of rock steps. It wasn't very far away. It was down next to a creek or a branch which came right out from under that mountain. And there was a big ol' spring box. *(Harold Sutton)*

In Western North Carolina, the Silers were really pioneers. They came over from Buncombe County to Macon County. They were among the very first settlers there. My great-grandfather had the first house in Macon County that had glass windows. Long before the Civil War they started having family meetings.

One of my family came over with a companion with the idea of starting a little store for the Indians. They came into what was Indian territory in which is now Macon County and built a little shelter. One of the men said, "I bet the Indians are

45

aware that we are here." They didn't have long to wait before their suspicions were confirmed. One of the Indians came and told them they would have to leave as that was Indian territory. My great-grandfather said, "We come as friends. We have things that your people would like to have, cloth, materials, implements, saws and hammers, and things of that nature. You might drive us out, but there will be others that will come that may not be so friendly." The Indians said, "We'll talk again." They had a powwow and decided that it would be the prudent thing to let these people stay. They were friendly, and they got along beautifully. My great-grandmother spoke the Indian language.
(Louise Morgan Rodda)

My grandfather settled up in the mountain country in the very northwestern part of this county. His father came from Dillsboro and settled out here by Laurel Springs. When my father was about three years old, my grandfather moved up into the mountain. I think he paid 150 dollars and an old long-barrel rifle (what they used to call a hog rifle)

for about five hundred acres of land. None of it was cleared. It was right in the wilderness.
(Delmer Rose)

Abe Enloe is reputed by mountain legend to have been the father of Abraham Lincoln. Abraham Lincoln's mother was Nancy Hanks. She worked at the tavern or inn that Abraham Enloe ran near Sylva. He owned the inn, and Nancy Hanks was a serving girl in the inn before she married Lincoln.
(Harold Bennett)

Abraham Enloe lived in Rutherford County. Nancy Hanks worked for him, and the story goes that Nancy got pregnant. Well, Grandma Enloe didn't like that too well (Nancy was sort of the servant in the family), so she got rid of Nancy. Nancy moved to Kentucky and married Tom Lincoln. She had the baby Abraham and changed the name, of course, to Abraham Lincoln. Supposedly he was Abraham Lincoln, the president. Whether that is true or not, nobody knows. But the Enloes did live in Rutherford County and Nancy Hanks did work for the Enloes. *(Dan Moore)*

Dogwoods, maples, and oaks along Buck Creek, McDowell County

When Nancy Hanks became pregnant, Mrs. Enloe raised all sorts of havoc. Abraham Enloe hired Tom Lincoln to take her over the mountain and marry her. He gave him a team of mules and some money and they left. The baby was born the next year. Abraham Enloe was six feet, six inches tall and stringy. Everybody knew that Abraham Enloe was the father of the baby. Then, when he grew up, he became president of the United States. Colonel Morrison here in Western North Carolina and George Shuford, who did all the land titles in Western North Carolina and who lived to be 105, knew that Abraham Enloe was the father of Abraham Lincoln. They have pictures of all the other children of Abraham Enloe here in North Carolina, and you can't tell any of them from Abraham Lincoln. They are all six feet, six inches tall, and all look alike.
(Landon Roberts)

Restored cabin belonging to Kay and Bill Wilkins, Plum Tree, Avery County

This was the West. My mother was born in a log house. My grandmother and grandfather had one of the first houses built out of sawed lumber on Jonathan's Creek. My mother was born in 1880, and her sisters and brother after her were born in the "new house" as they called it. The house that my grandfather and grandmother built in 1881 or thereabouts is not in existence. It burned several years ago. But, the old log barn that she built while my grandfather was collecting taxes in Pine Creek one summer is still in existence. It's the one just this side of the eastern line of Maggie Valley. There are two buildings there. One is a barn and the other a corncrib. The house that my mother was born in was built before 1838. There was a deed for the property in 1838 that called for the house and fruit trees. They were Little John, Buff Apples, and Rusty Coats. *(Frank Ferguson)*

We first belonged to the Cherokee Nation, then we belonged to Spain, then we belonged to France. Then after the Louisiana Purchase, we belonged to the United States. Then during the Civil War, we belonged to the Confederate States of America. Then we belonged to the United States again. We were at one time in the State of Franklin. The Blue Ridge was the eastern boundary. The Virginia line was the northern boundary. Georgia was the southern boundary. And there wasn't any western boundary, just the wilderness. The eastern boundary was just the top of the Blue Ridge between here and Crossnore, between here and Newland, the dividing line. The water here runs into the Mississippi, and the water on the other side runs into the Atlantic Ocean. *(Ivor Vance)*

The first slaves that were brought to Yancey County were brought by General Wade Hampton. General Wade Hampton's great-grandson married my aunt, and they lived in Little Creek in Yancey County. Most of the people who settled this mountain didn't believe in having slaves, and there were only a few people who owned slaves. *(B. Hensley)*

THE CIVIL WAR

As the Civil War approached, these people living in Appalachia were confronted with the possibility of a war. They realized that they'd never had it so good and they had made the nation. Therefore, they would stay with it and defend it which meant that during the Civil War, they supported the North. When the war was over, then of course, they identified with the black Republican Party and they became a despised minority, both culturally and politically, occupying the backyards of Southern states. It was customary then in the capital towns to pass laws in such a way that any benefits that might be available to anybody anywhere would not be shared with the Appalachia people—those rebels, you know, those traitors. And that went on down to 1950. But we were cut off in all these states who had no sense of solidarity. We suffered more from the Civil War than any other identifiable group—and didn't know it. (Cratis Williams)

History said nothing about us, and we sank then from a literacy level higher than that representative of the country to the lowest level of illiteracy—or highest, whichever way you're looking at the scale—by 1890. But the fact that we continued in the main throughout the region to support the Republican candidate, to identify with the Republican Party, accounts mainly for our poverty and neglect.

In time we became a land open for exploitation because we had a lot of wealth buried in the Appalachian hills and the finest timber stand in the world. Because we were despised, it seemed all right to trick us, if possible, to get all this wealth out of our hands without leaving anything for us. Millions of cars of coal and other valuable things were hauled out without leaving any taxes behind at all to support the people who were being exploited. And no tax was paid for denuding our mountains of fine timber.

The history books in the states told how the blacks suffered. We knew the fate of the plantation owners. We knew what happened to the fine culture which certainly was exaggerated in retrospect. We knew what happened to all that. We knew what villains the Yankees were, but nobody said anything about the mountaineers. We have one of the richest histories of any subculture group in the country, if not the richest. And it's identifiable and traceable. It doesn't become lost in speculation. *(Cratis Williams)*

During the Civil War, there was an unusual situation in East Tennessee and Western North Carolina. Many of the people were related. Practically all of them had come from Virginia, had emigrated west to find something that they could live on. It was a quest for survival. They chose different sides in the Civil War. Within my own family that happened. A lot of East Tennessee and a lot of the northern part of Haywood County went with the Northern forces, the Yankees, the Union. And most of the southern part, south of Cataloochee, went with the Confederates. And, actually, there were relatives fighting against relatives in the Civil War. This was just a personal feeling that they all had about the South or the North. Of course, none of them owned slaves, or very few of them in those days. Very few slaves were owned in Western North Carolina, so I was told by my father. There were pretty good-sized homesteads. But, this was tough farming. This was mountain land—tobacco, corn, and that was about it. *(Harold Bennett)*

Here's what happened. You take my grandfather Burleson. He deserted the Southern army and joined the Yankees. Now my granddaddy Houston drew a little government pension. It was either twelve or fifteen dollars a month. Well, Joe Burleson, whenever he came back out of the Northern army, drew maybe one hundred dollars in pension, and he drew it as long as he lived. So the difference there might have been what caused a lot of fellows to desert the Southern army and go to the Northern, hoping for better benefits if they lived through it. And it worked out that way.
(Myron Houston)

The Civil War was a genuine civil war in Appalachia because not everybody stayed with the Union. Some of them supported the South. Some didn't want to have a thing to do with either side and hid out for the duration and became despised by both groups. **(Cratis Williams)**

When you look at census records, you see families that existed before 1860, and then they're gone by 1870 or the widows have remarried and they have other children. But whole families just disappeared. I never realized there was that much impact here. I

Snow-covered ridges, Blue Ridge Mountains, Yancey County

think that's something that people don't realize. They think of the mountains as a place where people hid out and weren't involved and didn't fight or were Union sympathizers. *(Rose Marie Feimster)*

They didn't own slaves. They were fighting for honor and duty. It was their duty to answer the call. Do you know how many lost their lives?—529,332. The biggest city in North Carolina in 1860 was Wilmington, with 5,000 people. Where'd they all come from? North Carolina lost more men than any other state out of the nine Southern states. We were the first at Bethel, first at Gettysburg, and last at Appomattox. We didn't want to get in the war. We didn't know what we were fighting for.
(Ivor Vance)

There were some people who were drafted into the Confederate Army, and they deserted and became what they called "bushwackers." They plundered the homes and the property of people who were faithful to the South. There were a lot of people killed by the bushwackers, and a lot of people killed the bushwackers. I knew an old man in Mitchell County, Uncle Reuben Young everybody called him, who had been in the Confederate Army. He said he came home one day after service, had a furlough and needed a bath worse than anything, so he started to bathe in a tin tub in the house in the middle of July. His son hollered to him and told him the bushwackers were coming. He said he had to jump up in his birthday clothes and hide. The only place he could find to hide was to crawl under a haystack in the middle of July in his birthday clothes. He said the bushwackers stayed around a long time and he never had such a miserable time in all his life, but that made him a more staunch Confederate and a more staunch Democrat.
(Sam Ervin)

She (my grandmother) said they like to have starved to death during the Civil War. They couldn't buy bread, flour, or anything. They boiled potatoes for bread, Irish potatoes, and they had dried beans.

Back then they didn't can food, they dried it. Their daddy never came home. They captured him or killed him or something.

There were graves over there in the field with brick around them. We picked cotton over there, and I asked them why they buried people there. One of the men that owned the cotton field said that they were soldiers' graves. They were killed and buried here. The war came right through Lincoln County. Grandma said they never heard tell of their daddy any more. Grandma went to her grandparents to live 'til the war was over because they didn't have anything to eat; it had been stolen.
(Bertha Lowe)

I will be eighty-nine years old in February. My grandmother worked with the doctors at Murphy as a young woman. During the Civil War, her husband—he was quite a bit older than she was—had to hide out from the Yankees. They came to her house. Her oldest sons were just lads and they dug a hole under the house. They pried up the plank and dug a hole and put a box in there and saved their meat. They took their cow to a cave in the mountains up somewhere beyond Murphy, and the horse, and hid them out to keep the soldiers from taking them. The Yankees came to the house searching for Grandpa, and they'd have killed him if they could have found him. He hid in a cave. She would go every chance she got and carry food to him. The winters were so cold, but he couldn't have a fire because he was afraid they'd smell smoke and find him.

After Grandpa died, she raised her family by delivering babies. She delivered more babies than those doctors at Murphy because she did all the country work. The doctors couldn't get out. She rode a horse over the mountains and went through with panthers screaming and bears running across the road in front of her. She had to ride at night. If they went after her for anything, she went to help. They'd take an extra horse for her to ride.

With Grandma's oldest daughter taking care of the younger children, she took care of mothers and babies and patients that she could look after, to help out in money matters or food. She took anything anybody had that she could use to help. *(Harriet "Granny" Echols)*

There was real split during the Civil War. My father's people were for the Yankees; however, they didn't fight for the Yankees. My mother's people were Rebels to the core. My grandfather fought the Battle of Bull Run. My grandfather on my father's side joined the Confederacy. He was a Union sympathizer, but he joined the Confederacy. I saw where he had applied for a pension in 1914. He didn't die until 1922. He applied for a pension in 1914 and got fourteen dollars a month.

Kay's [Wilkins] family ran an underground railroad. Her grandfather English would help slaves and white prisoners that had escaped. He'd hide them during the day and tell them how to go at night and who to contact that would hide them the next day and then at night would give them directions until they reached the Union lines. *(Ivor Vance)*

The people up there are people of rather strong convictions. They didn't have many slaves, and a lot of them felt that the Civil War was not their war. In other words, they were against slavery. They owned no slaves, but a good many of them would come down. We had in this county a lot of them that would come from what's now Mitchell and Avery counties and join the Confederate companies here. After the war, most of the others joined the Republican party. If you do find a Democrat up there, you find a person of strong convictions. The Confederates joined the Democratic party.

Zeb Vance was very much loved by the mountain people, and all the people of the state for that matter. He was a member of the Know-Nothing Party before the war. He joined the Democrats later. He was very much opposed to secession. When it came up that he had toured the state and made speeches against seceding, well, I've been told by the older people over in some of the mountain counties that if Vance had come back after he came out for secession, that the mountain counties would have probably backed the Confederacy. This county was the last bastion of the Confederacy on this side. It was one hundred percent in favor of the Confederacy. Notwithstanding, the Union candidate defeated the Secession candidate by only thirty-two votes on the question of secession in January or February 1861. After Lincoln called on North Carolina to furnish troops to subjugate the seceded states, Vance always said that he was in Madison County, one of the mountain counties beyond Asheville, and as he was speaking of the Union, he raised his arm and somebody ran up the aisle and handed him a copy of the telegram of Lincoln calling on North Carolina for troops. Vance instantly realized that left North Carolina no alternative, so he was accustomed to saying that "My arm went up for the Union and came down for the Confederacy." These people said it would have been quite different in many of the mountain counties if he had gotten back and made the secession speech to them. *(Sam Ervin)*

POLITICS

The people's families who were Unionist are still mostly Republican. The Democrats were Confederates, Southerners. There were a lot of people that came into the mountains to hide. We couldn't get anything out of Raleigh because it was predominately Republican in the mountain counties. Actually, today we don't get our share of the road money, so far as getting the work done. Another reason for that is it costs ten times more to build a road where you have to blast out rock cliffs than what it does down in Eastern Carolina where you don't have to go through a big mountain of rock. *(Wade Brown)*

Mountain people usually take their politics very seriously. You're either a Democrat or a Republican and you're not supposed to split your tickets. You're not supposed to change parties and things like that. People mix up their tickets a lot more now than they used to. It used to be a pretty rigid, right-down-the-line business in the mountain area.
(Alfred Adams)

Alfred Adams

I've always been a Republican. But I'm going to tell you this tale though. You can tell it either way. Back when Carter and Mondale were running for president, Carter came up here and said he wanted to see the dogs. I took him around there to see the dogs and see the pups. I had a gang of pups then. He said, "What's their politics?" I said, "Democrat." He bragged on them and said, "They're sure pretty." Well, he left and brought Mondale back with him in about two weeks and said, "Let's go see your pups." We went out to look at them and he said, "Tell him what their politics is." I said, "They're Republicans." He said, "The other day you told me

they was Democrats." I said, "Well, they was, but they got their eyes open now."

I've got a sister-in-law's a strong Democrat. Oh, it makes her mad to tease her about, try to tell her to vote the Republican ticket. I was teasing her about being a Democrat. She's going to be a Democrat, she said. I said, "Well, just stay one then."

It's kind of like the two fellows out coon hunting one time. They treed a polecat. It was in a hollow log and one fellow kept trying to get that polecat out of the hollow log, and it was about to stink him to death. The other one says, "Let him alone, he'll stink his own self out directly." And I said [to my sister-in-law], "Evelyn, I'm just going to let you go [and be a Democrat]. You'll stink yourself out directly."

As a rule, sure enough, you don't know which one to vote for. I'm proud they've got two parties. You have to have two parties because one party would go haywire directly if you didn't switch. You need to switch back and forth. I don't care which one is elected now. They don't need to be in over two or three times. Then they need to switch around and put the other side in. They do better. If they switch around, then they feel like they've got a little competition and they got to do good, you know, to stay up, to keep everything going. It's good to change, ain't it? *(Grady Reed)*

We didn't have any voice in state government, very little. Eastern North Carolina, Raleigh, was more accessible to them. It was a long journey from Webster to Raleigh. They had to come by train. Even when I came to the University [of North Carolina at Chapel Hill], I had to go to Asheville on the train, change trains in Asheville, come to Salisbury and change trains, and then go to Greensboro and change trains, then go to Durham and catch a bus to Chapel Hill. People just didn't run down to Raleigh like they do from Greensboro and the eastern sections. It was a long, hard trip and therefore, people in the western part of the state didn't participate. That was one reason they didn't have as much influence politically as people near Raleigh who came into Raleigh on all occasions and knew what was going on. We didn't know what was going on in Raleigh. And most of the people in the mountains didn't care, as long as they left them alone. The western part of the state was isolated. Part of their lack of influence was due to the fact that they just didn't try to do anything about the political situation. They voted for the one of their choice, but after that, they pretty well left state government alone. They didn't participate.

I think most of the changes have been pretty good. Certainly, the area is no longer isolated as it has been for many years. I was a native of the county, the first governor since Zeb Vance that came from that area. [Governor James] Holshouser was from another mountain section, so we've had some participation. *(Dan Moore)*

———————

When I called Dan Moore for an interview, he had recently undergone an operation. He said that he was up and about, at the office working a good

part of the time, and to come on ahead to his home in Raleigh. He had been governor of the state at one time and had served on the state Supreme Court, so Raleigh had been home for him and his wife, Jeanelle, for some years. But after only a few minutes of talking with him, it was clear about where his real home remained. This was a true mountain man with all of the strength, practicality, sensitivity, and basic common sense wisdom seen in so many of these people. Jeanelle had been brought up in the mountains of Tennessee. Dan told me about growing up in the mountains, and they both described their later experiences trying to deal with outsiders' notions of the Appalachia in which they had grown up.

Their enthusiasm and belief that an accurate story should be told caught me up again and helped bolster my determination to see this project through. There was a real purpose to this book, and they understood it. Their encouragement helped me see that purpose more clearly.

Dan Moore's funeral was no less moving for me than Sam Ervin's had been. It was disturbing to find such wise and sensitive people slipping away. After hearing of Dan's death, Mother and I drove to Raleigh for the funeral. She had known Dan and Jeanelle for a long time. The streets were crowded, and parking places were hard to find. Again, there were people from all over the state who had come to pay their respects, but on the way out of the church I saw Wade Brown and Alfred Adams, who had come all the way from Boone. They had come as a gesture of their admiration for one of their own. (W. M.)

———————

Uncle Dave Snelson was a farmer out here. When J. Melville Broughton ran for governor, he didn't have any political allies up here. The whole organization was against him. He came up and found Uncle Dave Snelson and Handy Hipps, who was a lawyer. Handy Hipps had been superintendent of the schools and a lawyer and had come from Spring Creek over in Madison County. They decided they would help J. Melville Broughton when they saw him. They made an agreement with him that they would help him through the primary and through the election. They told him, "If you are elected, the one thing you will have to promise to do as your first act as governor of North Carolina will be to pave the road from Leicester to Spring Creek." He said, "Oh, I'll do that if you'll help me and I get the nomination. When I am the governor of North Carolina, that will be my first official act."

Broughton won the primary; then he won the election. So these two characters, Handy and Uncle Dave, went down to the inauguration. As soon as the inauguration was over, they went over to the governor's office and they said, "Governor, remember when you were our friend up in the hills, you made a promise to us?" J. Melville reared back and said, "Boys, I have to tell you there's been a little change in my plans. If you can come back in two or three years, I will see what I can do." So the two of them left, and they drove all the way from Raleigh and neither one of them had spoken until Uncle Dave turned around to Handy and said, "Handy, we shot us a bird, but it was all feathers."

In another true story, Zeno Ponder, a Democrat, had sued Mr. Cobb, the chairman of the Republican party. He claimed that the Republican had slandered him in that he had been accused of stealing the election. Mr. Meekins, my partner, represented Mr. Cobb. We pled the truth of the allegation and subpoenaed 2,300 witnesses, everybody who was entitled to vote in the town of Marshall.

We put all these witnesses on the stand and asked, "Are you a registered voter?" and "Did you vote in the election?" and so forth through the whole 2,300 of them. There were two other plaintiffs. One of the plaintiffs was a fellow by the name of Rice. He lived up on a creek near my farm. As it turned out, evidence showed that Mr. Rice's father had been dead eight years but had voted in the last two elections. So, I asked him, "When your father came back to vote in these elections, did he come by to see you?" Eventually, the jury found in favor of Mr. Ponder for 40,000 dollars. But, they answered the issue as to damages to the other two fellows at four dollars apiece. Their damage was four dollars. So, they were known as the four-dollar men in Madison County. Everybody that met them on the street would say, "How about letting me borrow four dollars from you?" *(Landon Roberts)*

In the old days, effective politicians attended every funeral, and they would be sort of like preachers. They would go to every prominent person's funeral, go out the door, and shake hands with everybody as they came out, just like a preacher does. **(Landon Roberts)**

Barn on Edminsten farm, near Boone, Watauga County
(Opposite) Frank Ferguson in his Waynesville law office

THE DEPRESSION

Oh, when I came to Franklin, the Scott Griffin Hotel was fairly new. They had dances once a week, and they were big affairs. But pretty soon the Depression hit. The bank closed. Nobody had any money. Times were just horrible. Without a milk cow and garden, you didn't eat very well.

During the Depression, a family we heard about took the boards off the outside of the house and burned them. They were cold. They had a lot of children, and they practically burned the place up before they moved out. It had been a lovely house. Franklin had a time during that Depression. People who were on a salary were the ones that were the best off. Our bank didn't close until 1932. Most of them started closing around 1929. We finally got it open without losing everything. Then it was so much longer before we recovered. It was longer coming, but then it was longer getting over it, too.

My husband, Dick, finally got a job with the government searching titles for the Forest Service. He was getting 178 dollars a month, and he didn't get that. He had to put it into Jones and Jones (his law firm) because they were still trying to keep the firm going. He was the building and loan and insurance

Letha Hicks

agency. He had to go to Murphy, Bryson City, and Robbinsville, and he'd be gone the whole week. They worked until twelve o'clock on Saturday. He'd come home Saturday afternoon. In the meantime, I was trying to run an insurance agency, building and loan, and whatever else Gilmer [his brother] couldn't get done up there. Dick would come home usually at two o'clock on Saturday, and we'd go straight to the office. Times were really bad. *(Lois Jones)*

The Depression in Asheville was worse than any place in the world except Miami, Florida. Miami got over it, but Asheville never did. The Depression was hard, but most people had their own homes. They were not paying rent. They couldn't buy clothes, or many of the things in the world, but if you don't have anything when there is a Depression, you don't lose anything. When you are going from zero, you don't lose much.

I had an old uncle who was unmarried. During the Depression, he helped people. Anyone who didn't have a cow, he would give them a cow and they would take care of the cow. He said, "You have to feed her and when she has a calf, I'll take the calf; you take the milk." At one time, he had about two hundred cows out.

The Depression was very personal to me because my father had always been very active. When they closed the banks, I can remember my father coming home and playing solitaire. It was terrible.
(Landon Roberts)

We always had something to eat during the Depression. It was hard. Back during the Depression

and even World War II, they had sugar rationed and lard. But we killed hogs then, and we rendered all the fat into lard. Then you'd can it and it'd keep good, you see. *(Grady Reed)*

Now in the Depression we ate just as well as we did in prosperity. The cattle didn't bring as much, and the sheep didn't bring as much. But, as far as eating, we were making it at home. We put up a lot of apples and things. *(Alfred Adams)*

I married at about twenty-one, I guess. Through the 'thirties, the Depression, we had a good time—no money, no clothes, but I farmed. Grew plenty of vegetables, bought me a cow—paid twenty dollars for the cow on credit. There was an old lady who would come here about once every week or two and spend the night. She lived by herself, and she just loafered over the country and carried the news around. She'd give you the news, and you'd give her a place to stay.

People were pretty good back then, neighbors were. They knew how people's circumstances were. There was nothing to do and only a little farm work. The only way in the world that you could get a day's work would be to help somebody on the farm with his crop. Chances were you would just have to swap out with him. If he did hire you for money, it'd be one dollar for a whole day, ten or twelve hours, however much daylight there was.

I went down to one man's farm. He was teaching, and I knew that his crop had to be taken care of. I said, "I'm sure you're going to have to have some help taking care of your crop since you're away, and I'd love to do your work." He said, "Well, all right, provided you'll work for what I can get it done for." And I said, "How much can you get it done for?" He said, "Seventy-five cents a day." I said, "Okay, when I'm not busy, I'll work for that." It was one way of getting a few pennies, you know. So in just a day or two, he called me—wanted me to go do a day's work. Well, I went down there early and worked all day, and he came in from school after four-thirty and did whatever he needed to do 'til six o'clock; and at six o'clock he came out to where I

Salad beginnings: cabbage, peppers, and tomatoes from the garden

was, and he says, "Well, it's quitting time and you agreed to work for seventy-five cents." I said, "Yes." "But," he said, "I'm going to give you eighty." For a whole day! And I mean ten hours. Eighty cents for ten hours. That was eight cents an hour! He gave me a dollar a day for the rest of it.

My wife was taking care of the home. If it hadn't been for her, we'd have starved to death. She was one of the best cooks. She could fix one of the best meals, it seemed like, with the least to do with. Of course, I grew vegetables and stuff, and there was plenty of fruit in this country back then. Everybody nearly had a few apple trees. We even had trees here on this place, and berries and stuff like that; and we gathered all that. She put up a lot of canned stuff and made jellies. We ate better than people do now, better food actually.

It cost fifteen dollars then to deliver a baby. And I was in debt for doctor bills for three years. I'd pay a little along, but I actually wasn't out of debt for three years with Dr. Horsley. And, bless his heart, every time I'd try to get a job somewhere—jobs were so scarce, somebody was always ahead—he always gave me a good recommendation. The only jobs I ever got were on his recommendation, and he never would accept pay except, "Now are you

sure you can spare this?" Oh, he was good to me. There were a lot of people good to me.
(Monroe Ledford)

Jeanelle and I were married in 1933, which was the worst of the Depression. We went to Washington and New York on our honeymoon. The only reason we could go was I was local counsel to the Southern Railway and had a pass to ride. I had exactly one nickel in my pocket when I came back, and there wasn't any money. I met a client of mine on the street and he told me, "Dan, I owe you eighty dollars and I collected eighty dollars this morning." He said, "I can't give you all of it; but, I'll give you half, and I'll keep half." So he gave me forty dollars, which really helped tide me over. You could live for a month on forty dollars.

Banks were all closed during the "banking holiday" when Franklin Roosevelt closed all the banks. Money was just nonexistent. Up in the mountains most of the people made their own living farming, or at least they had a good-sized garden. They all had cows, pigs, and chickens.

A lot of people couldn't raise money to pay taxes. I was county attorney back in those days, and we just had to let the taxes sort of slide to keep from

selling everybody out for the taxes. I remember Southern Railway was our biggest taxpayer. I went to Atlanta, Southern's headquarters in the South, and got them to advance their 1932 budget, so that we could keep the jail open and pay the county officials. That's when the state had to take over the schools, if you will remember, in 1930.
(Dan Moore)

You just couldn't get hold of any money at all, and if you didn't have any money, you couldn't get anything else. It was just trying, that's about all; and you didn't accomplish much. Most of the people got along fairly well in the mountains back in there, but there was a time there when people would work for twenty-five cents and put in ten hours a day. Only they couldn't get it. There wasn't anybody to hire you for twenty-five cents. There was just hardly anything there for a while.
(Raymond Presnell)

We didn't have money. I had a Sunday dress. We called it a Sunday dress, and we had about two everyday dresses. Whenever Lorina went to school, while she was in school she'd wear my dress during the week. Then I'd wear it on Sunday, and she'd have to wear an old one to Sunday School. We had a hard time. We made our own clothes or a neighbor who was a seamstress made them. I worked plenty of days for fifty cents. *(Lillian Hooper)*

View ascending to the summit of Mount Mitchell

ISOLATION

Storm coming near Glendale Springs, Ashe County

Well, I was two years old when we moved to Jackson County. I was born in 1906, so I started school when I was about six, in 1912. At that time, we were pretty well cut off from the world to a large extent. The only way you had to travel then was on the train. That particular area of the state had only been served for about fifteen or twenty years by railroad. Up until that time the only way to travel was by horseback, carriage, or wagon. Jackson County when I was a child was very much like it was one hundred years prior to that time, no electricity, no telephone, no radio, no central water supply or sewer. It was a rural section. But, that's not to say it was a bad place to live. We had a good time growing up. You had to entertain yourself.

Due to the fact that the railroad missed Webster and came through Sylva, there was a movement to move the county seat to Sylva. In 1913, as I recall, the legislature approved it. That was about the end of Webster when the county seat moved. The courthouse, of course, closed down. Nobody much had

any business in Webster, and gradually Webster died out really as an active town. *(Dan Moore)*

I went down the Golden Manor Road about seven miles down the highway toward Marion and was looking for something we call Bee Rock. It's a right well-known place among the mountain people where there used to be a lot of trout. I stopped to ask directions at a house. There was a girl by herself. She wasn't over seventeen and she had a little baby. Her husband was off working on the road. She told me she had just shot a rattlesnake that was killing her chickens. She showed me the snake. She'd put it in a jar to show her husband. I asked her if she'd ever heard of Little Switzerland, just seven miles away. Had she ever been to Marion? Yes, once in her life she'd been to Marion. That was about ten miles the other way. She never had been out of the hollow anytime except that. Just think of that! That was not over two or three years ago, a short time ago.

That makes me think of another funny story. An old mountain man up here had heard that the train had come through. You know how mountain people always would stop and pick you up if they had a wagon full of cabbages or potatoes and you were trudging along the road. I think he thought he'd get a ride on the train. He wanted to go to Marion. He went down to this first tunnel here and stood there until the train came thundering around the mountain and went right on into the tunnel. Later somebody asked him about it, and he said, "Well, he weren't neighborly at all. He see'd me a-standing there. He just said a loud 'T-o-o-t' and run right straight in his hole." *(Louisa Duls)*

Sometimes you will pull up in someone's yard, and they have the house built four feet off the ground, and you can see straight underneath it. That's where the children play in bad weather, underneath the house. And that's the way I grew up. Our neighbors and friends never visited our home between two o'clock and four o'clock on Saturday afternoon because that's when the children took baths, and we took them on the back porch of the house in a washtub. We had a well on the back porch. But, we didn't have any type of television or running water in the house or anything like that. And back when I was eighteen years old—and this was in 1970—we lived in a house that did not have indoor toilets. We still had an outhouse. And this was in the mountains of South Carolina. I brought kids home from school and would tell them where the outhouse was, and it didn't mean anything to me. I was never belittled by it or ashamed. It was just something I had known all my life. Growing up in a large family like that, in the mountains, I think we do garner values that I'm sure other people do; but our pride comes from a history of dealing with harsh conditions.

I honestly remember going down and busting ice in a creek and washing diapers out on a scrub board in the winter, and taking them and hanging them out to dry, and then going out and getting them once they'd frozen and putting them up behind the wood stove. Working from sunup to sunset was the way. My mother sent us out. There were eight boys. People would come pick us up in the morning, and we'd go and hoe in their gardens all day long. They'd feed us dinner, and that's what we worked for because Mama wasn't home and she couldn't feed us dinner. We worked all day long doing that. There were ten of us, eight boys and two girls. The youngest was three months old and the oldest was sixteen when Daddy left home. *(Mike White)*

I live in a school bus way, way back in the mountains. We have a washing machine, but we ain't got no power. We have all kinds of animals up there, and we can catch one anytime we want to. All you have to do is put out some feed on the ground, and they'll come out and get it. All you have to do is run toward them. They just sit down. We catch squirrels, birds, rabbits, and all kinds of stuff. Even snakes. . . ground snakes. You can even handle a ground snake. (Child)

Smokehouse

JUSTICE AND THE LAW

The system of fairness and law and justice in the mountain area transcends established law and order. The Appalachian people have been, through the Scotch-Irish ancestry and possibly the Germanic, too, suffering depredation, cruelty, and shabby treatment from entrenched authority. A long time ago they learned they were not welcome in court. When they arrived, they were enemies. A long time ago they learned that somebody else handled the judge, not they. If they wanted real justice, they couldn't depend upon the crowd in the county seat or in the state capital to give them justice. (*Cratis Williams*)

In the old days, people secured their knowledge about what was going on in the outer world by going to court. They had what was called "courts of pleas" and "quarter sessions," which met every four months—that's where they got the name "quarter." They were run by justices of the peace. Everybody who was a justice of the peace in the county was a member of the county court. They not only discharged duties like having supervision of roads, but they also would select three or four of their best members each time they met to hold court, and they'd try cases before juries with lawyers around. The judges delivered long charges to grand juries about what was going on in the world, and they gave their views on everything, and so did the lawyers. People used to go to court to hear the lawyers. If they had a big case, they would probably spend half the time talking about their views on subjects other than the case. That's the way people got their information, that and political meetings and churches. That's all they had to amuse themselves. The courts have been a great educational feature.

They had Court Weeks, and it was a great boon to me because it made me one of the last circuit riders. It was sort of difficult to get to these mountain counties in those days. So, when the judge and lawyers from elsewhere got there, they just stayed all week. At night they'd just sit around with nothing to do, and they'd swap stories. I accumulated a lot of good stories from there. (*Sam Ervin*)

In my father's day we served three meals a day at the inn, seven days a week. In the old days, it was a little bit different. In the Court Week days, it was just packed and jammed. All the lawyers would be there, the judge and the solicitors. All ate together in the dining room. Some of them came for years and years. As a kid, it would fascinate me to sit and listen in that lobby to hear these men talking. It wasn't as great in my day as it was in my mother's day. In her day, Court Week was just everything. People would look forward to it year after year. I guess court was twice a year. The men would leave the farms to come to court to listen to the trials. It used to be pretty rough, too. They'd have fights and free-for-alls. The courtyard used to have rocks around everywhere. There was no pavement. I've heard Uncle Frank say that there wasn't a rock on this square that hadn't skinned somebody's head. They'd get to drinking. They'd bring in white lightning; then first thing you'd know, there'd be two or three fights.
(Rush Wray)

Jackson County Court House, Sylva

We had two sessions of court a year, one two-week term in the fall and one in the summer. Occasionally they'd have another court when they'd get some big murder case or something. When I started practicing law here, two courts a year was about it. They'd come in from all over the country to court. They'd come and ride horses and hitch their horses to trees. And these medicine-selling, snake-oil people would have their things here. There'd be somebody out under one tree selling medicines and maybe down on the street. The old jail was right across the street. That old house right across the street was the jail. They had a well and everybody'd go to that well. It was the only public water they had in town.

They'd have an interesting case. Maybe somebody'd rob somebody or kill somebody, and the courthouse would just be packed and jammed. You couldn't even get in the courthouse. It was a big event then. It was a social event. A lot of them would come to court and not even go in the courthouse. They'd come to buy. My daddy would come to buy a horse or sell a horse, or something. That was the only way the farmers had of meeting. It just lasted then for two or three days. By the middle of the week, court was pretty well cleared out and folks would leave and that would be the end of it. *(Wade Brown)*

Some of our people came to get away from the law. There was a feeling that people tend to their own business. There was originally right much resentment of anybody telling a mountaineer what to do, whether it was the law or anybody else. (Bob Phillips)

I can remember when Marion's daddy would ride a horse and come to Court Week at Boone. It was a big day for him. They'd trade horses and they'd gather there from all over, everywhere. I remember a number of times that his daddy would come on Monday morning on his horse, and he would come and stay all night there at home, so he could be at court again the next day and trade and jabber with the men. We were glad to have them. It was company. We just brought up a few more cabbages and potatoes. That was what they were used to. They would have just the two Court Weeks, one in the spring and one in the fall. *(Lyda Coffey)*

Do you want me to tell you about the tale of the lawsuit when we had two sheriffs? This was in Madison County, North Carolina. One was a Republican and one was a Democrat. One had the keys to the jail, and the other had the jail in his possession.

There was a big trial as to who had won the election. Judge Parker was the trial judge. Someone made the statement that the jury came from Yancey County and were all Democrats. At the conclusion of the trial, the Democrats won and Elmus Ponder was made sheriff. During the course of the trial, various voting irregularities had been gone into. One man named Andy Gosnell testified in the morning, and then they allowed Mr. Eldridge Leake to cross-examine him in the afternoon. He admitted that he had committed seventeen felonies, including murder, rape, arson, and burglary. Then Mr. Leake read the final question back to Andy Gosnell in his slow drawl and said, "Mr. Witness, have you ever pled guilty or been convicted of any offense that I haven't asked you about?" With which Andy reared back; you could hear him bouncing off the back of the room, "Mr. Leake, I believe that you have covered all the crimes that I have committed, man or boy, except the time me and you got caught with that load of liquor over on Laurel." Judge Parker refused to laugh in court and he said, "This court will take a five-minute recess." He went out and slammed the door, and you could hear him banging on the inside of the room. *(Landon Roberts)*

Well, that's a tale! For twenty years, I did not know that Eldridge Leake was the revenuer that had caught Andy with a load of liquor over on Laurel

Proud mountain man with sickle and hornet's nest, Little Canada, Jackson County

and that Andy had enough sense of humor to tell it in court and make people think that Eldridge Leake had been into some devilment as a young man. *(Jean Roberts)*

I prosecuted a man once who had walked up behind someone in front of the courthouse on a Saturday morning in Marshall, put a gun behind his right ear, pulled the trigger, and killed him. This happened in front of the courthouse on a Saturday morning with the streets packed. Everyone who was around at that time was scared to death of the defendant. He had a very bad, mean reputation. Back in those days juries were hard to get in Marshall that were honest. I got a jury that was not totally honest. Apparently, the defendant's family were able to work on that jury. As I was prosecuting the murder, a lady who was on the jury told the judge she had a toothache. She went to the dentist during lunch hour and came back sort of out of it. He had given her some narcotics or something. At any rate, the case finished, the judge charged the jury, they went out and stayed and stayed. Finally, they came back and said, "We are hopelessly dead-locked." I learned later that she had held out for "guilty" and all the other eleven jurors wanted to free the defendant. There should have been ten witnesses at least to the fact that the guy walked up behind the man and pulled the trigger at the back of his ear and killed him. After the next election, the legislature changed things and got a different jury log. They tried the man again. He pled guilty and got a prison term. But that's the sort of unusual justice you had in Marshall.

The Oconoluftee River runs right through the heart of the Cherokee Reservation, and a lot of the Cherokee over the years have kept bears for the tourists. I remember one case I defended, my partner and I. Susie Sharp was the presiding judge. This bear was named "Minnie the Bear." This fellow had stopped at a tourist place outside Bryson City along the Oconoluftee River and had bought a Coca-Cola and was feeding Minnie the Bear through the cage. He would take the Coca-Cola away and he kept doing that two or three times, so she swiped him and just caught him in the eye and took his eye out, Minnie did. My partner and I were defending Minnie in the case. The funny thing about the case was there can be no ownership of lands on the Cherokee Reservation. No one owns the land except the tribe. Therefore, they were never able to prove who owned the bear. It was a strange case. We won because they could not prove who owned Minnie. I thought Minnie had a right to come back at this guy. But that's an odd story. *(Harold Bennett)*

VIOLENCE

It's like the mountain feuding; there was some, you know. It was like there was not much law. My mother said she could remember when they had a reunion and the sheriff came to the reunion on top of the mountain at Glenville, and they put whiskey in the sheriff's car and sent him back down the road. They just drained his gas tank, filled it up with moonshine, and sent him back down the road. It's weird, but if you think for one minute that they're not tough, just don't call their hand. It's like the fellow said that carried a gun all the time. He said, "There's one thing about a gun. You very seldom ever need it, but when you need it, you can't go home and get it. The one time in a lifetime you need it, you can't go home and get it." Of course, most people disagree with that, but there's some people who live by that code and they do that type of thing. It's a carry-over from the mountain business. Some of the Scotch-Irish, and the people here right now are probably descended from the same people fighting it out in Northern Ireland. It's unreasonable violence in a way. I have lived in a strange world. I guess they were violent; there's no question they were. They would make you a proposition if you messed with them. *(Jimmy Moss)*

Mother always said she believed in this business of mean blood. She believed that there were certain groups of people, certain families in this whole area, that you can almost trace every bit of violence in the whole area back to those two families. Some were just really violent people. In other words, when you confront him, he immediately comes alive. It's just like it was instant pudding. **(Jimmy Moss)**

Did people feud with each other? No, I don't think so. Never where I was living. *(Mamie Hall)*

It depends on how narrowly you want to define feud. Very few feuds came to a great climax with an enormous battle in which one side won and the other retreated or disappeared. Very few did it that way. Most of them smoldered along, and there might be a generation or two when you'd think the feud was gone, and then suddenly it'd pop out again like a volcano. I don't think feuds proceed on an intellectual basis. I think they proceed from one incident to the next on the basis of personal conflict. There were more in Kentucky and West Virginia or southwest Virginia. There were more up that way, and they were more violent, more dramatic, but they existed down in here too and still go on down here. There was one out near Valle Crucis that was the basis for Patrick Hughes's Pulitzer Prize-winning play in 1922 called "Hell Bent For Heaven." *(Cratis Williams)*

I don't know much about it. But, ol' man Vance has told me about his uncle over near Linville Falls killing a man. They had a feud, and they shot it out with old rifles. They'd just shoot one bullet at a time. One of them stole a pig from the other one, and that started the feud. Vance says his granddaddy, I believe it was, killed the other man. That's been four or five generations ago now. They're not feuding in Avery County or anywhere else in the mountains that I know of. We're not clannish, and they're very friendly. The people in the mountains here and everywhere I've been in the mountains—I've been to most of the mountain counties—are not clannish. I don't think they ever were much clannish. *(Horton Cooper)*

Now, we never did have but one duel fought in this section that I have any record of. That was fought right up the road here, between here and Joe Al's store up there. At any rate, this duel was fought over a woman. *(Myron Houston)*

Why, you could get killed up there now without too much problem. You sure could. The sheriff was killed up there where liquor stills were. It's been twenty years since he was killed. They just blew him in two with a shotgun. You don't know of anybody going in on them like that. A lot of them people up in there can't read or write their own name. They never had any schooling whatsoever, no education at all except what they learned through life. I know people today, when they go to sign a check, they sign an X on it. Some of them are worth quite a bit of money today. And you won't beat 'em out of a dollar. But they still can't read or write their own name. If they give you a hundred dollar bill to break, they know if you give them the right change back or not. They might not be able to count it as fast as you do, but they can figure out whether you beat them or not. *(Unidentified man)*

Graham County, over here, was something else when we came here. You just got out of line and somebody laid the lead to you, that's all there was to it. There's so many people here—their families have intermarried. So if you're talking about somebody, you might be talking about their relatives. *(Unidentified man)*

Most feuds occurred in West Virginia and Kentucky primarily, but there were feuds in Western North Carolina. There were some families that just did not like each other, and that would last for several generations. They would have rock fights and sometimes gun fights, that sort of thing. For example, two families I know of were bitter enemies. They had rock fights. The kids had rock fights all the time. Sometimes the adults had fights too. Not the Hatfields and the McCoys, but rocks can hurt. *(Harold Bennett)*

Do you remember hearing the Frankie Silver story? Well, Frankie was a Stewart and a very pretty girl. Anyhow, she and Charlie Silver lived in a cabin over there and Charlie had a habit of going away, hunting he claimed, and staying a week or two at a time. It was along about Christmas, and he went away and stayed a couple of weeks. For some reason, she thought he had gone off with some other woman. She was there all alone, and her imagination probably filled in the space in between, and she decided he was disloyal to her. As far as I know, they just had one child. He came home and had been home maybe for a few days. He went out in the snow and cut up a pile of hickory wood to keep her warm while he was gone on another trip. He came in tired and wet and laid down before the fire to dry himself. There was an ax up there he'd been using. The small child was there, and he pulled the child up on his chest, and both of them went to sleep. While he was asleep, it occurred to her to take the ax and cut his head off. They said he jumped up—she didn't quite get it off the first time—and said, "God help the child." I don't know how he could have said it. She killed him, and then she had to dispose of the body.

First, she tried to burn it, and it wouldn't burn very well. She just kept building the fire and trying to burn it and couldn't get it all to burn. Then she tried to put the remains in the puncheon. She broke up the old puncheon, the old floor pieces, and tried to bury the remains under the puncheon. Finally, she took some of his internal organs down about half a mile below where there was an old rock pit. She dug a little hole right there and buried the rest of him down there. Well, she put on his boots and walked about a mile down the river and walked up to the edge of the river and took the boots off and waded across the river. She went on up the river two hundred yards and crossed and came back another way to make it appear he'd walked into the river and drowned.

And then, of course, the neighbors began to wonder about what had happened to him when he didn't show up. They finally went to the house and saw some of his blood on the puncheons and poked around in the fire and found some bones and some teeth. Of course, after that, they notified the proper authorities and had her arrested. They

Winton Shular's chopping block, Caney Fork, Jackson County

took her down to Burke County, and tried her. She was hanged in Burke County, and her body was brought back to Gillespie Gap for burial. But, anyhow, she was perhaps the only woman ever hanged. *(Bob Phillips)*

One day Wanda and Jimmy Moss took me for a drive through the backwoods areas of Caney Fork and parts of Little Canada. We had just eaten a huge breakfast of fried country ham, grits, red-eye gravy, biscuits, Larry Bixby's honey, scrambled eggs, and freshly made applesauce. It was hard to leave this comfortable table surrounded by the Mosses' daughters, Caroline, Jeanna, and Suzanne, and their son Michael. They were all in college or past that point. Jeanna's husband, Doug, and Caroline's fiancé, Danny, were there, as well as a couple of neighbors who had stopped

by. We had all been swapping stories, and it was pouring rain outside. The gleam in Jimmy Moss's eyes as he described the Shular family whom we were going to visit first in Caney Fork finally roused Wanda and me out of our seats.

It was a cold, wet day, but the leaves were still vibrant. We eventually made the turn into the "road" up through Caney Fork. Luckily, Jimmy's truck had four-wheel drive. The scenery was spectacular. The path we took wound alongside a fast-flowing stream that gushed and bubbled over rocks strewn in dramatic patterns everywhere. The white water seemed to illuminate the brilliant colors of the autumn leaves. Little branches with brightly colored leaves were swept into the water and churned their way down over the rocks. This was probably what most people would call a branch or a creek; it had not yet turned into a river, no matter how magical or powerful it was at this stage.

As we wound our way up the mountain, we came across rustic barns with cattle hiding underneath for protection from the rain, and apples dripping with raindrops. Wanda and Jimmy waited patiently as I jumped in and out of the truck to take pictures. They were just as caught up in the visual excitement as I was, even though they had lived with this all of their lives. After a while, we arrived at the top of the road at the Shulars'. The house was perched on a hillside near the stream. Nearby was a newly chopped pile of wood with the ax still launched in the top. (We found out later that Winton, in his eighties, had just chopped this for the stove.) We left the truck and made our way up the steps past the white picket gate and chestnut fence to the house. Winton, Vena, and their daughter, Eulala, greeted us and invited us to come inside. Jimmy stayed on the porch with Winton, but Wanda and I went inside and looked at beautiful quilts, gorgeous bedspreads made from flour sacks, hand-woven rugs, and freshly churned butter. We drank milk fresh from the cow and ate delicious hot sweet bread along with it. Later, we went out on the porch to join the men who had gathered and listened to more tales of logging, hunting, and all sorts of things that came to mind on that beautiful, rainy day.

When we left, the rain was subsiding and foggy clouds shrouded the mountainsides. On our way to Little Canada, we saw a small family cemetery at the crest of a mountain. Even though the fog was thick, the colors of flowers on the graves could be seen from far away. There must have been a Decoration Day recently. The terrain was rugged and became somewhat foreboding as we made our way through Little Canada. Even though the hillsides were alive with color, things seemed different here. The surrounding peaks seemed to close in somehow, and a sense of mystery prevailed.

This has always been an isolated and violent area of the mountains, and the physical features of the area seem to enhance those feelings even upon one's first encounter with the land here. At one point while we were driving along, we saw a man at the side of the road with a sickle slicing weeds away. I was excited and wanted to take a picture. Wanda and Jimmy were alarmed. They didn't think that this was such a great idea, but Jimmy stopped the truck anyway. I jumped out and asked the fellow if I could take his picture. He nodded and with a smile somehow made a slash with his blade and proudly held up a hornets' nest for his photographic pose. Things aren't always as scary as they seem. (W. M.)

_____

RELIGION

The first to come into Appalachia were religious dissenters. Most of them identified with a congregation, with Protestant congregations. Many, however, would have nothing to do with religion. They were tired of it. They wanted nothing to do with it, and so they came to Appalachia in order to escape it. Many Appalachian families from that day to this have been unchurched. Others came rebelling against Catholicism or over-formalized religion of any kind, including Episcopalianism.

The abandoned Free Will Baptist Church, Big Laurel, Madison County

They felt that ornate church buildings, elaborate holidays, special dress for those engaged in religious activities, all were the workings of the devil and they'd have nothing to do with that, so they had little shoe-box churches that were very plain inside and the ministers dressed just like everybody else. The ministers themselves—the people themselves—worked all week in the fields with them or at the factory, or whatever happened to be around.

This kind of religion satisfied the Appalachian person who embraced some extreme Protestant theological point of view, and, of course, this led to schisms and divisions. The result has been that more religions have been born in Appalachia than any other comparable geographical region that I can think of. There's no way to document this, but it seems pretty obvious that all this also in some subtle way is connected with the quality of mind that the Appalachian person has. The one who rebels has a certain quality of mind. Our ancestors all rebelled. That's why they were here. Those who rebel are touched in the head some way. So we have been touched in the head all the way along. And yet all of us accept others as God's creatures and worry in terms of their own individual deserts without regard for what their ancestors were. Consequently, illegitimate children have always fared extremely well in Appalachia because that's not remembered. They're accepted solely on the basis of what they themselves are and how they themselves interact with others. *(Cratis Williams)*

We didn't have a church. Used to, we met in the schoolhouse. We met in the schoolhouse for a long time, the Presbyterians did, before we built a church. The church has played a predominant part in changing the people. The Presbyterian Church had a high school, still have, at Gray Valley, and a lot of young people from this area were sent over there by Mr. Luke, and they'd finish high school over there. Lots of them would never have been able to finish. *(Helen Rose)*

He tended to seven churches, Mr. Luke (John W.) did, and such bad roads then, you know. He'd have these Christmas programs every year. I remember one Sunday morning, we got up early and started out. That was back before we had any sand on the roads. We went to Ebenezer and he preached there; then he went on out to the schoolhouse (Morgan School house) and preached there; and I walked on across to Bethel Church, that's Bethel Presbyterian Church; I don't know how I found my way through there. And I had Sunday School while he went down to Millers to preach there. He come back up from there and picked me up and come on—hadn't had no dinner now; it was getting late in the win-

Fresco at St. Mary's Episcopal Church, near West Jefferson

tertime; mud was about eighteen inches deep. We went to Deep Creek church; he was to preach there that night. It was after dark and the people there had already had supper, but they fixed us some supper. They cooked turnips, and those were the best turnips I ever ate. We ate supper, and then he went on up to Deep Creek to preach. That's the way he used to be. *(Delmer Rose)*

The church was a powerful influence on the people. Practically everybody went to church. They were very loyal to the church, and the church was the center of social activities. The church and the Masonic Lodge, back in the early days in the mountains, those two institutions were the foundation of the social activities of the people who lived there. Largely there were Methodists and Baptists in the mountains. Although they did not have much money, they used to do what they called "pounding" the preacher. They brought him food of all kinds, saw that he had plenty to eat, paid him as much as they could possibly pay him. Any time a man had trouble in the family, whether it was sickness or death in the family, or fire, the whole community rallied around that man or that family and divided whatever they might have in the way of clothing, food, and they swapped work a lot. Neighbors would chip in and do it. It was very much like the frontier days every place. They had to help each other as there was no other help available. And really that was frontier land in those days. *(Dan Moore)*

I started preaching in my middle forties. The majority of the people on these mountains are deeply religious people. Church was just as much a part of our life as eating and sleeping.

It had never entered my mind to preach the gospel, but one day the Lord called. It's hard to put into words. To another person who's experienced it, he knows exactly what you're saying. It's an impression. You feel it right in here. To begin with, I thought it was my imagination. But it stayed with me, and after a while I was convinced that it was real. Then I said, "Lord, you've got to be kidding!

You know I'm in my middle forties, I haven't got much education, I've settled down here, making a living, got a good church to go to, and I've got the rest of my life all planned out." It wasn't that I didn't want to do what the Lord wanted me to do as much as I felt I was the wrong man. I never said a word to anyone. I didn't even tell my wife because it was something I had to settle myself. I couldn't get it from other people. In my case, it was just a matter of God applying pressure. It came stronger and stronger. I got to where I couldn't even sleep really. So now I'm pastor in a church thirty-two miles from here.

I also grow apples. There must be a thousand sermons in this orchard, every bit of it. A fellow at Southern Seminary in New Orleans is writing a book on bi-vocational pastors and wanted my story. I told them that I was just as much a preacher when I was on my job here as that full-time fellow was when he was on a golf cart. It really serves the same purpose. I didn't mean that hardly like it sounds. I don't mean to say anything against the full-time preacher. To be full-time in the ministry, you've got to have a break some way. You couldn't deal with people continuously and with their problems. And if you love them and care about them, you're involved with all the emotion and everything that goes with it. So most of the so-called full-time preachers take maybe one day a week, and they go off and fish or something that they want to do. And I work and serve the same purpose. I do it more than one day a week, but I'm available when my people need me. I don't have anything that keeps me away. If they need me, I go because I have the advantage over the bi-vocational preacher who's got to check with somebody else before he can go. The distance is a disadvantage in some ways, but there are advantages in some ways. They don't call unless they really need you. A small country church can't afford a parsonage and a full-time salary either. *(Jonah Parker)*

I was Missionary Baptist. That was the Old Baptist, the ol' timey Baptist my daddy belonged to. What tickled us younguns one time, Evi Law was a preacher and he was Old Baptist. He didn't believe in these other denominations. Johnny decided he'd join—what was that where they baptized them three times?—the Dunkers. And we went up there to the mill pond, and Johnny like to have whipped two or three of us girls when we got back home. They baptized him and put him down on his knees in the pond. They'd dunk his head over and say, "In the name of the Father," and get him up; and they'd dunk his head plumb under and, "In the name of the Son," and then back up; the next time, "In the Holy Ghost and Amen"; and they then would take him out. Lilly or some of them laughed when they dunked him over one time. He like to got strangled. She giggled, and Johnny was about to lick all of us. He heard somebody sniggle over there. Me and Corrie and Bertha told him he didn't hear us sniggle. Now the Old Baptists, they'd preach the Bible. You can't say they didn't preach the Bible. They'd hold their revivals and have big revivals. There was no collection in the church. Never heard tell of it 'til I was way grown. They'd give them many a bushel of corn and a ham. I guess Papa gave him some money once in a while. I didn't see him do it. But I do know they gave him corn and put it in the wagon. *(Carrie Johnson)*

Well, now, I remember one of those fellows telling me he got "churched." In that church, if you didn't do like they wanted you to—that's the Hardshell Baptist—they would put you out of the church. *(Annie Winkler)*

Sure they would. If you did anything wrong, if you did any meanness, they'd take you off their list. *(Carrie Johnson)*

Well, the Primitive or the Hardshell would not let their members visit other churches and had a lot of rules. They "churched" people; it was very common for them to "church" people.

That meant that you were no longer a member. The most famous person they "churched" around here was our poet laureate James Larkin Pearson, who in his youth got interested in socialism, and

when he came up with an idea or two, I don't know what church it was now, but they "churched" him right out of the church because he had some socialistic views not according. Baptist churches, you see, are independent. They are their own boss and they elect their preacher. The Baptist is independent; he is a Baptist. The Roaring River Baptists were Baptists on their own. Nobody was telling them how to do it. They chose their preacher, and they got rid of him when they wanted to. So that makes a difference. *(Annie Winkler)*

We've got Presbyterians, Episcopalians, Pentecostals, Methodists, and three kinds of Baptists. We've got Primitive Baptist, Missionary Baptist, and Free Will or Union Baptist, whichever you want to call it. The "hard shell" is Primitive Baptist.

What I use for an illustration, [is that] you plant a garden and I plant a garden. But, we don't either one plant just alike. Maybe I'll use a certain kind of seed, and you use a little different kind of seed but still grow the same thing. And that's the same way with these denominations. We all believe in the same God and the same Christ.

The story is that when this country was first settled, people built log cabins, churches—predominantly Baptist. As soon as they got some paths that you could ride on horseback, the Methodist circuit rider came; and as soon as they got roads that you could drive an automobile on, the Presbyterians came; as soon as they got railroads built, with Pullmans, the Episcopalians came in. **(Delmer Rose)**

I guess the Baptists are the very worst people in the world to drink and hide it. *(Jimmy Moss)*

My father was a Baptist minister and, of course, we children had to walk the chalk line. *(Hattie Oates)*

They didn't approve of hoedowns. We're all Baptist. My grandfather wouldn't even let them pat your foot. I'll tell you what. I was about five or six years old, and I'd never heard any music (except you just sung the old songs in church). My mother took me down to her sister's. They put us to bed real early so they could have what they was going to have. I was asleep and woke up, and I heard the most beautiful sound I'd ever heard in my life. I jumped up in my petticoat tail and run in there. The woman had a guitar, and another had a banjo, and the man had a fiddle. They were playing and singing. I'll never forget how pretty that was. Imagine a child that old never heard any music.

Back when I was growing up, there were a lot of small cabins, and people lived in there and had children. I was a grown girl before I ever heard any of the facts of life. Everything was carried on in a modest, decent way. The boys grew to be grown boys, and they were almost sexless. They had to live among each other, and they were taught to be decent. And, boy, they had to toe the mark, and the girls too. *(Carrie Burnette)*

Baptism in the Baptist faith is symbolic. There are several symbols involved in it. To begin with, it's a test. It's telling the people looking on of the step you've got to take by the fact that it symbolizes burial and resurrection. "That old person that I once was doesn't exist any more. He's dead and buried. I'm a brand new person" is the symbolic message. "I have been cleansed. This doesn't cleanse me, but this is telling everybody what has already happened to me." There's something else. Out there in that moving water, under the skies and trees, you gather around and have this service; and there's a feeling of closeness with nature. You can't get close to nature without getting close to God. There's something there that you can't get

inside. The river is real ornery. It gets up, and it changes the water, but usually there's a sand bar that people can stand on. The water gets deeper gradually and goes to the other side and there's rocks sticking out of the bank and trees hanging out over the bank and the sun shining down. To have any kind of religious service outside close to nature is real special to me. We don't baptize in cold weather. I would if they wanted me to because I enjoy it that much. But we usually wait until summertime to have a baptizing. *(Jonah Parker)*

I don't believe the church work ought to be left out of any account of this area. We're very lucky to have a Methodist Church right in the center of Valle Crucis and the Episcopal Church on the side of the hill up here. And that little rock church there. And then we have a Baptist Church on the Clark's Creek Road and the Seventh Day Adventist and Christian Church. I didn't mention the Lutheran. Every one of them was here when we were growing up. I'm a Methodist so we went to the Methodist Church to be married and had an Episcopal minister come down to our Methodist Church to marry us. *(Howard Mast, Sr.)*

I'll never forget when I was "saved." I was small for my age at twelve. The parents were getting the children ready and they ignored me as though I hadn't been there. And there, I felt so burdened. We started home and I thought we'd never get there. I thought, "If I can get in bed, I'll be all right." But I wasn't. I couldn't sleep, and I got to talking to the Lord. I told Him I didn't want to go to hell, that I wanted to be His child and would He forgive me. And that burden just left me. I was light as a feather. I've never had that burden any more. I've had lots of other burdens. I had a lot of trouble raising a family, but the Lord's always with you ready to help you if you'll depend on Him and let Him, that's for sure. *(Lena Shull)*

I don't know that it [snake handling] goes on in North Carolina. I suspect that it does right over here on the edge of Tennessee. As a matter of fact,

Tuckasegee Wesleyan Church, Jackson County

in some of the local papers in the Kingsport area, if you read the want ads, you will see ads for serpents. They say that the true believers shall take up serpents and not be harmed and drink poison things and not be harmed. They drink strychnine and some of them die. East Tennessee State, with a grant from the Tennessee Art Commission, put together the most fantastic film on snake handling you've ever seen. I saw the film, and it was the most unbelievable thing you've ever seen. But the interesting thing is that although it's a contrast from the idea of taking care of widows and orphans, it's the same thing because it is taking literally what the Bible says. The bottom line is that those people are doing what the Bible tells them to do, and there's not going to be any change even if they all were to go to prison or all died. That would never, ever change. It'll be a long time changing. *(Rebecca Councill)*

We say "our church," but this "our church" is "Christ's church." I don't believe in changing things around every way. I believe in sticking to the Bible and not getting up there and preaching about fairy tales. Preach the good ol' Gospel, that's what we need. The way I see it and understand the Bible, anything we get between us and God, our children, our husband, anything, then we're worshiping them instead of God. If we keep our temple, our body, clean, we wouldn't be afraid for Christ to walk in; and that's the way we've tried to bring up our children. God forgives you of everything except sinning against the Holy Ghost. The sinning against the Holy Ghost, the way Bob and I see it, is saying that things done by Christ were done by the devil. I say you really have to repent. There's nobody here on earth that is without sin because until we've been changed from this sinful body into the spiritual body that Christ has for us, then we're in sin and we ask God to forgive us daily. *(Myrtle Merrell)*

DEATH

It was a matter of a courtesy. You never left a dead body alone. When I can first remember, the community did everything. They washed the body; they dressed it. I can remember at least one home-made casket. Even after undertakers got involved, I remember them coming to the home to do the embalming. And the neighbors would come in and sit with the body all night as a courtesy to the family, just caring and being there. *(Jonah Parker)*

The Sitting Ups, when someone dies, become the reason for being together. When someone dies, everyone knows about it. Marriages do not bring you together like death does. The families don't get together for a marriage nearly like they do for a death. When someone dies, that is really the time for catching up, seeing people that you haven't seen, of visiting with relatives and family.

And then they have Decoration Day where they go to the cemetery and work like slaves seven or eight hours cleaning off and planting and putting down artificial flowers, I mean all over the cemetery, even for people they don't know who have been dead a hundred years. All day Sunday they have singing, preaching; it's unbelievable. **(Mike White)**

We have Decoration once every year. In every cemetery we have a certain day, and we all go and put flowers on the graves of old friends and par-

(Opposite) Cemetery at Saint John's in the Wilderness Episcopal Church, Flat Rock, Henderson County

ents. Back in the old days, we didn't have any undertakers. We had to bury our own dead. We had to bathe them and put their clothes on them. Almost all the stores kept the casket handles, and they would make the caskets out of wood and line them with white material. And they had to bury them. There wouldn't be a preacher near, and there wouldn't be flowers in the wintertime. When summer came and everybody could get out, they had Decoration, and they went and put flowers on the graves and had a sermon preached, and they'd all come together. You could sort of stand it like that. In those days, they didn't even preach funerals much. They just gathered at the house and took them out and buried them. Now we have Decoration at every cemetery. Almost all of us are related to somebody in that area.

I have seen the time when it was awfully hard to bury your dead. The ground would freeze, and sometimes you'd even have to build fires on the ground and thaw it out as you went, digging down. Now we have ministers to come and preach, and we have lots of flowers. The graves are just covered with flowers, some from the florist; most of us raise all kinds of flowers. Our dead are never forgotten. *(Carrie Burnette)*

At Sitting Ups people go to the house and sit around the body. They will have groups of people who sing. Everyone else brings food. Children and everyone go to the house. All night there is singing and witnessing and talking and sitting up. That's why it is called a Sitting Up. You sit and wait for the spirit to leave the body. You are with them during that time and the body very seldom ever sees the inside of the funeral home. They don't do any embalming or cremation or anything like that. That would be taboo, destroying something that wasn't meant to be destroyed that way.

The people have used that person's life to make theirs better because he is responsible for the Sitting

Up. He is responsible for the singing and the gospel music, the witnessing. So many times someone will be saved during that night. To them that is the ultimate of your life to be used after you are gone for the betterment of others. Say a man preached all his life and countless people were saved. He died, and at the Sitting Up others come to the Lord or are saved. That is remembered. People remember that the Lord really used him. That's the way they see it. The Lord used him after he died to bring these people to Him, and that was the purpose of his life. *(Mike White)*

through the field and took those two little caskets on a sled to the cemetery and buried them. They couldn't get up there any other way. That was in February. We didn't have a funeral director then in Watauga County. The neighbors just took care of funerals. Three or four of the neighbors helped bury the little girl and little boy. The grave was dug with just shovels and manual labor. *(Lottie Greene)*

A funeral used to be an all-day thing. I can remember when my father went into the Second World War in 1943 and my mother used to take me to the

Reed family bible

In 1917, when my oldest brother went into the Air Corps, I'll never forget that morning when he left. There was snow on the ground, and back then we didn't have a highway commission like we have now. Different people on the road did their own work. That was the day when Dave and Nora Ray's little Cecil and Mary were buried with diphtheria. They had to take the children to the cemetery, up there to Ray Cemetery, on a sled. They went up

funerals with her. I've been going to funerals since I was seven or eight years old. A funeral used to be held like at ten o'clock in the morning and they would preach two to three hours. Then the women, other than the immediate family, were in the church and all the men were out at the church cemetery. Church and the cemeteries were connected for years. When the funeral was over, the men would bury the individual. Many times we would leave the funeral home to go to the funeral in the forties and be gone four and five hours, you know, leave in the morning and come back after lunch. Of course, that time has been cut and probably a funeral service will last an average of thirty minutes now. It's a lot different. *(Reg Moody)*

Let me tell you a little story about one of our mountain friends, old Uncle Isaac Holifield. I think he is typical of the mountain people in his sort of stoicism and his fatalism. You know, they all were

a sort of, "Well, I reckon." One time Aunt Sally was telling him about the death of a friend she had down in South Carolina. She talked and exaggerated her grief a little bit. After a while he couldn't stand that sentimentality much longer and this is what he said, "Miss Sally, 'taint no use to take on so. Like the leaves of the trees, we all drop off, one by one, and when your time comes, we'll miss you for a spell; then we'll forget." I think that's very typical of the mountain people. You just have to accept death and whatever kind of rough life you'll have, or pleasant life, too. *(Louisa Duls)*

Tombstones in cemetery, Wilkesboro

somewhat fatalistic. You have to accept life as it is and don't romanticize it very much. One day he was sitting on our porch here, talking to my aunt who was a maiden lady. He was a widower then and used to come and spark her on Sunday afternoons. That's what they called it. He was a man of very few words, and Aunt Sally talked without stopping. They'd carry on a one-sided conversation all Sunday afternoon. He'd put in every now and then

Some person from out of town said that he came to Sylva and stayed all day and said, "I wonder what people do here for recreation?" Then he drove up to Moody Funeral Home and probably saw three hundred people standing out in front of the funeral home that night. And he said, "Now I know what they do. They go to the funeral home." We have about 225 funerals a year, so most of the time there is something going on. People question the "visitation" a lot and say they don't like it. One of the comments I hear is it's not a thing in the world but a social gathering, and that's exactly what it is. But it is meaningful, and it has a purpose.

I was born in Sylva in 1935, and my grandfather P. E. Moody was in the funeral business and in the furniture business. In 1922, my grandfather went into the furniture business. Then they sold caskets in furniture stores, and that's the way most Southern funeral homes came to be. People would come in and buy the casket and take it home and put the person in the casket. Prior to that they made their own caskets, but when they found out they could come in and buy one at the furniture store, they would come in and buy it and take it

home. He would give them pedestals and grave straps. They would take it home, and they would handle the funeral in the community.

It used to be that when a death occurred in the community, it was a total community activity, and it was at the church, around the church, and in the home. They even tolled the bell. When somebody would die in a rural community, they would go and ring the church bell. That way everybody would know that somebody had died. Then they would all get together and dig the grave. The person who died never left the house. They either had a home-made casket or they bought one at the furniture store and took it back out there. It was a community thing, a family gathering time. *(Reg Moody)*

Herman and Mabel Estes, Clay County

MARRIAGE AND INTERMARRIAGE

He brought out a Colt .44, the old Frontier Special. I said, "I'm not interested in that thing." And while we were sitting there talking, the door opened, she [Mabel] walked in, and the gun trading went up the chimney. Now that was on January thirteenth. I saw her every night but one 'til the twenty-fifth day of May when we were married. I'd hurt my shoulder and she came to see me that night. She tells me now, "I wasn't a bit interested in that other boy." But I made up my mind he wasn't going to get his foot in the door anymore. *(Herman Estes)*

I grew up and married. I never saw a girl I wanted to marry until then. There was just one girl in the world that I'd ever seen that made me decide to get married. She lived in Roan Mountain, Tennessee. It wasn't exactly love at first sight, but it came near being that. It developed into real love in about three months. I didn't date her but three months, I think. Then I brought her to North Carolina. She died fifteen years ago, maybe more, I've forgotten. Yes, I had seen many girls, but I hadn't fallen in love with more than fifteen or twenty of them. *(Horton Cooper)*

My wife was a neighborhood girl, a lot younger than I. When I went into the service, I guess she was going into high school. And four years later, I came back from the army and she was graduating. We got married in 1950. Ever since I can remember, I've known her. It's just one of those things, local boy married local girl, I guess. Been married thirty-four years. Her family were neighbors of my mother and daddy. And their mother and daddy were neighbors of the other mother and daddy. They all grew up in the same area, and they're all buried in the same area. My daddy is buried within five hundred yards of where he was born. You can see my mother's home where she was born from where she's buried. *(Frank Norris)*

Cass and Virgie Wallin

I'll tell you how my grandfather and grandmother became engaged. They used to have quilting parties in this area, and the girl would piece a quilt. My grandfather and grandmother went to a quilting party. He had been in love with her, but he was like I am. Evidently he was timid. Every quilting she'd go to, he'd be there. They were at a quilting once. They always shook the cat at the quilting. Before they took the quilt off the frame, they would all help quilt, and the young fellows were there watching. They would get around and hold the edges of the quilt and somebody would throw a cat on it and the cat, of course, would become frightened and jump. The nearest girl that it jumped out at would be the next one married. The cat jumped out nearest my grandmother, and he didn't say anything. So she finally went out to get a drink on the porch, and he sauntered out there and said,

81

"Martha, do you suppose that cat was right?" And she said, "Well, all cats are right." He said, "I'll just go and get the license." And that's the way he proposed to her. It wasn't any proposal at all. And they hunted a preacher. There weren't any divorces around in this area when I was a young man. When a man married a gal, he stuck with her, fighting or not. *(Horton Cooper)*

My grandmother said that she remembered when she was fifteen or sixteen years old, maybe younger than that, thirteen or fourteen, and they were having a picnic where all the girls made picnic baskets. They would take them up in the valley and have a big picnic and auction off the picnic baskets to raise money for the church. The boys tried to get their girlfriend's picnic basket. She had made a basket, and they were sitting there, and all of a sudden these two men on these two big horses came riding up through the valley where they were. They were real tall-looking gentlemen, a man and his son. The younger man was seventeen or eighteen. He started trying to get her dinner, trying to pay for her dinner, but her father kept overbidding him because he didn't know who the man was. Her father overbid him and got the food so she couldn't eat with him, but he ended up being her husband. (Caroline Moss)

I was married at home. It was the fifteenth day of June, four o'clock in the evening on a Saturday. Preacher Sam Jennings came there and stayed and married us. Mama got a wedding supper for us. Didn't invite but just a few of us there. Just went in the living room, stood up, and the preacher mar-

Grady and Delia Reed

ried us, and that was it. We had to go and get a license, drive to Sparta. I was eighteen.

When I first started to school, as little younguns four or five years old, he'd get me by the hand and come around and be barefooted, and he'd hold the books. Had a little first reader or ABC book or something, and we'd wade the puddle and just splatter all over. And we'd get home and they'd say, "Carrie, who's your sweetheart?" And I'd say, "Cliff," and they'd ask him and he'd say, "Carrie." And we knew each other and were together all our lives. We were married fifty years; we were married long enough. The day I was twenty-one years old, Claude was three weeks old. He was born eleven months and two days after we were married. My baby is seventy-nine years old. *(Carrie Johnson)* ["Aunt" Carrie (Johnson) celebrated her 100th birthday in June 1987. She is the daughter of a Civil War veteran. W.M.]

They serenaded us. Nobody knew except Grady's mother that we were gone to get married. The first night when we got home after we got married, Grady had to go check on the cows. He had to milk a cow on our wedding night. It was just pourin' rain, but he had to go milk the cow. It was dark, and we had to light the lamp. We had oil lamps. And we sat there and ate supper, and the door opened, and the hall filled with boys. It was dark and the lamp was the only lamp we had at the time. They came in, and you couldn't see anything except their eyes and their teeth. Now they were going to have a good time, and they kept teasing Grady. They finally got him to go outside. They had him on this pole, riding him down the road, and he just went right along with them. There wasn't a bridge down yonder, so they were going to ride him through the creek. He didn't care because he had on a pair of rubber boots and they didn't. He told them to "Go right on." In the meantime, I was sitting in here. They'd look in at the windows and enough of them stayed here to keep hollering at me, telling me, "You're next. We're going to make you ride in the wheelbarrow." But they didn't get that done. I never did go out; I never did answer them. *(Delia Reed)*

I had a first cousin by the name of Dolly Triplett. And Dolly and Ora were walking along together, and Dolly said to me, "Willard, would you like to have my place?" I said, "Better than the first feet in heaven." And she stepped out and I stepped in, and we went together. Her [Ora's] dad never did want me to have her. Sneakin', slippin' out, and makin' love is the best love there is. I wanted to treat her dad like a man. I went and asked him for her. I said, "Me and Ora has decided to get married and I wanted to treat you like somebody." And he said, "I ain't got nothin' to give away." I said, "I'll steal her." And he said, "You'll pay, too." And I sure did. Now, that weren't yesterday. *(Willard Watson)*

We've been married sixty-two years the fifth day of this last October gone by. I kind of like her, though. She's as good a biscuit baker as I ever was acquainted with. She'll be eighty the fifteenth of December, and I was eighty-three the first day of June. The morning the boy was twenty-one years old, I gave him a twenty dollar bill for a birthday present and I said, "Son, it takes a long time to raise a man, but it don't take very long to raise a young fool." (Willard Watson)

They'd usually slip off and get married. Then both families would pout for a week or two, and then everything got all right. You know, nobody ever thinks anybody is good enough to marry their children. That's the way it was. You see, a girl wasn't out at night without some of her people. When you walked your girl home from church—and that's where your social life was walking a girl home from church—you walked her home and her people would be right back there. Oh, you could steal a kiss, but you weren't by yourself. They were close by. People looked after their girls, looked after them closely. *(Alfred Adams)*

Ora and Willard Watson on their porch at Deep Gap

I'll sing you a love song, "A Pretty Fair Miss."

A pretty fair miss saw in her a garden
A very fine soldier come a-riding by.
She stepped up and thus he addressed her
Saying, my pretty fair miss, will you marry me?

No, kind sir, a man of honor,
A man of honor you may be.
How can you impose on a fair young lady
Who never intends your bride to be?

I have a true lover gone to the army
And he's been gone for seven years long.
But if he stays yet seven years longer,
No man on the earth could marry me.

Perhaps your lover's drowned in the ocean,
Perhaps he's in some battle field slain,
Perhaps he's taken another girl and married,
His face you'll never see again.

Well, if he's drowned, I hope he's happy,
Or if he's in some battle field slain,
Or if he's taken another girl and married,
I'd just love that girl that'd marry him.

His fingers being long and slender
All from his pocket he brought his hand.
Says here's a ring that you did give me
Before I started to the war.

She threw her lily-white arms around him
And prostrate at his feet did fall.
Says, you're the man that used to court me
Before you started to the war.

Yes, I've been on the deep sea sailing
And I've been sailing seven years long,
But if I'd stayed seven years longer
No girl on the earth could have married me.
(Cas and Virgie Wallin)

You see, back then the man wore the britches; he
was boss. I was raised up that way. He [Marion] was
raised up that way. So no wonder he's had the hand
of me seventy years because we were both raised
that way. *(Lyda Coffey)*

I never cease to admire the women of the mountains. They worked hard in dual roles. My grandmother would be the first to rise in the morning,
prepare the meal, help milk the cows, come back,
clean the dishes, and go to the field with us and
work as hard as most men would work. She might
leave thirty minutes early and come in and prepare
the lunch. We would come in and, depending on
the number of hands that were there, she would
either eat with us or wait until we had eaten and
then she would eat, clean the dishes. The men
would take a small nap, sleep an hour or so. Then
she'd go back to the field and work all day. And
that was not unique by any means. Yet she found
time to do all those things required of a mother
plus be the worker and true helpmate. So the
mountain women have a big stake in that society. It
was part of their culture. The man was thought to
be the head of the house, and he ruled the house
sort of like an old patriarch. Any time we were
walking anywhere, Grandmother always walked
behind Grandpa, never up beside him or in front of
him, always behind him. Today Grandmother still
takes care of my grandfather. She knows nothing
else but that. We all had certain responsibilities,
and I think that has helped me. Everybody had to
pull their part to make the unit turn and make it a
viable family. *(Charles Michael)*

Raymond Presnell

For a long time, I have heard about inbreeding among the mountain families of Appalachia and seen examples of it depicted in movies, so I searched for this as I covered the area. Such incidents were scarce. This indicated to me that inbreeding among these people has been overemphasized in literature to the point of inaccuracy. As a result, only a small segment of this book addresses the issue. To dwell on this or overemphasize it would be inappropriate. (W. M.)

There are inbred people in all of the western counties, but nobody is going to tell you that they married a cousin and this, that and the other. We have a lot of inbred families, particularly in the counties that around the turn of the century were isolated. *(Harold Bennett)*

There were close family ties. It used to be in my younger days that everybody was proud to claim relationship with some of them. And everybody was. Nearly everybody in Avery County used to be kin. The majority of people two or three generations ago would just go out and marry the next-door neighbor's girl, or up the road. The roads were bad and the automobile hadn't come yet. Very few of them married their cousin. (Horton Cooper)

You know all places where they inbreed, you just get bad business. People that live in the area, most of them are Scotch-Irish or English. They all come from about the same place. Most of the people that live in this area have been here a long, long time. Just a few years ago they married third and fourth cousins. They definitely were kin. The gene pool

after a while gets so there's similarity, and I think you pick up on it. I'd say a good half of the people now are marrying people from out of state, so it'll all work out. You know, it wasn't a gross inbreeding where brother married sister. It was a subtle thing, really something that no one would pay that much attention to. *(Jimmy Moss)*

Helen and Jonah Parker

A lot of them married cousins, first cousins, second cousins. My Grandpa Parker married his first cousin. Everybody had big families. Of course, sometimes you got pretty anxious to get your daughters married off. So they married real young. Real young a lot of times.

The women worked hard. They'd get up and get the fire started, eat breakfast and go milk the cow and get the whole family up and fed and go work all day and come back that evening and go through that same procedure again. Come in at lunch and cook dinner. I don't know how they did it. *(Jonah Parker)*

Martin married his daddy's brother's daughter—pretty close kin. Now, I married pretty close kin. Three of us married in the family. My brother and sister and me, we married all in the family. Me and my brother married the two sisters (second cousins of ours), and my sister married their brother .They were our cousins, and we were all Presnells. *(Raymond Presnell)*

Enclosure laws came about during the 1880s, as I recall, in Kentucky. It would have happened differently in other parts of the mountains. That meant that people became isolated because before that, the cattle kept everything grazed down. If you were interested in that blond-haired girl with the blue eyes you saw at the country church last Sunday and you wanted to go around and slip around so she could see you, you simply hopped on horseback and went straight up the mountain and down, and there she was. That was good because she represented a different family line. When he courted and married her, he went outside his own gene pool. *(Cratis Williams)*

When we passed the enclosure laws, you couldn't go over the hill like that. You had to go down the stream—the road was at the bottom of the stream—three miles, and then down the next little river three miles, and then up two miles. That took time. Instead, you became interested in your cousin who lived on the adjoining farm, so we became infamous for intermarriage. Now, we were probably not any worse than rural people generally are, so far as I've been able to tell; but we were doing it when others had stopped, and there's nothing so shameful as to be caught doing what other people have just learned not to do. (Cratis Williams)

It depends on the strength of the family how damaging intermarriage really was. There was sufficient weakness genealogically for many of the families to become degenerative, and they were noticed. Outsiders, of course, looked for them. They were noticed and reported, really throwing things out of line for us, leaving the impression that there was more degeneracy among us than there really was. So far as I'm able to tell from examining figures, we had no more degeneracy among us than rural Americans everywhere.

Now in my own community, there was a lot of intermarriage, starting in my own background. We didn't bother to count kinship beyond first cousins. If we did that, we excluded ourselves. Some of the girls I courted before I left my valley, I didn't consider to be any kin to me at all. Later on when I became interested in attributing kinship, I discovered that a girl to whom I was engaged to be married, in fact, was a triple third cousin and a second cousin. It depends on how you look at it. That's not distantly related. You have an inroad into a common gene pool through four entrances. And, you see, that can cause some trouble. It can also work to one's great advantage if it's a fine gene pool. Those people who are pretty, intelligent, handsome, successful, mean you're likely to be too. In fact, you're likely to have just a little more edge in competition than other people because you're bred to it. *(Cratis Williams)*

PRIDE

Boyd Payne with game rooster

The native mountain folks have pride, I guess you'd call it, the idea that I've earned what I've got. I don't want any handouts. Those old mountain folks made it a point at the corn shuckings. He would come help you shuck your corn, and you went and helped him shuck his. Most people weren't concerned with how long it took. If you didn't work but an hour at yours and you worked all day at his, you didn't worry about that. You were helping him with his crop. This was true in every area of helping each other. Everybody helped everybody else that needed it, and that didn't bother them. *(Jonah Parker)*

The people who settled here in the mountains, the people in general, brought three things with them. They brought their gun, they brought their wife, and they brought their Bible. They brought their gun for self-preservation, food, and defense. They brought their wife for making the home and spreading the family name. The Bible was brought for two reasons. One was the religious purpose of it, but also it was the schoolbook. *(B. Hensley)*

It's a shame that these people have been called ignorant because the things that they know about life are so much above ignorance. To me there's just a world of difference between being poor in New York and being poor in the mountains of North Carolina. What's a poverty level? Is it when you can't walk out on the street because you're afraid you're going to get hit on the back of the head, or that you can leave your house unlocked for a month and not worry about it? And we have that in this area. Of course, it's changing a lot. People should understand that pride, patriotism, is not something to be flaunted, but it's not anything to be ashamed of. It just is. It's what we are.

And I think most of the parents around here try to teach their children to fight. I mean, they grow up fighting, fist-fighting. My mother told me, "You

*Lonnie and Carrie
Burnette*

fight for it." I had four brothers who were in the service during Vietnam, and all of them volunteered. It wasn't a case of, "Should I do this?" They grew up with the idea that if you were threatened, you fought; and I think that's the way a lot of them were. I have aunts and uncles who really hate the idea that people think they're stupid or ignorant because they still hold onto the backward ways—you know, what we consider backward.

I'm thirty-four years old and I went through college and everything at a time when people said, "You don't talk right." Growing up, no one in our family would dare make fun of the way another person talked, would never think about it because that was unheard of. You did not make fun of other people. They were here for a purpose and you were here for a purpose. That was the way we were raised. *(Mike White)*

Now there's a lot of people who think that mountain people are so poor they can't hardly support themselves, and it's just not so. I'd rather be back in the mountains like this than anywhere else. My younguns can grow up without people complaining about them making a racket.
(Lula Mae Owenby)

When a mountain person is slow to answer, it probably isn't because they don't know the answer but because they want to be sure that it's right. And I have seen many instances when mountain people stood very courteously and quietly while somebody behaved outrageously. Then the person from the outside thinks he was too dumb to know what happened. That isn't the case at all. It's just that the mountain person is better behaved than the other person. It's just good manners. *(Rebecca Councill)*

Here is what I have found out in ninety-one years. I have seen time and time again Yankees come out of the north into these Appalachian Mountains and decide they were going to make it to suit themselves. I have never seen one succeed yet. These old mountain people will listen to their malarky, and there's a hole right straight through their head. It goes in one side and out the other. (Herman Estes)

The mountain people are just the finest people you'll ever meet—honest, hard-working craftsmen. I think we have some of the smartest people I've ever encountered. They were making things before anyone else ever knew how. They made their own plows. They made their own mule harness. Anything that they used they made, their pots and pans, forks and knives. They invented everything they used, their lamps and lanterns. The old farming way of life in these mountains historically is way advanced as far as today is concerned. I know there is technology and that today's standard of life surpasses theirs. But in their time, it did not; it didn't even come close to it.

I think one of the most innovative pieces of equipment I've ever seen is what you call a "hillside plow." It was a plow that you plowed the hillside with. You went backwards and forth across the hillside. You didn't go around it like you do a field because the hillside was so straight up, you couldn't go around the hillside, unless it was a knob. You could go all the way around a knob. If you just went straight back and forth across with a normal plow, you could only go one way. With the "hillside plow," they'd go one way and then they'd turn the foot over and go the other way. They took one plow and invented a way to flip-flop the foot on it, and they could go back the same way they came—creative. And they did it all with their hands. They didn't have all these highly sophisti-

cated pieces of equipment to make it with. These are things that I think stand out in our hills of North Carolina. I think it's a dying trait, I really do; and it's sad.

I've been blessed in a lot of ways, and I'm pleased with my accomplishments. Anybody who's doing anything has a desire to be the best at what they do. That's where you get your good feelings and your happiness. You put enough effort, enough sweat and work into it, until you've accomplished what you set out to do. *(Junior Johnson)*

We just didn't want people to think we were poor and had to sell. It's the same way today about work. I worked for three years at the Chalet here, and I never said that I was at the desk or anything like that. I always just said I was helping out. If they don't need us to help out, we don't work. We don't want to feel lower than somebody else. I think it's because of the way our forefathers were treated in the old countries. They fared so bad in other countries. When they came here, they were determined they weren't going to bow to anybody.
(Carrie Burnette)

They were too proud to engage in what we call barter, you know, commercialism of any kind. If you wanted to buy a dozen eggs or a pound of butter from them, you could not go right to a mountain family and say, "I'd like to buy a dozen eggs." She just wouldn't give them to you. She'd say, "I ain't got none." But if you would talk a bit and say, "What a cute little girl this is; and how'd you raise such a big dahlia; and how many hens have you got?" After a while you might say, "Well, I just haven't got an egg in the house to make a bit of cornbread for dinner. You reckon you could spare me one as a favor?"

Then she'd call one of the younguns and say, "You go look in the hen's nest." And she'd get you up a dozen eggs. But you had to go in that circulatory way. You'd pay her thirty cents a dozen in those days. She'd let you pay her, but it's just that the approach couldn't be, "Now, here is some poor person having to sell eggs, and I'm some rich person." Now, it had to be, "Well, we're friends and neighbors and you'll do me a favor because I need it." I think that's one of the first things we had to learn about the mountain people. It's a thing I like about them, too. They're still like that somewhat, but there are some exceptions. *(Louisa Duls)*

We feel like we have benefited from our heritage and our bloodline. Our people lived off the land, and somehow it was instilled in us to have that same tenacious dig, you might say, to survive and do and live. I know that today people seem to have a tendency to think if they can get a living given to them, it's much easier than getting out and working for it. I just don't believe that they would have survived very long back in those days. We're very proud of our heritage and thankful that we had this

type of people in our background. I still look at those mountaintops today and think of a lot of the things that were passed on down to me and my family. I know it's beneficial to us even today in a modern age. *(Jack Brinkley)*

You know, I'm not afraid to die now. A fellow from Durham wanted to buy my house up here on that side of the mountain. And I said, "Well, I wouldn't let you rent fish." Later he came back. He bothered me for ten years. I said, "I'm not going to sell you this property. I don't know of a house much better to die in than this stone house." And he said, "I ain't going to bother you anymore." But it took him ten years to figure out I wasn't going to sell. *(Tom Oates)*

Johnny Lewis milking Betsy

INDEPENDENCE AND SELF-SUFFICIENCY

You see the people had to do their own thinking. They were isolated for want of good roads for several generations and did their own thinking. Their individuality and isolation compelled them to do that. My father was a great defender of them because he practiced law up there all his life. He got mad one time seeing a letter in a church magazine criticizing the mountain people, and he wrote them a letter. He said, "The only difference is that a lot of those people started over to Kentucky or Tennessee to settle lands and the linchpin broke on the wagon, and instead of being a blue-grass aristocrat, they became a mountaineer, but they're good people." I think the greatest characteristic about mountain people I know is individuality. And the thing that's most alien to them is being stereotypes. They're not stereotypes. No two of them are alike. *(Sam Ervin)*

After I was working and was making good money, relatively speaking, in 1960 to what other people were making, I was visiting my grandfather. He noticed that I had a considerable amount of money with me and asked me to save some each month. He said, "Charles, if you'll develop the habit of saving some money each month now, you'll have a lot." I was trying to explain to him that I had a car and gas and food and so forth; it cost an awful lot to live. In fact, I spent over 1,000 dollars a month just to live. He said, "What do you think I spent last year as my total expenditure?" Knowing my grandfather, I didn't think he spent much and I said, "Probably 1,800 to 2,000 dollars." He looked at me, and he said he spent 362 dollars total and half of that was on foolishness. So a lot depends not on what you make but what you do with what you make, I found out. He's independent; he's a man of his word; he has a lot of pride in what he's accomplished in his life. This may not be considered by some measures of standards to be a highly successful life, but in my view, [it has been] a very success-

ful life. He's been happy. He's been healthy, and he's been self-sufficient for the most part. He is ninety-six years old, and he still raises his own garden, still works his own garden. *(Charles Michael)*

The mountain people are very independent people. If they tell you they'll do something, they'll do it. And if they tell you they aren't going to, you can depend on that, too. Mother's family was part German and part Dutch, I think, as far as I know anything about them. They lived down in Wilkes County. One of them had a colt, and he wanted his daddy to let him run it in a rye patch. The old man wouldn't let him. He threw a rope on his colt and headed up the Blue Ridge and came up in here and settled and never did go back to see his people until he was married and had a boy old enough to ride behind him on a horse. So you see I came out of a very contrary bunch of people, very resolute. *(Alfred Adams)*

The people who you have interviewed are more or less like myself. If I believe in something, there's only one way in the world that you can change it. You've got to prove that I'm wrong, and then I'll come over to your side. I'll bet you that nine-tenths of the people that you've interviewed feel just exactly like I do. *(Herman Estes)*

They don't push. If they think you're pushing them, they'll resist even if they know it's good. I guess that's the way they survive. Some good Christian people that are just as good a people as you can find anywhere can get plumb ornery if you try to change their belief in anything. They believe what they believe, and if you oppose them, now you're opposing them. They won't give an inch in what they believe. *(Jonah Parker)*

Everybody is a specialist. You don't have generalists any more. You have specialists in medicine. My grandaddy was a doctor. He did everything from set legs to cure dandruff, or try to cure it.

But everybody's got their own little niche now, and I think you lose a lot of the versatility that was characteristic of the mountain people. They did everything. A hundred years ago a family could move onto a tract of land that no one had ever set foot on before. They'd cut the trees, hew the timbers, build the house, thatch the roof, build a fire, cook, haul water, wash clothes, make their own clothes. They'd till the fields, preserve whatever they got out, and they were pretty doggone self-sufficient. If you're self-sufficient, you can become independent. If you don't have to go to the bank and borrow money, you become awfully independent. They had a mule and a wagon, probably, that they could ride in, and also take it wherever they needed to go to get salt or flour or carry corn to the mill to get it ground into meal.

So they were, in effect, jacks of all trades. They could do it all. Some did some things better than others, so they did it for all of them, for example, a blacksmith. Some guy might have been able to split white oak and make shakes out of them, or shingles, better than others, so he did that. There was some bartering going on. It was a big event at our house when somebody paid my grandaddy in cash. People in this part of the country tended not to have a lot of cash money to begin with. And then you had that Depression, which further reduced the flow, so a nickel was pretty hard to come by. But in a way they were probably better prepared for a Depression than a lot of other people in that they could make a living. They could eat. They might not be able to get a pair of shoes, but they could sure put bread on the table and survive. *(Jim Ryan)*

They used to grow a lot of things. Some of them would sell potatoes and all such stuff as that and make enough to live, and kept cattle and everything. It used to be that years ago everybody kept chickens and had their own eggs, kept cows and had their own milk and butter. Now they go to the supermarket and get everything. *(Hal Oates)*

There is no reason in America to have any welfare whatsoever, except for disabled people, because you can teach anybody to make a living. The government has done more to make lazy people than any other thing on the face of the earth. Such marvelous people came out of the Depression, the people who survived the Depression. If they had been wealthy, they might not have been worth too much. I could take a young man right now, put him there in the shop and tell him he doesn't have to do a thing but make that knife the rest of his life, and he'll do a good job. He can make a living making that knife. He could make a living carving anvils out of wood, 'cause I know that. (B. Hensley)

Nowadays you can get work off the mountain. Everybody fares pretty good. Nearly everybody owns their own home. They have their own garden. They kill their own hogs. They have their own cattle. Of course, we don't milk them much anymore. We're not too much dependent on the outside. That's one thing about the mountain people. They can do anything that they set their minds to do. *(Carrie Burnette)*

A tree fell on me down here years ago. I was cutting wood, and that tree would not fall. I drove three wedges in it, and it just stood there. I had my chain saw with me and looked up to see if it was lodged in anything. And there came the awfulest windstorm you ever saw! I saw it was going to hit me. And I just turned my back. It hit me. I kept working under that tree and finally turned around and got out from underneath it and crawled to my truck. I couldn't hardly get in it. I'd holler, and no one ever came. Finally I got up in the truck and blew the horn. My son came, and he brought me to the house and washed the blood off my mouth. He got me over there to the emergency room at Boone, and they X-rayed me and liked to have killed me then. *(Stanley Hicks)*

Most of those old mountaineers are pretty tough. You have to be to live, to survive. *(Dan Moore)*

Cass Wallin

WORK ETHIC

I quit school to become the plowboy. I did the plowing when I was fourteen. Of course, back then when a boy graduated from the hoe to the plow, he thought he was a man. He was proud of it. I really believe that we don't know what life is like until we experience some hardships. That's a side of life that a lot of people miss, and it serves a good purpose. Whether it grinds a man up or pommels him down depends on the stuff he's made of. The rough places in life tend to be good for us. (Jonah Parker)

We were taught to be content with what we had and be glad that we had it. I read a little thing one day that said, "Contentment is not what you would love to have, but what you have and are thankful that you have." I don't miss a thing because we had a lot of love, we had plenty of clothes, we had as nice a clothes as any of the children. I was never embarrassed in my life. I was taught to take what I had, ask no questions. I was glad to get them. We were just taught to be thankful. *(Lottie Greene)*

The mountains never had a lot of farming. People had their gardens. Everybody had a garden, but there weren't many big farms. A lot of people didn't want to accumulate much. They just wanted a cabin, some land, their gun, and just to live as they wanted. *(Lewis Green)*

We have always had the poor, fairly well-to-do, and the to-do's. We have all three. They were all natives.

As for newcomers, so far we've been fortunate enough to get the type of people which are assets. Of course, once in a while, you'll see a black sheep get through, somehow. But on the whole, I'd tell them to find a place just as close to Valle Crucis as you can and move in with us. We'll try to be good to you. *(Howard Mast, Sr.)*

I was one hundred years old the fourteenth of May. The mountains have been good to me, and the people, too. The ol' mountain people are awfully good to you. I like 'em. They'll just do anything for me. They're the best ol' things you ever saw. *(Mamie Hall)*

And in these mountains, Roy [my husband] said that what they ought to have done to Brushy Mountain was bar it up, keep everybody out of it, and leave it for the animals. People had such a hard time making it, but they've come out of it now. Well, we had a hard time when we first came here. Me and Roy both worked, and our children every one of them worked. *(Bertha Lowe)*

I'll tell you another thing, that working don't hurt you. If anything, it's going to make you stouter. It's just different. People ain't working nowadays. They're just playing and going naked. (Bertha Lowe)

(Opposite) "Aunt" Carma Reed on her porch

HONESTY

They were Christian people. They built their own churches, very strong on religion. And Grandpa Smith used to say, and Great-Grandfather, too, that a man didn't need to sign his name. His word was his bond then. *(Jack Brinkley)*

I have enjoyed living here. I've got a lot of good friends, and there's a lot of good people here. I've been away from here, but I just didn't like it. I just like the mountain people on the whole. They're just exactly what they are. There's no two-face about them. If they tell you anything, that's what they mean. If they don't like you, they don't like you; and you know it. And if they like you, you know that, too. And they'll treat you good. I really like them. I wouldn't live anywhere else. I like it here. (Clifford Casey)

Perhaps because of the severity of the climate and location and isolation, competence was admired. You hear comments like, "So-and-so just won't pay you at all, just will not pay his debts, but he can really play the fiddle." You know, this admiration of competence came about because they had to rely on each other. That brings about a wonderful tolerance for other people's mistakes and quirks. I think there's real forgiveness. I think that one of the things that I am proud of is the fact we have this ability to separate the things somebody might do that we don't approve of from them as a person. You don't hate the person. You just wish they didn't do that. *(Rebecca Councill)*

As long as the man was honest and kept his word. The saying, of course, was, "His word's as good as his bond." That was what they said about a man that was honest. They always managed some way, although money was in short supply. The average family always managed to pay their debts, and if a man promised to do something, he did it. By and large the mountain people were truthful. They were honest and you could rely on them if they promised you something. If they promised to come to work for you, they would be there.

And they were independent in that they did not want to be harassed by anybody. They felt like they were independent, and that spirit developed, I think, because they had to be independent to make a living. Each man had to rely on his own effort because we didn't have any industry and you did not go to town to get a job. You had to make it with what you had. They were independent and

Bertha Lowe and granddaughter Jodie Handy

I love fall! Those first days when you feel fall in the air. It's my favorite time of year. I get this feeling of urgency. I think I inherited that from my ancestors who lived in these mountains all these years because when winter was coming on, they had to get the crops in, everything stored away, and get prepared to survive the winter. It was urgent, really. And I still get that feeling in the fall.
(Jonah Parker)

I think that a lot of people have that image of mountains, of these poor starving people and these houses with dirt floors, but that's not the case. Nobody starves in the mountains. People grow food, and it's everywhere. They raise gardens, but a lot of them hunt and fish. If they don't have money, they still have all these things. They can go out and catch fish or kill a deer or do something like that. It's not like they go out and kill a deer and waste it. They eat it. I feel like it's bad if you go out and hunt animals to kill 'em and not use them. But if you use them for meat, I don't see anything wrong with it at all. My husband loves to deer hunt, but he would never kill an animal just for the fun of killing it. (Wanda Moss)

A lot of times when the moon is partly shining, with the clouds shaping it out it'll go off. Well you'll be walking along and you will see a rock or an old stump of a tree, or stuff like that; and if you're scary, now, scary of seeing something, you'll get to looking at that, and you'll imagine there's a pair of eyes. There's a head, and then when you see the head, there's a pair of eyes. Then you'll study a little more and there's a mouth; then a little more and there's the body, hands. Now a haint is something you imagine. But a ghost is a real thing. (Ray Hicks)

The river used to stay iced over six weeks at a time. It was so cold back then, and you could take a wagon and horses and go from here to Spruce Pine on the river without ever getting off. They used to go down after freight. And the boys at the Presbyterian School would build a fire out here at night and they would skate. That was one of their activities. And they would ride us on their shoulders, you know, and they'd push us on chairs, just a regular chair we'd turn upside down. You'd sit on the rails and they'd push us with the chair. And I couldn't wait 'til I grew up so I could date these boys, you know. But, after I grew up, we didn't have them. [The school had burned down.] (Kay Wilkins)

That was the greatest thrill on earth when the time of year came to pull your shoes off. My mother would never let us go barefooted until we saw a catbird. She said, "When catbirds come, spring is here." So we'd look for that. We thought it was plenty warm enough to go barefooted, but we had to produce a catbird or let her see one.
(Quay Smathers)

they were hard workers. I have felt like some of those virtues have disappeared. This progress, as it is called, has come into the mountains like the rest of the country. I don't think those old-time virtues are quite as strong as they used to be. *(Dan Moore)*

I'm very proud of this area. It doesn't make any difference what they're doing, what business they're in. They can be in the whiskey business, anything, that American tradition of honesty is still there. *(Junior Johnson)*

You cannot legalize morality. That's one thing the mountain people used to be very high about was allowing their neighbors to do what went on between each other—"That's your private business." Like home brew—making home brew—that's your right to make your own liquor or anything you want to. *(Mike Phillips)*

The honest acceptance of people is the most durable, the most easily recognized across-the-board characteristic. I would account for it solely on the basis of Calvinistic theology, which emphasized the goodness in the presence of the human personality. That had to be respected both in the face of the man and in the face of the woman. So we accepted people because they were God-like as they presented themselves to us, knowing all the while that they have evil in their heart, that Satan lives there and that we might expect anything from them. We typically are not surprised when the preacher runs off with the deacon's wife and things like that. This is ol' Satan working, and he's present in everybody's heart. Socially, we emphasize the acceptance aspect. *(Cratis Williams)*

A GENEROUS SPIRIT

They were friendly. They would help each other if they needed it. They always had time to help each other. A good neighbor was counted as one of the best things that ever happened to you—to have a good neighbor and to be a good neighbor.
(Ola Miller)

There wasn't any money made back then. You didn't have to have any, only to pay a little tax. We'd go to the Beech [Mountain] and get a hog and bring it up here and share it. I'd go to work for people, and my wife, too, and work for twenty-five cents a day. And I'd work for fifty cents on the farm to get enough money to pay our taxes. I sold eggs. We'd give milk and butter away to people that needed it worse than we did. Back then, people helped one another. *(Stanley Hicks)*

We truly do have a lot of poor people that are almost invisible. Now the local Jaycees have a Christmas shopping tour each year. They looked forward to that so much because they got names from various social service agencies and took the children shopping. The extraordinary thing about those children was when they got in the store, before they bought anything for themselves, they wanted to buy a doll for their sister or gloves for their brothers or something for their mother. I think this speaks to the need of the human spirit to be generous, to give rather than to take.

At one time, the wife in one of the families at Meat Camp had a long, dreadful terminal illness, just disastrous. Their neighbors went in, and they didn't do what I would do, which is fix a casserole or bake a cake. They did those things too, but they went in and tended the family's garden. They canned and froze that family's food. Even after working all day themselves in their own gardens, they dug that family's potatoes. It was neighborly. Those people just did the work as if it were truly their own because they felt the responsibility.

Before there were organized charities, the people gave their money to the church and the church decided what to do with it. It was a real simple, down-to-earth formula that worked. Now, of course, everything is so complicated, and because of all the public funding, people don't feel that responsibility for their neighbors that they used to. And that is so sad. Because of the isolation, that kind of thing did hold out in the mountains a lot longer. It's gone now, virtually gone. If you read old church records, time after time you will find accounts of widows or orphans, and the admonition to take care of them is taken absolutely literally and seriously. Those early churches accepted the responsibility for those women and children just as seriously as any husband would have done. They did see that their needs were met, and so there was no need for an organized government effort.
(Rebecca Councill)

And Daddy always kept a car there at the house. If anybody got sick, they could come and get the car. I don't care who it was. They could get the car and go to the doctor in it. That's what it was for. If there was somebody sick and needed to go to the doctor, needed to go the hospital or something, they drove the car. He had a car there and everybody was welcome to it. It was a wonderful life, really. I'd like to go through it one more time. I really would. (Leon Johnson)

In the community, the neighbors would check to see if they had seeds to plant, if it was planting time. They shared their seed with them. They'd have their "workings," we called them, shuckings,

Harold Jenkins delivering peaches

chopping. If there was sickness and the family got behind with cultivating their crops or whatever, all the neighbors would come in and catch them up. You'd work like a slave all day and have the biggest time. Now that's gone. *(Jonah Parker)*

You never knew who was going to come for dinner. You sat yourself down and you shared what you had. I've seen the time when there would be fifteen and sixteen at dinner on Sunday at Mama's. It didn't seem to shock her. You usually got something ready on Sunday. They usually got up a fat hen. They killed it and made a big pot of chicken and dumplings. And they had what we called "shucked wings," leather britches [dried beans], and they were soaked and ready. They had all kinds of canned fruits and they made a cobbler. Everybody had plenty to eat and enjoyed it.

My grandmother used to say, "There's two classes of people, the leaners and the lean-ons." Some people are always looking to lean on somebody else, somebody to take care of them, somebody to help them. And there were others that everybody leaned on. They could take care of themselves and have something to help others. I think that's another thing about the mountains. Everybody is not really created equal. Some people have the knowledge to know how to make a living and some just don't

have it. We've always been very tolerant toward anybody. Nobody ever goes without if we know. We help each other. *(Carrie Burnette)*

Newland used to be called the Old Fields of Toe. You'd never lock a door because it was absurd. A neighbor may need something. They'd usually walk miles just to come by and see you. They'd usually come to spend the night, have dinner and everything else. Everybody switched back and forth getting together and helping each other out. They isolated themselves from the rest of the world but not from each other. *(Mike Phillips)*

Mountain people you couldn't tell them from lowland except by their friendliness, their desire to help one another. They're mighty good at that. They've got an independent disposition too. Neighborliness I guess you'd call it. It is gradually disappearing as the population increases. *(Horton Cooper)*

And we had good neighbors and made better than some people do now. Neighbors back then would come in. If one in the family got sick, your neighbors all round would come in. If one in the family was sick, they'd come in and hoe your corn fields out for you. All they wanted was their dinner. They came and helped people. Now people live right close to you, die, and you don't know anything about it. Somebody else may tell you. People now don't care for one another like they used to. All they want is just a big time themselves. If they're all right, they don't care about their neighbor. But people are supposed to care for one another and love each other. *(Lilly Wykle)*

The country merchant would let you have things on credit until the fall of the year when you sold your cattle and your crops and things. He'd ride his jobbers 'til then. It had been an awfully hard year, and nobody had made anything and crops hadn't been much good. This old man named McBride got on his horse and rode down to the local merchant's and told him to come outside. He got out there and

ol' man McBride said, "You're going to have to pay your company and a lot of people are not going to be able to pay you." The country merchant handed him a Coke and he [McBride] said, "Here's some money you can use awhile." And the merchant said, "Well, I'll be glad to have it. You'd better count it, and I'll give you a note." The old man just turned his horse around and said, "You just count it." You wouldn't find that happening now!
(Alfred Adams)

We've lived here ever since 1920. We were married December 30, 1917. When we bought this place, we only had two hundred dollars to pay down on

it, the whole farm, the whole mountain in through here. So Bill was seven months old when we came up here that fall. We have worked and struggled here for sixty-eight years on December 30. I am eighty-nine and we're both old, but I am thankful to be up and able to go yet. I never fail to thank my Lord for blessing me to be on my feet.

Marion would make enough to pay a little more on the farm. It took years to pay for it. Hard work, too. Oh, we struggled. Never thought much about it. Didn't realize, you know, that it was hard times. Everybody was alike, so we never even realized it. Even when we lost some money we had in the bank saving to pay the next payment on the house every year. We lost some money. Everybody did. I'll never forget how things picked up after good old President Roosevelt was elected. We got to getting a little money off what we had, what we raised.

The bank closed. And then Mr. Roosevelt just brought it right out. I always loved him. *(Lyda Coffey)*

It was nothing like the Christmas we made our paper chain and put it on the tree. We popped popcorn and made our own chains. We took innertubes and cut out squirrels and things. My aunt helped to make them and we stuffed them. They were so pretty hanging on that tree. We made some candles, but we didn't have many candles too often. We had two up on the mantel, and then we had a Christmas stocking and we made it. That was some kind of a pine! We just went out in the field and got it, and it was so pretty. I took paper (crepe paper) and twisted three different colors around. We didn't have electric lights, but I'd been quilting, and I took my quilt and put it in the center of my house. I'd twist the crepe paper around the branches, and I hung some mistletoe and then they got under it. *(Lillian Hooper)*

Oh, yes, I remember before Brenda was born, I think it was a hundred and some pumpkins I toted up, then pulled a whole field of corn, and then picked some apples. I never worked for anybody 'til my younguns were big and I went to hiring out picking apples in the city. You see, the girls helped us get ours done. Why then I'd hire out and make a little extra. *(Bertha Lowe)*

If you look back on it now, you'd think we were having a hard time; but nobody ever told us we were having a hard time, and we thought we were getting along fine. My father was a leader in the community. He was on the school board when they finally got a school. He was a director of the little bank at Blowing Rock, and he and my mother helped organize the First Baptist Church in Blowing Rock.

It was a fascinating time to grow up. I remember the first automobile I ever saw, and now they're going to the moon and so on. Now, I've seen all that. *(Wade Brown)*

The day before this last Christmas a year ago, I lost my billfold. I had my Social Security card (the old one) and had never lost it. I hated it awfully because the ol' lady had given me a fifty dollar bill for a Christmas present exactly a year earlier, and I wouldn't spend that for anything. I carried it and took care of it. It had a one dollar bill in it that was exactly a hundred years old, and it had five twenty dollar bills doubled together. I had enough extra to pay my light bill. I hope one thing—that the man who got my billfold had a gang of little children so they could have a happy Christmas. We always were lucky. We always had plenty to eat. When the ol' woman goes to the grocery store, I tell her, "Buy anything you want to eat because we're not taking anything with us when we leave here." *(Willard Watson)*

Never did have nothing much. Just kind of been from hand to mouth, but, my, how I've enjoyed it. But I've had a lot of help looking over me from above. *(Monroe Ledford)*

(Opposite) Snow-covered Grandfather Mountain profile, Avery County

Watch for Fallen Rock

Mountain Living

ANYONE WHO HAS EVER TRAVELED THROUGH THIS AREA has seen signs saying "Watch for Fallen Rock" or "Falling Rock Area." They are all over the place, and for good reason. Although the soil is very fertile here, the rocks and steep hillsides can make farming and transportation difficult. One day, Caroline Moss took me to visit her fiancé's father, who was plowing a potato field with a pony. She thought that this would be interesting for me to photograph, as so many farmers still use mules and ponies for plowing in the mountains. It was a wonderful scene, but Johnny Lewis's description of the futility in trying to cultivate many of the steep and uneven grades found in mountain fields was even more illuminating. I had heard of farmers being killed when their tractors had overturned, pinning them underneath. Johnny Lewis described these dangers but also said that because of the terrain, fields often had to be so small that a tractor could tear up a good portion of the crop in turning rows because there was no place to turn around outside the field. He had some nice tractors that he could use in many fields, but this was not one of them. He laughed and said, "This might take a little longer, but it sure beats a hoe."

Since farming has been so difficult, most mountaineers have always had at least two jobs. They kept their gardens and found other work to bring in cash from the outside when they could. Since there was little industry, many had to go down to the lowlands to work in furniture factories or cotton mills. Some went off to work on highways that were being built. Some found jobs locally. Grady Reed is a good example. He has worked at a meat-packing plant for years, raises hunting dogs, and "keeps a garden." Most people would consider his garden a full-fledged farm, but this is just part of his routine. He and his wife, Delia, love their life style and have enjoyed sending their children to college.

Since there were few ways for people to get cash, some turned to making or bootlegging moonshine. (Moonshiners were the makers of the liquor, and the bootleggers sold it.) People had been making liquor legally in mountain stills licensed by the government for many years before Prohibition came in. It didn't seem fair to have this source of income taken away, so some mountaineers just ignored the law and went on ahead with their business.

(Opposite) Warren Moore and Letha Hicks

More industry has come into the area in recent years, and tourism has expanded, providing opportunities for more local jobs. But it is still frightening to find yourself behind a truck as it struggles up a steep, curving mountain road. And this brings to mind how landlocked this area still is and the difficulties involved with future development here.

Many of the changes have come about as the mountain people have adapted to their environment and tried to make good use of things that were available to them. Faye Dancy and her husband walked me through rows of Christmas trees they were cultivating. They both have other jobs. An orchard owner had an assistant drive me on a golf cart through vast orchards of apples, peaches, and plums. They were happy and proud to show me around. It was glorious; the trees were laden with fruit and the peaks of ridges could be seen over their tops. Another time, Bob Phillips walked me through his orchard and explained the difficulties in growing apples now that sprays had to be used to fight off insects and diseases. This hadn't had to be done in years past. Jonah Parker explained grafting to me. Until he did, I hadn't realized that prized specimens of apples had to be grafted onto seedlings in order to produce the desired variety one wanted. All these conversations gave me newfound admiration for the farmer and his abundance of factual knowledge.

I learned about a lot of other things on these trips. After a while I could taste the difference between sourwood honey, locust, and many other varieties. I learned about pickled beans and real red-eye gravy. (Coffee grounds are used in it!) I tasted various kinds of moonshine liquor, from white lightning (corn liquor) to peach or apple brandy. The latter were usually mixed with, or chased by, some RC Cola. A small sip of these potions was usually plenty for me.

I was sent home with all kinds of preserves, pickles, pumpkin and apple butter, tomatoes, apples of all varieties, fresh ground cornmeal, mountain cabbages, and hot peppers. These were all gifts from the people I met. One day Lottie Greene even presented me with a quilted pillow she had made. It was near Christmas, and she thought I should have a present. Ethel and Harold Keener sent me home with some prized ginseng. I've never met such generous people in my life. One family was worried about my driving back to Greensboro after dark. They knew that it was a few hours' drive, and, as I had to get back and teach the next day, I couldn't stay the night with them. So they sent me off with a little supper that I could heat up when I got home. These are just a few examples of generosity from people who have made it through hard times and want to help others.

I sat by wood-burning stoves in country stores and heard stories about the area. People from different parts of the community were always coming in and out and telling jokes or offering advice. They told me about interesting places to visit and photograph and gave detailed descriptions of how to get there. They also told me about people I should interview and often introduced me to them. I loved stopping in at Roses' store in Glendale Springs. They always made me feel at home and protected from the cold weather outside or from whatever else I might run into on the road after I left them. The Houstons live in a house just beside their store near Spruce Pine. It was comforting to drive up and find them there. In an area where houses and people are so spread apart, the local country stores provide a sense of community. People from all over stop in, and everybody knows everybody. At least the store operators do, and they introduce everyone. Eventually, new people become familiar to those who have been there longer. Business is not as brisk as in the old days because of the big chain stores that have come in, but the need for these gathering places is still there.

Willard Watson

GOOD THINGS FROM THE GARDEN

There ain't but two kinds of pie I like, though. Cold pie and hot pie.
(Grady Reed)

Well, I tell you, a cushaw makes a mighty good pie. It's got a harder shell than a pumpkin. I bet you've seen 'em. Some of them's got necks, and the meat is just as hard. It's not as dark a meat as the pumpkin's. My, they make good custard. I like them better than I do the plain pumpkin. We don't grow them any more. *(Delia Reed)*

Well, we ain't planted 'em is the reason. It used to be, we had the cornfield full of pumpkins and cushaws. Well, if you spray your ground, why that kills everything. Yeah, if you make pumpkins now, you've got to get out and make some hills and plant them and just let them run everywhere they want to go. You can't put them in the corn and spray it because that spray will kill the pumpkin.

Anyhow, we raise in the garden 'taters, corn, tomatoes, beans, well just about anything you want to, salads of all denominations, onions, bell peppers, squash, and cabbage. You can raise about anything you want to here. *(Grady Reed)*

Here's my garden. I just planted it, and it started growing. I've dug up all my rock; I built the lower side up this summer. Had the upper part last summer. And I had some azaleas up there that I'd bought; dug them up and brought them down. Went to town and got me some more and put them around. They got froze this spring, part of them; some of them didn't. My garden here was partly red clay. There was a lot of manure put on it last year, but there wasn't a speck put on it this year.

I'm pretty bad with the signs, yes I am. Because you can plant things then, they grow so tall. You plant things to grow in the ground, potatoes and things like that, on the dark nights of the moon; and then light nights, you plant things that grow on top of the ground, beans and corn and such. And I've got this calendar, and whenever I plant anything in my garden, I go and mark down the date that I planted it to see how it works out.

My garden's real wet there, and I couldn't get nothing planted. I couldn't work it, and I couldn't get the weeds out or nothing. I took my hoe and made a little furrow about that deep and planted corn and that row of beans down there. The ground was just mud. But I laid off this little shallow furrow and planted my seeds in there and turned the hoe over.

Now you see how it is. You see. Everybody has tillers and things to clean their garden out. But if mine's weedy and if I can't get it cleaned out and I've got to plant something, I'll put my row through it, plant it, and then if I come down here, any time I come if there's a weed growing around my plants, then I'll pull those weeds out. Here's some squash. See the way I do my weeds, I pull them up and pile them up. And this is creasies. They grow in a field—used to grow in cornfields. I don't know what's making mine die but that it's so wet. Used to, you'd go out in a cornfield and you'd get all you wanted, wild stuff. And I love them better than turnip greens. Turnip, mustard, any greens—have to be cooked more than spinach. Now as soon as I pile my weeds up like that, I get my wheelbarrow or bushel basket and take my tater digger and I'll pick them up.

Here's tomatoes and lettuce. My onions almost rotted. It's too damp for them. Cabbage and broccoli. There's my limas. I love those frozen. And I put my ashes in my bucket in the winter and set it on the porch and then if I have potatoes or anything I

122

(Opposite) Nanny Suttles in her garden

put the peelings and everything in the garden. Those potatoes have come up from potato peelings. And I noticed one out there at the end had a potato on it. Looked like about that long. Those two rows are the ol' timey field corn. I love it. I love creamed-style corn, and I love the field corn for that because when you cook it, it gets thick. With sweet corn, if you want it kind of thick, you'll have to thicken it with something or another, but field corn you don't have to do it. And up here's my three hills of butternut squash. They take a lot of room to grow. But weeds, weeds, weeds. I get my 'tater digger; when things is high and I can't bring my wheelbarrow in to them, but I'll haul them on the edge, where they'll rot.

For a while we had about twelve or fourteen cows in here. They got out in my garden, five of them did one night, and the hateful things, they just broke my cauliflower, broccoli, and cabbage. I came in the house and called Doug and told him to come down here and help me get them cows before I killed them. I bought me a little fertilizer and put a little fertilizer in it [the garden]. I never worked my potatoes; never hoed them a time last summer; and I never hoed them potatoes this summer. Laid my rows off with a hoe, but I keep the weeds pulled out of it, and it grows. I had potatoes before anybody else on the farm, and they planted theirs in March, and I didn't plant mine 'til April. I've got a calendar and it has signs to go by planting, of the moon and the signs of the bodies and this, that and the other. *(Nanny Suttles)*

Well, I've got cabbage and beans and tomatoes, peppers. This last summer a year ago, my husband brought one tomato up off the vine weighed two and one half pounds, and I got one weighed two and one half pounds. A piece of white bread, a piece of tomato would just cover it up. He's got some tomatoes set out now; the tomatoes are supposed to be eight inches across when they get grown, but I doubt they get that big. Some of the yellow ones got almost as large as the big ones we raised. *(Ruth Settles)*

The drive out to Letha Hicks's house was long but very beautiful. It took me almost into Tennessee along the Pigeon River, with views of paint-brush combinations of brightly colored leaves reflected in the water and majestic rock cliffs towering along beside the road as a reminder of the blasting that must have been done in order to carve the highway out. They were also a reminder of the strength that still emanates from these peaks. Later, after turning off the highway, I crossed over a stream and traveled up a dirt road for a few miles until I found Letha's house.

She was out in the garden when I drove up and greeted me with a smile. She didn't have a phone, so my visit was unannounced. I introduced myself, explaining that a mutual friend had suggested that I interview her about her growing up in the mountains. Within a few minutes, I felt as though I were talking with an old friend. She has a kindly nature but a mischievous sparkle in her eyes. As she told me about her life, she walked me around her property, stopping at each variety of apple tree to give me a sample taste. We sat on the porch and she told stories of bears in the apple trees and beehives, of decoration days and family reunions, and of learning to read from True Story *magazines.*

Life had not been easy for Letha, but she didn't seem to think so. It all seemed to be a marvelous adventure for her. She was full of energy and humor and the idea that life would follow its course. On later visits I would look at new quilts she had made. The one on the frame always looked the prettiest. She called the quilting room the deep freeze because there was no heat in that room. The kitchen and living rooms each had wood-burning stoves. She would go out and get water from a spring close to the house. Everything was comfortable, and there were wonderful meals of fresh cooked cabbage, hot peppers, tomatoes, and other good things from the garden, all accompanied by milk and cornbread. When I last saw

Letha this past fall, she was very happy that she had "gotten water in the house last spring." Her older sister (aged ninety) had come to live with her, and they were getting along well.

I'm still looking forward to going hunting for ginseng with Letha. She knows about some good places. (W. M.)

Oh yeah, we lived on a farm and we raised what we ate. What we didn't raise, we didn't eat. There were nine boys and one girl. We had a rough time, but everybody had a rough time. We sold very little stuff. We raised enough to feed the cattle through the winter and had to make enough to feed the mule so we could make a crop and we used him to pull our pulpwood, to log with; and that's where we got our money. We'd cut pulpwood and log; and we'd have to use the mule to pull it out.
(Clifford Casey)

It was '34. Up until the Depression people looked after themselves, but the Depression changed the average man. They started all these WPA's [Works Progress Administration], CCC [Civilian Conservation Corps], and all these welfare-type programs. Make-work programs is what they were.
(Dan Moore)

Oh, there was no way people with a spoonful of energy would starve in this area if they knew how to survive.
(Wanda Moss)

The first job I ever worked on was the WPA. I started on that. Then I just went from that to one thing and another. But still farmed during that time too. We grew a lot of the stuff we ate. People in the mountains have always had two jobs. People this day don't know what work is.

Tomatoes and beans from Grady Reed's garden

They'd make a living at home, and then they worked on public jobs to have money to buy their coffee, flour, and clothes and things they couldn't do at home. People used to have all their milk, butter, meat, potatoes; they canned stuff; canned their beans. They raised all that. If they didn't, they didn't have it. *(Nelson Cabe)*

When it was summertime, we'd have big black pots that hung on an iron post, and build fires under it and boil your clothes. And when they canned beans, you'd put beans in the can. People would put twelve cans in a big tub and put cloths all around so they wouldn't shake, and press them down and boil them three hours in that tub, and they'd keep. A whole lot easier to can now than it was in that big tub. You had to put a fire under it and keep it going.

Back before I got married, the way I bought my clothes, we had a big field of wild strawberries; now you talk about good! And my grandpa would burn them off in February to keep all the weeds killed down, and there wasn't no briars and no weeds, just solid wild strawberries, thick, big as the end of your thumb, as sweet as they could be. I'd go out in the fields and pick them red strawberries and cap them, tote them up that mountain, three gallons at a time, to Dillsboro; I really did. A dollar a gallon; save up enough money and go buy my clothes and lots of other stuff. That was before I got married. I've done well to be held up like I am as much hard work as I've done. *(Lilly Wykle)*

Peaches from the Brushy Mountains in Wilkes County

PUTTING THINGS UP

Pearl and Gayton Marshall's "can house"

They didn't can back when I was growing up. They dried everything. There was very little canning done. Beans, corn, everything they grew they dried that couldn't be preserved in the ground. Dried beans were called "leather britches." They dried it, and just as soon as you put the water back in, it made a kernel of corn or green bean again, dried fruit, dried peaches. They had dry houses just like they had smoke houses. They had a dry house out here, and they had a kiln. You build a fire and then add your coal and put these sheets, put your stuff on it to dry. Put it in that building, keep a fire under it until it dried. You didn't burn it, you just dried it. They'd take these layers of fruit and put in that dry house and dry the stuff. The thing they put it on was a screen made in a wooden frame; just slide it in there. Put your fruit on it and slide it in there; when it got dry, take it out. I remember a spring house, dry house, and a smoke house.

The spring house is still standing. That's where you kept all your butter, milk, whatever you had to keep cold. Water stayed cold and run through it all the time. You'd bring the stuff that you were going to put in there like your milk and stuff that would freeze in the jar because it wasn't moving; but the water was moving and it didn't freeze.

See when I was a kid growing up, I had to get up in the morning before I went to school, carry in the wood for Mother. If it was wash day, we'd carry the water in a pot outside the house. Now if it was too cold, she washed on the kitchen stove; boiled the water. She boiled your clothes. You got a stick and you punched the clothes. We had a granary, too. Everything done at that time was for a purpose. *(Frank Norris)*

Honey, we took apples and put them on a thread and hung a nail behind the stove, or wherever you wanted to hang them. We'd hang them on the clothesline. You'd be surprised to know how they dried in the sunshine. We'd have to take them in at night, you know, on account of the dew. *(Lottie Greene)*

I can remember back before we got cans when I was growing up at home and Mama dried everything. She dried pumpkin. She'd cook a great hunk of lean striped meat, good fresh pork, and then she'd soak that pumpkin and then cook it in that, and I can remember how good that was. And then somehow or another somebody invented cans and we got to canning. One awful bad winter, though, they had all the cans sitting in a closet, and so much of it froze and busted open. *(Lyda Coffey)*

Yeah, I made many pickled beans. You don't cook them done, you just cook them and you put them in a jar and you put one tablespoon of salt to a half-gallon and then you pour water over it and they pickle. You do kraut the same way—you know, cabbage. Now I can my kraut as I cut it; put hot water and seal it. But pickled beans, you've got to let them set, and you've got to keep the brine up on them, 'cause if you don't, they'll mold, and what's mold on top won't be good. You've got to tie it up good 'cause gnats gets after things like that, vinegar, anything that's sour, gnats gets after it. And they'll get in there. *(Bertha Lowe)*

She cooked, dried a whole lot of leather britches. And you'd pick your beans; if they were dirty, you'd wash them, let them dry, string them. About middle ways of the bean, through the bean, you'd stick a needle with a long thread on it; and you string that full of beans and hang it up somewhere where it'll dry, and it dries and makes leather britches. Trouble of it is cooking them. You could soak them overnight and then pull them off the string, put them in your pot and parboil them, I guess two hours. Take them out and wash them; then put them in your pot and put in your meat and your salt and cook them the rest of the day 'til dinner. They were really good. **(Sue Oates)**

I canned. I made twenty-four cans yesterday. I made apple jelly. I made a gallon of juice and I made two five-pound pokes of sugar, or ten pounds of sugar to the gallon, and three boxes of Sure-Jell [fruit pectin]. I don't know what makes the difference. The other day I dumped fifteen cans out of a gallon, but sometimes it just turns out thirteen. I don't know whether it's the sugar or what it is. Maybe it's signs of the moon or something. I just let it come to a boil every time and then put my things in it. Why, I don't know. I guess it's sometimes, you know, the moon. You know people go by the signs. *(Lillian Hooper)*

I counted ninety-six big hams hanging to the joists and then the side meat and other stuff was packed and hung everywhere. There wasn't a place left in there, I don't think, that a piece of meat could be hung that there wasn't a piece hanging. Back in those days, all you had to do was just turn your hogs loose in the woods and let them get their own food, the acorns and the chestnuts. Well, them hogs would get so doggoned fat they couldn't walk. They'd [farmers] take one horse and a narrow sled and go out into the woods, shoot down a big one, stick it, load it on the sled, and bring it in and butcher it. The next day, maybe they'd go two or three times in one day. They really had good ham meat to eat then, and it was cured right, cured the old-fashioned way with just plain salt. You know, over the years, I used to raise quite a few hogs myself—and I've cured meat about every way I ever heard tell of it—and I finally ended up going back just to the plain ol' salt. That's the best flavor. *(Myron Houston)*

In the wintertime we'd cut the ice off the lake and put it in the icehouse. They had no way to make ice back then. And they packed it in the sawdust. That kept almost into the summer. *(Pearl Marshall)*

We used to dig a big ol' hole and bury the potatoes. Just put them in there for the winter and cover them over and throw dirt on top of 'em. You had your potatoes then when you wanted them. Just go down and get you some. *(Lillian Hooper)*

My daddy buried his potatoes. He'd just dig a hole in the ground and cover it with straw and pour in potatoes and then cover it up. But ordinarily it'd not be too much above the ground, not too high, but there'd be plenty of straw, or if he saw fit he might put something else over the straw and then the dirt over it. But he'd always cover it up, and of course, in the spring of the year we'd go out and take out the potatoes and replant them. *(Lottie Greene)*

THE COUNTRY STORE

I built it in 1937. It used to be a general store; it's just a staying place now. See after the big stores went in, there's no way a little store can compete with them on prices. They buy it in carload lots, you see. We buy it in case lots, and we don't get the price that they get by any means. We reduced everything down here to feed and gasoline, practically. As long as it maintains itself, why we'll try to keep it open. It gives us something to do, something to look forward to. You set both of us down here looking at four walls and not a thing in the world to do, and I don't know what would happen in a very short time. *(Myron Houston)*

All the kids know me as Aunt Ruth, and we know them backwards from their mothers and daddies and grandparents, all the way up. And we're always Aunt Ruth and Uncle Myron. *(Ruth Houston)*

It's been the community meeting place, you might say, ever since it's been here. In fact, this community has grown up an awful lot since this store first started here. But back in the beginning, there weren't near so many stores in the country, and we didn't have these big supermarkets. We really did a nice business here for a long, long time.

Well, I'll tell you it used to be that I had a market for chickens and eggs and meat. I used to barter an awful lot here on eggs and chickens. And the state turned around and they passed a law now that I can't buy a dozen eggs from you and sell it in here, without violating the law, without its being checked and counted before they'll allow it to be sold. There was no exchange of money whatsoever. They would take whatever they wanted in trade and that was it. I wish it was like that today, but now with all these restrictions. It just helps us meet our grocery bill and light bill and things of that nature.

Country Store (has since burned down), Cranberry, Avery County

130   *Wood stove at Phillips's Store, Little Canada, Jackson County*

There's not enough volume of business to pay much. I really had a nice stock of merchandise here for many, many years, but things have changed and we can't change along with it. We just don't have the means to do it with, and we're not able to take care of it. We're getting up in years now. *(Myron Houston)*

Bob Banner's store, I never thought that there could be anything like that— shelves, you know, with canned stuff and all kinds of overalls and clothing out on the counter, and candy and showcases. And just to see that, never could I imagine ever anything being in the world like that, never. Today I could see New York City and all the glamour of all these things, and go through a big city and all these stores—self-service stores like we go to today in Boone—and it's nothing to me compared to the excitement that was going in there and seeing all that. I'd never seen anything before, you don't know how that looked to me. I thought, "Nobody else in the world has got anything like this. This is the headquarters of the whole world, and nobody knows anything about it but just me and a few around here!" That's just the way it was, now, to me, to learn how to buy things and how that trading was carried on. (Raymond Presnell)

I can remember well the old cracker-barrel days. They had a big barrel full of crackers. And they didn't wash their hands every time they went in the cracker barrel. They got a paper sack; a paper poke is what the mountain folks called them. They'd get that poke in their hand and dip out a quarter's worth. You could get a great big bag of crackers for a quarter. And when we had soup, if we didn't have cornbread, we had crackers. And all those barrels and kegs were around a big pot-bellied stove in the store, and there's where the men ganged up and chewed their tobacco. And they had buckets with ashes in them to spit in; they didn't have spittoons, but they had to have something to spit in. They'd chew that tobacco and get around the cracker barrel. They'd eat crackers; they'd eat cheese. By then the bought cheese was coming in. *(Harriet "Granny" Echols)*

Yes, that's all the stores we had, of course, were country stores. And I can still remember the smell of this country store and the ol' cracker barrels and the nail kegs, and they sold meat and the rawhides. Had 'em all in the same store. Had to dip it all out and put it in a paper bag, you know. And if you were out away from home and had to get your lunch, well, fix a piece of cheese and open a can of sardines and a can of tomatoes and sit on the counter. And sometimes the merchants would give you crackers to go with them. Just reach in there with their ol' hands that had been in meat and nails and stuff and hand you the crackers, you know. I don't know whether germs were available in those days. We were immune to them, I reckon, and we survived. . .I don't know how. *(Bob Phillips)*

My daddy bought roots and herbs of all kinds, and all kinds of furs; people would trap for rabbits and minks along the rivers, muskrats. But, I remember my daddy's store having nails drove up in the ceiling, and it was hanging full of rabbits that had just been killed. Then the furs, of course, they skinned the animals and would board those on boards and hang them up. He had a big warehouse, and I remember that room just hanging full. And in the store he sold all kinds of groceries and big buckets of candy, which you don't see any more, and he had shelves of overalls. I remember the overalls and the ol' blue denim shirts which have come back after all these years. They would trade their leaves, dried herbs, and furs for groceries and clothing; and my daddy had, even, shoes. I remember lace and all kinds of notions, and a big wooden showcase with the glass top full of notions, thread and needles and all kinds of fancy lace, which if we had today would bring a fortune. *(Faye Dancy)*

Had a little country store up there. You'd take the eggs up there. He made one trip to Canton every Saturday and took his eggs and stuff to barter with. If you'd go up there, you could get cloth on a bolt, get you enough cloth to make you a shirt. When your shoes wore out, you told him you wanted enough shoe leather to half-sole a pair of shoes. And he would take his knife and cut that off. You'd buy what you called "sprigs," little sprigs, little nails—that's what you half-soled with. And they had a last [a form shaped like a foot], and your daddy would half-sole your shoes. Every family had a last. If they didn't, they'd go borrow one from a neighbor and they'd half-sole the shoes. And anybody that chewed tobacco, the tobacco came in little wooden boxes, little square wooden boxes; and in that box the pieces of tobacco had little marks marked off on them and had little cutters. If they wanted a dime's worth of tobacco, they'd stick that in there and mash that lever and cut it off.

My grandpa ran a store, and you could take a can down there and get a gallon of kerosene oil or a lamp chimney or a lamp wick or shoe-sole leather or a piece of cloth, a little black pepper and stuff like that. They bartered at the country store. They'd take eggs and they'd take butter. There was just not any money. Most of them kept it at home in a sack and buried it, a lot of them. A lot of these old folks had more money than you might think saved up. *(Quay Smathers)*

I had my brother-in-law in here one day and these little ol' boys brought a chicken in. He bought it, paid them for it in candy or drinks, or whatever they wanted. Well, he took it out and put it in the lot. In about an hour or so, they slipped out and got that chicken out of the lot and brought it back in and sold it to him again. And they sold it to him three times that day now mind you. Well, the fourth time they brought it in, he recognized the chicken; and his byword was "ding it." He said,

"Ding it, boys, I bought that thing three times already today." *(Myron Houston)*

If they could go back to the '40, '41, '43 years, 'cause there wasn't no money! We'd tote eggs to the store—a penny apiece—and get a penny's worth of candy. And, I never will forget, there was an awful big bootlegger lived right close to us, and he stayed at the store all the time. Mama had extra eggs. So, she said, "Now, if y'all want them eggs to take to the store, take them on." So we all had us an egg apiece. We had to walk a footlog to the store—across the creek to the store. All of them got across, and I fell at the end of the footlog and busted my egg. And this bootlegger, he was known to be a mean man and all like that, but he had a heart as big as a side of a mountain. I went on to the store and all of them got their candy. He said, "Leon, why ain't you getting no candy?" I told him I dropped my egg. He give me a nickel. And I never will forget it! But a nickel's worth of candy back in the thirties and forties—early forties—it'd do you all day! I bought a nickel's worth and that was a big bagful, you know. *(Leon Johnson)*

I had a restaurant over across the river and up here too. I moved up here in 1922, in April, 1922. I lived over there ten years and then came up here. But I sold the cafe out down there. I had one side groceries and one side dry goods and a filling station. I kept it open until I bought this store up here and moved up here. It was sort of funny; you know people could not advertise. But, mine advertised itself from the smell. They were building roads, and all these state trucks, they'd go over in Sylva and spend the night and come here and eat their breakfast, and we'd have a large crowd, and then they'd come back here for supper and go on into Sylva. I cooked for the school and everybody. I'd cook thirty or forty pies, and maybe they'd last a few minutes. And I cooked big cream pies for about a quarter. I cooked every kind of cream pie, from blackberry and peaches and apples and everything, besides butterscotch and chocolate and lemon and that kind. *(Granny Moss)*

ROADS AND RAILROADS

They'd drill these holes in the rock by hand, take these big drills that had a flat place on them. And two men would stand there with these big sledge hammers, and one'd hit here, and the other one'd hit when he'd come up, just like they used to do on the railroad driving the spikes. And they'd drill those holes down sometimes twenty or thirty feet deep in the rock. They'd pour the powder down in those holes, and they'd maybe load fifteen or twenty holes, and just blow off a whole rock cliff. It'd just shake the whole country. Now, the way they do the blasting on these new highways, you can't ever feel it. But they'd load them just as heavy as they could, and it'd just throw rocks all over the country. It was very dangerous, but that was the way they built roads then.

Back then there was a toll gate right below my home. They had this house that was built on the edge of the road, and they had a big long piece of timber that would reach all the way across the road. Of course, the road wasn't any wider than this room. They just had the horse and buggies. And these folks kept the toll gate. They had it swiveled on the side opposite the house, and on the other end of the big piece of timber they had a box built and filled with rock. They had a rope on this end; and, when folks would come and want to get through, they had to pay a quarter to get through the toll gate. The folks that lived there (we never did keep the toll gate, but it was on our property) they would come out of the house, on the porch, and unhook the piece of timber. They had a long rope attached to it, and they'd let that timber up. The rock on the other side would weigh it down, and it'd raise then. The people would pay their quarter and go through; and then they'd pull that back down and fasten it. That was the toll gate.

Even before that, they had to work the road on what they called subscription. Every able-bodied man would have to work on the road one or two days a year. That's the way they kept the roads up.

If they didn't do it, they'd find them and fine them. It was fixed so that they could make them do it. And if somebody had something else to do and didn't want to work, he could hire somebody to work for him and get away with that. You see, all the roads were kept up by the counties. I remember when the state took over the highways in North Carolina. Before that, they were what they called county roads. Each county took care of its roads, and of course some of them would do a better job than others. Some of the roads would be muddy, and you couldn't get from North Wilkesboro to Boone in a day's time. I remember when I started practicing law, I went to Wilkesboro to be sworn into the federal court. I had an old Model T that I'd bought for fifty dollars and coming up the mountain, I'd have to stop every once in a while to get a bucket of water to cool it off. It took nearly all day to come up from Wilkesboro. And you know they referred to this area as the lost provinces.
(Wade Brown)

These roads, most of them that are in the mountains now, were first blazed trails. Now the way you blaze a tree is to take your ax and whack off the bark about that long and about that wide, six or eight inches. And that became a path; that is, when people began settling not far apart and the houses were maybe a half a mile away or a mile away. And these blazed trails became paths. And later a few wagons, when wagons came into the mountains, the first ones were called wool wagons. They brought up the farmers' wool when they sheared in the spring.

A road that wasn't a path was a wagon road because at first only the wool wagons came into the mountains. Even when I was a boy they were still sending wagons drawn by horses. Some of them were drawn by oxen as far away as Virginia and South Carolina to swap their commodities for things needed, groceries and commodities like bolts

133

of cloth. And then later, as the wagon roads developed and grew and came across to other communities, they would bring more bolts of cloth, store-made shoes. They just swapped.

But as land became more thickly settled, the state of North Carolina passed what was called the Road Law, and it compelled men from eighteen to forty-five to work a certain number of days a year on the wagon roads. As the population increased, the legislature lessened the number of days. When I was road-working age, we had to work four days a year, two in the first six months and two in the other. You could get a substitute worker. Before I began working the road, the state law was from eighteen to forty-five, same as for members of the militia. They also drafted men for the militia a long time after colonial days. I never worked the road but about two or three days in my life. I despised it, despised the idea of paying taxes like that, so I got indicted two or three times. If you paid the dollar a day for the days you didn't work, they'd turn you loose. I guess they'd put a person in jail; I forget. They knew who should work. They'd go to the tax books at the tax collector's office at the county seat.
(Horton Cooper)

Mountain path in winter

Roads are most important to mountain people because the roads always go up streams. They are the only thing that's on a level in the mountains you know. The streams are on a fairly good grade so roads are always built by a stream. If someone tries to close off somebody's roadway in and out, there is going to be a fight invariably either in court or with fists. That's the best grade you can get. You've got big hilltops otherwise.
(Harold Bennett)

This was the only route between the Ohio Valley and Florida. You either had to go through Knoxville, Tennessee, or Raleigh, North Carolina, or through Plumtree. Believe it or not, Thomas A. Edison, Henry Ford, and Harvey Firestone have driven through Plumtree on their way to Florida. So they got an organization together, and they wanted to advertise it and mark it. It was still a dirt road. And Jim Mayberry came up with the name that they selected. They called it the Appalachian Scenic Highway. It came out of Erie, Pennsylvania, [down through] Pittsburgh to the corner of West Virginia, Virginia, here, and on through Georgia, and ended up in St. Petersburg, Florida.
(Ivor Vance)

When the North Carolina Blue Ridge Parkway came through, from that day on, there was a clear break from backwoods into rural America to where it is now. Once the Blue Ridge Parkway came through, the whole character of the area changed. It not only offered jobs for so many of the young men who then moved into the area. If they married up there, they took their wives away. Otherwise, they moved away and married and lived away. Many continued to follow construction jobs wherever they went, and many of them just followed and settled in the new areas. Because of the rule that partially made possible bringing the Parkway through North Carolina, it was agreed that the view would not be cluttered by all these signs. Homes were moved off of the Parkway, and away and down. Many of the exits were closed, and they had country roads that ran parallel. Now this made more of a change in the area than we might realize. Once you are having to move your home and change, it was so traumatic that many people moved completely away. You have the feeling that there is less population because you do not see the people. But their homes are there, they are just tucked down in the coves.

Their homes have changed, though, because instead of dirt floors, now they are of modern construction and have modern conveniences in them. Now there is a world of information.
(Emma Sharpe Jeffress)

The stagecoach used to leave Franklin at four o'clock in the morning, and it would bring people here to Dillsboro, and the suitcases would be on the top and the driver sittin' up there to keep the horses in a row. It used to come over here when I was nine or ten years old. The driver let me hold the reins in my hand, and I thought that was something. They would bring the mail to Dillsboro here and put the mail on the train. *(Bennie Reese)*

I remember well a long time before the streets were paved in Sylva. I helped pave the streets. Drove a pair of mules with an ol' dump wagon and hauled dirt in that and dumped that dirt in there, and then

they'd drag it down and finally got it in shape to pour concrete on it. Yeah, it used to be back when I was a kid, Sylva was just a loblolly [mudhole] when it rained. *(Grady Reed)*

Back in the horse and buggy days, there was a man that always came through here selling a cook stove like this. Home Comfort was the best stove you could buy at that time. They had a buggy and had a sample setting on the back of the buggy. And after there got to be cars, these old Ford Roadster pickups, put your stove on the back and go that way. It was a little stove, made just exactly like a stove, but it was little, you know, for a sample. And that man said, "Well, I'll tell you, if you've got a car, you ain't got time to stop and talk. You pass the road and say, 'Hey, you want to buy a stove?' And of course they'd say, 'no', and on you'd go. But if you stopped to stay all night with them and talk to them, you can sell them one." And that's about right ain't it? *(Grady Reed)*

The daughter in the family had gone away to college and had met a young man from Texas. They had fallen in love and were engaged. The Texas family was coming to meet the girl's family for the first time. This young man and the host were sitting on the front porch and looked down and here came a station wagon, a huge station wagon, with everything except horns on the front. It came across the little bridge and was barely able to get across it and pulled up into the yard. The people got out and everybody greeted and were introduced. Then they went inside to eat dinner, which was, of course, in the middle of the day, the traditional big meal in the mountain culture.

After dinner, as is also the traditional culture, the men went out on the porch to sit and smoke and chew or whatever, and the girls and women did the dishes. So the young man, the girl's father, and the prospective groom's father were all sitting out on the porch and the fellow from Texas had just not quit bragging from the time he got there. He had not quit trying to tell them how big and how wonderful Texas was and how rich he was. Apparently

135

he thought he still wasn't getting through and said, "You see that station wagon out there?" And the fellow said, "Yeah." He said, "I can get in that thing early in the morning at sunrise and drive all day long, and at sunset I still will be on my property." And the fellow from the mountains said, "I had a car like that once." *(Rebecca Councill)*

I was fourteen years old and I left home, and I thought I was a man. My cousin didn't have no shoes, so I stole a pair of my uncle's old shoes and had to cut the toe so he could wear them, and we walked from here to Boone. Later on at Shull's Mill me and him got on a "log dinky" and went right on to the mountains. When we got to the camp, we was happy and we didn't know nothin'. Now when we got to the camp, there was a lot of fellows there we knowed that helped us along. Well, we got up the next morning and went out. I never will forget our foreman, the boss man's name was Doc Harvey. I asked Doc for a job. He said, "What can you do?" I said, "I'll try anything you've got." He said, "Come on, I've got your job." We went out there, and he showed me what to do. I wasn't big enough to carry a keg of railroad spikes; he gave me a peck bucket, and I put two spikes on each one, four spikes to the plate, and keep the tools along for the men to get ahold of, and that's my job.

And I kept the tools right to the place, and one day he got gone, went off somewhere or another, and I picked up a spike-driving hammer and was driving spikes when he come back. Now my job, I had it right to the plate, and he come back down and he said to me, "Watson, if you keep on, that spike driving hammer's going to stick in your finger." I laid it down, never said a word, went on and kept my job just like he told me. And he was gone again one day, and I still had my job catched up, and he come back and catched me driving spikes again. But my job was up; I had everything right just like he told me. And he come down there and he looked at me and said, "Watson, you just drive all the spikes you want to drive." And I did.

(Willard Watson)

You might say that the railroads have come into this section during my lifetime. The Tweetsie, I believe came to Cranberry in the late 1880s. The CC&O Railroad, this one down here at Spruce Pine, was started in 1884 and finished in 1908. In fact, the first locomotive that crossed the Blue Ridge crossed in the year 1908. Whenever they got the line finished, they started the first locomotive out of Erwin, Tennessee. When they started to build this railroad, they started in Elkhorn, Kentucky, at one end, and Spartanburg, South Carolina, on the other, and they met here on the Blue Ridge through these Blue Ridge tunnels. I don't remember the exact date. Anyway, the date the locomotives came from Erwin, everybody in this country came. They'd walk twelve to fifteen miles to see that locomotive. It was the first steam locomotive to come into the section. Well, it was the awfulest crowd. My daddy said they rode horses from all over the country.

He rode a saddle horse that he had down there to see it. He said when that engine came up the track, the horses stampeded and half of them broke loose and you never saw such running horses and the men around there trying to corral them. Well, the engine set there for quite a while and the people just kept feeding in more and more. An old lady walked out to see that locomotive. The locomotive had pulled in and stopped before she got there. She walked all around it and looked at it first one way and then the other, and she said to somebody standing close by, "That thing'll never start." Well, my daddy said about thirty or forty minutes after that, the news came for them to proceed on across the mountain with the locomotive. Said the engineer reached up and pulled the bell. Whenever that bell clanged, the ol' lady jumped about that high. Well, when he caught the whistle and gave it a pull, she jumped three feet high again. And then he opened the throttle and the steam blowed out both sides, and he said she ran backwards until she fell down and turned a somersault backwards toward the river. *(Myron Houston)*

Railroad tunnel near Dillsboro, Jackson County

LOGGING, TIMBER, AND TANNERIES

In 1864 the first sawmill that came to this country was brought in here by the Silvers family on Big Crabtree. The biggest chestnut tree cut in America is right out here on the mountain, right down here on Armstrong. It took twenty-two head of horses to pull that tree. Now, you cannot describe that until you see twenty-two head of horses, because, you see, I grew up in a day when all the logging in this country was done by horses, oxen, and these little engines, shay engines. *(B. Hensley)*

The largest poplar tree was cut over here at what they call Bear Wallow. You could have four squares of square dancers on it. [Four squares of couples each.] It was something like twelve or fourteen feet in diameter. At that time, the biggest cross-cut saw they made was a ten-foot cross-cut saw, and it wouldn't even come anywhere close to cutting it. Well if you ever want to see the largest poplar trees that grow now, go out to Joyce Kilmer Memorial Forest near Robbinsville. *(Mike Hensley)*

Most people used cattle to do their logging. Used to take a load of lumber from here to Asheville with them. 'Course it took two days, one day to go over, one to come back. *(Hal Oates)*

There's a flat flume from here to Dillsboro. It brought wood all the way off the top of that mountain. We had certain days. Cut a big amount of wood up here on the side of the flume. Well, maybe you could flume your'n today, and maybe somebody else's next day, and somebody else's next day. And maybe two or three people might flume it that day, but still they had a way to identify it. And then they had to have somebody down at Dillsboro [to receive it]. *(Grady Reed)*

They built flumes. They'd take poles and build them in kind of a V-shape. One of my uncles in my wife's family had a big flume over here on Mount

Celo, and they'd turn these logs loose and it would hit a—I'd have to describe it to you. Now, this was the wedge and here built the flume like this. Now they'd turn these logs loose just as fast as they could turn them loose; that would go down and hit this and split it up this way. The log would lay over like this, and it'd hit two more and split it four ways. The reason why I got to see a lot of this was because I made special tools for logging equipment and stuff for the sawmills back when I was real young. And then after the war, after the Second World War was over, then they began to use bulldozers and tractors and skidders and winches on tractors, so all this equipment is gone now. [The old skidder was a type of sled on which logs were placed to keep them from digging into the ground as they were pulled along by the horse.]

A pickeroon was the little tool that's got a handle in it that looks like a pick that you'd dig dirt with, but it doesn't have but a pick on one side and it's hooked. There's a lot of names that are lost in the pages of history because they are no more used. If you said "grabskip" to the generation of today, they wouldn't know what you're talking about. A grabskip is that which they used when they put the heavy logs in with the grabs. [A set of grabs consists of two hooks that are fastened with a chain (varying in length) that are clamped into opposite sides of a log.] They took one end of that "grabskip," and they knocked the grab in the log and the other end was pointed. They put it down between the log and gave it a tap or used it, you know, like bursting wood. They carried this tool on the horses, and they'd make up a big trail of grabs, and they'd go off this mountain linking them together. They had these horses trained, and this was beautiful to watch because they had little places cut out; and these horses would go to what they called "cutouts," and you'd say, "Jay-ho." Now Jay-ho doesn't mean anything to anybody except that horse. That horse knew that when you said Jay-ho

Ralph Morgan's Saw Mill, Jackson County

at that next hole that he came to, he would leave the main trail and they'd step out and the logs would pass them. Those logs might run on a quarter of a mile, and maybe they'd have to take the horses around and down another trail because they'd go off these rocks. But they'd stay together. That was a lot of fun. *(B. Hensley)*

The way that they got most of their money was they got out pulp wood, a little bit of pulp wood, and acid wood and tanbark. That was probably white, chestnut oak that they used for the bark, and the tannic acid came out of it too. Well, tannic acid came out of tanbark too. It was a chestnut oak. They had these hide places where they tanned, a tannery; and they used it to tan the leather. There was a tannery in Sylva. They would mica mine a little bit too. There was not very many ways to make cash money. They didn't need a lot. A hundred dollars would do them. *(Jimmy Moss)*

Well, Daddy said their family put logs in the flume. There was a flume all the way down Green's Creek. He said all the way from the head of Green's Creek to Dillsboro. There's one that came down each

creek that goes down and joined right below our house where the creek comes together. Everybody had certain days to flume. They made extra money selling the wood and digging the mica.
(Wanda Moss)

Well, they didn't have any money. They got the sawmill coming in there, and they paid twenty-five cents a day for a sawmill hand to work at the sawmill. The sawmill, that was the only way the boys could get money to buy their clothes or anything. *(Mamie Hall)*

My husband and his son-in-law hauled cardboard up here to Mead Corporation. He made it good in that paper, better than he did getting that cord wood. He made good money, but he just had to get out a whole lot of wood. But his son-in-law got him a job, and he made it better on that. It was easier. All he had to do was load it and unload it, haul it. Getting that wood and pulling that cross-cut saw (there wasn't no power saws then), pulling that cross-cut saw was hard and rough on you, but that's the way my husband had to make a living.
(Lilly Wykle)

Now, I helped cut 'em years ago after they were already on the ground. We'd have a six-foot cross-cut saw, and we'd only have about six inches of that saw stuck out of the logs. I can show you stumps where they've been now, and I'd bet money that they're six and eight foot across. And you couldn't give the lumber away. Chestnut lumber, even when this house right here was built in nineteen and forty eight, was considered cull lumber. They didn't want it. We used to make acid wood. That was the forerunner of pulp wood. That was the only thing they would buy was chestnut. *(Harold Keener)*

Years ago when they had tanneries, in the spring of the year when the old oak trees would peel, they'd cut the trees and peel the bark off and haul that. Anything to make a dollar. **(Hal Oates)**

Timber on the way to market

There was an old tannery in Old Fort, and when it closed down, it hurt the little town. It burned down. That was the livelihood of that whole country over there. A man would walk five or six miles from home to work at the tannery and then walk back in the evening. The gathering of the bark was one of the main cash crops in this area. Then they took the log that you got the tanbark from and made crossties for the railroad. *(Roscoe Bradley)*

We needed all the extra money we made because we farmed in the summer, and my brother, John, would cut railroad ties because it'd give him something to do. He didn't make much out of it, so he told us, says, "Girls, come and help me; we'll get out and cut." Well it'd be in the fall and in the wintertime; sometimes snow was on the ground, but not bad cold. You can't cut down trees if it's bad cold, you know, frozen. And he kept a good cross-cut saw and about two or three double-bit axes, good and sharp. So he'd help us get a tree cut down. Then Myrtle and me, we would saw it; and he would trim the limbs off and trim us a trail down the log. And we'd saw it as he would trim it up and trim us out a trail to it, you see, and mark off the logs. And we'd go right ahead and do it back over on the side of those mountains. It'd be rough getting them out. The only way you could get to them was a mule or wagon or something. And if a little snow'd be on the ground, we'd go out and pick up one end of them crossties and walk under it; pick up one end and keep walking, stand it up on its end and turn it loose; and it'd go way down the mountain, just a scootin'. So we done that in the fall and winter—done pretty good with it. Of course, he had to hire us a team of mules and wagon; we didn't own them. But he'd get them, and you'd have the logs bunched together, the crossties. I'd help him to load them on the wagon. *(Nanny Suttles)*

We'd cut telephone poles. We used to have to do all that with horse stock or steers. You'd get up before daylight and feed and be ready to go, hook up your team and head out and you'd be at the woods by good daylight and work 'til dark. Cut telephone poles and skin them out. Then you had to haul them to the railroad on a wagon. Haul them with horses, mules or steers, whichever you had. And crossties, you'd hew them with an ax. Go to the woods and cut down a tree that was a foot or so through and hew it up into crossties. Hew all four sides of it and skin them out and haul all them on a wagon. Then you'd haul them down to the railroad where they shipped them. You might get fifty cents apiece for them when you got them to the railroad. *(Nelson Cabe)*

MINING

Grandfather mined mica always. The Ray Mines are up in the mountains up on Mount Celo. He had thousands of acres back there, and he started as a young man. He was very much interested in minerals, that sort of thing, and he was mining mica there for many years. Of course, feldspar was there too, but in that day they didn't know. . .feldspar wasn't used for anything. My mother said my grandfather used to say someday he knew that mineral would be used for something. And you know, in later years they went back and reworked all of the old mines and salvaged the feldspar. They then began mining feldspar because feldspar sort of took over and mica sort of waned and went down. **(Rush Wray)**

And, of course, today mica is back as far as demand because it's in so many synthetic things. But in the old days, mica was used after electricity came, then for insulation, all the irons used some mica in them, and things about an automobile, there were certain things that mica had to be used for; and then feldspar was used for the bathroom fixtures. All the glass on porcelain was made from feldspar, and spark plugs in cars. Feldspar's still being mined, but this area here is just about played out. There's not much, nothing like when I was a kid. They were mining everywhere, but there's very little mining any more. Not too much damage was done because the mines—even the Ray Mines, which was one of the larger ones for mica, they had some tunnels and went back under the mountains some—but most of it was sort of surface mining, small

operations with just five or six men working, that sort of thing. *(Rush Wray)*

Tarheel Mica Company is the only industry we have. That's what's given us our post office all these years. And they've employed more than they do now, 'cause it's really down now; but all of that was a living for most of the people in all of the mountains around here. They walked to work. They came and walked every day to and from work. They always began at seven-thirty and always closed at four o'clock. They were in full force during World War II. They used to have a dam that would run their plants. The water was so much, it looked like a lake then. And they used to have boats, when Daddy was growing up, on the river. And he has pictures of the women all in their white long dresses and white hats riding in the boats, very picturesque. The dam washed out; they built it back, but the last time it washed out, they're not using that for power anymore, so they just never did build it back. So the river's way down now, along with the people. The valley's been drained. I love it this way. I just like it like it is. *(Kay Wilkins)*

The iron mines were first discovered by a man by the name of Reuben White in 1821, and he didn't do anything about it. Then in 1827, there were two brothers out of Tennessee up in here hiding from the law. One of them was looking for some ginseng and he stumbled across the vein, and he did something about it. And at that time, the state wanted things like that developed. And if you'd find a deposit of iron ore and produce as much as five hundred pounds of pig iron, the state would give you 3,000 acres of land surrounding it.

They had a furnace at Cranberry, and they didn't use coke; they used charcoal in the furnaces. They had that 3,000 acres of woodland so they worked as high as eight to nine hundred men at Cranberry, but most of them worked in the mountains cutting wood and hauled it in and made the charcoal. And others worked in the mine. I never understood how they could drill a hole in that iron ore rock with a hand drill. It's so hard. I remember when they used steam drills before they had air jackhammers. But that rock is so hard. Take a piece the size of a basketball, you could hit it with a hammer as hard as you could hit it, and the hammer'd bounce back in your face. *(Ivor Vance)*

Mitchell County at one time was, or maybe still is, producing more mica than any county in the United States. Well, I've seen mica mined ever since I was old enough to remember anything; it's been mined on this place. There's probably been more money spent looking for mica than has ever been found and gotten out of it. The best way of finding mica they've found yet is some ol' fellow that's

worked with it all his life. He can tell you more about where you might find mica than the engineers that come in there.

Feldspar mining started when the railroads came because feldspar is a very heavy substance. Now the processing is done here into a fine powder sort of like flour and they ship it to Pittsburgh and other places where they make it, a large percent of it, into glass bottles. Most of the bottles you see are made of feldspar. Quartz and feldspar and limestone are the basic ingredients to make glass. Feldspar is a lot of it, and most of it comes from this area. Maybe we ought to add one other thing to the minerals, and that's the kayolin business. It's a white substance; it's usually got some grit or dirt or something in it. It is the basis for our dishes. The glazing on it is made of molten feldspar poured over the dishes to give it a glaze. *(Bob Phillips)*

Farm scene, Yancey County

TILLING THE NEW GROUND

Well, the farmer, he just gambles; he don't know whether he's going to make it or not. *(Bertha Lowe)*

Oh, it's changed a lot. Of course, we farmed here in these mountains. I do most of my farming now down off the mountain where I can do it with machinery. We used to plow with horses and turning plow, cultivator and hoes; and now you never put a hoe in corn. Plant it, and spray it, and forget it 'til picking time. People have just about quit farming around here. They're all on public work. There's no place to farm much and no money in it; and you take this younger generation, they want money. *(Walter Winebarger)*

In the eastern part of the state, I can get on a tractor and plow all day on level ground. I can plow for days and work and grow beautiful fertile fields. It's level. Up here, you try to plow around the side of the mountain on a tractor! *(Mike Phillips)*

I cultivate with a mule. Tillery proved that you ought not to be using a tractor over in here, didn't he? Turned it over and killed himself. **(Boyd Payne)**

I used to have considerable honey in stores, but for the last ten years I've sold most of it here. A few people have started to sell in stores, but I've not been hauling any out to stores much for the last ten years because the country stores went out of business. The big chain stores took over and didn't buy in such small quantities. I used to raise produce and potatoes and sell to the country stores. And they would buy about anything you could raise and take to them. But when the big chain stores took over, they claimed they got everything from the warehouse, which was off maybe in South Carolina or Charlotte or headquartered somewhere or another, and they didn't buy anything. So that cut out most of produce hauling and what we used to call peddling—get out, you know, and go from store to store and find out what they wanted. It didn't really go completely out 'til about '60, I guess.

Most of them [peddlers] had cabbage and potatoes and apples, Irish potatoes especially, and some other vegetables, even parsnips, carrots, most anything, green beans especially. Snap beans were one of the beans they generally had with them when they had cabbage and potatoes. They had as much a variety as they could have with them, so if they didn't buy one thing, they maybe had another they could sell. Back then, the farms had little orchards about, and they didn't have to spray the trees so much and had fairly good apples. But that went out pretty soon; they had to get apples in from orchards that sprayed. But they used to, a lot would buy apples around through the country and load up forty to fifty bushels of apples, and potatoes and all that to make a load and make a round. Maybe they'd be gone three days, sometimes longer. *(Raymond Presnell)*

I've butchered hogs and cured beef all my life, too. I've done that as I've went down the road. My daddy was a butcher. And he used to buy ol' cows and fatten them up, butcher them and sell them. They've sold out many a doggone cow; load them on the pickup; he'd have them cut up; go out in the country and sell them. Make a little money on it. *(Thurmond Sparks)*

My mother used to, they started a truck through here picking up cream and we sold cream, she sold cream. And they finally years later, I don't know, maybe twenty-five or thirty years later, they started coming through here with the milk truck and we'd sell a little bit of milk. That's when we got started in the dairy business. *(Mabel Sparks)*

I built a Grade A dairy and went all out. I built that ol' barn down there. *(Thurmond Sparks)*

I milked cows ever since I was eight years old. We sold milk to Coble Dairy here in Wilkesboro. I have milked twelve cows with my hands. But most of the time I had some help. But sometimes I'd get caught where I had to milk them all by myself. He'd [Thurmond] be gone or something, be farming or something and not get in and help me milk. *(Mabel Sparks)*

When the Farmers' Federation was going on, Mr. McClure got it started. It was for dairies and chickens and everything. They had a big broiler place up there in Asheville and would buy people's fryers, and a big ol' freezer locker, and they'd rent that to put meat in. And then he got this knitting thing started up for the women folks and got all the women started knitting. They'd pay us ten dollars to knit a sweater. And they'd furnish everything, directions and needles and yarn and everything. *(Nanny Suttles)*

I think that a big step forward as far as the people of Wilkes County were concerned was the poultry business. A friend of mine, Fred Lovett, took it on himself, through his father's little poultry business, and some friends of his that were in it. That's the Holly Farms that was formed and created and brought forth. And you about have to put all the responsibility on Fred Lovett for that because he's the one that could foresee what could really happen in the poultry business. Of course, him pursuing that was a tremendous influence on the people that were in the whiskey business. It gave them an

(Opposite) Clifford Casey plowing with his mule

opportunity to get into business for themselves. They could stay home and get off into something else and make more money at it than they could in the whiskey business—and that was the poultry business. If I had to say one thing that contributed to this county and basically was a big help in people getting away from the whiskey business, it'd be the poultry business. *(Junior Johnson)*

We hadn't never had no layers. We started one time to, we thought we was going to put in layers, but we didn't. And he later built the biggest chicken house that we had. We've never raised nothing in it, just the broilers. They made pretty good money with them layers. *(Mabel Sparks)*

When I was a kid we'd rake up the chestnuts, put them in a sack and we'd sell them a quart or pint at a time. I'd go with my uncle in a T-Model truck and go down there, and he'd sell a pint of chestnuts for a nickel or a quart for a dime, and you'd never sell a gallon. My grandfather had a chestnut orchard. Everybody had a chestnut orchard, just like apple orchards. Some bug of some kind killed them all—a worm. They say maybe in time, they may come back. I've got eleven chestnut trees in my yard, but they're Chinese or Italian chestnuts. Nothing like that. They never get big. Now we find back in the mountains, you can find a chestnut tree that's grown, and it'll bear chestnuts maybe two years; then it starts dying again. *(Frank Norris)*

Had a lot of chestnut trees back in those days, and I went out many a time after a rain and the wind would blow, you know, and blow the chestnuts out, and you'd pick up a half a bushel at a time. And when we'd go to market in the wagon, we'd take four or five sacks of chestnuts, you know, and go down to the cotton mill and peddle our apples and 'taters and chestnuts; had a pint cup and sell them for ten cents a pint. *(Bob Phillips)*

We raised shelly beans and cabbage primarily for market, lots of corn and potatoes and small amounts of tobacco. Burley tobacco has become

John Lookabill picking corn, Meat Camp, Watauga County

the primary source of income in this county now, primary source crop. It's controlled federally by allotment, which has kept the small farmer in the market. And this climate in the mountain grows a different kind of tobacco, of course, from down in the eastern part. They grow flu cured, and we grow broad leaf, burley, which is a broad leaf and a higher grade of tobacco. *(Charles Michael)*

My father built that in the late 1890s and 1900. He put out thousands of young trees and had wonderful apples; and he shipped apples all over the country. He had to make the farm pay off in some way, so apples did . . . and he knew how. They had the trees sprayed and pruned and kept small like they had to do. Oh, I can just smell those apples 'cause we had huge beds in that basement. It was a tremendous basement, went under the whole house. They had apple beds almost half as high as this room just filled with hundreds of bushels of apples, and the odor of those apples just permeated the whole house. My father shipped apples; they were select apples 'cause he had special crates made, little wooden crates. And those apples were wrapped in individual tissues and said Wray Villa

Farm, Cane River, North Carolina. And he won prizes at the World's Fair in Paris. *(Rush Wray)*

At one time apples could be grown without spraying or much care. You'd just plant the trees and go out and gather the apples. The insects were not so prevalent. One way or another, everything's being changed about; and all the diseases and insects anywhere in the world are likely to end up anywhere else in the world. We have to put on a scientific spray program and do a lot of other technical things to keep apples growing properly now.
(Bob Phillips)

They're growing acres and acres of Christmas trees, which has become a primary source of income. When I was growing up, no one ever sold a Christmas tree for anything. Now it's one of the primary markets in this county and Ashe and Avery, primary source of income. So with those kinds of changes comes some good things as well as some of the bad. *(Charles Michael)*

We have 75,000 or 80,000 Christmas trees. We just got into it about four or five years ago. It's a lot of work. You have to spray them and fertilize them. Then there are all kinds of diseases and mites and things you have to spray for; and you have to trim them. Then the year before you cut them, you spray them with another kind of spray to make them greener. I didn't know that 'til this year. We've never got into that 'cause we don't have any old enough. But there's a lot more work than people think. You don't just go out in the woods and cut a tree. It takes seven or eight years for a good tree.
(Mikie Miller)

I've lived here about sixty-four years. I'm the fourth generation here. This mill [Winebarger's Mill] was built in 1840, the best that I can find out. Those old people didn't keep too many records. There was some man here wanting to talk to Dad a few years before he died, and said his dad made the pins to pin the first one together. And I spoke up and said, "Could you tell me when that was?" And he said 1840. Anyway, I'm the fourth generation. Dad lived to be ninety, and he learned all this like me. He helped his dad all along. My great-great grandfather built it. Well, it's the only one [working grist mill still operating] I know of in this county. There might be one down in Wilkes that runs on water. It's all run by water.

There's been a lot of grain that went through this old mill here. I don't guess this hollow up through here would hold it. People still bring their grain here to grind. But people have quit raising so much; nobody farms much any more. If they do, they send it to these big milling companies. Well, I just make it one way or another. It's pretty hard living. I farm and raise the stuff, then grind it. And I buy some. Raise a little tobacco. Just work around, maybe plow for other folks. Work all the time from daylight to dark and after; it's really pretty rough. People still come to the mill. But like I said, those days are gone. Somebody would come maybe ten or twenty miles. It'd take all day to get here. They'd leave at three or four o'clock in the morning and get here about three or four in the evening. And we'd grind that and have him ready to go back the next morning. *(Walter Winebarger)*

MAPLE SYRUP AND BEEKEEPING

We did make maple syrup and sugar. We worked at that at times in the winter. We'd bore the trees with a brace and bit; and we'd take a bigger bit, and bore a slant down this way and bore it in there pretty deep so it made a cup. And then we'd take a smaller bit, half inch or something, and bore it so that it went into this hole, and then the hole would fill up with sap until we bored this new hole in; then it could come out. We would take an elder stalk and instead of pushing all the pith out, we would hew down like that 'til we got down about halfway through the pith. We left this up here about two inches on one end that we didn't cut into the pith. So it would run down this elder pipe and drip into the container, whether it was a wood trough hewed out or buckets of any sort you might use. But generally we had troughs hewed out; cut down a tree and cut blocks off it about three feet long and split it in the middle and hew the wood out of the center part, chop it out and make a trough in this wood. The linden troughs were porous enough that the sap would run out through the wood. And so my daddy had to dry them a little. Then they'd close that so the water wouldn't run out of the ends of the troughs. And they would get full; we'd have

dippers to dip this into buckets to carry in, and he had a way fixed for the mules to haul a steel barrel on kind of a sled. He'd go down by the trees, and he could go up through the woods with this, with one mule. The tank held about forty gallons. And then we had a wooden boiler like a molasses boiler. We boiled that sugar sap down the same way as we boiled the cane molasses juice.

Then we'd take it across the mountain to Banner Elk. Bob Banner had what would be now a country store, but it was in the town of Banner Elk, and the biggest store there was and near about the only one there was in that area. And my daddy did a lot of trading there, buying supplies we needed, all the things we needed, there. And Banner would give him "due bills"; didn't pay any money hardly ever for sugar or syrup. He generally kegged it in small kegs, and he sold it to tourists. And he (Daddy) would get enough; we'd get enough to buy us supplies to do us all year, with a period in the wintertime.

There were a lot of maple sugar makers on the Beech Mountain. We had all the trees there that we could tend to. It was a job; it was hard work. You had to cut wood and bring in there to keep this fur-

148   *(Above) Raymond Presnell's bees   (Opposite) Larry Bixby "robbing the bees"*

nace going, boil that down. It took about a bushel to make one pound of sugar. My mother would do that. After it had boiled down to a pretty good syrup, she would make this on the cook stove, the cakes and all, put it in the skillets. So she made the cakes of sugar on the stove out of about two skillets, ten-inch covered skillets. Put that syrup in there and boil it and test it by dropping, after it began to get to a certain foamy-type situation, into a cup. If it went down through that cold water and it hardened into a ball, it was ready to take off and put in the cake pans. It was hard enough then to make a cake of sugar. And they'd take it off the fire then and stir it until it began to grain. Then they'd put this mushy sugar into these little cake pans.

(Raymond Presnell)

The first thing I remember was how I was fascinated by bumble bees; and I probably wasn't a year old. And then anything that was said about bees, it was fascinating. I gave it all I had because it was interesting to me. The word "bee" had something of fascination to me and then to see them, it was something I had to know about. I guess I was about twelve years old before I got them to really work. And then I found the bee tree and got my daddy; my daddy was awfully interested in hunting bee trees. He loved the sport of hunting bee trees. That's where a swarm goes into a tree; it may come out of another tree. That's where they split up to make increase and they swarm generally in the early part of the summer. And a portion of them go and put up a new home in a tree, or maybe in the wall of a house sometimes, if it's a convenient place for it, a cavity. (Raymond Presnell)

When they swarm, they come out. It used to be thought that you had to beat pans or ring bells to get them to settle when they'd come out. They start coming out; they hatch queens, and they raise what's known as virgin queens to start with. They are the first queens. And when they are going to get crowded and the time comes, generally the first of June or along the last of May, they'll want to swarm if they're strong enough. So they will start queen cells then. Before that they only have drones. They'll start raising some male bees in early summer or spring, and brood which hatches the worker bees. And then when they go into swarms, they will make a different kind of cell, and maybe they'll start from five to twenty-five of these queen cells.

And the queen will lay an egg in there and they will feed her a special food to make her develop into a queen, which if the same egg was laid in a cell for workers, it would be a worker bee and it wouldn't be a queen. But they put this egg in this cell and they feed her royal jelly, which is a special food that causes her to develop into a queen; and it is a fertile egg. The drones are from infertile eggs. The male bee is the drone or king bee, and he doesn't work, and he doesn't have any stinger. He doesn't fight, he doesn't do anything. He's just for the purpose of mating with the virgin queens. A worker bee is from a fertilized egg, and the queen is from a fertilized egg. And the only difference between the queen and the worker is the royal jelly that she's fed during her larva life. From the time the egg hatches from an egg into a larva, it develops very quickly, and the queen can develop into an adult bee in sixteen days from the time the egg is laid. Now if they're going to swarm, the old queen that's in there (her mother) will probably go out with the swarm, if she can fly; and if she doesn't, the first one of these virgins that can go, goes with the swarm. And then if they swarm again, another virgin goes out later on.

Sometimes this one hive will swarm three times before it quits. So if the old queen goes out, one of these virgins takes over and she mates and goes to laying and she kills all the others if she doesn't mean for them to go out in the swarm, and she doesn't go. She'll go with the swarm if she's going to and leave these others, not kill them. But if they aren't going to send out any more swarms, she tears down and destroys all these queen cells. If there's another virgin hatched, they fight a duel. One of them gets killed, and it leaves it with one queen to carry on the whole colony. She can lay up to 5,000 eggs a day, and they can have as much as 75,000 workers at times, or maybe 100,000 at times. The workers do all the work. The queen doesn't do anything but lay eggs. Drones don't last over a year. I don't know how long a drone would live if they were left to their own and were fed, but they're driven out and starve to death in the fall. None of them winters over, so they can't live a year, and six months would be a good long life for a drone anyhow.

The workers ripen the honey. Generally the older worker bees do go out to get the nectar. They come in with a load, and they give it to one of these younger bees, and it takes it in through its out-parts into its honey storage and keeps it in there. They get in formation, and the bee can let it come out here between these mandibles in this current of air. It warms up as it gets in here; it's very warm air. They have to dry it down pretty fast or it'll go sour; so they know how to do it, and they do it. They've got to keep working; they work day and night to keep that air current going through there. They're fanning it in through there and back out. It's enough to blow a lit match out. No doubt they use some of this nectar that they are collecting. But when they go out, they have enough honey in their stomach to keep up energy to make the trip, three or four miles away and back with a load. What they let go through there gives them the energy to fly.

Scout bees go out to hunt for a source, and then they come back in and tell the others where they found it. For instance, you think about a beehive or a colony of bees; a colony of bees is above a certain stage. It's called a colony after it gets up to 15,000 or 20,000 bees on up to 75,000 or 100,000 bees. It's proven by test and experience that it takes 360 pounds of honey to do a colony of bees a year, and that's a lot of honey. But it takes a lot of energy to do all this. The colony takes 360 pounds whether I get any or not. *(Raymond Presnell)*

My dad used to keep, well I know he had about sixteen stands of bees, and we'd put them big ol' tin cans about that high, you know, and fill them things full of honey; you couldn't hardly pick one up. You know honey's heavy. Reach in there and get a big chunk out of there, and then have a big ol' glass bowl. We'd put it on the table and get it gone and get another can and fill that bowl full again. And it would set right in the center of the table all the time—big lid over it so nothing couldn't get in it. *(Grady Reed)*

Larry Bixby tending the bees

MOONSHINE

Oh, there was moonshining. In the old days, you see, they were allowed; why all of the area had a still. The help were paid on Saturday night. They were then given a pint or something of moonshine or brandy, whatever they made. They'd have a still right on the place. They were allowed. It was just like you had a license or the government would grant them a license to make liquor. It was made for the government, and it'd be sent other places, but I'm sure a lot of it slipped out the back door to somebody else. There was really no way of making any good cash money—everything was bartered. So many of them just didn't have any other way. (Rush Wray)

They had plenty of liquor. They was makin' liquor up there when we went. There was six government distilleries right in a row up and down that creek. A whole lot of them didn't know how to write, and they'd bring the books and come to our house and get Papa to write for them, run up their books, and do things for them. (Mamie Hall)

They called them Revenues back then, and they rode horses, didn't have no cars. But you could make liquor for the government, back about I'd say in the twenties and all the way up until Prohibition. (Thurmond Sparks)

Old copper still

The people at that time largely were dependent on farming or lumber, or wood products. It was hard work, it was hard to make a living, and hard to make any money. People that lived in that area didn't realize that they were poor until many years later when Uncle Sam convinced them they should be on welfare. Up until that time, they all made their own living and were independent.

Some of them made it by moonshining, but you couldn't much blame them when they were so far removed from any market. The corn couldn't very well be shipped out, so they used it for bird feed, for their livestock, or in a few cases turned it into moonshine. That was, in the early days, one of the thriving industries throughout the mountains. That is about the only cash crop a lot of them had. There was very little market for the produce because everybody had their own little farm and they grew their own food; so for the surplus they had, there was very little market. Transportation facilities were, to say the least, inefficient. If they had a surplus of corn, for instance, they would have to bring it sometimes twenty or thirty miles to the railroad to ship it, and the only way they could get there would be by wagon. So for any surplus they might have, it was much easier to convert it into white lightning and transport a gallon rather than several bushels of corn.

The earliest settlers thought that it was their own business. They were independent. They didn't feel like the government should tell them what they should do with their property, or what they should do with their products from the land. And they felt that they had a right to do as they pleased with their own land and the products of their own labor. They didn't feel like it was any sin, even though it was against the law. *(Dan Moore)*

In the days of Prohibition, Morganton was surrounded by still sites. Incidentally, you had a lot of that in these other counties, and the people felt like they had a right to make their corn into liquor. It was easier to market it that way and carry it out, and so they were grateful for that. I've got a story in my book about one of them that I've always loved.

We had a federal district judge from Greensboro, James E. Boyd. He was a very able fellow, but he had a love for having fun with people. He loved to kid everybody, lawyers, witnesses, jurors, everybody. He was holding court in Statesville and had what we called the Burke County moonshiners convention down there, trying all these old moonshiners. They had this fellow, Joshua Hawkins, one of our mountaineers, indicted for running a still, and he was sitting in the back of the courtroom waiting for the district attorney to call his case. When the district attorney called out "Joshua Hawkins," he started down the center aisle to be tried and Judge Boyd said, "Mr. Hawkins, are you the Joshua who made the sun stand still at Jericho that the Bible tells us about?" And ol' Hawkins said, "No, your Honor, I'm not the Joshua who made the sun stand still at Jericho that the Bible tells us about. I'm the Joshua who's accused by the district attorney of making the moonshine in Burke" As they say, now they can't compete with store-bought'n whiskey. *(Sam Ervin)*

They made moonshine back there in the time of Prohibition. My granddaddy and one of my uncles, they made it. It wasn't good to do, and I think they'd all been better off if they hadn't've done it. One of them especially got an awful bad sentence in the penitentiary, and it really worked him over, it just ruined him. And he had done pretty well and had a good living and everything, and he made it mostly making liquor (he called it liquor), but it was moonshine. Prohibition was that law, you know, when you couldn't get government liquor like you do now. And so it's never been real profitable to make moonshine since then. Because, you know, people couldn't get any. And, of course, a lot of them made stuff that wasn't any good; it was poison. They adulterated it with all kinds of stuff. And some of them used this ol' rubbing alcohol. A lot of them drank it 'til it killed them, and they didn't ever know what killed them. They'd maybe have a little good liquor with it. And a lot of them put aspirin in it, a lot of aspirin and washing powders, yeah, they put lots of ol' wash powder in it. To

153

make it have more effect and make it bead, you know. They'd shake it, you know; if it beaded, they thought it was real good. And they'd just add suds on it and they thought it was the real stuff. *(Raymond Presnell)*

Well, they'd use it; you never saw anybody drunk, but they drank it all the time. In the morning, if it

tain there. And we'd take the corn down there and get him to grind it on that mill. He had bought a steam boiler to run the sawmill and the grist mill to grind the corn.

And he made liquor around the hollows about and everywhere around. But most of it he made, he made out there and got to run it off with the steam out of that steam boiler where he ground the corn.

Doug Wallin, Sam White, Michael Ann Williams, Stanley Hicks, Hamper McBee (squatting), R.O. Wilson, Ben Entrekin (with basket), and Jack Wallin at Mountain Heritage Festival, Western Carolina University, Cullowhee

was cold, they'd take a pretty good drink and go out and work all day. Kept the blood circulating. *(Stanley Hicks)*

My great-uncle moved down there, put him up a little shack, and lived there on the creek with his son on his son's place. He had made liquor, and made right smart money, and got by with it pretty well. He had some problems, though; the Revenues came on to him a lot of times. He had a mill, though, up on the mountain that was run by steam; that's where we took our corn to get it ground for meal. My great-uncle had the mill up there about a mile below my daddy's place on down below my granddaddy's place on the moun-

He and my granddaddy made good liquor and brandy. So he was making liquor there at the sawmill where they had sawdust and slabs and all this. Often, some of them fed the slop to hogs after they had distilled it and got the alcohol out of it. Then it was just meal and mash. And often there where they emptied the stills, they'd leave this old mash in the branch. It'd be just a bunch of old sour-smelling mashy stuff, looked like cornmeal mush, in the streams there and around where they'd poured it out. There would be yellow jackets and bees collecting some substance for their food

(Opposite) Willard Watson with a typical still used for making moonshine

out of it. So where my uncle was making the moonshine there at the sawmill and grist mill, he'd dig a pit under the floor of it, dug a hole out to put this slop or mash. It smelled loudly, and I guess he didn't pay much attention to it.

But often somebody would get mad, or they would be paid a little maybe, to report where somebody was making it, to the Revenue. And so somebody had reported him and said they had evidence that they should come and search. So they came, and one of them was a man that I worked for, Dave Wooten, "Ooten," they called him. He was overseer on WPA, and he was one of the Revenue men that came to my uncle's place out there to tear his still out. So he told us about it there when we were working; that was about 1940 when he told us about this. He said there were several of them, and it had been reported that my great-uncle had been making liquor. So, they were around there. He caught them and told them to get away, get off his place. They were stomping around there and didn't find anything for a while. He had these old slabs, and they would turn anyway, you know; one side's rounded and one flat. He covered this slop over in that area there where they fired the boiler. He covered this hole over, but he had filled it up with slop where he'd emptied it. And so then he covered it over with slabs, he put sawdust on it so it just looked like the ground; it didn't look like anything there but just the ground, sawdust and stuff to sort of keep it from being muddy.

So they were stomping around on there and some of those slabs turned. They went down in it. They got awfully mad. It made them awfully mad because they went down in there no telling how deep, right into that old stuff. And, oh, they came out of there cussing, telling what they were going to do to him; they were going to take him on with them. And he got out there, got his high-powered rifle, and laid it up on the fence there. And he said, "You come 'ary a step towards me, and I'll shoot you." They didn't come. Wooten told me that he told them, "Boys, he means it; we'd better get away from here." And they went on. So finally he worked around and paid out right smart, you know, gave

them maybe a half a gallon of liquor and so on and paid out right smart of money, and he got out of it.

Going back to the meeting, though, and churches, and so on like that, it seemed they were sincere, a lot of people. They seemed to be sincere. And though they'd get into all kinds of things, they didn't seem to maybe get into anything but what them and the Lord both couldn't get them out of it. But they generally, if the Lord didn't get them out, they managed some way to get out with the help of the Lord maybe. But they were very sincere about going to church and taking part in supporting it.

It was a way to make some money pretty quick, you know, and a right smart of it pretty quick. It was very slow and hard if you made it really any other way. *(Raymond Presnell)*

To make peach brandy, you just ferment your peaches and run it through the still. You don't use a copper still. Stainless steel is best. I never have liked copper. A copper worm is the only thing I'd ever use. I like copper for the cooling system, but otherwise, I don't want no copper. And definitely you don't want no copper that they have now because they put something in it that'll poison you. Now if you could get the old copper like it was made years ago, it'd be different, but they're making it different.

Look at my fingernails. I've been working in 'em [peaches] all morning. See you've got to take that peach, and you've got to get the seed out. And then you put the juice and all that into a barrel. Then it ferments, and then you've got to take the liquid and pump it in. You don't strain it. You just pump it in the still. If the seed was out of it, you could still the whole peach, but them seeds don't make good brandy. It takes three days to ferment.

To make corn liquor, you've got to heat your water real hot and mash the meal in the box. You make up a big thing of corn mash, or mush. You take a big box of water and get it real hot; and then you pour cornmeal into it and cut it in, and what it makes is mush, corn mush; it's a lot thicker. And then you let it set there, and it cooks real good overnight so you can mash it down and let it sit 'til

in the morning. All right, then go in there and add you some water and break that up real good. And that's hard to do, breaking it up, because it's a cake. It sat there overnight and baked. Then you put your corn malt on it; I do. If I make corn liquor, that's the way I want to do. I'll crack my own corn; take it and have it ground; and make my own malt. (What that means is that you take corn, ears of corn, and you shuck it off. Then you put it in water and let it sprout like bean sprouts. Then you dry it, grind it up, and that's corn malt.) Then put you some rye flour on it. Put that on there and then watch it head, prettiest thing you ever seen. Foams up and everything. I had some, last I mashed over there. I mashed rye and it was seventeen inches, the head of it. Makin' liquor is hard work!
(Unidentified man)

Did you get a picture of my license here? Federal license. This is state licensed. All this here is government stuff. There was an ol' boy, I done forgot; I cut that out of the paper. He was making white lightning; I believe he was over across the mountains someplace, and he was testing it there. You make gasohol out of that still. That's what I'm doing. And it will burn, too. *(Thurmond Sparks)*

Moonshine's always been here. Back when we grew up, when I grew up around this area, we'd go to certain areas; we could always get a bottle. We could buy a pint of whiskey for a quarter; a half a gallon was a dollar. You had quite a few suppliers around that you could buy the whiskey from. Even when I was just a little small boy, I had the knowledge of where to go and what to do. They were very particular who they sold it to. If there was a drunk in the vicinity, or something like that, they didn't sell it to him. But the most of our whiskey that we got, we went down to Wilkes County. Still, most of it is made in Wilkes. All that whiskey that I knew anything about was in the area next to the Wilkes County line in the Caldwell or Globe section, somewhere like that, that you could go to the mountains and get. Someone could go down there

and bring it back up here. I can remember buying whiskey for one dollar a gallon.

If you drink enough anything, you'll get sick off it. But you wasn't afraid of it. You never had any poison whiskey 'til after World War II. Then they made it in old car radiators to make it fast, production-wise. Now you take a man, go out here and make thirty to forty gallons of whiskey, it'd take him three or more months. See, he'd have to make his beer first, then distill the beer and hide it from the cops or law. If he made some that he wouldn't drink himself, he wasn't worried about getting poisoned. I don't think it's as bad now as it was. It got bad, you know, after World War II when it started making people sick and getting poisoned from it. Up North they called it bathtub gin, and here it was white lightning. And people would get "jakeleg" from drinking the stuff—too much lead in it, made it through radiators and things. And they'd make it in old galvanized buckets or galvanized stuff, and there was lead in that—zinc lead. It wasn't made in a barrel, wooden barrel, the way the moonshiners used to make it.

They'd make a box, put the beer in it, cover it with something, and let it work out that way. Generally, it was made around old sawmills. They put the box in the sawdust or somewhere where it could ferment. Then they had to cook it. They had a cooker. When you see a picture of a still, you see two parts of it. You see one over here, the cooker; then they got a worm run from the cooker to the condenser. The condenser condenses the boiling steam; the steam comes over and it goes into a liquid. It has to be cooled as it goes. And when you cool the steam off the boiling beer, it goes into liquid, which is alcohol. Same process in the lab today. You go to the college and they're going to make some alcohol to burn a lamp over here. They boil it off and make—same process. *(Frank Norris)*

You just didn't double-cross them people. If they were out there, they were making an honest living, making liquor. Only

thing they was doing was taking the government out of a little bit of tax money. And if you reported them people, you would send them to prison. Their families had no way of making a living while they were gone. And they didn't like that. And they didn't go to prison if they could help it. They'd just soon shoot you as look at you if you crossed them. You just kept your mouth shut about things like that. And you lived a whole lot better. They'd give you anything they had long as you was good. . . you know, as long as you went along with them. If you didn't go along with them, they'd kill ya.
(Harold Keener)

kill him. My granddad had a lot of good friends and had a lot of authority over there, and he talked the boys into leaving him alone, letting him go. But, they was about fifteen or twenty of them down there waiting on him. They'd a' killed him, too, if he had come down the road. They burnt his house down. They burnt his barn down. Now this is back in the thirties. He had a new Dodge car. They cut it down. They cut the tires off of it. They cut the body off of it with an ax. It was never moved from where it's sitting when they got through with it. He left and went to Massachusetts. Owned a chicken farm just out of Boston up there. He knowed he had to go. Smartest thing he ever did. He didn't have nothing left. But them people never did like him. He lived for quite a few years after that, and a lot of them was close relation to him. It didn't matter if it was his brother, his uncle, his cousin. . . they'd 'a shot him. They didn't care. *(Harold Keener)*

They had to make it at night to keep the law from seeing the smoke in the daytime. They used to have stills in old houses and such stuff as that. But, most of the time, if they were just a small operator like most of these old country people are, they just had it out in the woods. In a little ol' dark cove where a good spring was at. I know where one place was at; they made liquor, I guess, for ten years before they finally quit at that one place. A lot of people found it, but they wouldn't turn it in. The law couldn't find it. They'd hunt day in and day out for it.

You didn't bother the people as long as they didn't bother you. You let them go. After I got big enough to go squirrel hunting, if I found a still, I didn't tell people about it. I kept my mouth shut. Because them people didn't believe in running their mouths or turning anybody in or reporting them.

I had a great-uncle that thought he would be smart and clean Walnut Creek up. He had hisself appointed as deputy sheriff. No pay. Just so he had a badge and authority. And he cut out and he found a still, and instead of going and turning it in, the next day he went to hunt another still. Well, they was waiting to ambush him. They was gonna

There was a family lived there; they had two stills a-goin' all the time. And then the Revenue officers come in to raid them. They'd get one. If they just got one, it didn't hurt them too bad. They had another one ready. There was a big patch of laurel and ivy between home and their place; and we had some big brood sows there; now they can smell beer a long way. Them things'd get out and you couldn't beat them out of them woods. They'd go out there and they'd have to beat them back. They'd get in the beer. Above where I lived there, that was all mountain laurel then. They kept a man in there choppin' and burnin' just here and yonder all the time. And they had some big holes dug; and in those certain places, it'd be just smoke, didn't see no fire. That's where they made it. And they'd be a-burnin' right beside of them. They was hard to catch. But then bootleg whiskey was good. Wasn't any adulteration about it. Everything was made in copper. They had a man that made the stills for them, cut them out and everything, made them round; the neatest things you ever saw. They make them out of everything now. It's dangerous drinkin'. *(John Cooper)*

158

community that would report still places and get twenty-five dollars. So, we didn't only have to hide the still from the Revenuers, we had to hide from the people too. Because it takes a pretty dirty fellow to do a thing like that. We were working and tending our business. Now, if we'd been out here stealing something or harming somebody, it would have been a different story, you know that. We was just making whiskey. (Leon Johnson)

"Corn squeezin's", liquor being distilled in a working still

How did moonshine get the name moonshine? Making it of the night while the moon was shining. See, they'd sneak around in the night. Nobody would see your smoke and nobody'd see you. When you can make money off of whiskey you deserve every penny of it, because it's hard work. Our biggest problem making whiskey was keeping anybody from knowing it. We had people that lived in the

Used to be that years ago it was really a means of life. I was born and raised in Windy Gap. Down there you either worked at the sawmill or you made whiskey. There wasn't no other work. That was it. And there wasn't no ways to getting to town like there is now. There wasn't a half a dozen cars in the whole community. And people, they'd wait to get a job to make whiskey. And the people were well thought of. They provided. If somebody in the community was having it rough they could go borrow money from them. Northwestern Bank didn't know them. There wasn't no Northwestern Bank. I believe there was two banks in Wilkesboro one time when they sent my daddy off.

Look, the liquor business is gone now. But the best people in the world is the ones that did this. It was the hardest work in the world. You lug 150 pounds for a half-mile up through the woods, through across the hollers and things like that. It's hard work. There wasn't anything come easy about it. But we enjoyed it. I been in it ever since I was knee high to a duck. But I've sat on Saturday, when we wasn't in school, somebody'd be workin', and they give us two or three dollars to sit out on a hill. And, if we seen a car coming through, most of the time it was the law, we'd shoot a gun three times and run. For two or three dollars that was more money than you could make in a week, hoeing corn. But, of course they's some bad things about it too.

Every one of Mama's—and a lot of my aunt's folks too, and all my people, we come from a bootlegging family. And I reckon my daddy was probably one of the biggest in Wilkes County. And he did time too. But, it wasn't no trouble at all, you know, if you was down there [in jail]. You'd see at least thirty of your neighbors every day. It was half of Wilkes County, I mean half of the prison department came from Wilkes County, or people we messed with from Greensboro. Pulling time is the biggest thing. I was unfortunate enough to get captured twice. Course I made parole on both sentences. It seemed like we was on vacation. We stayed in the barracks. We stayed on the Air Force base. The first time I went in, from this country there was three hundred prisoners there and two hundred and sixty-some from Wilkes County. So it was just like going home. I had a nickname. It was Hickory Nut. My daddy's nickname was Tater. When I got out of the car, "Hickory Nut, I know'd you'd be on [down]. Been waiting on ya!" They was all glad to see ya, but they was glad to see ya go, too. Everybody was friends.

So after pulling time, I come home and got me a job in a grocery store in Harmony. Making thirty-five dollars a week in 1961. You couldn't live off of it. I worked on like that for two or three weeks with it at the grocery store, and my friend come by one day and said, "Leon, I got to go up the road and go to Wilkes to get a few cases." Said, "Do you want to ride with me?" I said, "I might as well, I'm as well-off in jail as I am out here broke." We bootleggers stuck together. Kinda like the Republicans and the Democrats. The Democrats now sticks together, and the Republicans sticks together. That's the way us bootleggers done. Hauled liquor for two years, I guess, two or three and never lost a drop.

They would lay on the roads and watch for us. They'd be up on banks to see what we had in our cars. And they could tell a liquor car because it sat up. It wasn't shaking all over the road. It run solid. It run smooth, and they was fast cars, most of them. So, they jumped a friend of mine down there about Yadkinville, and they run him about thirty, forty miles down there, and finally they caught

him. They blocked the road on him over there. And he quit and come on back home too then. It was really hard in the forties now! Even back then, I was making forty dollars a week down there, with the work. *(Leon Johnson)*

Well, see you'd have a guy over on the edge of Tennessee, and he would get whiskey from Wilkes, and he would sell it to the people in Tennessee or in North Carolina. There's an understanding between bootleggers. It's something similar, say, like bidding on construction work; the guys from the east don't bother the guys from the west. And the same way with the whiskey. The boys that lived in the west end of the county, they took care of themselves. The boys that lived around Boone took care of themselves. They worked together on it. A lot of liquor used to come through here from Tennessee, and it would be going to Winston or Charlotte, or some place. The law would chase them. They'd buy liquor from Tennessee, take it back, haul it both ways. Now the biggest bootleggers in Watauga County were people that hauled whiskey in here from Baltimore, Maryland, and places where it was legal, where they made whiskey legal in pint bottles. And they would bring that liquor into Watauga County by trailer loads, and then it would be sold out to different areas by the case. And this guy would sell pint liquor to people in the neighborhood. It was made in Kentucky. It was made in the same place where liquor is made today, only they'd haul liquor; they'd go all the way to Georgia with it and circle around to keep from being caught. They'd bring a trailer load of whiskey into Wilkes County, and then eventually it'd be funneled back into Watauga County, or they'd hide it in Watauga County and funnel it to Wilkes. The guys that dealt in it, well, most of them are living today as legitimate businessmen. When liquor became legal, they went out of the whiskey business and went into farming or whatever they were doing. *(Frank Norris)*

In bootlegging you'd get your automobile lined up, and then you'd go looking for a job. And I always worked somewhere besides doing this. This wasn't a full-time job. You couldn't just sit around on the street. You couldn't even support yourself. I wasn't married until '50. This was back in the 'forties. And nobody knew I was doing it because I didn't tell anyone. And the guy I was doing it for did not dare tell anyone.

There was the aspect of being honest about it; that was the whole thing. You didn't try to be dishonest. I wouldn't have done it if I thought it was hurting anyone. Well, there's honor among thieves, you know. The guy that I worked for, he furnished me; nobody else did. See the guy down here, somewhere else, he might have furnished somewhere else. But this guy here, he did this, though. Nobody else would dare do it. See, the thing was, you understood that. I didn't dare take this liquor and go somewhere else with it. *(Unidentified man)*

Everybody that dealt with whiskey had liquor traps. In other words, you'd walk in the place over there, you wouldn't know where they were. It's a place you hid whiskey. I had a shoe rack in a wall. Set your shoes on it. Lift your shoes off, the wall would go up into the ceiling and you could put a case or two of pints there, or fifths. Maybe you had an electric switch or electric clock or had a shower; you could put twenty-five cases under the shower. You had a shower. You could take a shower in it, but down under the shower was a cellar you kept your liquor in. And it was locked. It had two railroad ties and railroad wheels on it. You'd roll it off of that and put your liquor in it, pull the shower back and lock it and take a shower. People built those things. There was professional people that did things to break the law, I guess you might say. But yet, it was a way of life everywhere except

Watauga County. When they legalized whiskey in Wilkes County, they cut the bootleggers out, and they did to a great extent here in Watauga County. It wasn't profitable. But back then, it was profitable. (Unidentified man)

I didn't drink the liquor. If I drank liquor, I'd go get white liquor. And I'd drink moonshine. 'Course you knew where it was made and you knew who made it, and it was good liquor. To this very day, if it's made right, it's better than this other stuff. There's no chemical in it. It's just the pure, natural growth of alcohol. You grind the corn up, you ferment it, cook it; there's nothing in it but that. You don't have to use sugar. People didn't use sugar 'til they found out it was cheaper to make it with sugar. You could make more faster. I didn't haul white liquor that way. As long as the stamp was on the whiskey, the Federals will not bother you. The Feds would not bother anybody hauling tax-paid whiskey. This whiskey was paid; it didn't have the North Carolina taxes paid on it, but it had the Maryland, Kentucky, and Virginia taxes. And they would not bother you. See, the government, once the government got their money out of it, they didn't care what went with it. Down here it was the North Carolina tax and the sheriff's department of the county. So the state's the only one you had to worry about. They didn't dare touch those hotels. They would have caught me bringing it in to them, but they didn't raid the hotels. *(Unidentified man)*

He can tell you about all them times he built time; he ain't told you nothing about that. You think he's made so much money with whiskey. The first sentence, I reckon, that he built after me and him was married, I didn't even have enough money to buy gas to go to Winston. He was down there in jail and wanted me to come see him. I had to borrow money to put enough gas in the car to go down there. That was fifteen months, I believe it was. So I had to do by myself. *(Mabel Sparks)*

Don't let her tell you the story the next time around. The next time I went off, I was hauling moonshine then and I had a good trade and I had two cars—liquor cars. And she made more money hauling liquor while I was gone than I made when I was at home. That's what brought us out of the can. *(Thurmond Sparks)*

But I didn't do that! Your brother did the hauling. *(Mabel Sparks)*

Yeah. He come in and lived with her, him and his wife, and stayed with her. One of my late cars, they wore that thing slap out. When I come back it wasn't nothing. *(Thurmond Sparks)*

On this place, if I hadn't done that, he wouldn't have had a home when he come back 'cause it'd been gone. *(Mabel Sparks)*

One evening the ol' cow didn't come up and I was going across, way over across the pasture over yonder; and there's a big ol' deep gully over there, and I had to cross right at the top. Well, I seen something down there in that gully, and I couldn't figure out what that was. I knowed it was something different, and I kept going a little closer and a little closer. I got down there and it was a suitcase like thing or some kind of big bag. It was zipped up, and I unzipped it to see what it was, 'cause I didn't know what was going on. I knowed there was something wasn't supposed to be. And they had their lights in there, flashlights, and canned stuff, and everything, their sleeping bags that they had there. I couldn't imagine what in the world. And he was on over in the barn, or plowing or doing something over there with the tractor. I let the cow go. I went on over there where he was at, and I told him what I'd found down there, that they'd been watching the house. He come on to the house. You know, they got that stuff up by the time that he come out with that tractor and we went down there. I was going to show him where it was and what I'd found, you know; and by the time we got down there, there was nothing. Everything was gone when we got

there. They would have caught him that night if I hadn't come along there. See, I was following the cows and they knowed I was coming, getting closer and all. And what they done as I got closer to them, they ran way off down the holler and hid where I couldn't see them. They was watching me, but I didn't see them. *(Mabel Sparks)*

She said, "Come on, let's go over there and haul that stuff off." Yeah, we had a rough time.

I was, I'd say, about twelve years old when I started making liquor. A number-3 washing tub made me a load, all I wanted to carry, when I first started making liquor. My pa and grandpa made liquor too. Well, times were so hard back then; that was the only way you could make a dollar. You didn't have no public work out here to do. Just digging herbs, hewing crossties, and skinning bark. *(Thurmond Sparks)*

My father hauled it, but he had it made; he didn't work it, the shack himself. He'd always had somebody else do the making of it. But he hauled it and he'd always carry, my mother would go, and he would carry two or three of us children in the car. See the whiskey was in our tote. That's the way you would get by hauling it. We'd be riding it. He'd pay me so much each trip that I went, you know. That's the only way, you see, that we really made any money. There wasn't no other way of making nothing. See, the farm he had, the land was so poor. *(Mabel Sparks)*

The chicken operation hadn't never come in here. All you had was a few old yard chickens. *(Thurmond Sparks)*

The first time I've ever run from a still place, if you'd like to know about it, it was on a Sunday morning. I had a uncle, brother-in-law, and a cousin—they was changing shifts—they'd work all night and there was five or six people. Three worked one night. Three another. It was a brand-new still, but we'd add on sugar and make brandy too. So, they sent me in there to carry the breakfast to them that morning about eight or nine o'clock, you know, to the ones that went in at six and they'd stayed over and was loading the cars and helping them get things. The law came in and caught them. They never did come out. So I got almost to the still place, and I thought I saw somebody, and I thought it was one of the work hands, and I just kept on walking. I had my dinner bucket in my hand with country ham and sausage biscuits and a jar of coffee in one hand and I walked on up to him. I guess I was probably thirty-five, forty feet from him. His name was Villet—I never will forget him, he's a big officer—and he had on a checked shirt. And he stepped up from behind a tree, and I knew I done got in a hornets' nest. I turned around and throwed my bucket down—they run me—it must have been two miles before I ever did get away from them. *(Leon Johnson)*

I got away. I was thirteen years old. They run me right back by the house because I didn't have no other way to go. There was three officers. There were five officers down there, and they'd done caught five people. And I was the sixth one. And they was in there. See, one was just coming out to see if he could find the whiskey and stuff on the side of the road you know, where they had made it and carried it out. And, I'm a youngun going up through the woods there with a dinner bucket just as happy as a tree frog because it tickled me to death to get to go to the still place. (When they'd go and they'd put on sugar and stir the beer up, sometimes they'd let me—when I was eight, nine, ten years old—they'd let me on with it. It just tickled me to death.) They run me back through a briar patch. I never will forget it—I was tore all to pieces. I got in that briar patch. I was

scared to death too—knowed they was going to catch me, and I was give out and I just laid there. And I seen him coming on his hands and knees crawling through that briar patch to get me. And I want you to know, I've heard of people catching a second wind, and I reckon I caught mine. (Leon Johnson)

I come out of that briar patch and hit the main road and run the road for a quarter of a mile before I could get off. It was just big fields on both sides. And him right behind me. We both give out running up the road, and we both walked. When I got to the top of the hill and I got over on the other side where he couldn't see me, I hit the woods again. And they hunted for me down there for two or three hours. I was laying up on the side of a hill where I could watch them.

That was the first time I'd ever run from a still place. And, really, I guess it was the last time. Somebody'd shoot and get us out and we'd leave, you know, if they was coming in or something or we'd always have a watchman. And, you know crows in the cornfield, they got a watchman sitting up on a hill in a big high tree. And if anybody goes around the field that crow will let them know. That's the same way we was doing. We'd have a watchman stuck out there and if anybody got around close he'd just run through, or either shoot a gun and we'd leave. If we heard a gun fired three times, we left. If it was somebody squirrel hunting, we still left. We couldn't afford to take a chance, you know. We've run as high as two—we'd have two or three different still places at the time. And we'd work at one one night, and one the next. One one night, and one the next. We stayed pretty busy there for a while—nearly ten years. We hauled whiskey then for about probably eight or nine years. It just faded out. When liquor stores came in here, the whiskey business was over.

(Leon Johnson)

163

There are a few people who still prefer it, very few though. There's not much of it goes on any more. When I was in Washington, I one time asked Director of Federal Prisons Bennett, who knew more about prisons and prisoners than anybody I've ever known. I said, "I want to ask you a question (about some bill affecting criminals). I want to ask you this question and see whether or not you and I agree." I said, "My experience has been that the best people essentially that get into trouble with the law are moonshiners and people who commit murder on the spur of the moment with some provocation and never get into any other trouble." He said, "That's been my experience. They're the best people we ever get in the federal prisons, moonshiners." He said, "They'll tell you the truth, if they tell you anything, and you can depend on what they say. And then the mountain people who commit murder on the spur of the moment with sudden provocation are good people." He said, "There's a lot of difference between a moonshiner and a bootlegger. A bootlegger's a crook, and a moonshiner's an honest man." And I found they tell you the truth. The bootlegger was the man that sold it, peddled it around. And I've defended people that did moonshining, in my young days. *(Sam Ervin)*

I lived in a rough community. I was raised in a rough community. You kept your mouth shut. You didn't know what the neighbors done. If you did, you sure didn't tell nobody. 'Cause most of them made liquor. We raised the corn and sold the corn to 'em and they made liquor out of it. They was too lazy to farm. They had to make liquor to make a living.

We'd go to church. We had an old preacher to come there every Sunday. Fine old man. He would walk, I guess, seven miles up that mountain from where he lived at to preach.

This old woman there, she got religion 'bout three or four times a year. One time there on one Sunday afternoon, she was in there and the preacher got to preaching pretty good, and she

View over Snowbird Mountains, Graham County

tipped her dress up and she pulled a bottle of liquor out and slid it down the floor. She didn't throw it, she just slid it so it wouldn't break, you know. She said, "I'm through with that rotten stuff. I'll never fool with it again." A man stood up. I'll never forget him. He reached down, and he grabbed that and he said, "Thanks." Shore did. She didn't throw away much. She didn't want to waste that. Every time she'd get in church and get to shouting, you could bet your bottom dollar she had a run of liquor coming off. *(Harold Keener)*

Here's a story about that Andrew Gosnel. Old man Randall lived at the old home place about twenty years, and the first eighteen of them he stayed drunk all the time. One time I went up to see him. He said he had an old mule. The mule was a red mule, except the seat of the mule was white. It looked like the mule had just sat in white paint. The rump was white. It was the meanest old mule in the whole world. But he said, "Andy Gosnel was coming down the road and he had two jugs of corn liquor, one in each hand." He said, "Andy come down the road, and here come the State Highway 'Petroleum'. The State Highway 'Petroleum' was a-comin' and Andy saw 'em a-comin.' And, he jumped in the stall with that mule." And old man Randall said, "I seen the boards start flying off the wall on one side, and then they would fly off on the other side." He said, "I would have rather a-fit the whole State Highway 'Petroleum' than to have jumped in the stall with that mule." But, Andy was a good one.

When I was a boy, Jesse James Bailey had a Plymouth automobile and he put a bumper on it, which was about a two-by-eight bumper made out of wood. They would haul liquor out of Tennessee into North Carolina, and he would catch them on that Hot Springs Mountain, and they wouldn't stop. So, it is said that he would just get behind them and just push them off the side of the mountain. But Jesse would tell all these tales.

We have a waitress here who moves around this area. I've seen her in every restaurant in town. She says that her daddy was the village drunk over in Marshall. One time Jesse James put him in jail and said he had been such a drunk that he was going to keep him there 'til he sobered up. And after seven days, he was still just as drunk as he had been. Just as drunk as a hoot owl. Then they found out what he had done. They had put him in a cell next to the captured liquor, and he got him a rubber tube. He worked it around the jar and siphoned it out and was just having a wonderful time. The old drunk never was going to sober up, so they just threw him out. *(Landon Roberts)*

Those were poor days back then in 1933. I went to work. But in the meantime, I was making whiskey, but there wasn't any sale for it. I sold it for four dollars a case, many, many a case. It was bootleg jars. It was about five gallons to a case. I'd sell it for four dollars. I loaded several trucks like that. Wasn't any money in it. I wasn't doing too good with that, and then I went to the veneering plant and went to work. I worked there 'til the thing burned down, and I started back into the whiskey business and

started farming and doing anything I could to make a dollar. We lived somehow. We didn't get anything for our work, but at least it was an income to you. If you'd sat here in the house, you wouldn't have made nary an ear of corn. And if you got out and worked and gave somebody one and made you one, at least it was better than sitting here and not taking in anything.
(Thurmond Sparks)

They did a lot of trading. They'd bring eggs, and they'd bring chickens and trade chickens for stuff. A big thing was that mothers and wives would bring in butter. You know, they had cows and they'd milk their cows; and the homemade butter they would take to the store to trade for salt, pepper, sugar, and so forth, that the store sold, that you couldn't make or raise on the farm. My mother made soap herself; she didn't buy soap like you go today and buy soap. A lot of the clothes that we would wear she would make. You'd buy certain things that would come in sacks, and she would take the sacks and turn them into shirts and dresses for my sisters, and stuff of that nature.

So the moonshine was an absolute must in my family tradition of life. A lot of people think that in the position I'm in today, that I ought to be ashamed of it; I'm not ashamed of it. I'm very proud of the way I was raised in the survival type atmosphere I became accustomed to, and I still live with that traditional way of life. I don't plan on changing. *(Junior Johnson)*

I did it to start with for survival, and then I found other things that I could get into to make money, and I got away from it 'cause there wasn't any doubt it was against the law. At the time that I was growing up as a young boy, the law didn't have anything to do with it—it was starve to death or make moonshine. You couldn't find something to do around this area because there wasn't anything here for you to do other than just sit on a rock and starve to death. (Junior Johnson)

I was plowing corn with a mule and they came and asked me, said they had a race going on at North Wilkesboro, would I go up there and drive in it. I said I didn't know nothin' about driving one of them things. They said, "Well, what we're going to use is the cars that we've hauled moonshine in." I said, "Oh, well, if that's what you're goin' to use, I'll go drive in it." And, of course, you know, I did. I went up there; and then from that point on, it was a thing where people around in this area would go up there and run each other—kept challenging each other, that kind of stuff. I was good at it, so I just kept following up on it, following up on it. The only reason they couldn't get me to start with, I was better at that point in time than anybody else was. There was so many people that got intrigued by racing that was bootleggers 'til it created the atmosphere, and they started doing it on Sunday in the cow pastures. First thing you know, it just grew and took off.

Once you establish something like that and get it started, and people get interested in it from all walks of life, then, of course, the bootlegging part of it kind of fades into the sunset. But [the] something [that] intrigues it and gets it started is what makes it worthwhile. I think the bootlegging has to take the credit, or the blame, whatever you want to give it. *(Junior Johnson)*

Dew-covered jewelweed deep in a mountain forest

WILDCRAFTING

Cherry bitters is good for your stomach; and take catnip tea and make that for a little baby. You take sassafras, that's real good for your stomach, and make tea out of it. Make it out of spicewood and all. And the ginseng is good for high blood [pressure]. I've got some laying over there. I make about all of my medicine. And moonshine whiskey, now; I've got some of that. Moonshine whiskey and rock candy and ginseng torn up real fine, is as good a medicine for a cough as you can get. It's good for laryngitis. There was a woman here a couple months ago; she couldn't talk and said she was going to the doctor. I said, "I can cure it." She said, "What can you do?" Well, I said, "I've got some rock candy and whiskey and ginseng in there. I'll get you about this much and you drink it; and before you leave here, if you don't tell me that it's cleared your lungs up, I'll give you ten dollars." So she got some of it and it cut out all of that laryngitis. Well, you see, there's an herb that was created here on this earth that will cure any kind of disease. It was put here. But anything that you go to the drugstore or go to the doctor that they give you is made out of the herbs. It's made out of cherry bark, ginseng, sassafras, peppermint.
(Stanley Hicks)

Oh yes, they used herbs back then a lot. One thing I'll tell you that they did; they believed that if you'd wear a wad of "assafoetida" tied around your neck, you wouldn't catch those contagious diseases. Oh, I didn't like to wear it, and I promised myself if I ever had a child, it wouldn't wear it. *(Hattie Oates)*

I used to take boneset for colds. Make tea out of that and drink a cup of it cold at night. You might have to throw some cover off, but you'll feel better the next morning. *(Hal Oates)*

Well, Mama used to gather boneset. It grows in damp places along branch banks, out in fields.

Grows up in a stalk about that high, has a white flower on it. And she'd gather that and put it up for winter. It was good for flu and colds. Oh my gosh, it would kill you to drink it. She had it dried and then made a tea out of it. And catnip out there in my wheelbarrow, that was a baby medicine. She'd dry that and have it in a flour bag or something to keep it clean and make a tea out of it for the baby for hives and things. And there's a wild plant they call rabbit tobacco. Well, they'd get that, and if you had a toothache, you'd take it and bend up them stalks and put them in a pot and pour boiling water over it, put a cloth over it, and then you'd lay your face on it for your toothache. For headache, Mama'd always take a piece of brown paper bag and soak it in vinegar, put it in vinegar and let it soak to get that vinegar in it, and lay it on your forehead. *(Nanny Suttles)*

I'm telling you, I suffered with the toothache a lot. My jaws would swell up. I used rabbit tobacco, they called it "life everlasting." Make the poultice of cornmeal. Just stir it up in real hot water, and put you some rabbit tobacco with it, and put it in a cloth, and put in on your jaw. One way of keeping well was to give the children a glass of water every night before they went to bed. *(Lillian Hooper)*

Now, my people in my family have always been strictly opposed to alcohol beverages, and I still am. But now, my mother would make about a quart of blackberry wine, and when a kid got a upset stomach, she'd give him one teaspoonful. And it was as good as anything you could buy in the drugstore. It really done the job. My mother made tea for colds—sweet birch. Take that and cook it down and make like a tea. Of course, she would add a little ginger and a few other odds and ends and a little butter to keep it from burning the ginger too bad. And you'd drink it just as hot as you could stand it and you'd go to bed and sweat. Now it worked. My mama said, "Whatever ails you, castor oil will help it." She really believed it. Believe me, I know. But she would take, when we got a chest cold, she would take a, she called it a yarn rag. It was wool, a wool rag. And she would grease that thing good and grease your chest and hold it in front of the fireplace and get it hot. And you had to go to bed with it. I hated them things, they scratched so bad. But we survived, so it must've worked. Mama raised six of us, and my mother went to the doctor for the first time when she was seventy-one. None of us children ever saw a doctor 'til we was grown. So, something she used was right. *(Jonah Parker)*

We'd gather roots and herbs: peel bark, wild cherry bark, beechwood bark, beechwood leaves, bomgilly buds, may apple, bloodroot. Just whatever they were buying, we gathered. We sold to the Wilcox Drug Company, the same company that's here today. Only it's run by the fourth or fifth generation now. They sold the roots and herbs away from here. We'd make our own medicine out of them. We used the pine needles and would boil it down and make pine turpentine and stuff like that and put in it to make a cough syrup, honey sugar, whiskey, whatever we had to put in, I guess. **(Frank Norris)**

I must have went seng digging. Well, now I would love to show you seng. See, on this ginseng, all you keep is the root. And it sells. . . right now I think it's one hundred and sixty dollars a pound dry. And it started out in the fall of the year at one hundred and twenty-six dollars a pound. I sold two hundred and eighty dollars the first day. If I don't have anything else to do, I love to get out in the woods and hunt it. But it's still profitable, you might say. Now, I sold almost five hundred dollars worth so far this fall. I still got another two hundred and fifty dollars

worth. Some of it's not even dry yet. I got it yesterday. And, if a man hunted it full time and knows where to go and how to hunt it, he could make some good money. You know, this goes in most any kind of medicine you get today. Ginseng is in most any kind of medicine you get. You get out in these dark coves is where it really grows the best. In poplar groves. Around black walnuts out in the woods is one of the best places to find it. In the fall of the year it has red berries on it. When it's got them red berries, it's pretty easy to spot, and this time of year it's pretty easy to find because the leaves are turning just a gold color. They're just a different color from any other leaf you'll find out there. The leaves are almost like poison oak. *(Harold Keener)*

Usually, in the wintertime, when we was picking galax we'd stay for a whole week. The leaves are about like that and some shaped like that. And you stacked them twenty-five in the bunch, and forty bunches makes a thousand. And they would pay you so much a thousand. They used them for wreaths at that time. Floral wreaths. And they were shipped out all over the country from here. *(Pearl Marshall)*

I've often thought that those people should have left it [the fern] more to us, but there were no hard feelings about it. There's never been anything so beautiful as that woodland in the Beech Mountain there in those beautiful places where that fern grew so nicely. It was used for decoration purposes in many places like Florida, Georgia, all the South, of course. But these folks that bought it, they finally got to taking it to cold storage. They would buy it up in the fall in order to have it to ship out, when they got orders, to these places—no doubt.

And my daddy, we generally gathered fern. We would roll the log moss around it when we'd bring it in from the woods to keep from bruising it so bad. They would take that to Johnson City

(Opposite) Lady's Thumb, a wildflower member of the buckwheat family

Ferns covering forest floor

[Tennessee] on Little Tweetsie Railroad and put it in cold storage there and keep it until in the spring when they would get orders. They got four or five dollars a thousand for it, where we got fifty cents. But after all the expense they had in it, they didn't make a great deal with losses and shipping and the crates and hired help. If we could have got that, it would have been awfully good for us. I could gather about 3,500 a day generally, and maybe up to 7,000 when it was real good, before it had been stomped over—three dollars and fifty cents on a super day. And that probably took fourteen hours. But really it was to pack, to sort, which took practically as much time as it did to bring it in.

We started probably in September generally and October gathering fern, and we got about fifty cents a thousand; that was each leaf, each fern. We packed it twenty-five in a bunch, we called it. And I first learned how much it took to make twenty-five by fives, you know. We gathered when the snow was off and would bring it in and have a lot piled

in when it would come a snow. And back then it did come bad snow in the mountains, really rough weather for months sometimes. We'd get this out, and if it was gathered when it was wet, it would freeze together; and we'd have to lay it out and let it thaw. And we had an old chimney and fire, and we laid it out on the beds and everywhere so it'd thaw. It'd break it all to pieces; you couldn't break it apart to bunch it. We'd gather about five hundred armfuls and take it to a place and lay it down there. And then we'd get 3,000 or 4,000 or 5,000 or 6,000 or whatever, at a place and we'd do it up in a burlap bag left open. And then we could lay it on our shoulders and carry it home sometimes two or three miles, sometimes maybe more. We'd take it home and then bunch it.

After I got up in the teens, I gathered bark and stuff, and I would get up a little portion and save up; and where I'd work on Sunday to peel the bark and stuff and get a little cloth shirt occasionally. But we generally gathered fern. *(Raymond Presnell)*

OUTSIDE INFLUENCES

Although this area is mostly rural, there are some friendly small towns and some larger ones such as Asheville, Boone, and the Cullowhee area, in which colleges and universities lend a different flavor to the community. Asheville is a city that has had a cosmopolitan air for many years, as the area has always been a haven for tourists from different parts of the country. Outside influences have been present in various areas for a long time, bringing with them small enclaves of affluence.
(W. M.)

One thing that a lot of people didn't understand about the mountain areas is that we've always had a lot of out-of-state people there during the summer. High Hampton, that was General Wade Hampton's summer home. Highlands has been a regular summer colony for Atlanta for years. In fact when Bobby Jones was in his heyday, I used to go up there and watch him play golf fifty years ago. And so, those mountain people have been thrown with outside people for fifty, seventy-five, one hundred years. And they've been exposed to more social graces than a lot of people give them credit for. *(Dan Moore)*

There's no place like these mountains. There'll never be any place like these mountains. I reckon that's the reason so many Florida people come up here. *(Harold Keener)*

There's about 225 miles of Parkway in North Carolina. It goes all the way from Cherokee to the state line near Laurel Springs, about halfway between Galax, Virginia, and Mount Airy, North Carolina. Today the Great Smokies has approximately 14 million visitors a year, not necessarily different visitors.

The Parkway last year had about 23 million, roughly twice as many as the Smokies. The impact of the Park and the Parkway really are not that widespread. Two miles away from the Parkway, a big impact; twenty miles away, almost none. So, it's a pretty narrow sphere of influence that you find, not only here but all the way into Virginia. The Smokies probably has more impact in Tennessee than it does in North Carolina—not probably, it does have. Forty percent of all the people who go to the Smokies go to Gatlinburg. Twenty-three percent go through Cherokee. *(Jim Ryan)*

At the inn [Nu-Wray Inn, Burnsville] growing up, it was a fascinating sort of life. You know you just came into contact with so many people from all over. Even back then, I don't know how they came, but they did. In the old days people came and stayed for longer periods of time. It made a very interesting thing 'cause it was just sort of like one big house party, you know, most of the time. There'd be children my age, which was just wonderful, and we'd have a great time playing and doing everything. It was strange how they'd come back and then even after they grew up, they'd still keep coming, or their children. We've had ties in with many families. Over the years I've just known thousands of people. I was always coming up with that statement; we'd see on the map a little town and I'd say, "Oh, I know somebody from here."
(Rush Wray)

I like it [tourism]. I think it brings a lot of money into the county that they wouldn't otherwise get, because the tourist trade now means a lot to people in this country. Because in the summer, you see people come here to get away from the heat, and in the winter they come here to ski; and so we just have almost year-round tourists. We enjoy them because they come to our churches. They help support the churches and everything. We have a lot of people from Florida coming to our church in the summertime. *(Lula Wise)*

They [the mountains] ain't changed so much 'til the last few years. For quite a while I knew everybody between here and Dillsboro, every family. I could tell you who lived up and down all the creeks and everything about them. Now I don't even know my own neighbors that live around here. They're from Florida. Well, they call them Florida people, but most of them's raised up North, ain't they? New York, Pennsylvania. They go to Florida and they get dissatisfied there, and they come back here maybe from Florida. People like Florida, but it's just more of a vacationing place. They're making a vacation ground out of this, ain't they? This whole mountain area through here is just getting to be a tourist section, ain't it?

I can just ride over the country and tell you every out-of-state person here. There's several different ways to do it. One thing like private drives, you know. They'll either have a chain across the road or a big sign "Private Drive, Keep Out." You don't see that out of people born and raised here. They never think about puttin' up a sign "Private Drive, Keep Out" or putting a chain across the road. You've seen signs "Posted Land, Keep Off." You never did see them 'til they come. I felt free. I could go anywhere I wanted to through here and felt free. Now then I can go where these people here are and they'll say, "Hello there, ain't you lost?" "No." "I own this property here," they'll say, "and didn't you see the sign down there that said "Keep Out'?" And I'd say, "Yeah, I seen that sign, but I don't have to pay no attention to it. I'm with so and so hunting," or something like that, and just keep going.

Connemara, Carl Sandburg's mountain home, Flat Rock

And I've come up over here, been hunting; there's always been a public passway, a trail, through there and then the man that bought it [a Florida man] says, "What does this mean?" And I say, "Nothing, just hunting a little bit." "Hunting? Didn't you see that sign down there?" I said, "Yeah, I seen it." And he said, "Well, how come you came on? How come you're not turning back?" I said, "I live on the other side of the mountain and I'm heading that way right now. And this has always been a public pathway, and I guess it always will be." I still come the same way yet when I go there. And everybody else does, but he don't like it. He's sold out and gone, but other people live over there now. They're a whole lot different, but still they're a lot like him.

They don't know what you're doing in there, you know. They're used to, I reckon, big towns and maybe everything being stolen, I guess. Never hear tell of nothing being stolen around here. You can lay anything down along the side of the road, your tools or whatnot, and go back the next morning and they'll be there. But now it's getting to be you can't lay nothing down, but on account of there's so many out-of-state people coming in; somebody'll pick it up now, won't they?

I mean I'm not thrown' off on them, that's the way it's been where they's raised; and they're afraid the next man's going to get something off them here. Well, I've heard them talk about people here that they like to live here, and all that; say there are good people. I said, "Yeah, they are, but they always depended on one another and trusted one another to look after one another; never did have nothin' stolen; didn't back then, but they do now. That makes a difference, don't it? But, see, everybody's strange now; so many strangers. There's about as many out-of-state people on this creek as there are natives now. We counted the houses a while back, and I wouldn't doubt now that there ain't about five or six houses of out-of-state people. A lot of them's good people, but still it took a long time to get acquainted with them. *(Grady Reed)*

Everybody's friendly; everybody says they are. A lot of them's nice people, and then some's just different. They don't want you on their property. They don't want you to even go through their property. If there's roads been through there all your life, they still try to block you, stop you from going. Yeah, they put gates up where the road's been for years and years. People shouldn't be that way.
(Lilly Wykle)

The tourists help out a whole lot. What I don't like is these big men coming in and buying all the property here for almost nothing. And then if the people that's had to go away from here to work and wants to come back home, the property is so high they can't buy any of it back. They won't sell it to them back. I don't like that. *(Gayton Marshall)*

We can't blame the out-of-state people for wanting to come here. If the natives of this place here had kept their land, they wouldn't have been here. They sold them the land, and I couldn't blame them for buying it. (Delia Reed)

Blowing Rock was an interesting place back then because it was considered a tourist attraction. In other words, folks came to Blowing Rock. And most of the people that came, though, were from Lenoir or Hickory and Charlotte, Salisbury, and around in there. So many of the people who came to Blowing Rock and had homes used that as a summer resort, and it was so different then from the way it is now because they would come and spend the summer. Well, some of them had cars and they'd come in them; and the husband would come and bring them and they'd go on back to their work and come on weekends or every once in a while. And the wife and family would stay up here the entire summer. My mother kept boarders. She'd keep some of the summer people, keep them all summer.

They were summer folks and we didn't associate with them on a social basis because they were in a group—we were a farm family—I don't mean that they were not nice to us and so on, but they had their friends and we had ours and so on.
(Wade Brown)

When we first came here, there was a woman called Emma who had very blue, china blue eyes, and little gray curls here on her forehead. She used to come and work for us. Of course, if they worked for you, they felt they were just helping you out.
(Louisa Duls)

They didn't discover us. We knew we were here all the time. It's a funny thing. . .we have beautiful girls and young men, too. But, as far as I know, there's never been a wedding between them. We like each other. We get along well with each other.

173

They came down and wanted to buy milk and butter from my grandmother. She said, "Yes, I have milk for sale." So they said, "Will you deliver it?" Grandmother said, "Yes. The children can bring it up." We carried the milk up there and when we got to the porch and started in the front door, the lady said, Mrs. Deboe said, "Ya'll tired?" We said, "Yes" She said, "Well, just sit right down there on the steps and rest, and when you rest awhile, take the milk around to the back door." And we sat there a minute or two; and, my sister looked at me, and I looked at her. We got up and took off down the hill with our milk. They hollered. They said, "Where are you going with that milk?" We said, "We're going home." We took the milk back, and it wasn't long Mrs. Deboe came to see us and get the milk. She said, "What happened?" Grandmother said, "Well, you were trying to send my children to the back door. We don't go to the back door in this country. We go to the front door or we don't go at all." So from that time on, they had to come get their own milk. We resent that terribly.

There was one lady I nursed some at night, and she said that when she first came to this country they told her that she'd better get along with the mountain people because if she didn't, she couldn't buy anything. You can't get anybody to work for you. You can't get anything done. So if you know what's good for you, you be polite, nice, and decent to the mountain people. *(Carrie Burnette)*

My family first started going up there because my great-uncle was a prospector for a lumber company, and they were looking for large tracts of land. He was on horseback and came out on this ridge and saw what a magnificent view there was not only of the mountains on one side, but the valleys and the rolling country on the other. He bought some land and built a home there (on the Continental Divide). My father lived down here in Guilford County, and they were all fascinated by his stories of the area. They used to go up and visit Aunt Lizzie and Uncle Sam Boyd. And then my grandfather and my grandmother bought some land that was almost adjoining. We would spend the greater part

of the summer there at my grandmother's. Later on, my father was able to buy eight acres up on top of the hill adjoining my grandparents' land. Our view is the western rolling view. However, at the top of the meadow where my grandparents' land was, and up where my aunt's land was, you had the steep eastern view, which was quite precipitous. The kind that makes butterflies come up in your tummy. So you could, by which side of the road you were standing on, you could take the easier view or the frightening view.

My earliest recollections are of riding the long train ride to North Wilkesboro, and then we got what they called a drummer's hack. They were what were then called long touring cars that might have three seats, with these long isinglass flaps that had heavy snaps. When it rained, we had to hastily put these side flaps up to keep the rain from coming into the car and drenching us. I well remember how the curves on old [Highway] 16 used to frighten me to death, as I was sure the car was going down the side. However, the roads were much better by the time that I came along.
(Emma Sharpe Jeffress)

There were dozens of very fine mountain families living in Flat Rock, and the outside people got their land, bought it from these wonderful country people. So, I always laugh when they say Flat Rock was founded by Charleston people. My family all came from Charleston on both sides. My great-grandfather, C. G. Manager, owned what is now the Sandburg place. It was called Rock Hill in his day. Then Canton Smythe bought it and changed the name to Connemara. Another great-grandfather, Mr. Drayton, built Ravensworth, which is right across the lake from the Sandburg place. The house is now gone, unfortunately. Flat Rock was perfectly lovely. I'm glad I grew up in part of it. It was a luxurious, wonderful, summer resort. The life was really just delightful. Filled with "tennis teas" as they called them. We rode horseback in the mornings and we swam at the McCabes' place. Then it was the old King place. Old Dr. King was a marvelous man. He lived here year round. There was a lake up there. It's not a very big lake, but that is where everybody went to swim.

How happy we were to get back here! Kickin' our shoes off, we could go barefooted up here, until time to have tea with our grandmother. Then we were bathed and freshly clothed and not allowed to open our mouth unless we were spoken to.

Oh, the fun we used to have! We used to climb Glassy, always once a day, and we would go up the steep way where you would have to climb the sheer rock. We would take our shoes off, hold on by our toes, and go. We used to go walk up to Pinnacle, or ride up there. There were a lot of fine country people up there, mountain people. There was a Step family and whenever we went up, we stopped there because they had fresh churned buttermilk and cornbread. They would feed us. Oh, it was just a wonderful experience. I'm so glad I had it.

In my great-grandfather's day everything was brought by wagon. They came in carriages, and the house servants came in carriages. We all had ice houses, and the lake froze so deep that all of our ice was chopped in these lakes around here and put in the ice house for the summer.

Ravensworth was about one of the first places that was electrified, and that was quite a few years ago. We had gas lamps. And telephones, Lord, we didn't have a telephone in the fifties. We always had water in the house because there was a gasoline pump. We owned the head of the lake down there, and we had a gasoline pump. Pumped the water into the house, but we weren't allowed to drink it. We drank the well water. We used the other for bathing and all that kind of stuff. When I was a small child, we had outhouses. I suppose it was very primitive at one time, but we never thought it was primitive. We thought it was elegance. It was elegance.

They used to come the first of May and stay until the end of October. They would bring their trunks with them just full of things; also, an awful lot of food came from Charleston. At Ravensworth we had bins of sugar, hominy, rice, and coffee. All those things were brought by wagon up from Charleston.

The Depression changed the life in Flat Rock. It wasn't the same as it was before. People started coming up and instead of spending the whole summer the way they did, they started coming for shorter times and shorter times. I suppose they didn't want to keep children out of school, whereas it didn't seem to make any difference way back there. They used to have tutors for the kids. The time came when people did not have tutors, so when school started people left. And then, so many people who always came have died and their children don't want to come. There are still quite a few children who do want to come though. I call them children. They are in their fifties.

So, it has changed; and, it has changed a great deal. We have a lot of very nice retirees in Flat Rock. But they're not Flat Rocks. They think they are but they are not. They know more than anybody who's ever been here about Flat Rock, but they don't know really about Flat Rock—and it will never come back, ever. Frankfort Simmons said, "Flat Rock is a state of mind," and my cousin, Shallota Drayton, says, "Flat Rock is wherever a Flat Rockian is." That's just about true. Oh, I'm the luckiest person in the world to have had that. It will not ever happen again. Not ever. *(Elinor Gorham)*

PART FOUR

Where the Clouds Freeze on the Trees

Cherokee People

I HAD JUST DRIVEN THROUGH BEAUTIFUL ROADS WITH COMMANDING VIEWS and watched different patterns of light hit the hillside. Along the way, I had seen signs to Cherokee. At the entrance to the reservation was an intricately carved wooden sign, and I was curious to see what lay ahead. But when I drove into "downtown Cherokee," I was upset to see such rampant commercialism. I don't know what I had expected, but this was not it. I had never had the pleasure as a child to visit this place and be dazzled and amazed by an Indian dressed in full-feathered headgear standing out in front of a store to entice the customers to come inside or to relish playing with plastic toma- hawks and machine-beaded ornaments of various kinds. All of the glitter and blaring colors, tepees, and feathers seem romantic and larger than life to a child. They make eyes light up with fantasies and the imagination run wild. To a grown-up the same view can sometimes be a little different. It looked tacky to me.

I soon found that this was not the real Cherokee at all. It was only a small section dedicated to the tourist trade, which brings in greatly needed money to the communi- ty and provides jobs for the people who live there. I eventually met Goingback Chiltoskey, who had carved that first sign at the entrance to the reservation, and his remarkable wife, Mary. They and others introduced me to more people, and a truer pic- ture of Cherokee began to unfold. There could, of course, be many books (and there have been) written on this topic alone because this is a special culture within a culture. The Indians have had to endure the same hardships as other mountaineers but with even worse conditions as a result of discrimination.

Molly Blankenship told me stories of trying to get the right to vote. Carl Lambert filled me in on tribal history. Ben Bridgers, who is not an Indian himself but was acting as the tribal attorney, explained elements of tribal law and spoke about the apprecia- tion he had gained of the Cherokees and their culture through his involvement with them, their lives, and their problems. Dan McCoy described growing up on the reserva-

(Opposite) Rime ice covering trees in the Smoky Mountains, Swain County

tion and later participating as a member of the tribal council. He was filled with concerns about his people surviving in the modern world and keeping their heritage intact. I went to the Yellow Hill community meeting with Mary and G. B. Here, people expressed their concerns about the schools, what their children were doing in their spare time, alcohol abuse, and various ways that they could keep their community clean and litter free. They talked, too, of people who needed help in getting wood cut for the winter. Everyone was very outspoken and was given an equal opportunity to speak for as long as he wanted.

Goingback Chiltoskey carving

HISTORY

In 1838, after many court battles and arguments in Congress, the forced removal of the Cherokee Indians from land (held through previous treaties with the United States) in North Carolina, Georgia, Alabama, and Tennessee took place. Arguments ranged from those of Davy Crockett, Henry Clay, and Daniel Webster on the Cherokee side to President Andrew Jackson, who opposed them. The Cherokee Removal was later called the Trail of Tears because of the suffering that resulted during the arduous trek of these Indian people, under the supervision of U.S. soldiers, from the Smoky Mountains to Oklahoma.

Some people say that the discovery of gold near Dahlonega, Georgia, spurred the effort aimed at dislodging the Cherokees from land that contained hidden treasure. Others think that general feelings of ill will between the "white men" and Indians at the time provided the major impetus for the treaty of 1835. Many people hid out and stayed in the area; however, some were allowed to remain under the provisions of the treaty. Others returned to their homeland later. (W. M.)

One of the things that misleads a lot of people about Cherokee history is the drama, Unto These Hills. *The drama is almost all of the history a lot of people know anything about. Night after night the narrator would say, "Four thousand Cherokees were buried in unmarked graves from Georgia to Oklahoma." Well, that is just about multiplied by ten. I mean, by actual statistics, it was 400, and some died on the way out there. And it was natural to believe that some of those would have died if they had been at home. It was a tragic thing to uproot the people and take them away from their homes and their relatives and go to a new country.* (Carl Lambert)

Another mistake that's given out about these people here in the drama, it leads them to believe that all the people that are here descended from people who ran away and hid in the mountains. That isn't true. Where we're sitting here today, the soldiers never bothered a person because of a treaty in 1819. Only the people beyond the dividing line were affected. These people could go if they wanted to, but they didn't have to go. You could make application to the authorities to stay here. They would review you. Many of the Indians or part-Indian who stayed here were Indian women who were married to white men. Under the rules of the treaty, they had the right to make application. Most of the people who were left here were here legally.

There was one hitch to it. The state of Georgia and the state of North Carolina both passed laws where it was illegal for an Indian to own title to land. In other words, they figured that that alone would force them to go whether they wanted to go or not. (Carl Lambert)

When the original trek which began the Trail of Tears started, the Georgia legal setup made it impossible for the Cherokee to have a council meeting. So they went into Tennessee, just went over the line. A good spring of water would have made them stop there, I think. And they were probably tired. So they stopped there. The last council meetings were held there. How many people there were, I'm not real sure, but from there those folks were sent to the West. Fire was carried on the wagon or something because that's the way people had to get another fire started. You didn't always have a match to strike, and you didn't have two Boy Scouts to rub sticks against each other to get a spark started. So when they got to Oklahoma, they started a fire that's been kept constantly burning.

In 1951 a group of representatives, four representatives and the chief, left here with some other folks and went out there and got a light from that fire, flew it back to Knoxville, and then brought it over the mountain to Cherokee up to the mountainside theater and started the flame burning, which has been burning ever since. Our new chief who went into office this past October and the chief of the Western Band got their faces together and thought how nice it would be to take the flame from here to Red Clay and light a fire there so it would go back to where it started and we'd have a joint meeting of council. Well, that's what they did. They picked the sixth and seventh of this April [1984] and there's been a lot of preparation for it. Boys were chosen to represent the seven clans. Of course, the clan system has gone out of existence, but people know what clan they belong to, if they still belong to a clan. If they don't belong to a clan, they know what clan their people had belonged to. You belonged to a clan if your mother belonged to a clan. You did not get in through your father. It was through the mother. So there are people who know that back in their family was a certain clan. I don't know just how the boys were chosen, but I guess they chose two people from each clan, a runner-up and all, and so they had a service, a ceremony, last Wednesday. It was to be up at the mountainside theater, but it was raining. So they had to have it down in the auditorium.

They had quite a little service with the dances and all, and the runners took off with the light. It was lit, though, by one of the men who had gone in 1951. Another one is living, but he wasn't able to be there. The other two representatives and the chief are gone, but Leroy Juanita was one who went,

and Leroy was the one who lit the fire. These fellows ran with this flame 130 miles and a few more feet to Red Clay. They got there at ten o'clock Friday morning. We were just where you could see the men running up this little side of a hill and lighting the flame. We were also close enough to hear the council proceedings. They had an area where the council members sat and then an area where members of the Eastern and Western Band were allowed to come in. Back of that anybody could stand or bring their seats. So the hillside was full of people, which was wonderful. (Mary Chiltoskey)

I guess it'd be hard for any race to maintain their traditions. What traditions does the white society have in the United States? None, you see. They're immigrants, you might say. They have their own little traditions themselves, but as far as America itself, the American tradition is concerned, they had no basic cultures to hang onto. It makes it very hard to try to adapt to what they call "moving in the fast lanes" of society and to hang onto those traditions and cultures here, particularly with Indian people. Indian people think a little slower and act a little slower, and their life moves at a little slower pace. They like their life the way it is—from mountain food to the economics they're accustomed to. (Dan McCoy)

Many times in Cherokee were also spent with Bob Bradley and his girlfriend, Mona. We had a mutual friend who had introduced us. Bob was a member of the Cherokee Nation and had spent most of his life in the mountains. Bob has a great sense of the land and its magic. We spent wonderful hours as he guided us by car and on foot to beautiful places both within the reservation and outside it. He took my friend on hunting trips at night, and they would come back with vivid descriptions of running with the dogs and the closeness to nature that became a part of these experiences. Mona and Bob went on camping trips whenever they could and would describe beautiful walks on secluded trails and the animals that would happen by. Bob also pointed out paths and areas for me to explore by myself with my camera, as he knew much of my work had to be done alone. But he always suggested that I let them know when and where I was planning to go so that they could check on me, as it was very easy to get lost. He reminded me of the danger of the backwoods, citing people who had been found dead after being lost in the woods for days. (W. M.)

Snow-covered ridge

CULTURE AND ECONOMY

There is more Cherokee culture per square inch alive here than any ethnic group in the United States, and remember, all people are ethnic. But for any group of people, I say the Cherokee have more per square inch. I've had people come along and say to me, "Why, it's a shame the Cherokee have lost all their culture." I say, "What do you mean?" "Well, they've lost all their culture." I say if you can tell me three facets of your culture that you haven't lost, maybe I can tell you a little bit about the Cherokee and maybe why they've lost it, if they have. They've lost some, yes. And I can tell you why they lost it, maybe. And they say, "Well, no, we don't have any culture." And I'd say, "Well, you've lost all of yours. What are you worried about the Cherokees for?" (Mary Chiltoskey)

The feeling is that we don't contribute because we don't pay land tax in the county. But all of us spend at least eighty percent of our money off the reservation because all we have here are grocery stores (and the groceries here are higher than they are off the reservation; gas is higher). And if we're off the reservation, we buy gas and whatever we can. But, I feel like we are an asset to North Carolina. We contribute to them and I feel that when I leave this reservation, I'm under the jurisdiction of the state. When I'm on it, I am not under the jurisdiction of the state, but I feel like I am a contributing member, as are other Indians, and I feel that we are an asset to the state. And generally speaking, now they do consider us an asset, and so they do lots for us. *(Mollie Blankenship)*

One day, I stopped by to visit with Mary and G. B. Chiltoskey again. Mary had lent me some material to use with some of my reading students. I was returning these and had a picture for them. I was glad to find Mary at home, as she is out a good bit of the time. We sat down at the kitchen table and began talking. Mary was originally from Alabama and had first met G. B. when she was teaching at the Cherokee School. He had also been teaching in the industrial arts department. Over the years, Mary has become quite an expert on Cherokee history, and I was asking her about questions that had come up during the course of some of my interviews and relating stories of some of the people I had met in other parts of the mountains. I can't remember how the subject came up, but at some point, Mary began recounting the difficulties that she and G. B. had encountered in trying to get married. I wish that I had carried my tape recorder along. Evidently it was against the law in 1956 for a Cherokee Indian and a white person to obtain a marriage license in the state of North Carolina. They could be married to one another and live there but not obtain a license for the marriage in that state. Such marriages had to be performed in another state. So Mary and G. B. decided to go to Tennessee for their wedding. Their Episcopal minister in Cherokee helped them with the arrangements. He went over to Tennessee and married them in Saint John's Episcopal Church in Knoxville.

Earlier during Mary's engagement, she gave a speech to the League of Women Voters in Charlotte. Many of the women were friends and had known Mary and G. B. for a long time. They

Dan McCoy at Cherokee bingo parlor

were excited to hear about the upcoming marriage and some of them asked to see her ring. It was a beautiful ring that had been handcrafted by G. B., who had used the band from Mary's great-great-grandmother's wedding ring. Mary had been carrying it around in her pocketbook, wrapped in a piece of tissue until G. B. could place it on her finger at the wedding. As she was taking the ring out for the other ladies to see, she mentioned the difficulties that they were having in getting married in North Carolina. The other women were outraged. Mary and G.B. went ahead with their marriage in Tennessee but were pleased to hear that, within a matter of months, members of this organization had approached the appropriate state legislators and that the law had been changed. They felt that they had helped to pave the way for other couples. (W. M.)

Often the person that's doing the interviewing when they come to Cherokee has the mindset of a person of a hundred years ago. It's like the person who came and asked G.B. what they had for breakfast every day at the boarding school, but did not ask what would you have eaten that morning had you been at home. *(Mary Chiltoskey)*

I think I told him we had goverment gravy.
(G.B. "Goingback" Chiltoskey)

If they had asked what would you have had to eat if you had been at home, then they would have known something. But if you just ask the one question, you don't know a thing. They were picked up and taken to boarding school. Suppose you hadn't gone to boarding school. What would have been the outcome there? If you don't get both sides of the question, you haven't answered either question.

We get a lot of crazy questions. Usually people do not ask the question they want the answer to, but they don't know how to ask the question that they want answered. *(Mary Chiltoskey)*

183

I'll tell you, one time when I started teaching school down here and it was not long after that, I was outside, the tourists were just beginning to come in this area. A lady stopped and said, "How long's this mountain been there across the way from here?" I said, "I don't know; it was here when I came here." *(G.B. "Goingback" Chiltoskey)*

Now that's the type of question you get asked. What they want to do there is to see if the Indian can talk, and they'll ask a question just to get him to talk 'cause they don't believe he can. And one person asked me—she was one of these folks that came to the house that was interviewing—said, "Do you think an Indian makes a better husband than a white man?" I said, "How would I know?" She said, "Well, you're white, aren't you?" I said, "Well, how would I be able to compare; I've had only one husband, and he's an Indian, and I wouldn't want to swap him off for any other I've ever seen. Does that answer your question?" *(Mary Chiltoskey)*

I guess we were pretty isolated until after the war. Just before World War II, in the late thirties, they paved the road across to Gatlinburg, and at the beginning of the war, the tourists had just begun coming into Cherokee. And, of course, with the war, the travel was curtailed, and after the war, then was when we had all the business develop. I think maybe we had one motel with less than a dozen rooms before World War II, and with tourist travel after the war, we have an economy based on tourism now. *(Mollie Blankenship)*

Another thing about Cherokee is that people drive through, and they don't see anything except the "strip." They see stores and businesses, so they think that everybody in Cherokee owns a business and everybody makes lots of money. There are 5,500 people who live on the reservation and it's only 45,000 acres and most of those people live back in the coves. People don't know what their liv-

ing conditions are like, and they don't know that during the winter months, when the tourist season is over, there is more than forty percent unemployment in December and January. There's nothing for them to do. Most of the businesses are closed. The largest employer is the school system, like on many Indian reservations. After that, it's the tribe and the bureau—that is, local government. Most of the people with the good jobs either are in business or they work for the Bureau of Indian Affairs or they work for the tribe itself. If they don't work for one of those, they don't do very well, not well at all.

One of the ironies I've observed goes all the way back to the French and Indian War. The French were good about trading with Indians, but the English never seemed to understand it. The English gave them inferior goods; they cheated them on weight and quality and all kinds of things. When the white people settled this country and started to trade, they made the Indians dependent upon the trade items—clothes and metal pots. Indian women saw that iron pots for cooking were good and they liked the jewelry and cloth that was more comfortable and better than animal skins, so they rather quickly became reliant on those things. Indians learned about trade at the very beginning.

Now here we have Cherokee—and over and over I hear do-gooders complain about Cherokee and how awful it looks and what a dreadful effect it has upon the Cherokee and their culture. But on the other hand, the Cherokees have done what they have seen done to them. They've seen the trade and junk, and for 200 years they've been given junk. Now they're trying to make a living giving the junk back to the white tourist.

The Cherokee are great wood-carvers and basket weavers. The baskets are beautiful and they're very expensive. Some people complain about the price, but if they ever went with one of those women and saw how much work is involved, they wouldn't complain as much. They don't go out in the woods with her when she finds the tree and cuts it down and strips and dyes the bark. The easiest part of it is probably weaving the basket, and that takes hours. But that's the way with all crafts. *(Ben Bridgers)*

(Opposite) Goingback and Mary Chiltoskey, Cherokee

Rebecca Grant spent hours with me illustrating the art of basket weaving. She told me all about the various dyes that can be used to create certain colors. All of the materials came from nature. It was very important to keep a sharp eye out when searching through the forest and to gather materials at the time, since they could be dried and always used later. My admiration for these Cherokee baskets grew as Rebecca took me through the steps necessary in preparing the materials—cutting the strips to be woven, dying them various colors, and eventually weaving intricate designs into baskets of many shapes meant for different purposes. She had done this all her life and thoroughly enjoyed it. There was great artistry in her work, but she was very practical about it. I think that she knew that she was very talented and took pride in her work, but this just seemed to be part of a normal course of events for her.

Rebecca also knew a lot about herbs and Indian medicine. She took me through her garden and showed me all kinds of herbs that could be used for various purposes, as well as certain greens that were particularly good to eat. Certain things were good for blood pressure; others helped different ailments. I remember asking about an herb that had come up in conversation. A cloud had come over Rebecca's face. She said that this particular herb could be used for evil purposes at times, and she would not discuss it. People should not be made aware of these things, she said, and she certainly wouldn't be a part of it. This herb could be used for good purposes in a couple of dire situations, but otherwise should be left alone. (W. M.)

I still make baskets and use white oak and maple. You have to split the wood into segments. You may have to pull it apart and the ones which are thick, about an inch thick or in diameter, would make at

Rebecca Grant

least ten or twelve splits. You have to know how to do it so you won't break it up. I've been making them sixty years. I was about seven years old when I knew I could make a basket and sell it. Oh, that was the proudest day of my life! My mother used to make them, and I'd sit at her feet under the table. A lot of people won't let their kids handle a knife, and I've been handling one ever since I can remember. If you let a child learn early, he won't be apt to hurt himself. A knife is to make a living with in my family. I've got some good wood–carvers in my family. My son is one.

Once you get everything done, after you do this, you have to scrape it [the wooden splits]. It's got to be damp to work. My friend and I here, we'll sit and have shavings up to our knees. You work it while the wood's wet or else you won't have anything but a pile of kindling or shavings. We just sold baskets. We were raised on baskets, you know. My mother used to make cane baskets, and then she made baskets from plain white oak, and she made vine baskets. I make them with white oak now. When a person tells me that stuff is too high, I say, "Well, you make it yourself; then you'll ask more than what I'm asking."

After you gather them, you have to boil them about four or five hours at a hard boil and then you scrape the skin off them. They'll slip right off once they get cooked good, and then you have to run them through bleach water. That takes all that inner skin off, you know, because if you leave it on there and you dye the stuff, the dye will come off the skin. You get it to be red by dying it with blood root. I've got a butternut stump from a neighbor. I use the root to make black. The oak has got dye in it, tannic acid, and it turns stuff dark. You have to do all this before you can even dye it. You have to get this and scrape and you dye it, and by that time maybe you're ready. The actual weaving you can do in a day, a big basket. Generally, I experiment. I don't waste anything. Like I told somebody, I know exactly what the basket's going to look like before I make it, when I start. *(Rebecca Grant)*

On the reservation in the wintertime, unemployment gets up to forty percent. The tribe had a building sitting up there empty and costing them $3,500 a month. I presented my proposal [for bingo], and it went through. Some of the comments I had to make to the council, I knew it would be a very controversial issue. These bingo operations became very popular on other reservations, and I said to myself, "Why can't we have that here for employment purposes, for the tribe to make money?" A lot of people called it gambling. A lot of people called it games. The Seminole tribe in Florida had won their Supreme Court case.

After we were in operation for one year, the tribe had received over a million dollars. Just over a half a million of that was direct dollars to the tribe. Some of that money was indirect through labor, but every first of January we have to pay the tribe 150,000 dollars cash before we start a year's operation. Then we have to give them two dollars a head for every person who walks in there, every game. We have to give them 3,500 dollars a month, every month for the building. They call that an administrative fee. Then we have to give them a percent of the gross before anything comes off it. I've never paid the tribe less than 22,000 dollars a month and I've paid them as high as 29,800 dollars a month for that bingo operation. They don't have one dollar invested in it other than that building.

My motives at that time were not to be controversial, not to be radical, but to try to put something on this reservation that would stimulate the economy, make money for individuals through work, make money for the tribe, and also, where I could make some money. *(Dan McCoy)*

Bingo has had a tremendous impact on the economy here—side benefits, the business, motels, and the jobs it's provided, especially in the winter, will take a lot of people off our social welfare rolls.

The periphery of the reservation are very prejudiced against Indian people. And the feeling is reciprocated largely, or it was. Back when I was young, Indians just didn't marry outside the tribe; and it was frowned on if there were intermarriages, both by the whites and the Indians.
(Mollie Blankenship)

SCHOOLING

A lot of the old customs are fading away. The Indian Bureau here had the philosophy back whenever I was going to school to make a white man out of an Indian in one generation. You see, I had my mouth washed out with laundry soap many times about using the Cherokee language. Have to clean the bathrooms out or sweep the sidewalks off. Do all kind of work like that just for asking somebody what a certain word was.

Chief Nimrod Garrett Smith was chief at the time, and I guess we'll have to say that he was one of the most progressive chiefs the Eastern Band ever had because he was farsighted enough and saw that the salvation of the Indian was to get an education. He contracted with the Quakers from Indiana. They took a ten-year contract and built a boarding school. They ran a boarding school there for ten years.

Chief Smith sent letters out and sent people out that could talk both languages, all around in the adjoining counties, to try to get them all to move here so that their kids could go to school. That was how my great-grandfather and my grandfather moved here. My father was one year old when his father moved here. My father said that the Quakers ran the best school that he ever went to in his life. Every day that a kid went, they kept a record of it; and at the end of the school year, the Quakers had all these big bolts of fancy-colored cloth and everything, and they would look on the list and see how much attendence they had. That determined how much cloth the family would get. They'd have cloth to make pants and shirts and these bright-colored calicos for women's dresses and whatnot. So the parents were very interested in the kid going to school, not necessarily for him to learn but for him to get that cloth. My dad said that it was really colorful a few days after they got their cloth. They immediately went home and went to cutting that stuff up and sewing it. The men would have some of those bright colored shirts on, you know.

The Quakers went to the council at the end of the ten-year period to get a renewal on the contract.

School bus on country road

188

But they had made Chief Smith mad, and he vetoed the thing. The Council never could get a two-thirds majority over him, so the Quakers lost out. And that's how the federal government is in the school teaching business. Rather than see the school go down, the Indian Bureau sent some teachers in here. *(Carl Lambert)*

I guess in the 1880s or '90s they started a boarding school here, and all the children would come to boarding school. In the early days they stayed in boarding schools year-round. They were allowed to go home in the spring to help plant and then in the fall they were allowed to go help gather the crops and gather chestnuts and wild things. But other than that, they stayed in school; and when they finished elementary school, then they were shipped to either Hampton Institute or to Carlisle, which is in Pennsylvania. And when they left home, they usually didn't come back until they either dropped out of school or finished their education. I know in Carlisle they would farm them out in the summer to the farms around there. They'd go and work. They didn't come home in the summer. And we continued to have a boarding school here until 1954, and, I guess, beginning in the forties we had people from Seminole and Choctaw come up here to get a high school education. We didn't have a high school here until the thirties. Up until that time, I think we had the eighth grade, and after they stopped sending students to Hampton and to Carlisle, they sent them to Chilocco, Oklahoma, or to Lawrence, Kansas, for high school.

I know the theory is now that it's better for the children to be in the homes; but in those days there weren't many illegitimate children, just orphans. The boarding school in some instances took the place of foster homes, and the kids who had no homes stayed in boarding school year-round. The ones that had homes were allowed to go home. They were in boarding school only when school was in session, and then in my day they were allowed to go home on weekends and vacation and Easter.

They had a regular routine in school. They had food and they learned to work. And you can say whatever you want to, you can tell to this day the people who went to boarding school, you really can. Because when you hire them to do a job, they know how to do it and the younger generation doesn't. We have some children today who are not in stable home situations, and I feel that they'd probably be better off in a boarding school. But I don't suppose there will ever be another boarding school here. *(Mollie Blankenship)*

A schoolteacher is in a bad situation. If I'm manufacturing cars, in two weeks or three weeks I can see my end product. Schoolteachers have to sit there twenty years to watch for the end product, so they're in a bad situation. There's a lot of things that we need that we're slowly coming around to on the reservation. If it had happened ten years earlier, we might have been in a totally different environment here.

Our children can go to a Cherokee school or they can go to a public school, either one. We had some children in a non-Indian school off the reservation, and they invited me over when I was serving as chairman of the education board to talk to them. I talked to the Indian Parent Committee in that school. They wanted to know why, when those kids graduated from sixth grade, they were three-quarters of a year behind. When I went over the proposal the Indian Parent Committee had sent in, they had remedial in there, and they had math courses, and they had some English; but all this was supplemental to what they were taking in school. They also had cultural programs: food, arts and crafts, and language. When I got the proposal and started looking at it, the Parent Committee had picked all these cultural programs as their number one priority for their children to study. So the emphasis was put on that, and when they got to the academics of the school, the basics, the grades were from the second grade, one month behind, and the sixth grade, three-quarters of the year behind. In other words, when the kid graduated out of the sixth grade, he was actually about a fifth grader.

189

When it came my turn to talk, I said, "I'm going to speak harshly and you must listen and don't think hard of me, but I'm going to lay it on the line." There was a lady sitting there and I asked her if she worked at the school part-time. She said, "Yes." "You work at the Indian Village in the summer full-time, don't you?" "Yes." I said, "You cannot live on that job alone, can you?" She said, "No." I said, "You've got to subsidize your income with making baskets and cultural things." She said, "That's right." I said, "Suppose you lost these two jobs and you had to depend totally on your culture, your history, and your basket weaving, to live on." She said, "I couldn't live." I said, "That's why you've got to get this education. Hanging onto the culture and history and all this stuff of Indian people is very important, but you cannot eat it in the wintertime."

Another thing about Indian people. Indian people feel like they're forced into everything. They feel like they're pushed to go certain ways when really they're not. They just feel it because of the way they've been treated in the past. In today's time they're not pushed anywhere. They're given opportunity. *(Dan McCoy)*

When we went to school, we weren't allowed to speak the Cherokee Indian language, but now they're teaching it in schools, but it's hard for them [children] to pick up because they didn't hear it [at home]. We were put in school when we were about six years old. We went home on holidays and summer vacation for about two or three months in the summer. When we went to boarding school, we had to stay there. We were punished if we spoke the Indian language. And our mouth was washed out with soap. Yes, that's true. They thought we should learn the English language.

Now they're teaching it, the Indian language, in the schools. Even those little tiny ones. My little great-grandbaby came home the other day. He says, "Tacaga." I said, "Well, we'll try and get you some." He meant, "I want some chicken." Then if I tell him that he's wrong when he says something wrong, he says, "That's the way Mrs. Hardy says

it." So that's kind of going full circle. They're teaching basketry, pottery, and then they have the Indian Village where they show how they lived about 200 years ago—higher education. *(Cherokee woman)*

And here in my last few years, they've revived it [the Cherokee language] trying to teach it in the schools. It's just like whenever I went to high school, I took French for two years. I might recognize a little bit, but when you don't use anything, it just gets away from you, see. That was one of the things culturally that set the Indian back. Of course, they were trying to advance the Indian up into the twentieth century because he has to make a living and compete just like anybody else. A lot of people think that the government gives the Indian a check every month. That's not so. They have to get out and work and punch a time clock and everything. And if they buy a car, they have to go out there and make whatever arrangements there are to pay for the car, and they have to buy the gas to put in it, and so forth. But I thought that was really one of the sad things about the language. I dare say that there are very few people who can write the language now. [The Cherokees are the only American Indians with their own written language. It was invented by a Cherokee named Sequoyah.] The old-timers are dying off. Like I tell people, each time they take somebody to the cemetery, they're taking a part of history with them, and that person knows something that nobody else knows. (Carl Lambert)

TRIBAL LAW

The reservation's made up of six communities, and the tribal council is the governing body of this reservation just like the city council is in the city or the Congress and Senate is of the United States. The people elect representatives at large. There have to be twelve, two from each community (township). As many can run as want to from a community, but the two highest vote getters win the election. Those two go in to be seated on the tribal council. Among themselves they elect the chairman of the council who acts as the chairman, or speaker of the house you might say, or the chairman of the city council. Then they elect the vice-chief. Some tribes call theirs chairman and vice-chairman, but we call ours chief, vice-chief, and the chairman of the council. Those people are elected at large for four-year terms and as many people can run again at large in all six communities. The chief runs at large and is elected by the whole community, just like the president does.

In all the communities, the council members run in their respective communities. Then that makes up the governing body.

We have a judicial system here, our own court system, or law and order system. But the tribal council makes the laws. The judicial system enforces it. And we have the executive branch, which consists of the chief, vice-chief, and chairman of the council. The only thing the tribal court can't do is handle land disputes and assign land, because by ancient law it is written in the charter of the tribe that the tribal council is the only body that can assign land. The tribal council handles all land disputes. The court system will not handle them now. They will handle if I buy some land from you and fail to pay for it. They will handle making me pay for it, but the assigning of land has to be done by the council. *(Dan McCoy)*

I was born in Cherokee, and I was the first child born in the old hospital, the first hospital they had here. My mother was a registered nurse, and she came back here when she married; and I was born here. I was a member of the tribal council from 1947 to 1949, the first woman to be elected to the council. I've maintained an interest over the years in tribal affairs. *(Mollie Blankenship)*

I remember this old lady saying, "Ah, it don't make no difference what you think, you're an Indian; you can't vote anyway." And I made up my mind then, when I got old enough to vote, I was going to register and vote. After we came back from Oklahoma, I went down to register after I was eligible, another Indian lady and I. And it just so happened that the regular registrar was gone and she'd given the books to this substitute. So we told her we'd come to register and she wanted to know if we could read and write, and we said yes. She said, "You don't pay taxes." And I said, "Yes indeed, we pay taxes." Well, we paid everything but ad valorem taxes. So she let us register. Of course, we came back and told everybody we'd registered. The next Saturday (which was the day they registered people) everybody went flocking down there. Well, the regular registrar was there, and she wouldn't let anybody register.
(Mollie Blankenship)

When World War II came along, most of the Indian men volunteered. Some of them were drafted, but most of them volunteered for the service. And when they came home, they went to register, and

191

they wouldn't let them register. At that time we were very fortunate. We got a Bureau of Indian Affairs superintendent in 1945 whose name was Joe Jennings. They had an American Legion Post here, so he got involved with them and they contacted Frank Parker, who was an attorney in Asheville. See, the American Legion took up this thing of people not being able to vote. Well, the county people agreed that they could have a monitor in the room with the registrar and when the people came in to be interviewed, they could take notes; so they selected me. And I went down, and I'd take the name of the person. I took shorthand, and I'd take just briefly what the trend of the conversation was. I believe they were supposed to be able to read the Constitution and understand the Constitution. And they weren't even reading the Constitution. They were reading different things, and I'd always make a note of what they were asked to read. And Frank Parker then took all these notes, and they had a few meetings. They contacted American Legion Posts all over the state, and they backed us. So then they decided that we could register and vote. *(Mollie Blankenship)*

In Cherokee they have twelve people on the council. They're all elected from their six different townships. They have two from each township and they serve two-year terms. They sit basically as a legislative body; they pass the laws, pass resolutions and ordinances. They are the legal body with the sole authority to assign land or transfer land between their members, to approve leases, and that sort of thing.

They also are responsible for running the government, to appropriate funds. The tribe has a sales tax that is the largest single source of local funds. They are responsible for administering all the local public services. The tribe has their own police force, their own fire department, their own water and sewer department, their own garbage collection. They don't receive any services like that from the local counties, the municipalities of the state. They have provided their own without state money. The council is basically the equivalent of a legislature because its members pass laws, but they're more analogous on a day-to-day basis to county commissioners. The people go to the council meetings and stand up on their own feet in front of their council and they speak their minds, particularly the Indian women. There is never any doubt where they stand.

The interesting thing about their political decisions is that they tend to be slower in reaching decisions, and they want to hear things two or three times. The way they operate is a long-standing tradition for them in which these controversial social decisions are made based on consensus. They talk among themselves and compromise or work out a consensus. Very often a problem will be resolved not just by confrontation and one side outvoting the other, but by bringing the opposition into line so that they at least accept the result. While that doesn't work one hundred percent of the time, that's a concept and goal that they still continue to work for, sometimes unconsciously. In the long run, it's a much more satisfactory arrangement than the political adversary system and the judicial adversary system where you have two sides butting heads, and one wins and one loses. They're not interested in winning and losing, in that sense. They try to resolve the problem satisfactorily. That's been right interesting for me to observe (as the tribal attorney) because I would never have seen that work anyplace else. After a while I started realizing what was going on, and I'm no longer frustrated or worried about it. I realize now that they will simply fall back and regroup, and somebody will try a different approach.

The biggest problem we've had in our mixed bag of legal and political problems with the state has been one of communication and understanding. People have their own perceptions and a limited amount of knowledge and information. Information is a big problem.

If they are off the reservation, if they live and work in the city, they're just like anybody else. The Indians have no legal distinction or protection. It's when they're living on land owned or held in trust by the government for the Indian tribe itself that these principles apply. *(Ben Bridgers)*

LIVING CONDITIONS

Clouds enshrouding mountains in the Blue Ridge near Cashiers

When I was growing up, it was just like today, but we had our Indian foods. We had our bean bread and our chestnut bread and sweet potato bread. We had hickory nut soup. They'd just crack the hickory nuts and then take the meat apart and beat it up in a mortar and roll it up in a ball and put it in the branch to keep it cool several days. Then just put it in a container and pour boiling water over it. It was good. You could drink it sweet or you could drink it just like it was. They don't make it anymore. You can't hardly find the hickory nuts to make that kind of soup.

I learned to weave when I came to work at the Oconaluftee Indian Village. I didn't do that as a girl. *(Mary Shell)*

Mary Shell sat with me around a fire in a reconstructed log house in the Oconaluftee Village. (The Cherokees never lived in tepees.) She told me about her growing up and shared various recipes for bean bread and chestnut bread, which I would soon be able to sample at the Cherokee Fair in October. She had some at home, though, if I had the time to stop by. Later on, I went to the festival and watched Indian buck dancing at nighttime and ate chestnut bread, which had been wrapped in corn blades for cooking. (W. M.)

In the spring the ramps come up. They look sort of like an onion. They're garlic multiplied a hundred times. I think the odor must come out through your pores for days afterwards. If you cook them, they're not as strong as they are if you eat them raw. If you eat them, if they're cooked, you can't tell it too much. Usually, I drink a glass of milk after I eat one. *(Mollie Blankenship)*

Anywhere you got, you walked; there were no roads. There was a boarding school; that's where I had to go. You couldn't go seven miles and walk every day. I knew I had to go to school; that's all I know. I don't have any feelings about it. I had to learn to speak English. It was another language. We had to make a living; it's an English-speaking country—the United States—so that's what I did. My name is Utsvdv [U-já-duh] Chiltoskey. If you translate that, it means Going Back Falling Flower. Chiltoskey, that means Falling Flower in my language. The English didn't see that. There's so many things corrupted, names around here, by English. They don't even know what they mean. You've heard of Dahlonega, Georgia. To Cherokee it means "yellow." That's where the gold was found by a little kid, you know. And that instigated the removal of the Cherokee Indians west, which was a tragic thing. *(G.B. "Goingback" Chiltoskey)*

Well, as I say, when I first came to the Bureau of Indian Affairs, there was just one telephone line that went into this office. And my mother's cows used to get out and I'd be sitting at my desk typing away, and of course, in a small community everybody knows everybody. And somebody'd come in and say, "Mollie, your mother's cows are out; they're down there in the clover." The clover fields and cornfields were where the elementary school and gym and playgrounds are now. And I'd run in and tell the superintendent, "My mother's cows are out; I've got to go put them up." And he'd say, "Okay, sign an hour's leave." And I'd sign leave and go hustling down there and chase the cows down the road (my mother lives about a mile from here), put the cows in the barn, and come back to

work. Now we don't have any cows within five miles of the agency. The school used to have a farm when they had a boarding school. They raised cattle, and they produced the beef and pork and milk products for the school.

When I was young, you know, people had to raise their food and they would have work days, like when it's time to hoe. Nowadays we have either a plow, tractor, or rototiller. But in those days there were whole families that just went around from place to place, and they would spend the day hoeing out your cornfield, and you'd cook a huge dinner for them. I can remember enjoying those so much because you had fresh green beans and new potatoes and other vegetables from the garden. If it took two or three days, they'd come every day until they got all the hoeing done, and then they'd go onto the next farm. And in those days they had this free labor. They still have remnants of it in the communities. And they'll go around and, for instance, if some family in their community needs firewood, they will have a work day and they'll cut firewood, and then if they need home repairs, they'll repair the home. But in those days, nobody had money and they had to help each other. Now it's different. *(Mollie Blankenship)*

No disrespect to our older people, but [we need to] get our tribal council and our administrative office up there—chief and vice-chief—to get our younger people involved and get young people thinking more and more openly as far as opportunity is concerned on how we're going to compete with nearby towns as far as industry is concerned. The tourist industry in Western North Carolina is very big. We're part of it here, but we need to learn how to get our part of it so we can benefit from it like everybody else does. We've got to have business-like people in these positions in our government in order to do this. Some of the older people—their thinking is traditional, but it might not be totally in the concept of business. It kind of holds us back, you see.

All the land right here is owned by Indians and all the buildings are owned by Indians. A lot of them are leased out. A lot of people criticize and say the Indians are not running their own business. That's true in a sense, but at the same time, if an Indian person has a building here, they can lease that out for $20,000 or $30,000 a year and not turn a hand. Why not let them do it? That's the reason a lot of them are leased out. *(Dan McCoy)*

Mr. Muskrat's the superintendent. He heads up the agency here. He's had some experiences with his name. Our chief was named Crow, and another officer was named Hummingbird. They went into this hotel in Washington and went up to the desk and said, "Do you have a reservation for a Muskrat, Hummingbird, and Crow?" And the desk clerk said, "What do you think this is, the city zoo?" Then when they called for a reservation for their return flight to Knoxville, and said they'd like to arrange for a flight for a Hummingbird, Crow, and Muskrat, the lady at United Airlines said, "Are they in cages?" (Mollie Blankenship)

I grew up in a house; never did have a dirt floor. It was a log house and had a good floor on it, but didn't have running water. I remember carrying water a lot of times from the spring. We carried water in a couple of aluminum buckets. Didn't have a bathroom, had to go to an outhouse. I remember in the wintertime it'd be cold, and we'd get up in the morning and fix breakfast and had to break the ice in the water bucket to get some water to drink and in order to cook with it. Of course, there's a lot of people who had to do that around here. I'm glad I grew up that way, and I don't regret it a bit. Sometimes I wish it was still that way.

I come from a family of twelve children. I was second from the oldest. We lost two brothers and a sister in an auto accident. We had to pick berries in

the summer, pickles, apples, anything we could put up for the winter. And whatever we put up during the summer, we ate that winter with what we had raised on the farm. We used potatoes a lot of times as bread. We did have a lot of cornmeal at different times because we raised corn, took it to the mill and had it ground. I remember as early as say '53 or '56 when we put our first electricity in our house. Even here on the reservation, I would say within a fifty-mile radius, a lot of families lived like that. *(Dan McCoy)*

Everybody was real poor, but we were all so poor that we were all in the same boat. I mean, if you had enough to eat, you were rich—and had a comfortable home. Years ago we didn't have any good roads in here. We just had wagon roads, and the basket makers used to walk over the mountain to Waynesville and walk to Sylva to sell their baskets on the street. *(Mollie Blankenship)*

I think it's a very good thing to educate the non-Indian people on how the Cherokee live. The minute you say "Indian" to somebody, they think of tepees. The Cherokee people never lived in tepees. They lived in log huts. We had cabins built out of logs and mud. They were very warm. *(Dan McCoy)*

When my generation came along, our parents thought they were doing us a favor by not teaching us Cherokee. Now I'm still struggling to learn to speak Cherokee.

I do believe in Indian medicine. A long time ago, if you had an Indian doctor, no other nurse or medical doctor would be allowed to come in the house. And my mother (a nurse) said that when she went to visit someone and she knocked, or if the door was closed and there was no sign of life around the place, she knew that they had gone to an Indian doctor, so she'd just leave. But nowadays, I understand that they'll go to a medical doctor and then go to the Indian doctor too.

They talk about "Skillies." Well, Indian people, certain people, they said, can change into other forms. I personally have no experience, but I love to hear these stories. This one woman had been away to normal school, which prepared you for the teaching profession in those days, and she graduated and came home. And they were having one of these work days with everybody out in the fields; and they cooked this big dinner and they had

Split-rail chestnut fence

boiled corn. So she said that her mother wouldn't let her go in the field. She said, "No, you're educated now; you can't go in the fields anymore." So she was helping them clean up the dishes and things, and this big pot of scalding water was on the iron cook stove. And of course, we didn't have plumbing in those days. So she just took it up and walked out to the porch and slung it down the hill. And she said just as she slung the water, she looked, and there was a hog there. It was strange, not one of theirs; and the water went on the hog, you know, the back, and in a few minutes a neighbor came flying over—a neighbor child—and said, "Come quick, something's happened to Grandpa." And they ran over there and said he was just really suffering from his hip down, looked like he'd been

scalded. So her family thought that it was a "Skillie" and that hog was him.

And owls. They think that they can change into owls. They'll tell stories about owls—or animals that will be hit, and then somebody will be sick and it'll look like they've been hit on that part of the body. And this one man, I guess not too many years ago, shot a neighbor. He swears that he looked over on the hill and saw a bear and he shot this bear, and when he called someone to help him—he was going to go over and butcher it—there was his neighbor man laying there, and he'd been shot. And, you know, they all said well, that was a "Skillie" and that man probably was in the form of a bear. Some really believe that.

I really don't know too much about Indian medicine except that it's just using plants and herbs. For instance, the yellow root is really very effective with sore throat. It's bitter as the dickens. And then there's some kind of tea. I know if you have a congested chest, respiratory system, if you drink that tea, it tastes horrible, but it sure will clean out your system and ease your breathing.

There's also a plant (jewelweed) that you can use for poison ivy, and it really works because I'm highly susceptible. When I've got poison ivy, if it's summertime, I'll find that plant and rub it on me, and it relieves it. Indian doctors traditionally are treated at birth or soon after birth, and they're just brought up in the ways of medicine, of Indian doctoring. But that's sort of dying out.

There's still "conjuring," you know. Sometimes they feel like somebody's "conjuring" on them and they have to go see a "conjure man" to get counteraction. They still do that today. *(Mollie Blankenship)*

My wife ran a gift shop down here years ago, and a man and his wife and daughter came by and wanted to know where Amoneeta Running Wolf lived. Amoneeta was the medicine man who lived up there where I was raised. Well, they had another man with them driving a brand new Jeep station wagon, and the man told my wife that Amoneeta saved his daughter's life. He said all the other doctors gave up on her, said she was just about dead. And, he said, over a period of time Amoneeta sent him that medicine, and, out of appreciation, he bought him a brand-new Jeep station wagon to give him. And Amoneeta drove that station wagon around here 'till he wore it out. And he used to make a circuit. He'd go over into Tennessee and he'd go around into South Carolina and around through Georgia. And he knew people to contact to tell people that he'd be at a certain place at a certain time. And people were always coming here looking for him. He just died here a couple of years or so ago. He evidently was good. *(Carl Lambert)*

I just picked up about medicines from my mother when I was a child coming up. And like the cough medicine; I've learned that. It's just got some herbs in it, two kinds of herbs, the rats bane and the mullin (rats bane or pipsqueak or what do you call it, lion's tongue). You get those two together. A person's got a real bad cough and can't stop coughing, you give him that and he'll stop coughing after the first cupful. You have to drink almost a cupful. It works. You know then that you can go to bed and sleep all night without coughing. If I see mullin on the side of the road, I'll just pull it because I might need it sometime. If I've got it dried, it'll serve the purpose. *(Rebecca Grant)*

I never have wanted to live anywhere else than on the reservation. I don't think I'd be pleased anywhere else. I love the mountains and I love the water. The water keeps me here. I've been places you couldn't drink the water it was so awful. The mountains are beautiful, and a lot of them are medicine. *(Mary Shell)*

PART FIVE

For a Purpose

Culture and Society

I FOUND MYSELF IN PLACES CALLED BAT CAVE, SLABTOWN, POSSUM HOLLOW, Reedy Patch, Snowbird, Possum Trot, Sodum Laurel, and Standing Indian. The road would curve and a sign pointing to Loafer's Glory, Aho, or Bear Wallow would appear. Many of these roads took me along for miles after the blacktop had ended. My notes are filled with directions to follow various dirt roads and make turns at certain land-marks, all "after the blacktop ends."

One day I called Edd and Nettie Presnell. They gave me directions to their home in a far-removed section of Watauga County. Edd makes dulcimers, and his wife, Nettie, is a wood worker. I had also wanted to visit Ray and Rosa Hicks (no relation to Letha Hicks). They didn't have a phone, but Edd and Nettie had said not to worry because they lived close by and could direct me. Stanley Hicks, a cousin of Ray, who lived in another remote part of Watauga County, had already called them to explain about my book and that I might be coming by for an interview. So they were pretty sure that Ray knew about me, too. As I drove along the back roads that eventually took me to the Presnells, the unpredictability of the landscape struck me. I looked out over rolling fields dotted with cows. Then the road would narrow, turning upward, taking me past an old, deserted house standing close to the road. Banks along the roadside were cov-ered with scattered patches of snow. The trunks of bare trees looked like stalks planted in a white sheath as they proceeded up the mountainside. With the lush foliage gone, the forest had a clearer and more open look to it. Views of deep coves and larger valleys would appear as the road moved closely along the hillsides. Mountain homesteads were set in along some of the ridges and some could be seen nestled in the hollows below. Trails of light-colored smoke curled up from the chimneys, giving out feelings of comfort and security. Each turn in the road led to something new.

As I sat by the wood-burning stove at Ray and Rosa Hicks' house later that day, the images I had seen earlier added reality to the folklore Ray was artfully conjuring up for me. Before I knew it, daylight had faded and darkness showed through the windows from outside. Smells of fresh-baked pumpkin pie were coming from the kitchen. I knew it was getting late but couldn't resist listening to just one more story. After declining their kind offer of dinner but enjoying a piece of that good pumpkin pie, I was ready to start back to my lodgings near Boone. I knew that I had at least an hour and a half's drive ahead over unfamiliar back roads. So I asked if I might use their bathroom before I left. Rosa led me outside to the outhouse with a flashlight. When I walked inside, I saw that it was a two-seater. (What a practical idea!) Rosa suggested that I leave the door open, as this would not be a good place to get shut in and nobody would be around to see. I'll never forget the view from the outhouse door. Here I was, sitting in an outhouse perched on the side of a mountain overlooking majestic outlines of dark ridges that spread out under a star-filled sky. This was one of the most beautiful sights I had ever seen, and without question the best restroom I've ever encountered.

In thinking about the visual surroundings in which Ray and Rosa lived, I understood how Ray had come to be such a wonderful storyteller. In considering the rugged conditions the mountain people have had to endure, it's easy to understand that most of their energy had to be spent keeping alive and scraping a living out of the land. Imaginations were put to use in trying to deal with the difficult terrain and harsh elements. So it is surprising to find such a large store of imagery in the native folklore because so little time was available for its development. Trips into the backwoods and remote ridges bring about an understanding of how this imagery naturally flowed into the folklore. These mountaineers love where they live. They like to take walks through the woods and to notice the changes that constantly occur in nature. Their entertainment had to involve practicality, but that didn't mean that imagination and fun had to be left out. Music and dance were carried on most often in relation to a gathering where work was done, such as a bean stringing or corn shucking.

Tales were told. Three types of storytelling stand out in the folk culture of this region. In "Jack Tales," Jack would always find himself in a fix of some sort, but he would perpetually manage to save himself in some miraculous way and move on to other adventures. "Grandfather Tales" were used to teach young children lessons; and ghost stories and "haint" tales added entertainment at community gatherings. All of these stories reflect the mystical qualities that are so much a part of these mountains and their forests. They are also characteristic of the humor and practicality of the people who live there.

Strong bonds grew up between neighbors and friends due to the outward isolation and lack of transportation. Because of the hardships, people had to get together and help one another out. Small towns developed in relation to the rural outlying areas. There still are not many very large towns. The poor, "fairly well-to-do's," and the "to-do's" have always been in existence. Many mountain people didn't really care about accumulating much wealth. They just wanted to get along where they were at the time. Neighbors still have to help each other, and they don't seem to mind. Many times I would stop and ask for directions at unfamiliar houses way out on back roads. People were always helpful and knew where neighbors miles away lived.

DAILY LIFE

Everything we did was for a purpose, you see. Very little time was wasted like it is now. You didn't take a day off to do anything, let's put it that way.
(**Frank Norris**)

My grandfather's home place was built in the 1800s, still stands, and they still use the same spring house for refrigeration of milk and food products that we had in the old days. The water runs twenty-four hours a day. It's good, cool, clear mountain water that I think has the best taste of any water anywhere. In those days, life was considerably slower than it is now; and people had the time to go visit other people, oftentimes to spend the night, especially on Sunday to go and spend the day and travel many miles in order to get there, considering the distance at that time and the mode of travel. Most times we walked or either we had a horse and wagon that we often went in if we were going to someone's house. In the fall of the year it was quite common to have corn shuckings at various people's farms, and people swapped labor back and forth. *(Charles Michael)*

I was coming across that little ol' bridge. It was a couple of logs and then some little ol' planks.

Granny Reed's measuring cup

Anyway, I was coming across there, and we had aluminum buckets and I had both of them full of water and I fell. One hand went on one side and one on the other, and there I was on the bridge holding onto them buckets. I didn't want them to wash away.

And then, another time, I used to pick a lot of blackberries when Grady was gone. I'd pick the blackberries and bring them in, and I'd have to carry water to wash them. This day I'd picked two big buckets of blackberries, and I came in and I was tired. I kicked my shoes off and started toward the spring to get some water, and there was a big ol' beech tree and it made it dark and shady there. I got to that little ol' bridge, and guess what stood up in front of me? A snake. I'd heard of a snake standing on their tails, but that's the first time I've ever seen one. And it stood up that high, a rattlesnake. Ooh! What did I do? I came to the house and told Mrs. Reed what had happened, and she went with me out there and we took a hoe. I was afraid to hit it, and I wouldn't use the hoe; and she stood there and watched it. I went down this way to a neighbor's house. He went on up the road and got a man to come down here with a shotgun, and he killed it. And it stayed there all the time, the snake did. Never moved. *(Delia Reed)*

When I was staying with Mrs. Bryson, she stepped on a snake one time on a footlog going across a creek; stepped on a copperhead and it was laying right on the edge of the footlog, a huge log that had boards on it. And she was a little short woman and wore those black shoes; everybody wore the same thing. She stepped on that snake's head and she stood on that thing until they brought something to cut its head off. It wrapped around her leg, but she still stood there on its head. *(Jimmy Moss)*

They'd pile quilts on you, so many quilts on you that you'd wake up tired in the mornings. Tryin' to keep warm. *(Annie Dee Leatherman Smith)*

Well, I was down at the store one time and Mr. Stoner asked me, he says, "What does Bob do in the wintertime when it's cold?" I said, "Well, one thing he does is he reads his Bible"; and as for me, "I piece quilts." I says, "I piece quilts." And that's what the old people used to do. The women would card the wool and spin the thread and weave their clothing. Set the weave and keep the cradle in there. We've got the one that Bob slept in when he was a tiny baby. So in the wintertime that's what we did, made quilts and molasses candy and had candy pullings and bean shellings; gather up the beans. We'd have bean shellings and pea shellings mostly in the fall. But in the wintertime about all you would do was to keep warm. *(Myrtle Merrell)*

The house was L-shaped and you'd go across the porch, of course, the porch was covered. And you'd go across the porch and then over on the kitchen side, there would be a long wash bench. It would just be a shelf that would have two or three buckets of water setting on there, the washpans and everything, and soap; and you would wash there. And a lot of times you'd have a towel hung up on a nail or on a peg there on the wall. And the towel really wasn't a towel. It was a feed sack; it wasn't a terry cloth. See, all these old feed sacks, they kept them all and they laundered them out; they were soft and good. They made a good cloth. But they made socks and they spun wool and they had a spinning wheel and they used it. They did a lot of darning and made some cloth—had a loom. They lived in the ol' timey way. They were self-sufficient. *(Jimmy Moss)*

We had a wood stove in the center of the house, and you'd hang them up behind that little round-bellied stove and dry the diapers out. And when you got up of a morning, it was freezing cold in the whole house. That was the only room that was heated, so you ran in there naked, carrying your pants and held them up beside the stove 'til it got warm, and then you put them on. And that's the way you dressed every morning—you grabbed your clothes and ran to the heat. We didn't have but two rooms. My maw and the two girls slept in one room, and then the boys (we had two beds, one

single and a double bed), six of us slept in the bed, three at the foot and three at the top. Of course, in the summertime we didn't sleep like that because we slept outside or on the porch or anywhere. You couldn't sleep six people in a bed during the summer, but in the winter it was great—pile on top of each other. *(Mike White)*

You saw lots of woolen clothing, winter and summer. It was invariably black and dark. That was on the men. The women almost all wore long skirts, not to the ground but certainly to the ankle. They wore bonnets, ol' poke bonnets. I guess they had kind of a full back and came around and had a little brim. Now I'm not talking about hats; these are bonnets. *(Jim Ryan)*

We didn't have shoes 'til Christmas and it was getting too cold—unless they were left over from the year before, and usually from one year to the next your feet are too big to put in the shoes. But my dad did cobbler work, and he helped make shoes, and he had all the old-fashioned tools to work with. And they tanned their own cowhides and saved them to make leather for shoes. And our shoestrings also were cut out of the cowhide. You couldn't buy shoestrings like you do now.
(Harriet "Granny" Echols)

I was a right smart little chicken, big enough to milk, when I got my first shoes. Remember where they come from and remember what they was. Right around the toe here, you had a copper toe, and you got one pair a year, and they called them copper toes. They had copper around there to keep it from wearing out. I took care of them.
(Willard Watson)

**Homestead at the foot of Mount Jefferson
near West Jefferson, Ashe County**

SCHOOL DAYS

Independence, integrity, the willingness to work, and the ambition to improve their lot in life are characteristics. I think a lot of those mountain people have a lot of ambition. They had to have, to escape the hardships of life back in the early days, to try to improve their lot in the world. I think that is the reason so many of them really strived to get an education. They realized that in order to improve, they had to have an education. A lot of those boys and girls wanted it. *(Dan Moore)*

The first commoners were educated, and they kept the tradition of education alive. They did not believe in slavery. They did not own slaves. When the Civil War came, the schools closed. Many of them never opened again. There were communities in which it would have been dangerous to have had a school.

Since these people were educated, it looks as if they would have educated their own children. Some did; most did not. Even though the old trunks in the attic with horsehair on them had the Greek and Latin classics in them with the names of the ancestors inscribed on the flyleaf, nobody could teach in general after 1861 because the spirit of the community was killed. What was the need for education in the first place?

In the second place, we didn't have a hard nickel with which to subscribe to a piece of reading matter. We were so poor, we traded by barter. For some twenty years after the Civil War, every nimble finger in the family had to be busy being engaged in growing, working pelts for leather and spinning. The housewives made all the cloth, did all the sewing and all of the weaving. The husbands hunted, and they tanned groundhog skins and squirrel skins, anything they could get, for a little piece of something that could be useful. They even sawed up the horn to make spoons of because they couldn't get hard coin together to buy pure spoons or whatever. It's hard to realize that poverty. Now

you had some children who were educable, who were at the right age, and Grandpa who could teach them. But, bless your soul, you couldn't spare those children away from the work that had to be done if you were going to hold body and soul together. *(Cratis Williams)*

We had a school just a little ways from the house, down this way. And it was an old two-room school. We had old log-slatted benches; we sat on them. We had a little slate to write on. We didn't have a desk at that time. And the one teacher sat over there; he had a little desk, and he had his teacher's aides sitting in the corner. Every schoolteacher has got an aide now. You know what his aide was, don't you? A hickory stick. And don't you believe that he wouldn't use it! We had old outside toilets; we had one for the boys and one for the girls. You would carry a lunch. Maybe some of them had a basket; some of them had a four-pound lard pail. Some of them had cornbread with milk, cornbread crumbled up in it; and each one had a spoon. Maybe they had a sweet potato pie or a biscuit with maybe a piece of ham. And they all sat down and ate together. And in the spring of the year, when the corn came in, roasting ears, why, they'd all bring that; and by the time the fall of the year was over, you couldn't walk for the corncobs out in the yard. And we had an old water cooler. I guess it held about five gallons, with a little spigot on it. And we carried the water in two ten-quart buckets, I guess a good quarter of a mile. You've seen those little cups that slide up, fold up. You had your own drinking cup, and that's where you got your water. You drank it while it was fresh. By the time you carried it back up there, it certainly wasn't cold.

We had a wood-burning stove that sat right in the middle with a big, long pipe going up. And we had an hour's recess. When I finished school up there, that was a six months' [elementary] school. I had to walk about two miles, and the school bus came and picked us up there. And you walked down there, and they wouldn't have any place to get in out of the rain. If it was raining when you left home, you very seldom had a raincoat. If you got wet, you stood there and caught that bus. You stayed wet all day when you went to high school. That bus only ran six months a year, and [high] school was nine months; then it was get down there the best way you could.

The bus had ol' straight-slatted seats on each side, two big seats down the side here, and it was slatted, and you sat on each side. Then it ran up there and it came to the creek, the first branch up there; it was a mile and a half to the schoolhouse and about another half a mile to my house. But why it came there and stopped, I never will know. It didn't cross that creek. And we had to walk down there and catch it. And then we had to walk back in the evening in rain and mud. There weren't any paved roads up there. You just walked in the mud, and it would take you a half-hour to clean your shoes off. *(Quay Smathers)*

[The length of school often varied in different mountain communities according to local funding capabilities. Families often paid to send their children to additional schools or sessions of school to supplement their education.]

I walked from here to the highway, three miles from here to there. And then after I caught the school bus, it was just a muddy road. We'd go in the wintertime 200 or 300 feet; everybody'd have to get out and push; go on a little further, and we'd have to get out sometimes three or four times between here and Webster and push. We'd be stalled, but there's enough people on it to keep it going. It was slinging the mud, sling mud all over you. We'd get there in time to come back. *(Grady Reed)*

It was a big wagon, a two-horse job that was covered. I guess the cover on it was about fourteen feet. Cloth top. And you'd all keep warm with a brick. They had a pile of straw in the wagon bed, and that big heated rock in there for the children to keep warm. It was in the twenties. But now that was the school bus, the first one we rode, a horse and wagon. Walking to school, that road was just filled with little bitty rock, you know. Then, if you got one pair of shoes, you were doing well, when we was growin' up, young like that. It'd be a frost on it in the morning, and you'd be a runnin' down that road barefooted, hittin' them rocks and them feet cold. You'd hop down and get them [feet] up in your hands and warm them a little, and get up and go again. Then when we got down, the sun would be a–shinin' and it'd warm up. That was late in the fall. *(John Cooper)*

You got to school the best way you could, and usually it was by walking. I remember some of the boys bringing their horse and tying their horse in the tree outside the school. They always had to bring their lunch with them. They didn't have cafeterias and food service at that time. The boys that lived way back in the county, they had the biggest biscuits. I can still remember those biscuits with ham or sausage or something like that. The ones that lived in town had sandwiches and would swap it for one of those big biscuits. Nobody was hungry though. I don't remember anybody that was really what you call destitute. Their children were warm usually. They all had clothes good enough to keep the elements out, and most of them had enough to eat. It wasn't the very finest in diet, but they made out.

And, of course, at that time they had a county home. People that didn't have anything, that couldn't work, were sick, or old, moved to the county home; and they took care of them. There wasn't any welfare, but they did take care of those who couldn't take care of themselves. *(Dan Moore)*

For their lunch, they had what they call the half-a-gallon syrup bucket. And they'd save those buckets, had lids, and for their dinner they'd bring sweet milk and bread in that bucket and a spoon and eat their dinner. *(Pearl Marshall)*

School children, Jackson County

My school was on an island in the middle of the French Broad River (Blanner Hasset Island). It is the only school in America which is on an uninhabited island. The bridge goes across on the other upper side, upstream of the island. The school always had a teacher who guarded the entrance where you would go in and out. I had a boat, and when we would take the boat in with us, we could escape from this school. *(Landon Roberts)*

These children who came in on a bus got up at six o'clock to ride the bus in, and they got home in the afternoon about that time. They left in darkness and arrived in darkness, and they had the barn chores to do and house chores to do, and when they got through with that, then they'd eat. When they got through with that, they'd have a half-hour for their books, in those days around coal-oil lamps. Because of the way houses were heated, there'd be one room that'd be warm and they'd be around a little table in there with the whole family. The situation for study was just impossible, so many of them didn't study. *(Cratis Williams)*

It always bothered me to go back to school in the fall, and the teacher would say, "Well, did you have a good vacation?" I'd worked as hard as I could work all summer, and they called it a vacation. I mean we went to the field with a hoe when we was seventeen years and worked all day. Everybody had to work, you didn't eat if you didn't work. *(Jonah Parker)*

If you got a whipping at school, you'd get a whipping at home. Nowdays, the parents want to whip the teacher. So, I've seen that change. We stayed home to work occasionally during peak harvest time or planting time in the spring. A lot of times we'd stay out to help put the crops in, but to play hooky, we didn't do that. *(Charles Michael)*

There was six of us in my family in that little one-teacher school. The teacher taught all the way from the first grade through the seventh in that one room. She'd work with those of us that were small, and then she'd have the older students to take a group of us off in a corner and work with us. They helped her and worked back and forth. Had an old big cast-iron stove right in the middle of the building, and we'd have some fun sometimes getting out. They'd let us get out and cut wood, and we'd be glad to get out of school just to cut wood. We considered it a privilege to get out of school to cut wood for the stove. I never went to any teacher except my sisters until I was in the seventh grade. When I was five and a half, my older sister let me come. She was the oldest one, and then she got married to a doctor in Elkin. Then the next sister taught two or three years. Then another sister finished at Meredith College. And when she finished at Meredith, she came and taught a year or so. After that, Miss Pearl Hartley was our teacher from then on. *(Wade Brown)*

So many were farm children. We had to work on the farm, and school was from eight until four then. They were long days, but we had less months [in school]. I would say six or seven months, maybe, because it was late in the fall of the year and, of course, spring planting and all. But we didn't know anything about snow days like we have now. If we went, we went. We knew that school was going to be there if there wasn't but a half a dozen students. There wasn't anything to do except just to put on plenty of good warm clothes and hightail it into Boone. *(Lottie Greene)*

You'd go and stay 'til twelve and that'd count that you weren't absent, and then they'd let you go home and help work. Or you could work 'til twelve and go in at twelve. That's where it's bad now where you've got the school buses, you miss that bus five minutes, you just as well have missed the whole day. It's too far to walk. Back then you walked. If you got there two minutes late, that was all right. You were at school. *(Edd Presnell)*

My mother was a schoolteacher. We lived in a large one-room building. It was just a one-room building that had a small partition between the middle of it.

We lived in half of that building, and Mother taught grades one through eight in the other half of that building. A lot of the children after that went to Valle Crucis. They rode the bus off to the elementary school there. But initially, my mother taught all the children in that area grades one through eight; and many of those, surprisingly, have gone on and become very successful in their own right. Some have become attorneys. I think there is one doctor out of the crowd. Several of them have done quite well in academic pursuits since that time. So the open classroom that we know today—third and fourth and fifth grades together—is nothing new. It has a carry-over value of students helping other students in learning other things at the same time. *(Charles Michael)*

The first school I went to had seven grades and one teacher. When I was in the first grade, I think I learned more that year than in any other grade. Sitting there listening to the older students recite, and their history, and their geography and their arithmetic and all. I had one of these memories that I remember what I heard better than what I had read. I think that kind of school is a good idea myself. **(Piercy Carter)**

I learned to write some and to read fairly well before I ever went to school because there wasn't any school there close and, of course, they [my parents] wanted us to work. They didn't want us to go to school anyhow; they said it was too far. It was about four miles right down the mountain; I guess it was about 2,000 feet down the mountain, so they said it was too far; but it wasn't too far nor hard nor anything to go out there nearly naked and it nearly freezing and the wind blowing and gather this stuff. From two years on up, I guess, I was working in fern, barely could walk, barely could stand up by a bed that wasn't this high and sort this fern out, and I couldn't count at all, even to five. Then I learned to count to five, and five five's made twenty-five, and I'd put those bunches of fern together then. Get five out here and five there, and then I put the five together, and I knew that made twenty-five. And then forty of those bunches made a thousand. Just to think of how many twenty-fives it takes to make a thousand, I didn't know that for a time. But I did know forty bunches made a thousand. Forty times twenty-five made a thousand.

When I was about fourteen, I went to school, the first day I'd been to school. I had learned to read off tobacco cans and Roebuck catalogs and the almanac; and I'd learned to write my name, and even I could write a letter to somebody that they could read. I learned that, then I went to school. So I peeled some cherry bark, I believe it was, and bought—you had to buy your schoolbooks—and I bought what they called a First Reader. It cost about a quarter, and I took that down the mountain to school; and me and my younger brother started at the same time. And I went two months down there, and I read that book through several times. And already, before I went to school, I could read it by heart without ever looking at it. So then I went to school 'til I was about sixteen, seventeen. I sort of went through fifth grade, I guess.

One of the Presnell boys there, one of my cousins, had got out of the reach of the teacher, and he couldn't teach him any further, so they had a school right over the hill out here for boys, a boys' school. Preacher Mack, we'd call him; he ran the school. He was a Presbyterian preacher. And so this boy had come up here, and so I decided I would come with him and go to the school just sort of to be doing it. Got up some quilts; we had to bring our quilts. So we got a load of quilts, and I came with him. It took all day to walk from Beech Mountain over here, and we waded mud up this road; from there to Crucis up and even down the Valle Mountain. I didn't like it a bit. They had old books that were out-of-date. He had a library of old books that were probably back in the 1800s, and so we had to use those books. I didn't like them; there

were some small boys there that were sort of in my class, but they were studying these old books and I didn't have my books, so I couldn't get much out of it. So I waited; I stayed two weeks. Then they got off [for vacation], so I could go back [home]. I didn't come back to school; I didn't go to school anymore. *(Raymond Presnell)*

I maybe was in about the second or third grade. You know what we got for making 100 in our spelling lesson? We got to go down the road and throw rocks out of the road so people could travel it.
(Modeen Bradley)

They used the school for church. On Sunday we went to church and on Saturday morning once a month. Then on through the week we went to school in that house. We did that for several years until I was a pretty big girl. *(Carrie Burnette)*

I went to school about three weeks up here on Cold Springs. They sent me up there, and I stayed three weeks and went to school; and that was it. I went another place to go to school; went three days; stayed about three months. My sisters didn't make me go. So I didn't know P from B when I quit school. I just learned on my own. I got a bunch of old magazines. After they built these tunnels through the mountains, people gave us a bunch of magazines, *True Stories;* and I got to looking at those pictures, and studying those pictures, and I'd like to know what they were doing. And it'd take me a day to read one little page and then didn't know half what it said. Then a woman came from Kalamazoo, Michigan, and she taught me how to write my ABC's together, in writing. Wish I had gone to school now. I do. A lot of letters, I don't understand what they mean. I get somebody a lot of times to read them, to get the understanding out of them. You know, highfalutin' have got different words than what I've got. *(Letha Hicks)*

When I got through school, they wanted me to work some for social services, so I started working with them. I went down into a little area called Canada, which is down below Cullowhee near Tuckasegee. There were some families down there that had some children that had not been going to school. And they had sent a couple of people from social services down there to talk to them, and they had met them at the gate with guns. And they couldn't understand, you know. Why wouldn't he send his children to school? The girl was thirteen years old. Her mother had three other children who weren't in school. Her job was at home. It was not going to do her any good to go to school, you know. Of course, now, it's bad that the man makes the decision for his daughter, but his parents had made the decision for him. *(Mike White)*

The first library that ever came in this country wasn't as big as that bookcase. It had doors, and they had a lock on that door. You had to go and sign your name and get a book out. We were amazed and pleased to death to get those books. And we read and read. It was what they called a traveling thing. It circulated all the time.
(Carrie Burnette)

There wasn't any books hardly. You couldn't hardly get books. But we learned to read. Papa got little books for us to read. We couldn't get books at Wilkesboro; he'd go to Statesville every once in a while. He'd go down there and come back with a whole stack of little books. We were so glad to get them. *(Mamie Hall)*

My father would have us all together and talk to us before we started to school. He'd say, "Now school opens this morning. You get ready and go to school and behave yourselves. If any of you get a whipping, you'll get another one when you get home. And don't let me hear anything that you've been into. If you do, you'll answer to me." Now, we have a lot of people—not all of them—but if their child is corrected, and my goodness if, they get a switching, there's trouble. *(Hattie Oates)*

MacArthur Shelton, in the first grade at Marshall, had gone to school drunk. Well, I think he had taken something with him, too. He took a pint with him and got drunk at school. They spanked him and sent him home. Told him when he got sober they were going to spank him again.
(Jean Roberts)

I went to Lees-McRae. It was an elementary school at that time. I went over there to school when I was ten years old, and I stayed there about four years. I lived over there. We stayed in a dorm. It was a boarding school from ten to fifteen. They used to have school over there in the summertime. We were out in the winter on account of the building. There wasn't sufficient heat for a dorm to keep children in. So we started school in April and got out in November. I graduated from high school at Lees-McRae. It's a college now, you know.
(Florence Wilson)

The Presbyterians started a school for the mountain children at Banner Elk. I had two years there, and my sister had two years there. That was Lees-McRae. At that time it was just girls. You'd get up early in the morning, and somebody would take a wagon. You and the girls and their trunks, and we'd go all the way to Banner Elk. You'd get to come home two weeks for Thanksgiving. When it got real cold in the winter, usually they'd shut down, and you'd come home. But that was one of the first schools for any advanced school. We fared pretty rough. They had gardens and they had apples and things that grew on the place. Sometimes we didn't have too much to eat. Sometimes you'd just have a sandwich or something. But it was a good school. The teachers were very dedicated. We really got a good solid start to education. Work your way through. We did anything that we could do around the farm. We took rounds making bread. We had a laundry, and we took turns in that. All we had was one teacher that taught the cooking. We did the waiting on tables. That was part of our tuition.
(Carrie Burnette)

We had a high school in Webster. For instance, we had four years of Latin, four years of math, four years of English, and four years of history. We didn't have any of these extracurricular activities. It was reading, writing, and arithmetic, and was a good school. I graduated from that little school with I think about fifteen or twenty others. When I graduated and made Phi Beta Kappa from Chapel Hill, I was as well prepared as anybody.
(Dan Moore)

The YCI (Yancey Collegiate Institute) was the Baptist school. It was quite large. They had dormitories and they had students here from all over; they came from South Carolina, Georgia, Tennessee, Virginia. They had a very strong faculty. Graduates from either one of our local schools (YCI or Stanley McCormick, the Presbyterian school) were so far superior to some of the college graduates today because they had a very high standard and a very hard curriculum. For instance, four years of Latin and all the math. And, of course, we had excellent music teachers. I took music from the time I was five years old. I started taking piano before I ever started to school, and I studied piano and violin all the time I was a child. *(Rush Wray)*

———————

The Rabun Gap Nacoochee School was established to provide a good education for hardworking mountain families who would not otherwise have had the opportunity for a quality education that extended through the twelfth grade. The school was run like a tenant farm. The families raised crops to provide food, ran the dairy and cannery, and tended to the general needs of the school community. (W.M.)

———————

When we moved to Rabun Gap there was about fifteen farms, fifteen or twenty, I think. They would let families that had children come. They preferred families that had several children. There were seven of us, and they liked to have at least four children

in a family before they would accept them to move there. The primary purpose was for the educational part. They would screen them, come and visit. Dr. Ritchie was the president of it then, but he came to our house. I'll never forget it. We were picking cotton, and he talked to us maybe two hours or longer and said, "Well, I'll let you all know if you're accepted or not." It was in '38. In about a week he came back and told us that we could move.

The DAR [Daughters of the American Revolution] built three houses there at the school, and two new families moved in, and then they gave us one of them. It'd never been lived in. We had never had a new home. We were in hog heaven. We lived there eight years. They had a policy that a family could only stay five years and then they would let them stay the sixth year if they were good tenants and cooperated and everything. You had to cooperate with the school and had to do a lot of things they asked you to do. They expected you to go to all their meetings, and they expected all the children to be in all the classes and participate in the activities. But anyway, when we got our sixth year in, they told us we could stay a while longer, and that way I finished one year of college there. It was a junior college. They had boarding students there and community students. It was during the war and they couldn't get students. They couldn't get qualified teachers, and they had to just dissolve the junior college part of it. I transferred from there to Berea, Kentucky.

Rabun Gap's still a boarding school, but they have from the eighth grade on up through seniors, I think. It's growing. They have a new president. He says he wants to revise it and put back into practice some of the old things that they did years ago. But they just don't have the manpower to do it with. You can't take an eighth grader out and let him farm.

When I started into school, it was just a little two-room schoolhouse with one teacher. She would teach on one side awhile and give us homework; then she'd go to the other side and give them homework. It was hard going to school. In bad weather, pouring-down rain and cold and sleet, we didn't go. And that's one reason why I say, if we had not moved to Rabun Gap where we could go regular, I probably never would have gone even through high school, unless we had moved closer to a school. Daddy wanted us all to have a good education. That was one thing, he didn't care how we had to get it, we all had to finish high school after we moved to Rabun Gap. He was concerned about our welfare. *(Ruth Cabe)*

The Appalachian Training School [which is now Appalachian State University, part of the University of North Carolina system] has gotten to be one of the great universities of the state now. I remember when it was started as a sort of a private high school by Blan Dougherty and his brother, D.D. Dougherty. Blanford Dougherty was one of the most unusual men I ever knew. He was the educator, and his brother stirred up the money to finance it. He was pretty shrewd. I know he came down to the legislature one time. He'd come down there, and they'd give him everything he asked for; well, he didn't ask for much. I remember he told them, "Don't consolidate your schools because, if you do, the government can sue just one bunch of people. Just make them sue everything." *(Sam Ervin)*

Blan Dougherty organized or established this school in 1899, and he was president of it until 1954 (Appalachian State University). At one time people didn't think there was any necessity for an education. Then they got to the point where a boy and girl that had some ambition had to go away from there to get an education. That's the basis for this college; that's why it was established. Dr. Dougherty's philosophy was that he wanted every boy or girl that was willing or wanted an education to be able to get it. And this school was largely made up of boys and girls from around in the county and area. *(Wade Brown)*

I taught school. The way I got started teaching, we had two teachers. This lady teacher taught the primary grades, and the man taught the upper grade.

Her mother got sick two weeks before school was out that spring, and she had to go up and take care of her mother. I was in the sixth grade, and she asked me to take over her room and complete the two weeks. She paid me fifteen dollars for two weeks. Can you imagine that! She didn't get but about thirty dollars a month. I was teaching just one room, and I had all grades. I had a wonderful bunch of children. I was supposed to teach from the very beginning through the seventh grade. But I had students in the seventh grade larger than me, boys especially, and they wouldn't come. They quit. They were just larger than I was, and they didn't want to go to school, and they dropped out. *(Pearl Marshall)*

A lot of them did; some of them didn't care. Many parents didn't have any education themselves, and they believed in moon signs and these old-fashioned signs and magic. But most of them were eager for their children to learn. They wanted them to learn. Some didn't. Some families would keep the children out all day just to go to the store and get a cake of soap and do the family wash. Then some stayed out to dig roots, pull herbs, such as that. But the majority of the families wanted the children to go to school and they sent them.

I taught in a one-room schoolhouse for years. All the pupils were in the same room and they sat on benches. We didn't even have desks. They were divided into seven classes. The first one was the ABC class, then the primer came next, then the first reader [these were all part of the first grade]. Then came the second reader, third grade, fourth, fifth, sixth, and seventh grade. *(Horton Cooper)*

That was in '49 when I went to Canada Township. It was fine teaching school in Little Canada. I had a lot of people tell me they'd run me out of there. I never had people as good to me in all my life. I got thirty dollars a month. I paid eight dollars a month board. It was the best job a woman could get. Well, the men only got twenty dollars a month. *(Carma Reed)*

We had quite an educator in this county, Logan Patton, who came up right after the Civil War. He lived up there near Table Rock. He had an ambition to teach the young people, and he didn't see much opportunity to get an education in those days. And one night his father sent him out to the woodpile to get some firewood to keep an open fire going. And he started out to the woodpile. He had about fifteen cents in his pocket, and he decided he'd just go on and get his education. So instead of carrying the wood in, he walked fifteen miles down to the railroad here and got a train and went over to Tennessee. And he worked his way over as he went along. He went to Tennessee, and he finally got to Illinois and graduated. He stopped and worked there and went to school and graduated high school there. Then he went on to Exeter Academy, and worked his way through it. Then he went to Amherst College in Massachusetts, and graduated about eleven years after he left home. Then he came back home and as he passed the woodpile, he got up an armful of stove wood. He carried it in the house and said to his father, "Here's the firewood you sent me for eleven years ago." He had a son who was our county superintendent for about fifty years. His son had an expression I loved. He said, "Life is a grindstone. Whether it grinds you down or polishes you up depends on what kind of stuff you're made of."
(Sam Ervin)

I used to teach in a one-room school. I taught nine years. Well, there wasn't very many in each class. I had each one doing their own little thing and you just went from one class to another. We managed to get through somehow. Of course, when I first taught in that one-room school, I'd just finished high school. But after that, I went to Appalachian and got my teaching certificate. Then I taught school in a two-room school first, two rooms and two teachers. Then they used the picture method of teaching to read, you know. I used a picture method and sounds and phonics, but I didn't use the ABC method of teaching them to spell the word before they pronounced it because that's too slow. *(Lula Wise)*

It's enough to kill the little ol' younguns. It just pulls every bit of their strength going to school so long. Putting them in kindergarten; go from there plumb on through all of it. They have school all the time and keep the younguns' brains mixed up 'til they couldn't keep nothin' in their minds. I told teachers right up here, I said, "Now I'm going to tell you, as long as school goes, and grab up these little babies and put them in kindergarten and push and rush them early in the morning getting them there, stayin' tired; then it's just the same thing over and over, and that many years of school." I said, "It's too much." I said, "A child don't have time to get out and get something else in his mind." *(Nanny Suttles)*

There's been a greater improvement, I think, in the educational system in the last fifty years than anything that I've seen go on in Avery County in the last fifty years. They went from the one-room school to the consolidated schools. We have a consolidated elementary school, and we have a consolidated high school now, and they have a lot of opportunities that people didn't used to have. *(Lula Wise)*

CHURCH MEETINGS

We'd have to go to church every Sunday in that wagon. If there was preaching going on or revival, we went in that wagon on Sunday night and all during the week. My daddy was awful bad to talk, and back at that time the preachers thought nothing about quitting at twelve o'clock. He'd just preach 'til he gave out, and that was about twelve-thirty or one o'clock. As long as anybody'd stand and talk with him, he'd stand and talk. So I generally got my dinner about two o'clock on Sunday. I wore old button-up shoes. I remember my mother buttoning them. I don't know whether you ever saw one or not, but the hook went in and went through the eye and caught the button, pinching the top of my foot, buttoning my little ol' tight shoes to go to church. So I think maybe I kind of got disgusted a little bit with all of that. I don't go as much as I ought to. I feel like I went enough. Had to go out there and ride an ol' wagon back, sitting in a chair, getting in around midnight every night.
(Quay Smathers)

Johns Creek Methodist Church, Caney Fork, Jackson County

families that came to that church. And it wasn't long 'til you knew every one of them. That's back when they rode a horse. They'd preach at one church one Sunday [and another the next]. There weren't many preachers. They had a full-time preacher at Burnsville, but I don't know of another full-time preacher when I was a boy in Yancey County. They had a full-time preacher here at Spruce Pine and maybe at Bakersville. *(B. Hensley)*

We would do the usual things on Sunday morning like you do on the farm seven days a week. Then we would sit out on my daddy's front porch, and sometimes we would wait for the Perkinses to come along to ride to church in their surrey or we might walk; and I can remember my daddy carrying my youngest brother, he was too small to walk. That is just something, you know, that I grew up with. Of course, we had church services once a month, usually on Saturday. Our pastor would come, maybe from the western part of the county or maybe out of Wilkes County on horseback; and my daddy

I was fortunate to travel with my daddy when they built the churches because he was pastor at Booneford, Silver Chapel, Cane River, Riverside, Halls Chapel, Celo, and then he'd go to different churches in Crabtree. What churches he didn't pastor in Yancey County, they'd hold revivals. So it was a family. See, you go to a church like Booneford, well, there'd not be twelve or fifteen or thirty worked on Saturday just like he worked the other six days, you know—the other five days. And along about four or four-thirty, the pastor come to spend the night. The house was on a little down. It's not a field, but there's a big gate at the curve of the road where the vehicles were. The pastor visited Saturday night wherever he was invited, but, you know, they took time about doing it. It was a very common occurrence. Even after me and Bynum were married, they just had church at Three Forks once a month.

A few had buggies and if they were living quite a distance out, they would come to church in a wagon. But it was just a little bit too near to take the wagon, so we usually just walked or would wait and ride in the surrey with the fringe on top. Old Three Forks Church was one great big church.

There was a spring in the rear of the churchyard and they had cut off a tree, you know, and cut it down kind of like a little step, and the ladies would step up on that tree trunk. It'd be about that high, you know, to get on a horse. But back then, you know, they rode sidesaddle, and we had quite a few ladies that rode horses to Three Forks Church. *(Lottie Greene)*

At revivals they would have singing and preaching and praying, and they'd gather around the altar. We had an altar in the church and would gather around the altar. Lots of people would get saved and receive the Lord into their hearts, and they lived all their life from then until they passed away. *(Lillian Hooper)*

Back when I was a boy, at revival time this church had two services a day for a week. Everybody dropped everything. A lot of the people who had moved away, it was really a homecoming week for them. It was really a great time, and it got where people was so busy they didn't have a lot at church during the day and then at night. They eventually dropped it. They had services all at night. People were working other jobs. But religion has lost a lot with the times, you know, and not having time, things like that. When they first started having

night meetings, this didn't go when they had day meetings. There wasn't many things going on in the community, you know, work and that sort of thing, and everybody goes to the big meeting, regardless of who he was, what he done. If he wasn't interested in religion, he'd go just to be there and meet the family outside. Sometime you had to go out and calm them down, they were getting too loud, or occasionally the law would come out and calm things down. One particular bootlegger, they say, used to make his special brandy for the revival. There would be fights and stuff, but they came. Some would come inside, and their lives would be changed, so it wasn't all bad. At least they came to church. *(Jonah Parker)*

Used to be you had a Baptist Association. That's happened many a time in my day. Everybody in the county would come to that Association. It would last for three to five days. It'd last all week. A lot of them'd ride horses, a lot of them would walk. Some come in wagons, some come in buggies. But Dad'd go down there, and he'd bring a crowd home with him. I don't know now how many tables full it'd take to feed them all during the Association week.

We'd make pallets all over the floor here; the beds'd be full, and all the floors would be full every night that whole week. *(Grady Reed)*

I grew up thinking that if you didn't go to church on Sunday, there was somethin' bad wrong with you. You know, when you went to church Sunday morning, you had nothing else on your mind. Do your chores, wash, go to church. You'd have your bath on Saturday night and go to church. It was one of those things. It wasn't a chore; it was a pleasure. You'd see Grandmother there. When there was a sickness or something, you'd have a family gathering, but at church you saw everybody. How's

(Opposite) Reed family reunion, Deep Creek in the Smoky Mountains, near Bryson City; Irene Fisher, Delia Reed, Ruth Bradley, Rachel Sutton

your crops? How's your chickens? How's your cow? How many calves you got? And all that. That was church. The preacher would come once a month. You didn't have a regular preacher to stay in the church. When he came, that's when they had the meetings. If you had any business in the church, it was held on Saturday. It wasn't held on Sunday. Just the elders went, your old church people went. They didn't have baby-sitters, they took the kids with them if they had little kids, but the others stayed home. It was a different ball game from what it is today when it comes to going to church. People go to church today for many, many reasons. We went to church for one reason only—because we were brought up to go to church. We didn't have no other place to go. *(Frank Norris)*

These old mountain folks were religious. They believed in going to church. They believed in their Bible. My dad went to school three months in his life, and there wasn't anybody could pray a better prayer. *(Harriet "Granny" Echols)*

Webster Baptist Church, Webster, Jackson County

NEIGHBORLINESS AND COMMUNITY ENTERTAINMENT

Neighbors back then would help one another. They'd clear a field and all work together. We'd hoe their crop and they'd hoe ours, swap work. One guy'd have a horse and another guy'd have a horse, and they'd put the two horses together and have a team of horses. They'd plow the ground and put out a crop and hoe his corn or gather his corn. That's the way it was. There was no money exchanged. They exchanged labor. I worked ten hours for him, he'd work ten hours for me. *(Frank Norris)*

I've had some of the best white friends that have ever been. When we'd run out of a milk cow, didn't have a milk cow to milk for our family, if they had an extra one, we got it; and if we had one, they got it. When they got behind in their work, we went over there and helped them plow, hoe their corn, and catch up; they'd come and help us. *(Clifford Casey)*

During the time of World War I when the flu was so bad and was killing so many people, my daddy and mother came down with it. Everybody was, dying like flies you know; and everybody that wasn't dead was scared to death. And my oldest brother didn't take it; if he did, he didn't ever let it be known. It just hit you and knocked them down and they stayed down, and then you'd get up and go on. And some, it knocked them down and they stayed down; just a lot of them didn't get up. So he took care of feeding the cattle and milking and doing some of the cooking. And the Kellers, our neighbors, would bring some food over, but they wouldn't come in. *(Raymond Presnell)*

If somebody was sick, they'd come and sit up with them. You didn't go and come back. You went and spent the night with your neighbor; and if you had a bunch of children, they'd have enough beds or they'd put pallets down on the floor. And if it was

Saturday night when they'd spent the night, why they'd go to Sunday School the next Sunday and church. *(Quay Smathers)*

When I was a youngun coming up, if a neighbor got sick or a friend got sick, the neighbors all gathered up and would go see each other and fix his wood, get his wood fixed. And if it was in the crop time when they was making a crop and one got sick, the neighbors would go right in, all of them, hoe out his crops and fix it up. If it was in the fall of the year when harvest time come, if one got sick, they'd go in and do the foddering and fix the feed for the cattle in the winter. *(Willard Watson)*

Neighbors are not nothing, not a bit more like they used to be than nothing in the world. On back behind here, folks has lost the love for each other. What the cause is, is too much money. People used to do and go walk for miles and sit down and talk to their friends and neighbors for three or four hours at a time. Now they're all in a hurry. (Willard Watson)

They helped each other, and now people haven't got time to even go see the dead or sick or anything else. If somebody got sick around in the community, or died, why the whole community would go in and just take care of the crop or whatever needed doing. You don't hear tell of anything like that any more. There are so many up on this creek here, I don't know half of them. *(Walter Winebarger)*

It's a good place to live, and we have a nice community to live in. We have nice people. And I believe each and every one of us care for one another. It's a place to get away from it all. But I don't want you to say this is a desolate place, 'cause I saw that in the paper, and that made me sort of sick. You let something happen and you see how many people will come out. They'll come out in a hurry, and they'll get the word, and they'll be out in a hurry. So I really wouldn't class it as being a desolate place, 'cause it's a nice place. *(Helen Rose)*

We had a great patch of sweet corn. I give corn to everybody in the whole country, I reckon. The Florida man got some to go in his freezer and wanted to pay me. I told him, "No. I didn't raise it to sell, just raised it to have corn." There's a difference. If you raise it to sell, then sell it; but if you raise it to have corn and give to your neighbors, then you don't want to sell it, do you? **(Grady Reed)**

We had pretty good neighbors when we was growin' up. You know I think back when years ago when people was growing up and all, people visited more. They visited the sick to help. A man came in here yesterday, yes, yesterday. He said, "Don't you want us to get you in some wood and get you some in here? Is there anything you need from down at the store or anything?" And you don't find that everywhere. *(Zora Lyle)*

You had Sunday dinner, most everybody in the country had Sunday dinner for his neighbors. They'd all come in and eat dinner with you. They'd come and stay awhile, and they'd eat dinner, and left. We had a piano and people'd come; they'd never seen one, and they called it a "pie-an-er." They'd say they come to hear the little girlies play the pie-an-er. *(Mamie Hall)*

They'd bake bread and stuff. Daddy managed some way to get the flour. They'd bake that up into cakes and pies, and they'd go to taking Christmas about a

Letha Hicks and her sister, Etter Moses, on the front porch

week before Christmas. And then they took Christmas 'til January, two weeks of Christmas. They'd just go from one house to the other. And they had plenty cooked, and they'd kill two or three hogs. Mother made souse, cooked meat, fried meat; baked cornbread. *(Letha Hicks)*

218

We didn't have any square dances. We had candy breakings. We'd get different candy and put it in a box, break it up and then two would go to the candy and reach in and get a piece. And the boyfriend or girlfriend would reach in; and, if they got a piece alike, they got to keep it and get to draw again. And that was real fun. All of the house would be full of youngsters. We just had a good time. *(Lillian Hooper)*

We'd get out and play tap hands, hopscotch, and things like that. The girls would make a playhouse. We had playhouses and we'd get moss and make beds. We'd have them big enough for us to lay on, moss beds. And ol' broken dishes, we'd have all kinds of tables full of things and make mud cakes and pies. The boys would get out and play marbles, mumblety-peg. *(They'd take a knife and close up the blade and put it on your finger and flip it somehow or other, and the knife would stick in the ground.)* And they'd make their popguns out of elder bushes. When they'd shoot you with them wads of paper, they'd burn like a bee sting. *(Nanny Suttles)*

Played snowball and made snowmen and stick them on the side of the road and scare the horses. We'd make big ol' snowmen and set them on the side of the road, and the sheriff'd come along every once in a while. He'd say we had to tear them down, but we wouldn't do it. We'd tell him we weren't going to do it. They'd scare the horses. They'd just about run away. But that's what we'd like to see. We made all kind of swings, grapevine swings and everything like that. We'd find a grapevine hanging down, and you'd cut it off where you could reach it, and you'd hold on to that and swing clear across the road and back. *(Mamie Hall)*

Used to, people'd get big ol' wooden barrels, get big things, and cut them in two and make two big washtubs out of them. We stole a washtub and drug it to the river. We was too small to carry it, so we drug it to the river. And there was a bridge across

there from the Esmerelda Inn across the river. Go back over in them fields over there, well, that's where we lived. Both of the families lived over there. Well, we got our washtub out there and got it under the bridge where nobody could see us, you know. Nobody was looking under the bridge for kids. Well, we decided we'd take a sail, and we went to climbing in that washtub, and we didn't set down in the tub. We placed ourselves (four of us) so it would balance; but what kept it from turning over and trapping us under it, I don't know. But we went down the river. We had big times. *(Nanny Suttles)*

Saturday evening, a lot of times the baseball players of the community would get together and play baseball, and the community would watch it. Mostly you just worked. There wasn't a great sight of entertainment. It was sort of self-entertainment. *(Alfred Adams)*

I was grown before we ever had electricity. I can remember the first radio I ever heard. A fellow right up the road here got a battery set, and we all went up there one night. I don't know whether it was around election time. There was some big to-do, and we went and couldn't hear it. It wasn't any count. It wouldn't pick up anything in these mountains. I don't know when electricity came to this country. I guess it might have been in the twenties. *(Walter Winebarger)*

I know it was a wonderful thing when we first got the talking machines, Victrolas, more amusing than the television when it came in really. People knew more about it, and everybody wanted one, and not many people could get the money to buy one. There were a few that got them; and from all around, when somebody got one, they'd come in here every night and would listen to it. They were always glad for them to come and had a good time listening. You turned a crank; it had a spring, but the spring would break occasionally, so you had to fix it. *(Raymond Presnell)*

I used to ride my bicycle from back over there near Banner Elk to Boone on Sunday and back and spend the day with my mother's mother. I did that because I liked her house. It had electric lights and things like that, conveniences that I wasn't used to, and I thought it was nice to come to Boone. It was in the late forties, maybe early fifties, '49 or '50, somewhere along in those years when electricity came in. But we had kerosene lamps and we had battery radios. A favorite pastime on Saturday night was to listen to the Grand Ol' Opry and Minnie Pearl. And in the afternoon I always liked to hear the Green Hornet and the Lone Ranger and the ol' time serials on the radio. *(Charles Michael)*

When I was growing up, there was one radio in Dutch Cove. It was down at another person's house, and that was our entertainment on Saturday night. We'd go down and listen to the radio, the Grand Ol' Opry. It was an old battery radio, and you had to sit just as quiet as you could sit; and the sound would leave and you'd keep adjusting it 'til it came back. And that was the entertainment that I had. *(Quay Smathers)*

The fast pace, the way things were speeded up, I think that has changed our culture more than anything else. There used to be time to visit. You know, television's come in, and everybody stays home and entertains. They don't visit like they used to. Used to on Sundays, you know, everybody visits somebody. You go and sit and talk, share your problems, just visiting. *(Jonah Parker)*

Used to be everybody'd go see one another. Well, back when I was a kid, we'd go down to Grandpa's and stay all night. And then we had an uncle lived right up the ridge, right over there, and I'd go over there and stay all night, and they'd come here and stay all night. We could have went over there in five minutes, but still the whole family would stay all night with one another. Then maybe in a week or two, the other one would come stay with us. Have bean hullings; raise a lot of beans, you know, and have a bean hulling. Then we'd get out when

the wind was blowing and we'd pour them in one tub and then change back, and with that wind blowing, first thing you'd know, they'd be as clean as they could be. *(Grady Reed)*

We told tales for amusement. That's what's happened to the entertainment now. You don't have corn shuckings; don't have music or square dance, except what's on television or listen to the radio. They'd tell tales and get you interested in a tale; you'd get to where you were shucking corn without knowing it.
(Edd Presnell)

I've gone to a lot of bean stringings. I had a good many bean stringings. My mother and sisters always wanted a bean stringing because it was social life. We had many more corn shuckings, I guess, every fall. The girls and boys that were big enough would line up around the cornstalks, and they could shuck corn. The boys would take their hands and get a pile of corn for the shuckers so they could sit where they were. Yeah, after the corn shucking was done, we'd play games.

[At] quilting bees, lots of times, if they weren't busy, the men would go with their wives. While their wives quilted, the men would do other things; I've forgotten what. Maybe they'd have a log rolling on the day they cut new ground, and pile the brush and burn it. And then men would gather in with hand spikes, and they'd cut a good strong pole about six or eight feet long. The man that was going to have the log rolling would usually get the hand spikes and stick them up, stick one end in the ground in the yard and wait for the men to come. The women set a good dinner, ham, chicken, beans, butter, all kinds of vegetables, pies, cakes, custards. They had a whale of a good log-rolling dinner. *(Horton Cooper)*

I always enjoyed visits with Willard and Ora Watson. One morning I had set out to take some photographs of Willard. After taking my pictures, I went inside the house with Ora to look at some of her beautiful quilts. When I started to take my leave, they insisted that they had planned for me to stay and "have a little bite of dinner." And what a dinner it was! The table was loaded with all kinds of good things to eat, including hot biscuits and some of Ora's homemade strawberry preserves. It was only eleven o'clock in the morning, but they had been up since five, as usual, and thought it was high time for the midday meal. (W.M.)

I had a quilting frame. Ol' man Parker made quilting frames for me. They're just homemade ones. Neighbors all kind of helped me when I put my quilt in. The lady that lived right close to me, we'd put the quilt in, and then the neighbors would come and help me quilt it. *(Mamie Hall)*

A lot of people had quilting bees, but Mama always did hers herself. She said other people couldn't sew to suit her. She said they'd make long stitches you'd catch your toenails in. (Nanny Suttles)

We had bean stringing, corn shuckings, and everything. Put the corn whiskey down in the pile of corn. They'd take a gallon jug and put it down in this pile of corn, and the one that got to it first got the first drink. Then the one that got the most red ears and speckled ears got to kiss the prettiest gal. That's where I had the most fun at 'cause the girls didn't want that, you see. They didn't go for it. Up all night, you know, playing music and telling tales. We had fiddles and banjos and stuff. You talk about music! *(Stanley Hicks)*

Used to have corn shucking and pea hullings and bean hullings, and we used to make all the kraut, pickled beans, and bleach fruit, and it'd take you

Vena Shular with hand-crocheted mats displayed on a bedspread made from flour sacks

221

Nellie Mae and Walter Edminsten, Ruby Michael, Lena Shull, and Lottie Green, Watauga County

through the whole year. One particular time we boiled the molasses and set the molasses on the back porch, and the shelf that I set it on was kind of sloping, and it all ran out into an old shoe a-settin' down off the porch on the ground. I never will forget that. And we didn't have any candy pulling. The syrup all went into the shoe. *(Grady Reed)*

My daddy made his own molasses. Well first, after you raise your cane, you have to strip the fodder off it, cut the seed tops off, and then you have great big huge rollers and they roll together and string out the juice. A horse was hitched to a big long pole that goes around and around, and that gets out the juice. He's got a furnace down there with a molasses pan, and you pour it in up here. And he keeps pouring it in 'til it circles around and gets in all those different partitions. Then he boils them. You have to skim it. Lots of foam comes on it. Skim it, and when it gets down into the last one, it's molasses. And you have a bucket setting here with a cloth tied over it. He pours it on that cloth and strains it through, then you've got pretty molasses.

Now it costs about eight to ten dollars a gallon. He sold his for a dollar. *(Sue Oates)*

People would raise the cane in the community. Everybody didn't raise it, just one family out of maybe ten or fifteen; and they'd have the molassy boilings. Everybody would go about the time they got ready to put a boiler on, when they had their juice ground out and everything ready to boil. Then they would go and be ready to what we called "assault the molassy boiler." We would maybe cook it a little longer, some of it, and make us some candy, molassy taffy candy. We pulled it and made it real wide, and then we'd twist it around and break it in two. Made a great big stick of candy. It'd last you forever. It was really fun. It gave you a chance for your boyfriend to come see you. *(Faye Dancy)*

Everything was done in a family fashion; if your mother and daddy went, you went. In cleaning off a patch of ground, you'd cut the logs all down and you'd have the brush piled up and everything. And

222

Gristmill wheel, Old Winebarger's Mill, Meat Camp, Watauga County

you'd burn the brush and roll the logs out of the field. That's what it was. Back when people think of log rolling, that's when they raised a house, cut the logs and raised a house; but this was just clearing off fields. We'd all get together—we'd do it at night. The brush pile would light up the whole area, and it was a lot of fun. Everybody—the families were doing it; it wasn't just an individual. The whole community would get together, probably have a jug of moonshine around somewhere, and have some fun. *(Frank Norris)*

Used to build barns, a lot of them, out of logs. You'd get poles and get your stuff all ready and just have a barn raising. All your neighbors would come and help you build that barn. They'd notch your logs, you know, so they'd fit together.
(Nelson Cabe)

That was a log raising. They'd have their logs all pulled into the place where they were going to build and have them notched, and then they'd send out the word there was going to be a log raising. One ol' fellow that used to live in this community said that men would walk as much as thirty miles to go to a log raising, help build a house or a barn. And a pretty good size house, they put it up in a day. And at that time they split boards two feet long to cover with and put a roof on it in a day. And the ladies, they would cook big dinners and bring out to the men working. *(Phelps Merrell)*

People back then, see, had log rollings. Back when I built log houses and log barns and stuff, I helped build them. What they did then, see there wasn't any money, was go help each other. We'd have log rollings, corn shuckings. We'd go and gather corn, pile it up in a barn, and then they'd have a corn shucking. Everybody'd gang in and shuck that man's corn; next time they'd go to another one. Then they'd have log rollings; and if you were building a house, everybody pitched in to help build it—no money.

You didn't have to pay any tax, but you had to work about four days a month building roads, free

labor. That was a hand just the same as working.

But when Grandpa was alive, see, we didn't have stockyards. They'd just turn the market cattle and hogs, turn them out. If you had a pasture or something you didn't want them in, you just fenced it yourself. But now, then, oh my gosh, it'd be pitiful, you know; if you were to let something get out in a man's crop now, he'd die, have a heart attack. All that's here now; I'm talking about two-thirds of them, are here for the money. *(Quay Smathers)*

We always had one big day of the year, I guess it was July because it was hot. And you'd hear, "The thrashers are coming, the thrashers are coming." The women would get together in the neighborhood and cook the biggest—it was a dinner, it wasn't a lunch—the biggest dinner of the year at noon. And that's when the men brought the machines and came in and would do the thrashing. That was a big time of the year. And men, I think, would eat a lot just to prove that they could. Big affair of the year. *(Annie Dee Leatherman Smith)*

Everybody'd raise wheat. The thrashers would come and have their wheat thrashing. And if the thrasher broke down, say if it was here when it broke down, well, they'd have to cook dinner every day as long as that thrasher was broke down. Well, there'd be about five or six men with the thrasher. Then the whole community would come in and help thrash; feed all the men, especially one or two, out of each family all week. People didn't think nothing about it then, not a bit more than nothin'. But you take women now, if they had to cook for, well, say fifteen or twenty men, dinner every day for a week, they'd wonder what in the world they were going to cook, wouldn't they? *(Grady Reed)*

They used to have serenades. Anybody'd move into a new house, a family'd move in, they'd always serenade them. That was welcoming them in the community. Get cowbells and guns and run around the house and ring the cowbells and shoot the guns and stuff like that. *(Nelson Cabe)*

TOWN LIFE

Did you ever notice that nearly every county seat in North Carolina is thirty miles apart? You just notice it, from Marion to Morganton, anywhere. Bakersville to Newland, anywhere that you go, thirty miles apart. Just about a day's ride on horseback. (Ivor Vance)

Trust, Luck, and Bluff are three towns in a row that were named after a passing crap game in the back of a wagon. Trust, then Luck, then Bluff. Sodum, Relief, and Spill Corn are three other mountain towns. *(Landon Roberts)*

The post office [first] was named Pump. It was at a store where they had pumped the water. The water was pumped there with wooden troughs from way over at a spring. So, they named this one Pump, N.C. Later it was moved back up near where it is now, and it was Uncle George Wall had the post office. In those days they wrote with a pen that was dipped in ink, and he sent off for some material for the post office and instead of stopping his "P" where it should have been, it run on down into an "R," turned it into Rump, N.C. Immediately, they needed to change a post office name. At that time, we had a representative from this area at Raleigh. His name was Freeman, so they told him they wanted him to get a new name. He had a sister who was a wonderful person, very liked in the community, and so somebody said, "Let's name it Gertrude." And he said, "No, she wouldn't want her name," and they changed it to Gerton. So that's why it's Gerton. *(Modeen Bradley)*

Everybody would come to town on Saturday and the streets would be littered, shall we say, with where the horses had been. And then the side-walks—all the men then, it looked like, chewed tobacco; and they'd stand and talk and they'd spit. To get anywhere in town without stepping in something was a real feat. The sidewalks were brown. A lot of them made their own chewing tobacco. They grew their own tobacco. And they'd have a twist of it in their coats. All the men wore coats, it seemed, heavy wool stuff. Then on the weeks when they'd have court, it was just jammed. Everybody'd come to court, maybe more than on Saturday. *(Jim Ryan)*

I never did live on a farm, although we did always have, in those early days, cows and hogs, and always had a big garden, grew practically everything we had to eat. We lived on a farm economy, you might say, because we grew a lot of our own produce. I used to have to take the old cow to the pasture every morning and go get her at night. Milk the cow, slop the pigs, and feed the animals. We had a wood-burning stove, outhouses, and kerosene lamps. In my early days we lived about like we had for many years with very little change. All the so-called modern conveniences have been developed since then.

Webster was a very progressive town in its early days. We lived up one end of the town, and the school building was at the other end. I would say probably a half-mile. So, we had a plank sidewalk from our end of town down to the school building, which was really a godsend in wintertime because everything was mud and snow, and those walks made it possible to get back and forth. My older brother went to Chapel Hill [University of North Carolina] in 1916. I never will forget, one time the only way we could get to Sylva to catch the train was to walk from Webster across the mountain. There was a mail buggy that ran from Webster to Sylva to carry the mail, and the mailman would take passengers. But the road was so bad the horses couldn't pull the buggy to Sylva. And I remember distinctly my brother carrying the bag, walking across the mountain. There's a mountain between Sylva and Webster. He was on his way to school walking from Webster to Sylva to catch the American Branch to Asheville. And when he went there, they had to stop and change trains in Greensboro. They got off at Hillsborough and there was a little Branch line that ran from Hillsborough to Carrboro. And then they walked from Carrboro on into Chapel Hill. Nobody thought anything of it. *(Dan Moore)*

The sidewalks were plank, in front of the buildings. The first hardtop road that came in, came from about where the Tastee Freez is now up to where you turn up Water Street to the jail. That was the first hardtop road in Boone. There was a mud hole right in the middle of town. They had to hook steers to pull the cars through, what few there were. The old Tweetsie'd come in up there and then go back up. They had a turntable there. Tweetsie'd pull up on it and turn around. I never got to come to town that much. I don't remember ever riding Tweetsie until I was old enough to run her down and hitchhike it. We'd catch it going out of Boone, ride to Hodges Gap, and walk back. Oh, they didn't pay any attention to us. We'd just jump on.
(Frank Norris)

People all over Macon County, now, would come and visit the train on Sundays and bring big lunches in baskets. They would come with a buggy with a horse. Some would ride horses, and it was dusty around there. They would come and watch the train, and listen at it, and bring their children. On Sunday that was the place for them to come to see the train come in. It came up every day from Cornelia and come to Franklin, and then went back. It would stay there about an hour and let the passengers off. Whoever would get back on would then go to Cornelia, Georgia, and then catch a train, eastbound or northbound in Cornelia, where they would get off.

    A circus used to come in on it. A friend of mine and I got some peanuts and went up on this old

Porch at Ruth and R.O. Wilson's house

boxcar and threw the elephant peanuts. So, we run out of peanuts, and he ran down there and got some sawdust in his cap and put it in the snout of the elephant. He blew that stuff all over us, and we were scared to death. So we jumped down and ran out there behind the man, the old engine man, and we hid out there afraid somebody'd seen us, you know. So, that's as mean as I was. *(Bennie Reese)*

A hag show was like Barnum & Bailey's, only it was a small, two-tent circus. It had an animal tent and a circus tent where they had wild west shows at the end of the night, cotton candy, hot dogs, and all that stuff, outside the tents. Later they got to being carnivals more or less instead of circuses; come in with the gambling and all that, you know. We'd go up to the hag show, but we didn't have no money to buy tickets, so we'd go up and help put the tents up. They'd bring them in on trucks or wagons. I can remember when they walked the animals from Boone to West Jefferson and put them on the train. They'd go down by my house; the elephants, camels, and the donkeys, and everything walked. They'd have a big truck going down and if it got stuck, they'd take the elephants and push it out. *(Frank Norris)*

I was born in Franklin, North Carolina, in the old Macon County Jail. My daddy was deputy sheriff and we lived in the jail. In those days, people did. Then, of course, we moved out of the jail and moved on up a little farther out the street there in Franklin, right across the street from the courthouse. When I was a little boy, I used to slide down those banisters in the old courthouse.

There were just a few stores on top of the hill, no brick buildings, they were just plain buildings. You could go in those stores, and they smelled so good with candy and different things in there and all. Many houses on the main street had a picket fence around them and one of those swings that six people can swing in. And the porches would have chairs on them, of course. And people would go in and sit on the porches and tell all kinds of tales and stories about back before their time. That was seventy years ago or seventy-five. There were several hotels in Franklin, too.

I started shining shoes when I was nine years old. A man had a barber shop, Mr. Lester Conley. He said, "I'll let you have the corner in my shop, if you will keep the bathtub clean and keep the barber shop swept out." There was only one bathtub in town. Everybody on Saturday night would work, and they used to get paid, what little they got on Saturday night. So all of the men would come to the barber shop to get a bath for a quarter. Then, I would have to wash the tub out. Me, a little ol' boy.

One time I fell in it. I would shine shoes, and it was five cents a pair to shine your shoes. Back then they wore a lot of boots, fancy boots. I got fifteen cents for shining boots, and sometimes they would tip me a dime.

When I got a little older, big enough to lift a sack of flour, I went to work for Mr. L. C. Rhodes in his store. In the meantime, Mr. Rhodes had a theater too. It was called the Idle Hour Theater. They had silent pictures, and they would just run one reel at the time. And when they would change the reels, a girl would play the piano. We had the old Victrola then. She would put records on and play while they were changing reels. I worked for Mr. Rhodes in the store in the daytime, and he sent me down to the theater at nights to open it up and pick up tickets. It had a little fountain in there, and we sold ice cream. Made the best milk shakes with whipped cream on them and little chocolate drops. Then I learned to run the machine. It was a Power's model. You had to go up the little steps. It was up there, and the screen was down yonder. If the boy didn't show up to run the machine, I had to do it. I thought I was a big shot, you know. Me, a little ol' boy. I was about fourteen or fifteen. *(Bennie Reese)*

The Vances had a very fine saddle horse named Holly, and rather than take the horse back with them to Nashville, my father would keep the horse during the winter. Of course, we used him, and I rode him a lot. I think he was the fastest horse I've ever seen trottin'. In fact, he was a fine buggy horse. I delivered milk in Blowing Rock with the horse and buggy. And coming back down the slope from Blowing Rock through there by Appalachian Motel, now I was young and didn't care, and I'd turn that horse loose. He went around some of those curves so fast that the buggy went on two wheels. He was the fastest horse trottin' that I've ever seen; and, of course, I enjoyed him. I was just a teenager, and it was the nearest thing to hot roddin' now that you could get because he was fast. I delivered milk in Blowing Rock during the wintertime. In the summer they'd have him back, and I was in school anyway. *(Wade Brown)*

MUSIC

One thing that the people down here in this community and in the adjoining communities in the wintertime did was singing. We had singing schools; usually there'd be one here at Bear Wallow Church, and they'd have one over in the Middle Fork community and maybe down at Bat Cave. On Sunday afternoon we'd just get a crowd of young people together or older ones too to sing, and we didn't have organs or pianos much back then either. *(Hattie Oates)*

Shaping notes is an ancient practice. If people talk about Sacred Harp singers, that means they are identifying with a tune collection that is called the Sacred Harp. *Christian Harmony singers are identified with a book that is a collection of tunes called* Christian Harmony. *Christian Harmony happens to be seven-note singing. That is to say a diatonic scale with a shape or note for every degree in the scale. Sacred Harp has just four shapes, and it involves an interesting manipulation of the tetrechord.*
(James Dooley)

The obvious advantage that they argued is that you only have four shapes to know or use. Four-note singers and the seven-note singers usually don't have any trouble with either system. They are really traditionalists, but they are the people who enjoy singing. I am knowledgeable about this from my musical background and from my study of American music (my grandfather could sing the "four-notes"), but not from the practical standpoint of having grown up in a family that went to singings every week.

The first edition of *Sacred Harp* dates back roughly a hundred years. Then they were carrying on a practice that had been going on for some time. *Sacred Harp* was simply, in that day, a modern tune book for practices that were already in motion. What they practice today in *Sacred Harp* singing conventions, Sunday singings, and singing schools is very close to what you would have found if you were able to be transported back to those times. But on any given Sunday any weekend somewhere in the Southern part of the United States, you can find a singing going on of some kind, and it may be one of the more recent versions that are associated with note singing.

The gospel singing is a more recent phenomenon that grew out of shaped note singing. Some of the early gospel quartets grew right out of a close relationship with publishers and compilers of books and that kind of thing. Of course, today it's a big business. It was a religion. Quartet singing hadn't developed in this country until roughly fifty years ago. It has changed quite a bit, but it grew out of this musical tradition, too. *(James Dooley)*

There are two popular systems of shaped notes. There's the "fa so la" or four-note *Sacred Harp*, which is older, and the "do re me fa so la se do" or seven-note system as found in *Christian Harmony*. Looking at a page of shaped-note music, you find notes arranged on a staff with a time signature and a key signature. The duration of the note is, as usual, indicated by the notes being in outline or solid form and by stems and flags. Only the shapes are different; instead of just round or oval notes, you have (in order) trapezoid (do), crescent (re), diamond (me), right triangle (fa), oval (so), square (la), equilateral triangle (se or te), and trapezoid. What these shapes add to the information contained in conventional notation is an aid to sight reading the intervals between notes. Singers practice associating the shapes, note names, and tones

Kelly Smith, shaped-note singer

by singing through a piece using shape names rather than the hymn text. Instead of "Oh, bear me away on your snowy wings," they sing, "so do do do re do la so me so." As "Singing Billy" Walker, *Christian Harmony* author, said, "The end proposed is that the same name invariably applied to the same interval may naturally suggest its true relation and proper sound."

If you dropped in on a shaped-note singing and heard them singing in four-part harmony four sets of strange syllables, you might conclude that they're from a foreign country or possibly another planet, but really they're carrying on a tradition designed for the education of people on the edges of the American frontier. One of the problems with the regular notation system is that you've got to know what key you're in and worry about the sharps and flats. And more than simply going from this note to this note, you've got to know that this is a "C" and this is the "G" and all that. Shaped notes kind of eliminates the difference.

Most people can hear certain things real well. Most people can hear a fifth. So if you can hear a fifth, if you have two symbols for that, you can respond to the symbols. In other words, it's really an aid to singing by ear. If somebody gives the pitch, everybody can follow. The shapes help you sight read.

As you know, every time it goes from a little square to a little triangle, that's going to go hum (high), hum (low). It doesn't matter what key you're in. It's based ultimately on medieval singing, sort of like what the monks used to do [Gregorian chant]. A lot of the systems through history have tried to make sight reading easier, and this one was found to be a way to do that. And it is easy to teach. It can be learned by people who can't read, even words. *(Mr. Jan Davidson)*

At the first singing schools, they didn't carry a blackboard. They carried a chalk canvas, an eraser, and chalk, and generally brought a bunch of song-

Sue Ellen McGrew, Edd Presnell, Julie Ellen McGrew, Nettie Presnell, and Hannah Harmon

books with them. And they wrote the music, the lines and spaces and all the music, on this folded piece of canvas, using the chalk and the eraser. They generally had singing schools at churches. My first singing school was at Morning Star Church. We learned to sing the notes. That was in 1919, and I was thirteen. So I was very young. The leader used to have a tuning fork. I don't know whether you've ever seen one or not. The way that leader pitched a song, he never looked to see whether it was an A, B, or C. He'd look through his line of music and he'd find the highest note that he had to reach. Now he's got a medium in there. He's got to get that up high enough that it doesn't kill the bass; or if he gets too high, then he's going to ruin the tenor.

One time I started to go to Dallas, Texas, and enter their singing school down there, but I never got around to it. But in the last thirty-five years, I know of nobody teaching singing schools, only just the workshops like I've been doing. Over at Warren Wilson College, why I'd go over there for two hours every Sunday for maybe two or three months. There's more interest in shaped-note singing now than there's ever been in my lifetime. And they seem to sing it better. One fellow made the com-

ment over at Etowah. He said, "Those old people used to sing it like they heard their grandparents sing it." He said, "These younger people have not got any more sense than to sing it right." You know how you hear things handed down from old people. So that's the reason I say that their singing is better now. But they still publish the gospel song-books in shaped notes. A lot of those gospel song singers, the better singers, quartets, I believe if you'd take the piano or instrument away from them, that they'd be at a loss, because I don't believe that half of them—I know the ones around here that have the quartets couldn't sing. A shaped-note singer could sing it. I can sing any song that's written as long as it's in shaped notes. I don't care what it is. It might take me a time or two, but it wouldn't take too many times. You look at the time signature—3/4, 4/4, or 6/8 or whatever—if you look at that, you'll start right. *(Quay Smathers)*

Uncle Joe Hartley had some of his relatives that lived off and were coming to visit him. He wanted to have something special, so he goes up there above his house on that hill on Grandfather Mountain, they called it the singing ground. They had a get-together, and they had invited in a lot of singers from one place or another like Boone, and different places you know. And they'd have this singing. They started off with just a little group of people, and it has grown up now. I think they said one year they had 40,000 people. And that was a terrible crowd for the mountains. I haven't been up there since I broke my hip seven or eight years ago. I used to wouldn't miss it. It's the first Sunday in June. They'd gather up there, and people would come from everywhere after it got advertised. Then they have a lot of prominent people come. Billy Graham, and such people like that. And the Smith Brothers. People take food and they have picnics. They got to where they put up tents, so if it came a-raining, and they had these little old people that'd sell stuff all around the mountain, you know. That's been going for years, I'd say for at least forty years. Uncle Joe's been dead for years, but that old man started that thing just out of a family group of people. *(Florence Wilson)*

Bascom Lamar Lunsford was known as the Minstrel of the Appalachians. He catalogued for the Library of Congress all of the mountain ballads and folk songs of the last 150 or 200 years. He traced them all back to English origins. He and my father would play the fiddle and banjo together.
(Harold Bennett)

So far as I'm able to determine myself, this is the oldest native fully developed Appalachian ballad. This is a real ballad, a true-blue ballad that was created in Appalachia. It has an Appalachian ballad-maker and is sung in the Appalachian fashion. We can date it 1807. Appalachian people had been in the region less than a generation when this ballad was born. So I offer it as the first Appalachian ballad, the Vance song. Vance was condemned to be hanged, and while the scaffold was being made and the coffin was being built, he watched through the bars of the jail and he made his own death song. He stood on the scaffold and sang it, the ballad about himself, using a hymn similar to that of the old regular Baptist hymns.

Now Vance shall no more the Big Sandy behold,
Nor drink from its crystal wave.
The buck, the fawn, and the laurel gold,
The hunterman's found his grave.

The laurels blow on Flinch Mountain;
In the valley, the roses bloom.
This day shall Vance close his eyes in death
And be interred in the silent tomb.
(Cratis Williams)

I was about the only one that knew the old-time songs, church songs, and all; and a woman from Germany came down out there and made a movie

Wondrous Love, *shaped-note music*

of me over in Germany. Well, they got where I was singing and all, and they found that I was the only one that knew those old-timey songs. They said I was important to them; they had to have me. I got with a man there in Asheville and went on to New York and to Scotland. I performed there in Edinburgh. And they taped all those old songs, and they've got them all over there. They'd forgotten all those old meeting songs. I can sing with music or without it. They wanted just the tales told about how people lived back then, how they sparked, and things, you know. Now, I didn't have a car or anything. I told them that when the fall of the year came, I didn't have a car; I'd just go and pick me out some pretty girl and go chestnut hunting with her. We'd sit down and rest every once in a while and sing those old songs and have a good time. I had one I sung they liked.

Here's a Baptist preacher,
You can tell him by his coat
Don't you hear Jerusalem mourn?

Got a bottle in his pocket
That he can't hardly tote.
Don't you hear Jerusalem mourn?

Don't you hear Jerusalem mourn?
Don't you hear Jerusalem mourn?
Can't drop by heaven with a ringing in my soul
And my soul said—(break)
Don't you hear Jerusalem mourn?

My brother, Lee Wallin, worked with Guy, and they all the time joked with one another. So he sung this song for Guy Roberts.

Hello, Guy, what's the matter downtown?
There come a wind last night
And blowed the payroll down.

Tell me how long; can I get you now?
Will I have to wait?
Can I get you now?

Went down to the railroad,
Laid my head on the track,
Saw the train a comin',
And I jerked her back.

Tell me, how long?
Can I get you now?
Must I hesitate?
Will I have to wait?

Say, I was born in Cincinnati
In a rattlesnake's den.
My daily occupation
Takin' women 'way from men.

Oh, tell me how long?
Can I get you now?
Must I hesitate?
Will I have to wait?

Says there's not but one thing
That I can't understand
Why a bowlegged woman
Likes a pigeon-toed man.

Tell me, how long?
Can I get you now?
Must I hesitate?
Will I have to wait?

(Cas Wallin)

Now they have cloggin' and bluegrass. They can't speak of old-time music any more. They've got to speak of bluegrass music, which is all right, but I have no desire for it whatsoever, just like I have no desire for much of the gospel song. About the biggest difference you can find out is they want bluegrass just as far as they can go; then they try to sing with their voices so high and the leaders on their necks stick up like ropes. Some of these bluegrass bunches take these old-time songs and try to soup them up, which I'm not in favor of. I've heard some of these bunches take some of these old Christian Harmony songs, and they'll just make a mess out of it. My family's always made ol'-time string music, banjo and fiddle and guitar and bass fiddle. Ours is the ol'-time mountain music. In other words, it's not the bluegrass. We play songs; we don't sing. *(Quay Smathers)*

It's old-timey mountain music, when I think of it, 'cause that's what I grew up with, with just two or

Fiddler and guitarist rehearsing for performance at Mountain Heritage Festival, Cullowhee

three instruments, no drums or anything like that. No electrical guitars. One on the banjo, one on the bass. *(Kay Wilkins)*

Everybody thinks the best pickers are found in Mussell Shoals or Nashville or Hollywood. There are an awful lot of good people that I know here who can sit down and copy lick for lick off the record, but nobody's ever seen them unless they just go to their house for a picking. Nobody ever sees them or hears them, except in those particular instances, and they're very good. *(Ted White)*

Well, Daddy had played for years. He played all over the United States with a band. He put down the guitar and became a family man and worked. He played tenor banjo and after he put that down for a while, then he started up again. Liz (my sister) had a violin. She was taking violin lessons, and the violin teacher quit. She started playing fiddle. Then it was just she and Daddy playing, and then I started playing bass, and then my sister, June, started playing banjo. And we'd have people to the house. This was before we even thought about getting out to colleges or wherever we went to play, just playing there at the house, and it was a lot of fun. Then we started going out to all these different places playing. And I think that's the way a lot of people play, just at home.

We were on another album of the Haywood Arts Council. It's been a treat to see all the different musicians and meet good ol' people, just get out and have a good time. We're not in it for the big bucks. I'm a banker during the day. People around this area aren't in it to make money. They're in it to have a good time, and if they make money, fine. *(Cynthia White)*

I used to play for square dances all the time. Back in those days everybody went. I was working for twenty-five and fifty cents a day back in those days. Well, I could go and play for the dances and make a dollar an hour; boy, I was doing all right. That was quite an increase. Go out and hoe corn all day or mow all day or cradle wheat, rye, or oats all day and then go play about five hours for a square dance and come home with more than I made in the field. **(Myron Houston)**

We had square dances in what is now the famous Glendale Springs Inn, and we called it a lobby. It was a great big room, and it was just good clean fun. We had neighbors that made the music, pick a banjo, play the fiddle, and we'd dance. *(Faye Dancy)*

Now in my family, we square danced. It didn't make much difference what the church said about it, we square danced. We got a lot of back lip, backlash about it, but we square danced. My mother and daddy went to square dances, and we went to square dances. *(Frank Norris)*

Now we had square dances that were true square dances. None of this folk dance business. The mountain children today have to go to school to learn to folk dance. When I came along, the square dances were held in the home in front of an open fire with kerosene lamps or hanging lanterns. The mountain people themselves "made music." They usually had a violin, only it was called a fiddle, and, it was played totally differently from the way a violin was played. There was always the guitar, which was so soft and beautiful. These people made music at different occasions. It was not always just for dance. I have been sitting on a porch on a summer evening when the sun was setting, and twilight was beginning to come in, and whoever was there that happened to have an instrument would come out and strum the music and play on the fiddle. It was soft and beautiful. None of this raucous, hillbilly type of music at all. It was something to catch your heart. And most of the music they played were ballads. You learned to dance to the ballads, and you sang the ballads, and you crooned the ballads. They were stories. They were a form of oral history, and they created ballads of their own that were just local. *(Emma Sharpe Jeffress)*

Now we did go to square dances, but the church didn't like it. Talking about the changes, I'm so thankful that our church has changed and our people have changed. We do not set standards and expect everybody to live to them. But I got to dance when I was real little because there wasn't many girls. Now my father did not forbid us to go to

Stanley Hicks

dances. He was a deacon in the church. He thought it was fun because at Christmas time before he got married, he went over to the Sherrill Inn, spent a week, danced out a five-dollar pair of boots, so he allowed us to go. He did not allow us girls to go alone. We were chaperoned, of course, back then you were. Other than private dances in your own home, there was quite a crowd. They didn't have dope, but they had a lot of moonshine. I think that's the reason some of the old, straight-laced Baptist preachers—it was the circumstances, not the dancing itself, so they just said no dancing. The fact is, my daddy was kicked out of the church one time for going to a dance and fooling around. *(Modeen Bradley)*

Daddy would call the square dances, so my square-dancing, I inherited that, it came through him. Square dancing was our national folk dance. See the square dance is our dance. It didn't come from Europe. Now you have your line dances and all. They're English. But what we call our traditional square dance, big circle Appalachian-style dancing, is our own. In your big circle Appalachian dance, the caller is in the circle. Now your Western dancing, square dancing, the caller is on the back; and you only have four couples to a set. But in your big circle Appalachian-style dancing, you can have as many as sixty couples or as little as four. It's a wonderful dance because in your big circle Appalachian-style dances, you have time to think through your calls before you execute them, and anybody can dance. It's a real social dance.

I got my love of dance just from growing up right around here. And from Daddy. He loved to dance. He loved square dancing. Clogging is a new development. I innovated it into the big circle Appalachian style of dancing here. I don't think it had been done before.

Mr. Underwood liked the way our dance team danced, and he asked us if we would come over to the Cherokee Fair for the Indians, so we started over there. And we picked up a little buck step from them. They'd get me out there in some of these Indian dances, and we learned a buck step from some boys. The buck step is our basic step we used in all my clogging. That's toe-heel-back-front, toe-heel-back-front. From the buck step we'd go into all these other steps. And first thing you know, we had

a clog team rather than a smooth team. The clog step, I guess, came down from Ireland or the Scottish, but some steps we were doing similar to clog steps. *(Kay Wilkins)*

I had gone to visit Kay Wilkins for a second time in Plumtree. It was close to Christmas, and she suggested that I meet her at their restored cabin. She and her husband, Bill, didn't live there but enjoyed using it from time to time. The cabin had been beautifully decorated for Christmas, and we sat in front of a blazing fire sipping hot apple cider. The beautiful fireplace screen had been made by B. Hensley, who lived in nearby Spruce Pine. Everybody called Kay "Miss Kay." I'm not sure why. Perhaps it is a nickname given her by her students over the years. Her eyes glowed as she told me about the old days in Plumtree when they would have ice-skating parties on the frozen river, and her face filled with love when she described teaching local students the art of Appalachian folk dancing. She was proud of her dancers and had coached dance teams for various competitions for years. We had a wonderful time. Miss Kay exudes warmth and kindness. It's not surprising that she is well known and well loved by people for miles around. B. Hensley once told me, "If you don't love Kay Wilkins, you can't love anybody. If ever God reached down to a human being and just spilled a whole pan full of love and it just went all over, she is one of the few people. She gave her heart, her mind, her body, and her soul for the benefit of young people." (W. M.)

They never did clog when I grew up. That's something that commenced about twenty years ago. See, some of them started this clogging not over twenty years ago at the longest. What I do is years and years ago. See, when I grew up, back then there were no jobs. There weren't any jobs, so you had to do something. *(Stanley Hicks)*

FOLKLORE

Take any "Jack Story." You find Jack, a boy who is in desperation. His mother's a poor "widder woman," you see; not that only, but she's looking to him for support and he's rebelling. He's being lazy; she's having to fuss with him. He believes, however, in what we might interpret as the American dream. He believes that all is possible to the man who has the right connections mystically. Now otherwise we'd say religion, faith in God, church, and the like; but that's not true of Jack. It's pre-religious with him. It might be a stick that has some magic to it (this is Celtic). Now this is what gives spirit to it. He uses that when he gets in a tight spot. Always, that's what gets him out of trouble, that thing, that mystical thing. He pays no attention to it until he needs it. It doesn't seem to be a matter of concern to him until he needs it. Then he remembers, much like Mag remembered the old case knife in her apron pocket in another story. That's the mystical thing, that case knife will solve her problems. She remembered that just in time, you see, just as Jack always did. Both, however, are impelled by pragmatic matters. More than anything else, they must be pragmatic. This is Appalachia's story. *(Cratis Williams)*

The mountains now, at one time, was called God's Country, I was taught, where fritters grew on bushes. A fritter now, I've eaten them at my grandmother's down here on my dad's side. Now the way they first made their bread, after they got to grinding it, was in the old rock fireplaces. In the ashes in the rock fireplace, they would take their meal dough, rake out a hole, a place under the forestick or back stick, and pour that pone of dough down in there. They'd rake ashes back over it, and then rake some coals over it. That's the first skillet that was invented. The first skillet was in the ashes a-cookin' or baking. And they'd rake ashes back over it, and then they'd rake hot coals over the top of the ashes. Then the steam would come out; and you'd leave that there and check it and take that out. And I thought when I first saw my grandmother make it, those ashes would go in and ruin the pone of bread. When it got brown, you just brushed it a little with your hand, and rub it and blow. And that's the best piece of bread you've ever eaten in your life. Then a fritter came after they got the pan to fry in and then getting wheat flour, after wheat flour came into the mountain. And they took and made up a thin dough and fried fritters, they called them. That's the wheat dough fried up, and it'll melt in your mouth.

Now this tale was one of Jack and his hunting. So I put in, it was me that went with Jack. And so back in log cabin times I went down one fall, like it's been this time, now, like it was today, a pretty, beautiful day, what they called Indian summer. So I went down to see Jack, and he had his hog rifle out oiling it up, and I said, "Jack, are you going hunting?" He said, "Yeah, Ray." I said, "Could I go along with you?" He said, "I'd be ever so much obliged for you to go with me." So we took off and got in the woods and it was dry like it is now, no water hardly running anywhere in the mountain springs. So we got in those hot woods and were going along, and I got thirsty. We kept on walking and came to a few hollows and I checked them; we went on, and we came to another little deep one. I got down in the leaves checking for water, and Jack had gone on ahead of me. And so my fingers hit in something, and I hollered, "Hey, Jack, come back a minute." Jack came back and he said, "What's wrong, Ray?" I said, "I found something here in this hollow, running, but it seems sticky." And he got down, put his fingers down in it and rubbed; put it to his tongue. He said, "Ray, that's sourwood honey." And we went on up to the head of the hollow, and there was a big red cedar; it was around ten or fifteen feet through in diameter. And there had come a tornado or hurricane a day or two before that. And the swarms had got a beehive in that tree; it was hollow, and the branches on it was as big as big common trees, and they were hollow. And that hive had got in there, and it'd swarmed and filled that whole tree full of honey. And that hurricane or tornado had twisted it and busted the honey up, and it was running a branch of honey down about twenty feet from that tree. A branch of sourwood honey! And I got tickled, and I was tall anyhow, and I got tickled and staggered back a-laughin', a-lookin' at Jack look at that honey run. And I happened to hit a little sapling and bumped it with my body, staggering away, and doggone, confound it, it was a fritter bush, had fritters on it

Deer in forest, Grandfather Mountain

to eat the honey with. And so we took some fritters and ate some honey and went on.

And so we went on and came to the river and there was around fifty ducks swimming on that river and Jack says, "Oh, gosh, by dad, Ray, if I had some string, I'd swim under and tie them ducks' feet all together under the water and catch every one of them." So we took our shoestrings out and found some more strings in our coat pockets, and tied all them together, and Jack tied his britches legs so he could swim. And he dived down under that river at the edge and swam under there, and those ducks didn't see him, and swam under there and tied all those ducks, around about fifty of them, tied all of them together with that string. And when he came out among those ducks, that beat any quacking and hollerin' you ever heard in your life. He dragged them out on the bank, and

there he stood, and his britches legs just going that way—fluttering—and I said, "Jack, gosh what's in your britches?" And he untied his britches and had thirty-five pound of the prettiest trout fish that swam in here that you ever looked at, those little speckled trout—rainbow.

And so we went on, and going along we heard some wild turkeys hollering. And he eased out in the woods and me a-slippin' behind him. There were twelve, twelve big wild turkeys sitting on one limb. And he says, "Ray, I think I can load my hog rifle and split that limb with a bullet and let it spread open and their toes will fall down in between, and it'll close back and catch all twelve of them." And twing went the bullet and it split that limb and those toes went in there and it caught them, and he climbed that tree and took his knife and kept whittling and cut that limb off. And when he cut the limb off, the turkeys flew with it. And here Jack went through the air; over that limb the turkeys had so much pressure with their wings, they were carrying him. And so they went down off that mountainside and went down in a hollow next to the river, and me after them watching them fly with Jack holding onto it. And they got down there, and there's a great big hollow full of poplar timber; and the turkeys turned and came right back up with Jack, over me, in that beautiful hollow. And so I was running, trying to keep up to see if he lived or not; and all at once Jack got gone. And I was walking on up; I said, "He's gone this time; they've took him in the river; he's drowned."

So I was walking up about a fourth of a mile from where last I saw him, and I came by an ol' big snag, a tree snag, hollow with the top broke out of it. All at once a big black bear hit the ground, and it killed him. And I looked up on that, and Jack was sitting on top of it. And so he scaled down it. And so this is the story Jack told me now—what he told. He said, "Ray, I saw I was gonna be killed," and he said, "I turned loose and saw that big hollow snag and glided my legs like a calf and went down in there." And he said, "While I was down in that dark, I felt something furry." And he said, "I gave them the feel around, and it was two cub bears." And he

237

said, "I knew I'd die in there and you'd never know where I was, nor nobody else." And he said, "I know the mother bears always come back." And he says, "I waited a few minutes and here she came." He always picked up everything he saw and put it in his pocket, and he'd happened to pick up a one-prong eating fork. Two prongs were broken off and it had one on it, an eating fork, had one prong on it. And he said, "I saw a hole there, and I knew the mother bear was coming. When she got down to me, I seized on her and gouged with that one-prong fork, and she pulled me out of the top of the snag, and I shoved her right off."

And so we went on and we got in some deer, and he shot all his bullets at the deer, he thought, but he didn't get any. So we went on, and we came to an ol'-timey laid-up fence. There was a wild turkey on one bend of it, and a pheasant on another bend, and there was a big fox squirrel sitting on another bend of it. And so Jack says, "Oh, I wish I could find a bullet that I've missed." And he kept feeling in his pockets; he had plenty of powder left, that black powder. He kept feeling, and he finally felt right in here. He said, "By dad, I found one." And he loaded up that hog rifle. And I was looking around and turned from him kind of and was looking at that turkey and the pheasant and the fox squirrel, looking around, and Jack was gone. I looked out in the woods and he was between two saplings, two chestnut saplings, and had that rifle barrel between them. I said, "Jack, what are you doing?" He said, "I'm bending three crooks in this barrel, so I can kill all of them with one shot, with just one bullet." And so he bent three crooks in it and got down—kapow, twing, twing, twing—three ways it went and off fell the fox squirrel, and the pheasant and the turkey! And I looked and Jack was on the ground laying there, and I got him up. The gun just had the stock part laying there; it blowed it off. And so I got him up; he wasn't hurt too bad. We were there talking of what had happened, and all at once we looked down below us and there was a rabbit sitting down below, and it's dead. And the barrel had gone in and killed the rabbit. When it blowed out of the gun, it went in and

killed the rabbit. And I was standing there and heard something. I said, "Listen, Jack," —pick, pick, pick, pick, pick, pick, pick, pick, pick; and we stepped down in the woods, and the hammer on it [the rifle] down there was pecking a wild hog in the head.

And so we came on back and he got his dad's sled with a yoke of ox, and got two barrels to get two barrels of that honey, and took a cross-cut saw or the cold ax to get that tree cut down and get them two cub bears, and a rope to tie them with. And we went back by and got those ducks, and you know, confound, as we went through an old field growing up, we found those turkeys in that field, and he took a stick and womped them in the head. He says, "I don't want to kill them." He says, "I want to take them." And he'd just addle them every now and then to keep them so they'd stay in the branch with their toes, to show them when he got home, the twelve turkeys.

And you know what, about five years after that—he'd loaded up with peach seeds on the earlier hunt, and we had some in our pockets and shot those deer when his bullets gave away. You know what, about five years after that, I was down there and we took another hunt, and we took us a little dinner with us and got in the mountains and a fire got out and burned it all black. So we walked and he said, "We'll not find any game in this patch of woods. We'll have to get out where that fire hasn't burned." So we got to the top of that mountain, and he said, "We'd just as well eat a little bit right here, Ray." And he sat down on a stump, and I went on above him and sat down on a black log, I thought. And so I opened my dinner and had my pocketknife out to use it to eat with; and I just reached over and stabbed my knife in the log to stick it there to hold it. Right after I did that, I looked down and Jack looked like the stump was riding him off; and I said, "Jack, is that stump riding you off?" And he said, "No." And directly there came a tree between us. And I looked and, confound, I was sitting on a big black snake and thought it was a log. And so we went on and Jack hollered and said, "Hey, Ray, come here. Here's

238

some of the mellowest, ripest, prettiest, October peaches I've ever seen in my life." And I got to them to reach out to get me one to eat, and it ran off through the wood. Those peach seeds had come up and those deer hides were bearing peaches. They ran off through the woods. And so that was the last hunt I ever took with Jack. But the last time I saw him he was doing fine.

He gets into a lot of ways, but they [storytellers] told them so he comes out on top. *(Ray Hicks)*

Well, a Grandfather Tale hasn't got any Jack Tales in it. It's told to younguns, you know, about coon hunting and all of this and that. And then there's one back when we were younguns. We didn't get much time to fish. I liked to fish and hunt, but we didn't get time. So Dad went off to work, and I slipped off and went to the river. It wasn't far from the river, and I was catching these fish, throwing them out, caught a catfish, and threw it out on the bank; and it lay there and went [throaty noise] and flapped, you know. I got ready to go home and took it home. And I'd put it in water, and then I'd take it out and put in on dry land. And it got to where it didn't want to stay in water. And I tied a little string around its neck and I took it to school with me and put it in the desk until I got ready to go home. And there was an old bridge across the creek, and they had ol' yokes of cattle and wagons. And where they'd broken a board on the bridge there was a hole through it. And I went on across and had my little catfish right along behind me. I went across this bridge and got a way on out, and my string got weak, you know. And I turned around and looked and my catfish wasn't on it. And I went back to see what had happened to it. And do you know what happened? It fell right down through that hole in that bridge and got drowned. See, that's a Grandfather Tale to tell a youngun.

Another time, I went to the Watauga River fishing and I was catching these fish; and I hooked on one and I kept a-working and finally did get it out, a big ol' carp. Well, I couldn't load it on the truck. I got another friend and loaded it on the truck; brought it on home. And me and my wife took a chain saw.

They took the truck out yonder in the field. Took a chain saw and cut its head off, and she helped me clean it and came back and put it in the freezer. My neighbors out here, they raise pigs. And a sow got gone, and we hunted and hunted, and we couldn't find that sow anywhere. And we were hunting and I was coming back around this ol' fish head, and I heard [pig sounds]. And I went around and looked, and she'd gone in that fish head and made her a bed and had seven pigs. Now, that's what we talk about Grandfather Tales. And you get a youngun started that way, they'll sit and listen to you all night.

Another time, I was over here at Smith's store, and there was a fellow in there telling what a great fish he caught. I listened to him tell it. And I said, "I'll tell you what I did. I went down to the Watauga; and I was fishing and hooked onto something, and I pulled and I pulled and I pulled. Finally, the mud began to come up and directly it started out, and I kept pulling on it. When I got it out, it was a lantern that was still burning. It'd been down there since 1800-something." He said, "What a lie." I said, "You cut your fish tale down a little bit, and I'll blow the lantern out."
(Stanley Hicks)

My neighbor came in with that apron on like she wore, and the bonnet and the dress, and said, "Ray, when you get through with that, I want to tell you one" [a ghost story]. Well, when I got through, she started. She said, "Now, way down on the other side of the North Carolina line, on the Tennessee side, above Lincoln County, Tennessee, where I was raised, down in those dark mountains, there was a girl about my age, and we went around together." She said, "That girl wasn't afraid of anything. And there was a house hainted up on the hill from their home and all the persons that went to stay there, after the people weren't in it, said there came a man through the front door in on the floor here and stopped, just looked like a man, and said, 'Follow me,' and was gone. Spoke with a voice and said, 'Follow me.'" And she said, "Ray, one family rented it and moved in with their wagon and ox,

239

with a little plunder stuff they had; and they stayed one night. After the man came in and said, 'Follow me,' and then there wasn't anybody, they moved out the next morning." And she said another man then rented it and came in that day. And the man came in on them and spoke and said, "Follow me," and they packed back up.

And she said, finally, this girl that she'd went around with—her girlfriend—finally married a young man, her husband. They didn't have much. One of their neighbors gave them one of those ol'-timey, like I've seen them, wrapped rocking chairs where it squeaked, and some more gave them a cup and saucer apiece. (They called it a "sasser" then; they didn't call it a saucer.) And gave them a plate apiece, and a spoon and a fork apiece, and a little bedclothes. Their parents gave them one bedstead like they had back then. And he went off to a steam-engine sawmill, and it was so far he couldn't walk and work. He boarded in the shacks I've boarded in, to cut timber and work in the sawmill. And so he told her if she wanted, she could move in the house.

She took the stuff that they'd all given her and moved in on Thursday, I believe she said; and got settled down and was sitting just about, like she said, where I'm sitting from the door there. And the walking mailman had left a little newspaper. She was sitting reading it and turned her head and forgot all about what she'd been told about the man coming in. And she looked around and there was a man. She nearly screamed thinking it might be a man that'd harm her, you know. She said, "Law, that's that man I've heard people telling about." She turned her head back looking at the newspaper; and when she turned her head back, he was gone, no racket and no door opening. And she said she opened the door and stepped out and looked, and he's waiting for her on the porch. And when she got through the door, he went down off the steps walking, and came to the pailing gate (they had pailing around their house back then, where they kept the milk cow, you know).

And said she followed him to the pailing gate, and he just went through it. She had to unhook the latch on it and hook it back; and he waited for her out on the path. And when she got it hooked back, he took down the path with her following. So, got down the path a piece, and he's gone. She said, "Oh, after I followed him this far, I'd like to see where he went." Said she stood there and studied about ten or fifteen minutes and happened to think of what they called the smokehouse. Well, now, the smokehouse, was after the steam engine came out, was what they called the cellar. They took dry sawdust and that tongue-groove lumber and built it above the ground, and nothing would freeze in it on account of it's dry. And so she happened to think of it, and they called it a smokehouse on up then because they'd learned to smoke their meat in it with hickory wood. She happened to think, and turned up the path to it and opened the door.

In there in the aisle of that smokehouse cellar stood the man with his body burning alive—all over it, about that long—bright orange-looking-like glowing. Had the whole smokehouse lit up, it was dark as a dungeon in there with no light. Then directly his body just kneeled and floated over in the left potato box and then burned with a longer light, and really showed a glow of orange light, and went out and left her in there in the dark. And she came out of it. It was lighter outside, and she came back to the house and went to bed directly, read her newspaper. And it went on, and her husband that she'd married came in the Friday night from his work with a little pay that he got to get them something extra and some food. And he said, "Did you see that man, honey? Did you see that man?" She said, "Oh, yeah. I followed him." He said, "You followed him?" She said, "Yes, I followed him." He said, "Well, you take me where you ended up."

And she took him in that sawdust cellar and showed him where his body burned that way with the orange light about that long, and then he floated over where the potato box was, and burned really with an orange light, and then went out. And said he went and got some tools and tore off that tongue-groove lumber and that sawdust and dug it out and found 1,662 dollars in gold coins and bought the place and built them a new house on it.

If I had to go into a city and live, I'd soon die. I have a bad headache if I go to town. And just as far as I can, I stay away from places like that. That's one reason why I haven't traveled any more than I have because, well, I just don't like it. I just want to be in the mountains, and be quiet, and be left alone, and be free. (Nanny Suttles)

I quit school to become the plowboy. I did the plowing when I was fourteen. Of course, back then when a boy graduated from the hoe to the plow, he thought he was a man. He was proud of it. I really believe that we don't know what life is like until we experience some hardships. That's a side of life that a lot of people miss, and it serves a good purpose. Whether it grinds a man up or pommels him down depends on the stuff he's made of. The rough places in life tend be good for us. (Jonah Parker)

And my neighbor said, "Now, Ray, that's true." And she said, "Now why there ain't no ghosts anymore, Ray, like it used to be, all the people anymore put their money in the bank, mostly, and building and loans to draw interest, and none don't hide it anymore for God to show somebody that'll take it that needs it like they did, to get it. And probably he [the ghost] was killed for his money."
(Ray Hicks)

Horton Cooper

There were more superstitions afloat when I grew up than you'd imagine. Everybody planted their gardens and corn on the sign of the moon.

I heard these things during my boyhood days, I guess. For example, a mole on the neck means money by the peck. A horse half-drenched in water will become a worm. Leave a graveyard last, and you'll be the next person to die. An unmarried girl whose apron becomes wet as she washes the dishes will marry a drunkard. Stepping across a grave will prevent a baby's having colic. Shingles nailed on a roof will curl if done during the light of the moon. Meat butchered during the decrease of the moon will shrink badly when cooked. Chickens hatched in May will not do well. Hogs killed on the increase of the moon will give more grease. Dreaming of a wedding signifies the news of a death. If an unmarried girl can't cut a pie through in a single stroke of the knife, she will be an old maid. When your right hand itches, it indicates that you will soon shake hands with a stranger. If your left eye itches, you will soon be disappointed; if your right eye itches, you will soon be pleased.

When the dog star rises and sets with the sun, it's dog days. It usually begins the first of July. If you cut yourself, get a stone bruise on your foot from going barefooted, such as that, it won't get well.
(Horton Cooper)

This is what they call "dog days," you know. I think it was the twenty-fifth of July 'til the twenty-fifth of August. And it just rains about all the time then, and they say the snakes go blind during dog days. Says snakes is blind, and we'd always have to be so careful with them because we were afraid we'd get snake bit, and it was dangerous because we have a lot of bad snakes in this country. If kids had a little sore, we couldn't get out in the weeds and get that water on them because the water was poison, and you'd have an infection then. If you had a little scratch on you and get out in that wet, why it'd puff up. I don't know what caused it, but it would do it. Us younguns used to have them pretty bad because we'd get in the briars picking berries and get scratched. *(Nanny Suttles)*

According to Scotty Wiseman's song, an old hunter fell off the cliff over there and killed himself, and I believe his sweetheart escaped. And the song tells about his spirit still haunting the Brown Mountain over there. The Brown Mountain lights are spectacular. The government has sent investigators there, scientists, and they, the geologists, say that the lights are reflections of headlights. There's no history of them except oral history. I think the ol' man that they're named for is buried up there. They say that was before trains came through or automobiles came, but nobody can prove it. Made an effort to find someone that really could give the facts, something written back then, but there wasn't anything. The government scientists say that it's the air there that causes some kind of reflection of headlights and automobile lights. Sometimes the sky is just full of them. I believe now, since I've investigated, they begin about sunset; and I've stayed there 'til

257

ten o'clock at night or eleven. They become fewer and fewer as the night wears on. I rather think it's caused by fewer and fewer automobiles.
(Horton Cooper)

Have you read about the Brown Mountain light? I got the story from some of the Wisemans, Scotty and Lulabell. Supposedly a Southern planter went hunting in this wild land alone. Here he lost his way and never returned to his home. A faithful old slave came back and continued to search night after night with his lantern for his master from above. The old slave is gone, but his spirit continues to search from dusk to dawn. Nobody's been able to figure it out. Somebody said it was the lights of an automobile or a train or something, but it was so long before there were any automobiles or trains in this area. And if you go up— at night when it's not too cloudy and murky—you can go to the right point there, you can see the light. (Bob Phillips)

I can tell you about the Brown Mountain light. When I got up to where I was dating a little bit, I'd go out there; and we had—Dad bought—an old pickup to deliver milk in. I delivered milk in an old horse and buggy to Blowing Rock for a long time. But I'd have a date and go out and look for the Brown Mountain light, and it was awful handy. She'd say, "Let's go, let's go"; and I'd say, "No, we've got to wait." And we'd sit there and wait for the Brown Mountain light. It was an excuse to park awhile. There's incidences of it before we had any cars. And it was visible. It'd come along, and it'd start up over here in one section; and then it'd fade out, and it'd go off over here. Sometimes, then,

you'd have to wait for ever so long to see it again. And it was just as clear as could be—not a brilliant light, but just enough to see that there was a light there of some kind; and it wasn't concentrated like looking at a street light or something that way. It was just sort of a jumble of lights, stronger in the middle and then spread out over a space in time. The *National Geographic* sent folks here to study that thing, and various other scientific folks studied it, and they never did find out what it was. They had theories about it; but every theory they'd get, we could knock it out. Some said it was train lights from the train, but there wasn't any train in that area. It was over the top of Brown Mountain, and no train was in there. And some said it was some kind of phosphorus coming out of the ground; and the scientists, some of them, discounted that. And there've been numerous articles back then written about it. Nobody lived on the mountain itself then. They went over there to see it and couldn't see anything when they got there—not a thing, couldn't find a thing. There's several vantage points where you could see it from up on Green Hill about where the Green Park Hotel is now, and then there's a place right on the highway there, just before you get to the golf course, where you could see it then. Now there's houses built along there, and I don't know if you could see. And then there's a place over on the Parkway just beyond Linville that was recognized as a good vantage point. But you could just see it in certain places. And it was there! And nobody, so far as I know, has had any hard and fast explanation as to what it was. *(Wade Brown)*

Yeah, I know about the Brown Mountain lights. Well, they say that this light just comes up a certain time of night, you know, and just comes and goes. Nobody knows what it is. They think maybe some kind of phosphorus from some kind of woods. That's what some people think it is, but I don't think anybody really knows. It's just a mystery.
(Lula Wise)

HUNTING AND FISHING

My dad always told us never to kill anything you couldn't eat. And we didn't eat coon, so if we killed a coon, we skinned it to get its hide. Your pets then were dogs that would do something. It wasn't a thing that you just kept around the house to cuddle up with. It was something that you chased rabbits and groundhogs with, kept varmits off your farm, or guard dog. We'd go hunting, that was our entertainment. Fish and hunt—there was plenty of game. But 1940 killed a lot of fish—the flood water and everything. You'd just go out in a stream and catch fish. I mean, you'd go out and catch a mess of fish, you didn't go out and catch a tub of fish. People today, they want to steal them. We'd go out and catch what we'd eat. See, when I grew up, if you went hunting, you'd eat the rabbit, you'd eat the bird you killed, you'd catch and eat the fish. You didn't kill nothin' you didn't eat. *(Frank Norris)*

You didn't go hunting or fishing just for the fun of it. You went out to get some meat. And a lot of the families really depended on particularly the hunting for a lot of the meat, bear, and venison. Then the streams were full of mountain trout. Even in our old days we used to go to what is now in the Smoky Mountain Park up above Cherokee and catch fish 'til you got tired of catching them. *(Dan Moore)*

My father [Grady Reed] worked there for twenty-five to thirty years, maybe longer. He has worked as a butcher and raises a huge garden. He has never missed a day of work, and he is a coon hunter and a bear hunter. During the hunting season, he works all day at the factory house, comes home, feeds all his dogs, and he also has cows. After dinner, many, many nights he goes coon hunting. And sometimes, my mother says, he doesn't come home until five-thirty or six in the morning. Eats his breakfast, goes back to work, and does the same thing again. He has done that for years. He likes the coon hunting when you crawl through the bushes at night with a flashlight and find a coon up a tree. He doesn't bring them home very much anymore because the family didn't really care to see a coon every night. He hunts with other people always, and he always gives it to somebody else. *(Wanda Moss)*

I coon hunt and bear hunt. Raise all kinds of dogs: white dogs, red bones, and got blue ticks. We bear hunt, like right now, go out and run them. Right now it's legal to run them. And it's legal to coon hunt and tree them, but you can't shoot them there. You have to leave them alone. It is legal to coon hunt after the fifteenth of October. But that's early enough for the season to open. The snakes're just beginning to go up then; hot days they're still out crawling. I hunt a whole lot, and then come back and work the next day. I never have let it interfere with my work. That means if I worked today, hunt tonight, and work tomorrow, then the next night I'll sleep. But I don't never lose no work on account of going hunting.

Been taking about four dogs out. We had four the other night. Load them up in the truck, take them out there, and get them on the track. Hear them strike, barking along, directly get a run on, directly to a tree, and you have to stay in hearing of them, though. And then you have them barking right on 'til you shoot the coon. Last night they got after something, but they come back. We got a little late, but still, better to stay late and get your dogs before you come in, ain't it? We left at nine at night and got in about nine this morning. Gone about twelve hours, wasn't we? We made a pretty good round, went over on the Macon County side and run into some more hunters and took with them. We got back to the truck about three, and we sat there and nodded 'til daylight—took catnaps, that helps. Keep the motor running every once in a while to keep warm, you know, waiting for the dogs to come back.

From about three o'clock on. We got the coon out about one. *(Grady Reed)*

I never went coon hunting, but I remember there were some boys that came here one morning just as day was breaking and said, "We've got something treed out yonder on the mountain and don't know what it is and want to get a saw." We went out there, and it was a big ol' white oak, and it was hard to saw. We got there in time to catch the dogs and hold the dogs for them. The tree fell, and no coon came out. And we turned the dogs loose, and they just made a dash in there and commenced to bark. The thing was such a big ol' coon, and it was such a big ol' hollow tree. He'd got in there, and he didn't aim to come out. He just stayed there, and those dogs just commenced to bark. Well, Wade Hanson got up on the log and took an ax and cut a hole in it. He stood there a minute and said, "He'll stick his head out directly." And I said, "Wait a minute; let me up there." And I had Charles', the boy that stayed with us that summer, I had his .22 down there. I got up on the log, and directly I heard something rattle in there and looked. It just came and stuck its head out there right in the open. I was just standing up there over him, you know; I just put a bullet right down through his head and killed him suddenly, and we dragged him out. They said it was the biggest coon they'd ever seen. Oh it'd weighed forty pounds, big as a dog. *(Marion Coffey)*

I don't go at night; I wait 'til daylight. Lots of times they'll [coons] tree at night, and I know they're treed. Last year that little ol' black dog treed two down there below the barn. I went down there and I shot six shots at it, and I couldn't hit it at all. I came back to get the shotgun. There was a big one. I was afraid I'd miss it with a shotgun. My head would swim or something, and I couldn't aim it right. My neighbor came by and killed it. I thought there was just one. When that man shot, he had to shoot twice with that ol' twelve shotgun. He had to shoot the second time to get the second coon out, then didn't kill it. Had to kill it after it fell. And I

gave him the coons, both of them. It was cold and I was kind of nervous, you know, jerking. That was one reason I couldn't hit it with the rifle. I've been shooting squirrels with the rifle. *(Letha Hicks)*

I think that a lot of people have that image of the mountains, of these poor starving people and these houses with dirt floors, but that's not the case. Nobody starves in the mountains. People grow food, and it's everywhere. They raise gardens, but a lot of them hunt and fish. If they don't have money, they still have all these things. They can go out and catch fish or kill a deer or do something like that. It's not like they go out and kill a deer and waste it. They eat it. I feel like it's bad if you go out and hunt animals to kill 'em and not use them. But if you use them for meat, I don't see anything wrong with it at all. My husband loves to deer hunt, but he would never kill an animal just for the fun of killing it. **(Wanda Moss)**

We came to the awfulest possum track that had ever been in this country. There'd never been one like it before and hasn't been one since. It was as big as a dog's track. They set their heels down and make a long track, you know, a possum does. The track would be that long and be almost as wide as your finger there. And that ol' heel will show on a possum every time. I said, "Carl, we could get that thing if we had a mattock. You go up there and get a mattock, and I'll cut a hole in that tree and maybe make us a fire." It was the biggest tree that I ever saw of a chestnut. It was six or seven feet through at the ground and it was hollow; it was dead. So I commenced chopping there, and I chopped in and knocked it off.

I crawled over in there, and it was just as dry in there as it could be. There were dry splinters and every kind of fuzz, so I just raked a bunch of that stuff together over on the back side of that and struck a match to it; sat down in there and warmed my feet while he was going after that mattock. He came back, and I'd gone and cut a long pole to see which way the possum went from that tree. So we took the pole and ran it in, and we dug, and we

I pulled it out, and he killed the thing and brought it on up here and dressed it; and it was more than twice as big as any possum that I've ever seen. And I took it to Willcox at Boone, and he said that was the best that has ever come to this shop; that's the best pelt that has ever been. He said, "I'm going to give you two dollars and fifty cents for that hide." Well, an ordinary possum hide wasn't but fifty cents. *(Marion Coffey)*

Justin Reed and his grandfather, Grady Reed, with hunting dogs

dug, and we dug. We'd dig down, and we'd call the dog, and he'd stick his nose down there. If he could smell it, he'd bark, and if he didn't, we didn't dig anymore. We dug two or three holes, and the dog wouldn't bark. I said, "Give me that mattock; I'm going to punch its brains out here at this place. I haven't dug this right here yet." So I just took the handle and commenced jabbing it down in the ground and the dog started barking. I said, "Boy, I got close to him that time." So we dug on down there, and in just a minute we could see the thing's tail. We just reached down and got it. And Carl said, "Lord have mercy; there comes the possum."

Well now, since he's told his possum tale, I want to tell you my groundhog tale. I just walked off up through the meadow to get away from the house, to the upper tree up there where we had lots of apple trees at that time. And there were some old apples that still hung there; it was awfully late, though. And I got up to that other one, and I saw this little half-grown groundhog eating an apple in the grass; and I just stood there and watched it and looked at it, you know, straight in the eye and it looking at me. And I just kept easing up just the least bit, you know, 'til I got to it. I never took my eyes off it; and I grabbed its tail. That's the dying

261

truth; I caught that groundhog by the tail, and I brought it back down here. You may not believe it, but I caught that groundhog by the tail, brought it down here. And that is an honest tale, if I ever told one, every word of it. I bet that's the only groundhog that's ever been caught by the tail by a woman. *(Lyda Coffey)*

My favorite was squirrel hunting. I love squirrel hunting. I love squirrel to eat. I never used to go out and shoot things for the fun of it. I never even thought about that, considered that. And if I wasn't going to save the meat, I wouldn't shoot anything. *(Jonah Parker)*

We did a lot of fishing and stuff like that; we ate our game. It wasn't a thing where we went out and slaughtered game just to be slaughtering it. Like rabbits. When I'd come in from school in the evening, I had two dogs when I was just a young boy in my early teens. I'd take them two dogs and rabbit hunt 'til dark, and sometimes I'd get three or four rabbits; and we ate it. We didn't just throw them down and go on and leave them. And then I was in school, you know, Saturday'd come, I'd go squirrel hunting real early in the morning. Me and my brothers, and my father sometimes would go, and we'd come back, we'd have ten or fifteen squirrels. We didn't throw away hardly anything. Whatever we caught, we ate.

Back then, we mostly went possum hunting. I didn't know anything about coons 'til I was in my late teens. There wasn't such a thing as a coon; I never heard of a coon around this area until I was in my teens. I rabbit hunted and possum hunted, squirrel hunted, and that type of stuff when I was a young boy. Then when I got to coon hunting, because of the races, you know, and hear the dogs run a lot longer, I enjoyed that kind of stuff. So that's when I got into coon hunting. *(Junior Johnson)*

If you've never been a fox hunter, with a gang of dogs sitting on top a mountain somewhere, I guess it's the most relaxing thing that you've ever done in your life. You can hear all kinds of animals around you, you know, the crickets and whatever. And all at once that dog gets the fox up, and he'll run and he'll be out of hearing awhile. And you'll sit there, and you'll listen. You're hearing everything but that dog, and in a few minutes he's going to come into your hearing. Same way with coon hunting or possum hunting. You may stand on this ridge for an hour. That dog's gone. He's circling around trying to find the coon or fox. Then when you hear him tree, you run. You break, and you're gone. *(Frank Norris)*

The way I cooked it [squirrel] was clean it good and put it in some water and salt and cook it tender; and then I'd make gravy. Season it with butter and take some milk and thicken it a little. That's the way we always did it, but I haven't had one for so long I wouldn't know what squirrel was now. It's been years since we had one. *(Lyda Coffey)*

Back then there was, oh, millions of squirrels. When I was a little boy, I'd say eight or nine years old, my grandfather had been shot in the hip and shoulder during the Civil War, and he was crippled, and he would take me with him. I'd carry his gun; that's what he took me for, to carry his gun. I didn't do any shooting. We'd go out safe from the house, and he'd kill two or three squirrels and bring them back and cook them and eat them.

You know, if they had sickness or something, they'd go kill something like a wild animal that they could eat, and make a broth—like we use bouillon today. They were delicious. Oh, they made dumplings, squirrel dumplings, rabbit dumplings. Even since we've been in the restaurant business here, we had a big rabbit feast, made dumplings and gravy and biscuits. *(Frank Norris)*

They hunted a lot. That was their recreation. They bear hunted. It is still a big thing, deer hunting and bear hunting. There are still clubs for it. But back then it was really something because they had bigger game. They talk about bears that weighed 300 and 400 pounds, and now you are talking about a bear that weighs 150 pounds. *(Reg Moody)*

They'd have an annual bear hunt. My grandfather had bear hides hanging in the house or on the floor. They had bear traps. They had a big ol' steel trap they called a bear trap. Oh golly, if you ever got in it, it'd cut your leg off. They trapped them, and then killed them. If they got to bothering their animals, they would trap. I mean, if they'd come in and kill your pigs or sheep, or something like that, they would trap the bear. And if there got to be too many of them, they would have a bear hunt; and they'd go out and kill the bear with a rifle, shotgun, or whatever they had, go kill the bear. But we didn't do too much bear hunting in this area. Now bear hunting was over in Avery County, always has been. They've got bear dogs—I mean, dogs professional hunters use to hunt bears. They run those dogs until they corner the bear. The bear gets backed up, and he'll kill your dog. That's the way they hunt them today. They get on mopeds and every other thing going through the woods. That's not even sporting. *(Frank Norris)*

I'm not mad at no bear. It's like I say, the only thing I ever killed was for something to do with it—you skin the fur and sell the fur, or you eat it. What's the point of killing anything if you can't do something with it? (Frank Norris)

Now there's one bear got into bees over here in Macon County just across the mountain right across there where I've been today. And they got into Marion Michael's bees and tore about four or five gums up. And he sent for us to come over there and dog it. They struck it right there where the bees had been and run it around on the hill there, and it just reared up and commenced fighting the dogs right there. It was one of the ol' tame bears I reckon had been around the park so much. It wouldn't

run, wouldn't run from the men. You had to get out there and hit it with a stick or something to make it move on. And then it'd run around the side of the hill a piece, it'd stop again and fight them dogs. They run all day and then kind of scared it off from there, and it went off down the creek a little further and got into Beulah Mason's bees. I believe it was three or five stands there. It had them scattered, I mean, tore up so bad I couldn't tell how many there was. They had several stands left, but he had tore up so many of them. It picked up one and carried it up on a hill about 200 feet and set that thing down and eat that honey right there. You might think about one picking a bee gum up. He'd pick that up, and he had to walk on his hind feet up there and set that thing down.

We get up a lot of times way before daylight. Way back when we had to get up early, it used to be Dad to holler at us, you know, to get up early. He'd say, "Rise up and get your foot on the rock; it ain't daylight, but it's four o'clock. I know you're tired and sleepy too; hate to call you, but I got it to do. I ain't a-wantin' ya, but the cook do. Dawn's done rung, roll done called. Don't bounce none; needn't to bounce at all. So rise and shine, keep up the time. Get them biscuits in that oven; how I wish I had some of 'em. Take 'em to the table; put 'em in a plate; sop, sop, sop; don't be too late." That'd get you on the go in the morning. Bring 'em up out of the bed, wouldn't it?

We have bear and coon hunting season at the same time. Well, there's a space too when we don't get to hunt much, but that's right through the hot part of the summer. It's agin' the law then. Of course, people don't pay much attention to it though. Back here in the woods, they get in there and hunt any time they take a notion. Could get caught, not apt to, though. *(Grady Reed)*

I was deer hunting and I stepped on a limb. I'd walked up this treetop, about six feet, and just turned around and stepped on a limb to fix a place to sit down. It broke, and right backwards I came. And if I'd just hit the vines and stuff, it wouldn't have been so bad, but there was a pole about that

"Old Joe", brindle Plott hound, one of Grady Reed's hunting dogs

big. Gosh, I saw stars and just went out. I thought my back was broken. And these boys had gone to make a drive, to drive the deer through, you see, and I didn't go with them. I just stayed there to kill one when they came back through. And I hollered, and there wasn't anybody anywhere near. So I crawled over to my gun; I just threw it when I fell. I could move my arms and my legs, and I saw that my back wasn't broken; crawled over to my gun, got it, and unloaded it. That's the first thing I did. I got all the shells out of the gun, put them in my pocket; got my hunting coat and my hunting knife and got a hold of a bush and my gun and got up. It took me an hour and forty-five minutes to get to my truck. It wasn't too far, but I'd just go a piece and then lay down, just crying. And got to my truck and got back to the campground and my kinfolk's wife, third cousin, his wife hadn't gone; so she helped me get out of the truck and helped me to the camp and helped me lay down on the bed. The sweat was just streaming. And they came in when they came back, and then they got her husband to take me to the emergency room. Thank the Lord no bones were broken. *(Stanley Hicks)*

My dad [Grady Reed] raises hunting dogs. He has as many as thirty dogs at a time. When you go there it sounds like an orchestra because of the dogs barking. And they know his truck. When he comes up the driveway they all start to howl and bark. It's a major thing just to feed all those dogs. He feeds

them twice a day. He has dog traders constantly hanging out by the back door. There's always somebody there wanting to talk trading dogs, and he will talk all day long. That's part of his reason for hunting so much. He would train these dogs. And he got a lot of money for them. He had some as high as 2,000 dollars. Most of the time they went for a measly 500 dollars I guess. But I remember a few years there he sold some real expensive dogs that he had trained. He has never advertised in any way except by his own reputation. *(Wanda Moss)*

I used to grow flowers. You know why I don't now, don't you? Quit that a long time ago and grow dogs instead of flowers. The last flowers that I put out was up there under those windows, and they were the little dwarf marigolds. I went out there one day and a little pup trampled all but three of them and bedded down right at the end—ruined every one of them. So we've got dogs anymore. Many of a time Grady'd work all day, take his dogs and hunt all night, and then come back in and work all day. It was constantly that way. He'd sleep by the stove while I cooked breakfast. He'd come in and get the fire started in the stove so it'd get warm, and then he'd sit down in the corner by the stove and sleep in the chair while I cooked. *(Delia Reed)*

You'd lose a friend when you lost your hunting dog. And, you know, a hunting dog's life will average maybe ten years. It's a while, but yet today a dog will live twelve to fifteen years because he don't do nothin' but lay around the house and eat. *(Frank Norris)*

We slept with wild boars many a night. I'm serious. Lay down and go to sleep, and they'd come through the side of the tent. One night one of them came through the side of the tent and took a loaf of bread and went right on with it. Usually sows and boars don't run together except during breeding season. But this was in the spring of the year, and there were boars and sows together, which is very unusual. The sows are the ones you really don't have to worry about unless they have piglets.

One time one big boar just fell in right behind us. We could turn around and shine our lights on him and see him; he was that close. We could hear him back there sharpening his tusks. See they've got two little tusks that come out and they grow down and vertical, actually make a V from their upper jaw. Then the lower jaw is where the thick tusks, the razor tusks, come out. That's the way they sharpen them, they chop their mouth together and it forms a triangle. And, I mean, they're razor sharp.

This one didn't like it very much. He'd just come up behind us and keep popping that mouth. We'd turn around and shine our light, and he'd run off up the hill and come back down and come right on behind us. He was stalking us. See, Russian boar are one of the few animals that will eat meat. They'll eat rattlesnakes, copperheads. They'll even eat a human. Oh, they'll kill their own. At that particular time, in '62, '63, '64, in that period, they were still pretty pure. They'd been brought over from Russia over to Cooper's Falls, and then they brought the moose and turned them loose on the man's private preserve over there and that spread all through that region, too. The boars are so tough that a .22 bullet would bounce off their hide. It wouldn't penetrate. *(Mike Hensley)*

It was early in the spring and it was getting cold. We were cleaning that land right out there, and it got a little cloudy, and it went to snowing while we were eating dinner. I said to my nephew, "Boy, that'll ruin it." He said, "No, that won't have anything to do with the fishing." I said, "Well, we'll just go fishing anyhow then." So we went fishing, and we went down the road there to where the bridge is and commenced fishing there. We both threw our hooks in, and he went on down to the next hole and threw his hook in. I fished a minute there and came on down to him again. He brought the rod in again, and I said, "Oh, wait a minute; you're going ahead all the time. You take one hole. One hole's mine and one's yours." "Good," he says. So we fished on down. We went on plumb down to where the creek comes into the Parkway over yonder. I had twenty-six and he had twenty-five. Mountain trout was what they were. None of them were more than six inches long; they were the best things you ever saw, just to bite into one, you could eat the whole thing. *(Marion Coffey)*

You can pull a good one on the game warden, though; have your fishing pole out there, you know, tryin' to drown the worm. And he'll come over and try to catch you for fishing. Tell him, "No, I'm not fishing, I'm drowning the worms." You have to go buy a license. Well, I'll tell you; I've got my permanent license now. It cost ten dollars. But I got it when I was sixty-five. If I'd waited 'til I was seventy-two, it wouldn't cost me nothin'. But still I have to buy a fish stamp now. I can fish in a lake or anywhere where there are not no trout fish, but if I'm going to fish for trout, got to have a fish stamp. *(Grady Reed)*

Southern Railway had to build a new bridge above Marshall, and all my lifetime there has been a fish in the river that nobody could catch. They had to dynamite, and they killed a catfish that weighed about, I believe they said about a 120 pounds. It had eighteen hooks in its jaw. But everybody that had ever hooked it thought they had hooked a log. *(Landon Roberts)*

Me and Papa went fishing one time, and I was sitting right close to him and I put my hook in, and I caught the biggest thing. I didn't know what it was! I thought it was a snake, and I swung it up and over, and Papa told me not to lose it; it was an eel. And I'd caught an eel, great big ol' eel. And I didn't know what in the world to do with it. He took it over the hill and took it home. It tasted like fish. *(Mamie Hall)*

I was raised to fish in Linville Gorge. I started fishing when I was four. I stuck my feet in his (Dad's) hip pockets. I'd lock onto the back of his neck, and we'd traipse off through there. We would go down to Linville Gorge or anything in Western North Carolina, we just about fished. We'd come out of Linville Gorge at night with our fish, and the wildcats followed you out 'cause they could smell the fish. **(Mike Hensley)**

I was walking up this old road after they'd quit traveling. It was washed away, big gullies in it. And so I was coming up the darkest place in it, and there were timbers beside the old road. It wasn't a real dark night. I could see right to the end where it was coming to the field down there. And I looked before me and it looked like some boys had rolled a log stump in the road, and I kept looking at it. I said, "That ain't no stump; I believe that's a black bear." And so, that bear now was wanting to eat me, kind of. Now a lot of animals that will kill you—like a dog—will bite you if you run; but if you won't run, they won't bite you. But there's one now and then in the animals that'll get you whether you run or not, just like bees will sting. And so this bear was kind of wanting to eat me, or kill me, but he was waiting to see whether or not I'd try to run. I says, "I can't run. If I run it'll catch me in here right now, it's dark and in the timber, this thicket." Well, I was standing there. What would I do? Well, it'd look at me and I'd look at it. And directly it hit my sight about Davey Crockett. It's said he grinned a coon to death and he tried a grizzly, but he had to cut it up with his knife. He got hurt pretty bad, but he killed a grizzly with his knife. So that made me think, and I raised my hat and took a few steps toward that bear, grinning, smiling at it, and walked on up a little more, and it smiled back at me and went out through the woods. I grinned it away. That was true about Davey Crockett grinning that coon to death. And I grinned it away; it went out right into the woods. That's the truth. *(Ray Hicks)*

CRAFTS

Emma Wertenberger with quilts for sale by local craftswomen in her shop at the Squire Watkins Inn, Dillsboro

I think the crafts were probably never hobbies, maybe the whittling was. They grew out of necessity, like making the quilts because they needed the warmth and making the bedspreads because that was inexpensive. All of these things, I think, grew out of a necessity of survival. Even making things to sell was still not a hobby, but the idea of buying food. *(Rose Marie Feimster)*

Daniel Boone I [the first] was a blacksmith. He was what we call a logger blacksmith. He shod oxen and horses and mules and made trace chains and ram's horns and all of that stuff, single trees, for all the different logging camps. This is the way that he got into the mountains. *(Mike Hensley)*

I grew up beside the Boones at Burnsville. I was fortunate to be able to work with Daniel Boone IV.

He's dead. Marvelous person; he was a genius, probably the greatest blacksmith that ever lived in America. He would boggle the imagination of the mind with the things that he could build. He'd let me fiddle around in his shop. Then when I got out of high school and started working professionally, I started working with him. We were on the going out of the time of the horses and logging equipment. So as the horses and all faded away, then we got to doing wrought-iron work, and he was a master at that. Then he had the contract of doing the work at the Williamsburg restoration. That's how come I'm connected with doing work for the Williamsburg restoration. I've been blacksmithing forty-five years professionally. And I've done work for Abercrombie & Fitch in New York, Macy's in New York, Williamsburg restoration, and President Johnson's got a piece of my work, and Gene Autry's got a knife that I made. I've got work in England, France, Germany, Belgium, Greece, Hawaiian Islands, Philippine Islands, Formosa, and Zaire in Africa. Queensland, Australia, is the last job that we shipped, I guess, the farthest way. No, New Zealand. If you go to New Zealand, I guess you'd be coming back home. If you do good work, you don't have to worry. And I'll tell you another thing that amazes me. I've never shipped but one job collect in my life. It doesn't make any difference where the order came from or how much it amounts to, I just ship it to them, and I never worry about getting my money. It always comes back. I used to do a tremendous lot of different things, but most of the work that I do now is limited to what a person wants in a particular home. If he wants andirons, fire screen, railing, balcony, or light fixtures, I do all of that. *(B. Hensley)*

We were rooming right back of a cabinet shop, and I would go up there and piddle around and help the man do this or do that or do something else. Finally, one day the foreman said, "Herman, you've got a talent for woodwork. I've got three apprentices here and I'm allowed one more. If you want to, I'll take you on as an apprentice for eight dollars a month. I stayed on there four straight years and graduated as a journeyman cabinetmaker. I practiced that trade for fifty-one years, and I taught twenty-two of them. And when I was sixty-five, I quit. I mean, that was the end of it. I taught woodworking over at the Folk School at Brasstown for fourteen years. I loved it. I couldn't even begin to tell you how many students I had. But of all the ones that I had, I've got twenty-six of them that's still making their living at it. *(Herman Estes)*

The secret of carving is this. You have to know what you're carving. Let's say, for instance, you're carving a hog. You've got to know what a hog looks like. You can take that piece of wood and sit there, and when you come to his ear, you know just what they look like. When you come to his snout, you know what they look like. And when you get through, you've got a hog. If you don't know what the object is that you're carving, you won't get to first base. **(Herman Estes)**

The craftsmen are the least cared for people there are in the world. About the poorest people we have are craftsmen. And I guess they're about as independent a people as there are. That's why they're craftsmen. They don't want to be told what to do. They don't make a lot of money, but they can work at what they're working at when they want to, and they can quit when they get ready. You don't make that much money at it. Been making dulcimers. Just forty-nine years since I made the first one. That was a rainy-day job back then, to have something to do. I've got them in about every state in the Union, in Alaska and Hawaii, Tokyo, England, Germany, Norway, Zaire, and I believe I sent one to

Kenya. I just take God's resources and change the form of it. Sometimes you have to look at a piece of wood an awful long time. This one over here, I looked at it, held onto it for three years, before I saw something. Just a piece of wood, that's all it was. I guess if you timed yourself woodcarving, you'd probably make one piece and quit. Too much time for what money you get out of it. To make a dulcimer, you'd get it probably in two weeks. *(Edd Presnell)*

I don't know how long it takes. I've carved several of these bears, but I never did keep time. I don't keep time with anything I do. Carve a while, quit a while, then carve again. *(Nettie Presnell)*

G. B. Chiltoskey is one of the greatest woodcarvers in the world. G.B. Chiltoskey—I've been fortunate to spend hours with him. *(B. Hensley)*

I'm a member of the International Wood Collectors Society. There were only two people chosen that year. I was one of them, and the other was a guy from London, England. So I felt quite honored to be chosen. Carving has been my hobby all my life. I don't think anything about it, but I carve what people want.

I enjoy living. I try to live the best I can. I make my own furniture and everything you see, I made. The table there I made, the chest, and all the kitchen cabinets. I'm just thankful that I'm gifted to do what I want to do. A lot of people ask me about how long it takes to carve something. I don't know why they ask me that. I think a lot of people ask before they think; that's the way I feel about it. If you think, you look at the piece of wood. I started this about a year ago. How would I know how long it's going to take me to finish it? So many things I've got are unfinished. I've got a violin up there I started thirty years ago I haven't finished yet. But if I can make a violin, I can make anything. *(G. B. "Goingback" Chiltoskey)*

I've got behind on my orders. I've got better than 2,000 dollars in orders for dulcimers and banjos. It takes about anywhere from thirty-seven to forty hours to build a dulcimer. It takes me a week from the time I start one to get it out. I don't work many hours at it. It takes something like fifty hours for a banjo because there's more to do. I've got the first banjo I built when I was fifteen years old; Dad helped me. I've been building banjos off and on ever since I was fifteen years old. And dulcimers, I've been building them, I guess, about twenty years.

One fellow came from Washington and ordered six dozen banjos. And if you get that many orders at one time, there isn't any way of getting caught up. I've got plenty of lumber and stuff to do. When my wife was here, you see, I could get more done. By the time I clean up my house, cook a little and tend the garden and mow the yard, just don't have any time. It'll probably be a month before I get back in the shop and do anything in it.

I learned to build banjos and dulcimers from my dad. I guess he learned it from his daddy, but his daddy, my grandpa, never did build many. It's something that oughtn't to be thrown away; it ought to be carried on. I've some stuff up there I made for them in Washington. I've got a little dulcimer in a museum and banjos. "A Master Traditional Artist" award they gave me. *(Stanley Hicks)*

When I was a kid, before Mother died, we grew a little broom corn and made our own brooms. We'd make the round brooms, you know. And we'd grow more than we'd need, and there was an old crude broom machine a fellow had over here; and my Daddy'd take what we didn't want to make up there to that old broom machine and make a flat broom just like you buy out of the store. And we'd sell the brooms we didn't need, the round ones we made by hand and the flat ones too. As well as I remember, the ones we'd make by hand sold for about a quarter. And I think the one made on machine for people who could afford it was fifty cents. *(Monroe Ledford)*

I have interviewed the Foxfire people with my quilt work and chair-bottoming work. I did that chair. I did not do my chair like the bought chairs are. I made that pattern myself. But that one in there was a little bit different, too. It's one I made like I was teaching the Foxfire kids to do. A lot of the strips don't match, but they just left me the odds and ends, and I bottomed my chair with what was left. I learned to make baskets, but I'm not too good at basket making.

Now my grandmother had the loom to weave it [cloth]. And they went to the woods and these ivy bushes and the maple barks, and all the different colors came from the woods. They blended these juices together to make other colors. You see, we had the two basic colors, black and white, when cloth began to be made. Then they learned to blend other stuff with it, and they took the cooperas that you bought at the stores, and they put it in to set the dye. You won't believe this, but she

Some of Willard Watson's carvings

didn't have a pair of scissors. My cousins would come over there and get together with patterns, and if one person in the whole community got a pattern, everybody got paper or something to make a pattern. And they would spread that cloth and put the pattern down, and one would fold it like this, and the other one would take the pocketknife and cut. And Dad kept those pocketknives sharp so they could cut out the cloth. Not many people could own a loom. There just had to be one in the neighborhood. They were busy the whole time, making thread, dyeing the thread, and weaving. But just the best workers that knew all about this would gather and weave the cloth. Some would be making rolls to make the thread, and some would be out dyeing the thread and drying it and getting it ready to work up. Then everybody that did the work shared in the thread. When they wove the cloth, everybody got their share of the cloth. *(Harriet "Granny" Echols)*

My mother did weaving way on back. She made the most beautiful suits for women out of linen, white linen; and she made dress suits and made a lot of rugs. I was eight years old and used to ride a donkey and take a lot of rugs just tied all around that donkey like you do a horse, and take it up on Sugar Loaf. She'd get her money. They sent every bit of it. It all went out to New York. She was great on crafts. She did hand weaving on the old-fashioned loom. *(Tom Oates)*

We still do a lot of quilting. I've been quilting lately. Now our quilts, all of a sudden, are selling for a hundred dollars. *(Carrie Burnette)*

I'm working on them now. I have my scraps. This is just a—I'll call it crazy fashion. It's just cut them into little pieces and sew them back. I've got stacks upstairs. Oh, they're not beauties. One of them is; I have one that is fifty blocks, a block for each state with a state bird and a state flower and the date embroidered. I got 200 dollars for the one I sold. I've made a lot of afghans, but my eyes are giving me trouble, so I'm not crocheting any much lately.

I made all my children, all my grandchildren, and two of my great-granddaughters afghans and gave it to them. So a fellow has to keep busy. If you give up, you surely are lost. *(Lyda Coffey)*

That was the only social life my grand- mother had really. She'd get her friends, and they'd quilt. My mother, until just a couple of years before she died, always had a quilt going. In the valley, they'd come in in the afternoon; and, instead of playing bridge, they'd quilt. Get caught up on all the gossip.
(Annie Dee Leatherman Smith)

The Fry Collection. Those are the knotted bedspreads. Unbleached domestic, a rough kind of fabric, and the mountain women did the designs, a lot of them were original. They called them "knotted" because they also made the fringe from string and they used some kind of instrument, maybe even a stick, and knotted that thread, just beautiful. Before the First World War, a lady was in Blowing Rock visiting. Her husband was a professor at Vassar, I think, and she bought a bedspread like that from a woman on the street. She took it back home and was so fascinated that she set up a little shop, and for years, even through the Depression, she ordered bedspreads from women in this area. I guess they fed their families with them. The work is all hand done, but the materials are very simple and inexpensive. When Mrs. Fry died, her daughter found stacks—she'd given the shop up long before—stacks of bedspreads in the attic or somewhere that I don't think had been opened. Apparently she kept buying those, I guess to help those women. She gave them to Appalachian State University. They're just gorgeous. You can see different personalities in them. *(Rose Marie Feimster)*

Aunt Josie Mast had three looms in a log cabin. She and her two sisters some days would all be in there working those looms, making something pretty—bedspreads or dresser scarves, something nice; sold a lot. Back during President Wilson's administration, she made enough to furnish one room in the White House. *(Howard Mast, Sr.)*

Penland is where there is a handicraft school. My uncle Rufus Morgan, who died two years ago at age ninety-eight, started an Episcopal school at Penland, and his sister, Lucy Morgan, came there as the principal of the school. The academic part and the dormitory part, an outgrowth of her work there, was a result of her interest in doing something to raise the economic conditions of the people in the community through weaving and reviving old handicrafts. She brought looms and took them out to the people in the community, and they would weave and bring the products in. She would pay them for their labor. She had a little Runabout Ford with the truck in the back, and she would take the towels, scarves, and rugs, and bags, and things like that and sell them. She started quite a community project, and the people in the community built this little cabin called the "Weaving Cabin." It was really a community affair because people would donate, for instance, a day's work or three poplar logs, or anything they might have, stones for the fireplace and various things. And it really belonged to the people of the community. It was really a wonderful experience to know that and to grow up with it—where there was a neighborliness and a friendliness and an interest in economic conditions. The students that came there from the mountain area provided us all kinds of drama and stories. They were very wonderful people. But, anyway, the school grew and people from literally all over the world came. Now, the craft school is the only remnant of the Appalachian School, the Episcopal school which was founded originally for young children. *(Louise Morgan Rodda)*

The Trading Post is an outlet for the mountain people's crafts from an eleven-county area. This operation started in 1955 and was incorporated in 1958. And everything we have is either handmade, homemade, or antique. Mr. Archie Davis from Winston-

Salem and some other men were interested in helping the mountain people get an outlet for their merchandise. Since it has been in operation, it has grown from about 2,500 dollars a season to about 200,000 dollars in one season. And we now have over 500 producers that bring merchandise in for us to sell. One fall I wrote this lady a check for 160 dollars for her crafts; and she looked at me and she said, "This will help buy my oil for the winter." A lot of them do it just as a hobby, naturally, but most of them do it for a supplement, not just a hobby. *(Faye Dancey)*

The carvers of the school were all local people. It was a great help. The Folk School [John C. Campbell Folk School, Brasstown] was a great help to this surrounding country in here. People built new homes from carving. *(Mabel Estes)*

The idea of going to the State Fair in Raleigh came right out of this old noggin of mine. I said, "Let's get the crafts to the Raleigh State Fair from Western North Carolina." That first year we went, 1952, we got fourteen people to go. The last year that we were down there, twenty-fifth year, we had 105. Me and her would go over to that shop, and we would work as much as three months getting stuff to take to the fair. We got down there, and we opened up at ten o'clock and closed at nine that night. They put a counter in each door; they counted the people who would come. There were 36,000 people went through that building that day. It was hard work, long hours, cold weather. Sometimes the weather would be so cold we'd have to hang out blankets, old quilts, tarps, around the wall to keep the wind out. *(Herman Estes)*

You can go to college and get every degree there is in the book. You start dealing with the public, and they'll finish educating you. But we revived about six crafts that were gone. **(Herman Estes)**

PART SIX

Surviving the Mountain Rough

Progress and Problems

SO OFTEN, AFTER DRIVING FOR MILES OVER THE COUNTRYSIDE and being taken back years in time, I would return to the modern civilization of Boone or Asheville, where there were universities, shopping centers, fast-food places, and nice restaurants. Many of these had been there for a long time. Asheville has beautiful colonial homes and large buildings downtown. Many of these elements sometimes seem out of place here, but they are not. Change has come to this area as it has to others, although perhaps not as quickly. Because this region has such a strong culture, it is interesting to see how the people are trying to maintain those aspects of it that they dearly love in times of change.

I went to coffee houses and taverns and listened to country music with my friend, Jimmy Morton. Through him and others I met many of the younger people of the mountains and listened to their concerns. I admire their pride in their heritage. Jimmy introduced me to Merle Watson, Doc Watson's son. Merle introduced me to his parents and took me to meet Willard and Ora Watson. They were kin to him. He knew they would be interesting to interview and that we would become fast friends. Another time, we listened to Doc and Merle Watson play their beautiful music at the Wooley Worm Festival in Banner Elk, organized by Jimmy to raise funds for the volunteer fire department. A few years later, Merle was killed in a tractor accident.

I also went to mountain festivals where craftsmen and women from all over would meet to show off and sell some of their wares. They also came to enjoy their mutual companionship. People would gather in small groups to reminisce, pick their fiddles, or dance. On Saturday nights in the summer in Asheville, mountain musicians come in from surrounding areas and play music in the center of town. Everyone who comes to listen joins into square dances. I found beautiful pieces of pottery made by local artisans, lovely woven work, paintings, hand-carved furniture, and beautiful quilts. Many of these items had been made by both young and old natives of the area. Others had been made by young people who had moved into the area and had been "grafted in." A lot of the old culture still remains here, and most people want to preserve and celebrate parts of it.

(Opposite) Outhouses behind Meadow View Primitive Baptist Church, Ashe County

MEASURES OF PROGRESS

We were hoeing corn right up there in the field when the first airplane came through here. We heard it coming, and my oldest brother raised up and said, "That's an airplane." And we watched that thing til it went out of sight, and everybody in the country saw it go over that day; and everybody thought it went right straight over their house, but it didn't go over everybody's house. *(Grady Reed)*

People used to live very simply, but very rich in the same way. I can remember, we got the first TV in the whole area when I was a child, my family did. And all the neighbors would come in to watch TV. And I mean twenty to thirty people at the house to see TV. I can remember when we got the first refrigerator, and everybody would come to see the refrigerator because, you know, the spring boxes were where you kept everything cool. All the new influx of people, the ski resort, summer people, everything else that came in, has changed things. It's hard to be a farmer when you can make more money building houses for the tourists. It's a lot easier, too. You know, a dairy farm is seven days a week, twelve to sixteen hours a day. *(Mike Phillips)*

In 1950 we got our first refrigerator. Before that we had an icebox that you could buy chunks of ice and put in it. But before that, we carried everything to the spring. We just had a barrel, and we'd put our stuff in a jug and drop it down in there. If we had butter, we'd put it in a bucket, put a lid on it. Well, that was pretty good, though. It didn't cost a darn cent. You didn't have no money, and you could have something to eat. Now I've got to pay my light bill and my phone bill every month, or they'll cut it off. *(Bertha Lowe)*

A part of our confusion—maybe nationally, but certainly in Appalachia—is that we have equated exploitation with progress. Progress is a holy word; exploitation is an ugly word; it's mean; it's negative.

Progress is positive. If we can identify any kind of change with progress, then we can cross ourselves three times. So we very carefully try to do that to every kind of change that has occurred in Appalachia; and I guess those who are profiting from it all the time maybe are best at that. The wise old mountaineer who watches it go on, if he's not involved personally, can stand aside, and see what's going on, and interpret it with considerable wisdom. But once he does become involved, then, of course, he blinds himself. He puts on blinders and charges for what's going to be, in his opinion, the most profit to him. *(Cratis Williams)*

I see World War II as the line of demarcation, so to speak, between what used to be and what is today, the beginning of what is today. When World War II broke out, I was, I think, thirteen years old. I think that so many people from this part of the world went into the Army and the Navy and the Marines during World War II, and they, in effect, saw the big city. They saw Los Angeles and New York and all the other seaports, if they were in the Navy, like Philadelphia, San Francisco, Honolulu. So transportation, communication, everything, has made the world a lot smaller. That, coupled with the fact that so many people weren't satisfied with what they had had once; they had, in effect, seen the bright lights. There was not an immediate transition, but people became more affluent; they could afford to move out. They became more knowledgeable through communication, the advent of television in the fifties. People had more leisure time and more money. They could afford to go to Myrtle Beach for a vacation or maybe even to Miami Beach. And the jobs weren't here. You know, if you want to drive a big car, you have to have enough money to support that habit; and the jobs just weren't here. And then the people weren't satisfied with what essentially had been subsistence farming, and loggings. *(Jim Ryan)*

John Neil and Jan Davidson playing music at home, Webster

Bertha Lowe

In my lifetime we have become much more part of the whole world, the outside world. We're not nearly as isolated and as cut off. . .and that bothers me a great deal. It bothers me, for instance, at Christmas when I see children, including our little granddaughter, want the same toys that the kids in California and everywhere else want because they're all exposed to the wonderful advertising on TV. There's just no way you can put a fence around the time you like best and keep the rest of the world out.
(Rebecca Councill)

I talk about I'm going to drive out to Dallas, or I'm going to drive down to Atlanta, or I'm going to drive down to Orlando, or I'm going to drive up to Washington, D.C. My daddy, if he was alive, he would have only been in his seventies, he would still have a hard time comprehending that, because when he grew up it took all day to go to Asheville if you were going to drive to Asheville. Now we drive to Asheville in forty-five minutes. So, it has just totally changed. Everybody kind of talks about the

good ol' days. I don't know whether they were as good or not. My family didn't have anything in the good ol' days. Of course, it was simple. You didn't have the problems. The more you get, the more problems you have. *(Reg Moody)*

Honey, when I grew up in Wilkes County, I never seen or heard tell of a car 'til I moved to Ashe County. The first car that I ever seen, I reckon Heg Burgess, him or Don Williams, which one was it, had the first car. Well, I believe it was Heg had the first car that I ever seen. *(Zora Lyle)*

Well, I've had a car since I was sixteen years old, until a year or two ago I got so I couldn't drive. *(Everett Lyle)*

The furtherest place in the world is not any further away now than the county seat used to be. You can get on a plane and be there as quick as it used to be to the county seat. *(Grady Reed)*

In the teens and the twenties, the doctors all thought in the United States that the higher the altitude, the better it was for tuberculosis. So, the result was they built sanitariums all over the mountains around Asheville and other places in the west, and people did improve from high altitudes. This brought new people from various parts of the country into our area. Many liked it and stayed.

You'll have a hard time now finding somebody with both sides of their family born and raised in Asheville. *(Elsie Bennett)*

We're exceptions. I would guess maybe forty percent of the population of Asheville today came from somewhere else. It started back in the forties when the war happened. After the war, things changed drastically in Asheville. The population just completely changed. There were a lot of government agencies here, and a lot of people came to work at the photographic laboratory in Asheville, came to work at Oteen Veterans Hospital and at the National Climatic Center here in Asheville. They used to call it the National Weather Service. All of these out-of-town people completely changed it. Then industries came in, and they came from the Midwest, the Northeast; and Asheville today is quite different from when Elsie and I grew up.
(Harold Bennett)

All these people had always wanted something better for their children. So as soon as they could make what they could, they sent their children away to get a better education; and, as always happens there, you lured children to a different way of life, and they remembered that way of life. But that had not hit as badly when I was a child as it did when they brought the highway [Parkway] through. After that there was quite a change, and it became rural America. But, when I came along, it was still a very backwoods area in many, many respects.
(Emma Sharpe Jeffress)

This area has changed from a trading center to a dead rural section. There used to be forty or fifty Vances in Plumtree. Now there're three of us. And it's the same way with other families. *(Ivor Vance)*

When I growed up, there was three stores, three grocery stores in Dillsboro; and now there's not one, not nary a one. The one that my son-in-law owned had been there for years and years, and he retired. Ain't nary a grocery store in Dillsboro no more.

Yeah, we had a big farm up there. Oh, it's so pretty, big bottom after you get up there. Some places on the mountain's really pretty; after you get up there, it's level, you know. Big fields, wheat fields, cornfields, fields of taters, and all kinds of vegetables. That's the way they made their living. Had hogs, chickens, cows, raised their own meat, raised their own bread; thrashers would come every fall and thrash four, five, and six stacks of hay or wheat to make flour. Took their own wheat to the mill, had flour mills, ground the flour; about as good a pure bread as you ever ate, from your own wheat you raised. People don't raise it no more down here. A lot of them raise a little corn, but not everything like they used to. Had all their stuff made at home, didn't have to go out to buy very much. Had to buy soda and salt to put in your bread, had your own buttermilk.

Made our own dresses and things like that on the sewing machine. And you could buy cloth at ten cents a yard. It wouldn't fade no matter what you put—Clorox, it might fade it. Ten cents a yard, pretty print, checked, flowered, all kinds. Real good stuff, too, back then. Cost you one or two dollars a yard now. Times change. Really have changed since I growed up. *(Lilly Wykle)*

My father told me that my tenth birthday cost him more than his father had paid for all the land he bought from the State of North Carolina—ten dollars. I think he bought probably a hundred acres for ten dollars at ten cents an acre. In 1924, my tenth birthday cost my father ten dollars to buy me a baseball mitt, which was the same amount of money that his father had paid for his entire farm in Haywood County. You know, George Vanderbilt paid less than ten cents an acre for the Vanderbilt Estate when he got it from a land grant from the State of North Carolina. He sure did. Ten cents an acre. Amazing. *(Harold Bennett)*

Small farming has gone by the wayside with the change in times and large conglomerates of agricultural products. The young people have moved away from the land. Very few still live there because you can't make a living there anymore and they're not satisfied with the lifestyle that's accompanied by that type of life. When I grew up, and this may sound a little austere, but we raised most everything that we ate. We came to Boone just on occasion, and Grandpa would buy 400 to 500 pounds of flour and 100 pounds of salt, a couple hundred pounds of sugar for canning, and some coffee; and that was about the extent of our shopping. We didn't come to Boone more than twice a year generally speaking, even though it was only fifteen miles from our house. *(Charles Michael)*

The values of the land have gone up so much that a lot of people are really tempted to get cash for it. That is definitely breaking up things. The value of the land has gone up so much, too, that younger people who don't have land from their families, they're—now, see, people my age and younger want to live here. They don't want to go anywhere. They never have, but especially now. The jobs are available but even so, they can work hard and do everything their tradition tells them to do, and they still can't afford to buy a piece of land. To be a mountain person and not own your own little piece of land is—I know it doesn't feel right.
(Mr. Jan Davidson)

It's more populated. Florida people have come in. Now they have been an asset and a hindrance. I feel like they've run a lot of our younger people off by buying up the land and making land so high that they couldn't afford it. However, you look at that again; there were young people who were beginning to go to college and get college educations, and there was nothing here for them to do. There's no plants here; there's no steel plants here. There's no cotton mills here. We do have a rug factory here that makes carpet.

I guess the biggest change that you would say has taken place over the years is the farming. People have quit raising crops, corn, because they quit having livestock. Well, you could go to the store and buy a gallon of milk cheaper than you could raise your corn and feed a cow and be worried with getting up at five o'clock in the morning and trying to milk and then get ready to go on the job. People began working at public jobs. In keeping a cow, you had to get up of a morning, go milk, come in the house, take a bath, put your good clothes on, go to work, come back of a night, change your clothes, and go back to the barn. You could go to the store and buy your pork. Everybody had hogs. You could go to the store and buy your meat cheaper than you could raise pigs. You couldn't afford to have that much. Well, most everybody lives on ten to twelve acres of land. There's not all that many people that have a big farm.

When Nelson farmed, we rented. He farmed for several years, and we had a cow until I'd say '65 maybe. I would milk one time, and he would milk one time. And that wasn't good. You'll laugh at me for saying this, but a cow won't give good milk, won't give regular milk, if two or three people's messing with her. They don't milk alike, so the cow's milk would fail, go up and down. And then I went to work, and I didn't have time to fool with it either. That's one of the main changes that has taken place right here in this section.

Other than that, over the years money has gotten easier to get. I don't think things are as expensive now as they were back then when you consider all that you had to go through with to have it. I can remember when our grocery list consisted of matches, a can of kerosene oil, five pounds of sugar, a pound of coffee, and maybe a bag of flour. In fact, I can even remember when we didn't have flour. We ate cornbread because we had cornmeal at home. Now Nelson says he can never remember when they didn't have flour and biscuits for breakfast, but I can. We were sharecroppers. They have always lived here in this one spot and were, I guess, a little bit better off than we were.

I wish my parents—we never owned a car. If we went, we had to go in a wagon. That's the only way we had of going. And if we went to visit, we always had to stay one night and usually two or three nights when we'd go to visit our grandparents and our cousins and our uncles and aunts because there was no way of getting there and back. I can remember the first time we went by car. My uncle came and got us and we went to my grandmother's and spent Christmas. And that was the Christmas before we moved to Rabun Gap. It was also the first Christmas that we ever got anything for Christmas except a stick of candy and an orange and maybe two or three nuts. My daddy, some way or another, he had bought us all a little gift. It was hard for him to raise enough money to do that. But he didn't think anything of it. He'd say, "I've got these kids and I got to do." And then, you know, they had what they called the relief, which was just WPA. You've heard about it, I'm sure. They gave us food. It was similar to the program with all this food distribution now. However, I can't see any need for it now. There was a great need for it then. But, to my way of thinking, I wouldn't go back to the "good ol' times." *(Ruth Cabe)*

I'd say about ninety-nine percent of the change is good. About one percent of it you'd want to see back. But you wouldn't want to go back to a gravel road—oh, no. The money that was spent on the Parkway here, that's a great asset because of the economy. You think about the people directly or indirectly that a good living comes to from the travel on the Parkway. So with roads and schools and the things that we've done, we're almost one one hundred percent. That money is well spent. And you cannot build too good a school. You cannot build too good a road. Now we might do some things that might be a little bit unnecessary, but that adds to the upbuilding of your community and your economy; and it puts greenbacks in your pocket. *(B. Hensley)*

Just because you lived where there was no electricity didn't mean you couldn't go to college and have a modern home in the eighties. Western Carolina really influenced Cullowhee a whole lot because so many local people work for the university one way or another. Western Carolina University is the biggest employer in the county, so it couldn't help

but be a big influence. It's grown a lot in the last few years. *(Wanda Moss)*

The character of the area has changed. So many new developments, new communities, have sprung up over the mountains. So many people have moved in there. Now, of course, they have contributed a lot in many respects. And then on the other hand, they've spoiled a lot of the mountain beauty, I think. But I think it will continue as our population grows. They are looking for the very things that I mentioned: peace, peace of mind. Get away from the hurry, the pressures, and move out into a mountain area. Sort of go back to nature, but you can't go back very far because you'll run into some fellow that just moved in. *(Dan Moore)*

I almost feel like I'm in a strange community, you know. There's just very few of us old-timers. At one time I knew every house for miles around, and now I've got neighbors right down there I don't even know. There's several acres of ground in there that at one time I could have bought for 600 dollars, and now you couldn't buy it for a million. *(Monroe Ledford)*

One of the problems in Madison County, and one of the problems about politics, is that the school system and welfare constitute the two principal sources of income in the whole county. *(Landon Roberts)*

Some areas have changed, and I think for the worse. It's a perfect example of what happens when you have no control. And yet the reason you have no control is that everybody says, "Nobody's going to tell me what to do with my land." And it's a real dilemma. Everybody owes the banker and the finance company. It's a way of life. My memories and the values that I had instilled in me say, "Don't owe anybody anything." As long as you owe somebody either money or time or favors or whatever, then you're beholden to them. And as long as you don't owe them anything, then it's a gift if you want to do something for them. So all my life I've despised debt. *(Jim Ryan)*

The only reason that many people are not back in here yet is because nobody'll sell them any land. All this development has helped, and it's hurt us. It brought some employment in; it helped that way. And it hurt because it's raised the value of our property and we're having to pay more tax, and it hasn't done us a bit more good. And the people coming in has caused the price of everything to go up. And you wouldn't believe now, from here to Bluff City, Tennessee, ten boxes of matches like that cost you a dime more here than it does in Bluff City, Tennessee. *(Edd Presnell)*

I have seen mountain people that used to have pride and may not have had a whole lot, but were able to be self-sufficient. Now, they have resorted to no work and to taking welfare, families that I never thought would do it. As a matter of fact, they are embarrassed about it, to be seen; and they often sneak around to the welfare places and pick up things and don't want to be seen. And those same people now that once you could hire for a day's work will not work. That bothers me. It doesn't fit in with this mountain character at all. And I mean generations of people that I knew their fathers and I knew their father's father, who had a lot of pride and would not accept handouts unless needed. And now, three generations down the line, they expect welfare and will not work and do not have any pride in themselves. That's a change in three generations. (Charles Michael)

I've got a little house up there and a little piece of land, and I wanted to go back and live. The doctor says I can't live by myself anymore; I must have somebody with me, and I can't get anybody to stay with me; nobody'll stay. They've all got jobs, and they just ain't got time to fool with me.
(Mamie Hall)

I remember when we'd go somewhere on Sunday, we used to go to my aunt's house a lot and we wouldn't even lock the doors. We couldn't lock them. We didn't have locks. And we'd take a straight-back chair, set it under the doorknob, and prop it shut. It's a good place to live and all, but people just don't trust each other that much now. As a matter of fact, we have a security system at our house, and a lot of people do so, too. Most people do in the area. *(Faye Dancy)*

The water that I used to swim in is now polluted. Streams that you used to could kneel down and take a drink of, you dare not do that. And the water table itself has diminished by more than fifty percent in the last twenty years—by more than fifty percent, the water volume. It's partly due to more people and partly due to poor development techniques that have upset the balance of the water table. The large influx of population has taken more water. I rolled the brick and the block for this wing of the building that we're in, in 1954, summer work. And so, I've seen this college grow from—it was about 1,200 students, a little teachers college. We all knew each other; we all knew all the faculty. And now I've seen the transition into a university [Appalachian State University]. It's still a rather personable campus, though.

There has been a change in the attitude of people in the past couple of decades. It used to be you couldn't come through Boone without someone always stopping and talking to you, whether they knew you or not, to help you; but with the hippies in the sixties and the drug scene now, people are really frightened by outsiders. In an area where we never locked our homes for years, you must do so now. You'll be robbed if you don't. And we have

View of downtown Asheville, City Hall in background, Jackson Building on the right

our own share of crime. Because of the tourists, this has become a resort area. *(Charles Michael)*

But them good ol' days is gone and worse a-coming and nobody knows exactly what's going to happen. But I say this. There's going to be a downfall before we ever start climbing anymore, and it's going to be hard with young folks. And, in fact, young folks, they don't want to do nothing and they ain't a-going to do nothing until they get hungry; then they'll go a-hunting some. *(Willard Watson)*

My parents' generation were the first to have access to Main Street stuff and modern life, and that's what they wanted. Then I think the people of my generation have probably turned back a little more toward looking at the older ways. And the interesting thing about it, too, is that now we not only are looking at their lives and artifacts as museum pieces, but we're realizing that there's a lot of meaning in their lifestyle for our own time and just the

incredible wealth of wisdom you can't get from anywhere besides experience. So I think we're doing really good work in places like this [Mountain Heritage Center, Western Carolina University]. We hope so. There are institutions now that can primarily look at the past and try to learn from it, try to interpret it.

We've established a regional museum here, and we now are being able to go out into the communities and do more. We are finally mature enough to respond to the Foxfire idea by going back into the schools and helping other schools have some of that experience. That's the next big phase. More traveling to do and getting out and not just sitting here. If it were not for these private collections, we would be in a fix. We would have lost a great many evidences of our past. These are folks who went from a family tradition and taking these things for granted to the awareness that these things were passing and that they needed to be saved.
(Mr. Jan Davidson)

282   ***Virgie and Cass Wallin***

One of the conflicts that you have in the town [Boone, for example] now is the "professional mountaineer" as opposed to the real mountain person. One of the things, in my mind, that will separate those people from the real thing is that regardless of how many times they say otherwise, they really think that mountain culture is second class and when you put it side by side with other cultures, it will not stack up. But those of us who have lived here and know the culture know that this is not true. It is just that we can enjoy and absorb all the other cultures in the world but still know that ours is at least as good, if not better, than most. And I'm sure it's no harder on our culture than it is on anybody else's, but it is a shame to see us all become so similar.
(Rebecca Councill)

If you're going to do anything, a fund raiser or anything, they [the professional mountaineers or outsiders] always want you to "clog." Everybody's so sick of clogging. Lots of people do it, but you get so tired of watching it, you know. We don't really need another festival to demonstrate clogging. And I am convinced in my mind that no matter how much they deny it, they really don't have the confidence in our culture that I do. I know what it can withstand. And I don't feel threatened, or that my culture is threatened, by introducing anything else. It will be destroyed, perhaps, by other things, but not by that. And, of course, the other things that are making it hard for mountain culture to survive are making it hard for all ethnic cultures. The television, movies, the easy transportation, knowing from the very beginning of your life that you're not just part of a family or just part of an area, but that you're part of the world, and that kind of thing. *(Rebecca Councill)*

In the mountains when I grew up, you raised what you ate and ate what you raised. I worked on a job after my wife and I married in 1931, worked for two years for a dollar a day, and then worked on the WPA two years for seventy-five cents a day, ten hours. Now people can't live at thirty dollars a day. It's good times now; it's real good times. It's the best time we've had in history if anybody wants to work or do anything. *(Stanley Hicks)*

Times has made a change since my childhood days.
Many of my friends have gone away,
Some I never more in this life shall see.
Times has made a change in me.

Times has made a change in my old homeplace.
Times has made a change in each smiling face,
And I know my friends can plainly see
Times has made a change in me.

In my childhood days, I was well and strong,
I could climb the hillsides all day long,
But I'm not today what I used to be.
Times has made a change in me.

Times has made a change in the old homeplace.
Times has made a change in each smiling face,
And I know my friends can plainly see
Times has made a change in me.

When I meet my friends in that land somewhere,
Meet my many friends that await me over there,
Free from pain and care I shall ever be.
Times has made a change in me.
(Cas Wallin)

LIVING WITH CHANGE

You can't save the old culture. It's already gone. The old Appalachia is gone. The people who would have become blacksmiths all became car mechanics when the Model T came along. There are still some recollections, but the old ways do not exist anymore. If you find some of the old culture still around, let me know.
(Lewis Green)

In the folk speech of Appalachia, one will occasionally hear something that gives him a start because he doesn't know what it means. He wonders where it came from. The vowels have changed within the word so that it doesn't look like anything he knows, and it becomes a real puzzle. One such word is found in the mild euphemistic oaths that one might hear old Appalachian women use: "Aye gonnies!" You could look the place over and not find it. Well, "aye," of course, is a-y-e, and "gonnies" is a survival of guinea, the British gold piece that was currently in use at the time our ancestors came. Now the people who use it don't know that's what it means. They simply accept it as a mild oath.

A mountain person might say, "They! Look at that snake." Now if you're not a mountaineer, you probably would not have any question about that at all. The "they" would be just some kind of meaningless, neutral ablative, or what have you. But "they" must have a history; it must have a meaning. And what would be logical to explain that is "they" is a dialectical pronunciation of "thee" or "thou" and that literally means, "Thou, Lord, look at that snake."

Here are two examples of things that come out of Middle English or Old English. We syllabicate or pronounce the plural for certain words as Chaucer did. "Westes," for example, "restes," and the like. Now we do that only when the plural follows something like an "st" or an "sh." This is Middle English, and we do this rather widely throughout the area. We continue to use "them" as a demonstrative adjective. Well, this was done generally in Middle English times, probably down to about 1600. "Look at them apples." Shakespeare did that, as I recall, and Chaucer. We, of course, continue the old, old usage of objective forms rather than nominative forms following copulative verbs. The French do this acceptably. The English, artifically, have insisted that it not be that way, that we say, "It was I" instead of, "It was me." Appalachian people continue to say, "It was me." Appalachian people refer to themselves objectively, not nominatively, and place themselves first, without apology or condescension. "So, me and John decided we'd do so and so." The language is very descriptive. It sparkles with sharpness. *(Cratis Williams)*

They used double names in the mountains like the "rock cliff" and the "milk dairy" and "widow woman," things like that. A lot of them have peculiar names over there. My surveyor's name was Benjamin Harrison Frisbie. He said, "If you can take from my name, you can understand my age and the political affiliation of my parent"; and, it is true of most of them over there. You have Theodore Roosevelt Worley. Most of these people were named after presidents. They stopped doing that with Franklin D. Roosevelt. Since then, they haven't named many children after presidents. I don't know of many today. *(Landon Roberts)*

My granddaddy moved to Sylva in 1912 and built the house that my mother's sister still lives in, that I grew up in. It's still right there in town. He lived there the rest of his life and so did my grandmother. The town has changed, and it hasn't changed.

Physically it has changed very little. Mentally I think it's resisting change. I think a lot of people are in the same frame of mind. "If it's good enough for my daddy, it's good enough for me" type mentality and type of philosophy. I think it has a lot of potential. *(Jim Ryan)*

What remains? Well, a good many homes scattered through the mountains really have not changed a great deal. I can still name people, if they haven't gotten them in recent years, that don't have a bathroom. Lights have pretty well covered the mountains as has the telephone. But I think there are still examples, particularly in the smaller communities, of that independence and self-help of years ago. *(Dan Moore)*

Everybody in the mountains always farmed along with whatever else they did. You had to make ends meet. And we still have to. I haven't got that garden down there just for the hobby of it or pleasure. It's a necessity. You take anybody on low income. I really don't see how people make it on low income and have to go to the grocery store for everything. It's so high. I try to make enough corn so I can have cornbread to do me, and we have a freezer. We put up juices. We have all kinds of juice, grape juice, apple juice. And she fixes soups. I've got beans, tomatoes and corn, mustard and peas, carrots, beets, lettuce. We were both sick last year. Our garden flopped. We never preserved anything. We canned a few cans of tomatoes, and that's the only thing we put up last year. We never froze anything;

Lula Mae, Minnie Rose, and Brenda Owenby

The lighting is a lot better with electricity than it was with kerosene. Of course, we were used to lamps, kerosene oil lamps. I sewed many a night and did handwork and could see and get along all right. But I tell you what, now, once in a while I just go off and light a kerosene oil lamp, and I wonder how we ever did make out with it. *(Hattie Oates)*

we didn't have anything. Of course, we had so much stuff left over from the year before that we made it pretty good. But I sure hope the Lord allows us to stay able to put some up this year because it's getting mighty low. *(Clifford Casey)*

I haven't made any stack cakes in a long time. We used to buy this home-grown syrup, and we could

285

get that stuff for a dollar a gallon. They'd make it for one another. There'd be a person in the community who owned the mill to grind the cane, and they boiled the juice and made the syrup. And they would take a toll out of that syrup. That's how they were paid. And we'd buy it from the one that received the syrup. *(Delia Reed)*

The reason we quit making syrup, we could buy it cheaper than we could make it. That stuff sells for sixteen dollars a gallon now around here. *(Grady Reed)*

Churches are still about the same. They've improved. I mean there are better buildings, better heating and light and everything. Everybody's got better dwellings. The houses are built better. *(Nelson Cabe)*

Most every Sunday there's a family reunion or a church homecoming. That's something I think's coming back in. They don't have Sitting Ups as much as they used to. Once in a while you'll find a family where there's old people in the family still living that aren't able to go to the funeral home. They will bring the body back home. We've had one this summer where they sat up all night with the family. But it's very seldom that that happens. That was done before the funeral homes were equipped to take care of crowds. They still have revivals. They're a little different from what they used to be. They're not as numerous as they were. There'll usually be about one a year in most churches. Most churches give people a chance to make a profession or join the church every Sunday, which I don't think they used to do as much as they do now. *(Ruth Cabe)*

Well, every generation has a world as they find it, and as they leave it. I was here before fast food, four-lane highways, and television. I remember when there was no TV here. I also came of age, I guess, at a time when there was a great deal of presenting mountain people as poor national orphans who needed more help than other people—the

Great Society program and all that. At the same time, in order to justify that, the federal government and other programs concentrated very strongly on the negative aspects of life in the mountains. You know the cliché, pictures of destitute mountaineers, which we definitely had and still have. But I think two things happened. By designating the area as a special area, it allowed some of the social and economic problems in the area to be addressed by the government. But, at the same time, I don't know if it did a whole lot of good for self-worth. It's the same as in any other kind of attempt to solve social problems. We needed help, still do, but part of the problem that they're trying to solve came out of the migration of young mountain people, going elsewhere. These young people who were having to face that decision not only faced an economic decision as trading off against staying home, which everybody in the mountains wants to do basically, but because of this stigma attached to being a mountain person, a lot of them wanted to get out.

Now I think we're in a new phase where we place our cultural life somewhat on a pedestal. But I think it's presenting better self-images for people, and I hope that we don't go too far into how great it is to live in the mountains that we blind ourselves to real problems that exist here. We came to pass here in isolation without realizing that every aspect of the past is still with us in some measure. *(Mr. Jan Davidson)*

Mrs. Johnson was going to view poverty in Appalachia. She brought Liz Carpenter, who was her secretary. We had them at the Western Residence to spend the night; Mrs. Johnson, Liz and some of the others. They were coming to Jackson County. Going to Canada Township. I was governor. I had lived in Jackson County for fifty years or more, but they didn't ask me to go with them. They did ask Jeanelle, my wife. They didn't ask me anything about where they were going, but Liz Carpenter was explaining at breakfast just what had taken place that day [before]. She said they had gone into Canada Township and seen a Mr. Mathis.

Mr. Mathis lived in this little mountain cabin way back in the mountains. He was unemployed except for about a month at Christmastime when he cut Christmas trees. She went on about the fact that he had a TV but not to let that disturb you because that was the only contact he had with the outside world. And I said, "Liz, did you happen to see that mountain stream that ran through the yard." She said, "Oh, yeah, it was a beautiful stream." Well, I said, "if you had gone about a hundred yards up that stream you would have found out how Mr. Mathis makes his living." I said, "I defended him, his father and his grandfather all for moonshining." I said, "He has never cut a Christmas tree in his life. He wouldn't strike at anything except a rattlesnake fixing to bite."

President Johnson had made a trip to view poverty in the Appalachians and they took him to Rocky Mount, North Carolina, of all things. That was 300 miles from the mountains in the eastern part of the state. Some bright somebody had figured Rocky Mount must be in the mountains, so that's where they took him. He went out on a tobacco farm. *(Dan Moore)*

They didn't follow up very well down here. They really didn't, because they didn't follow up at all. They didn't contact anybody down here that could have said you've made a mistake, this is not where you want to go. Let us tell you. They could have called down to the governor's office. They would have said, "Well, we will be glad to make a routine out for you." Certainly with the governor, he was from the mountains. He lived there all of his life. Born in Asheville. *(Jeanelle Moore)*

They should have asked, "What should we do while in Jackson County?" They didn't. *(Dan Moore)*

I regretted that I was even with them because it was a little embarrassing for me. I was just sorry that I was there. But what could I do? If the president's wife goes and wants you to go. Being the wife of the governor, it was a fiasco itself. *(Jeanelle Moore)*

Mountain Church

When I was growing up, it seemed as if we were much closer to the land than kids are today. I think all of us grew up with a real appreciation for what nature has provided and can provide. We can remember how it was, and we liked it. They come now primarily for the climate and the scenery, but they don't have those values. They don't have that sense of belonging, I guess. To them it's "everybody's doing it; everybody's going to the mountains," you know. And cocktail parties every night; it's a big deal. And I go out and sit on the bank of the creek for an hour or two hours and never do anything more than maybe flip some bark in the creek and watch it go on down. (Jim Ryan)

It doesn't really seem like the same area because when I grew up, I knew everybody, and everybody knew everybody else. People started traveling through this area, especially on the Parkway. They loved it so much that when they made a trip through the mountains, they seemed to fall in love with it and wanted to stay here. They have found and bought land and come back here to live in this area. Then they tell their friends about it, and we have a lot more people, then, coming all the time. It'd be impossible, as fast as they're moving in, to know everyone. Most of them are really nice people. We accept them as neighbors and they accept us. *(Faye Dancy)*

It's interesting to observe ways that people adapt. If you go by T.R.W., look in the parking lot in the women's cars. You will see in the back seat, where the window is, trays of apples drying in the sunshine while those cars are parked. Economic circumstances dictated that they had to go to work in most cases. But, rather than give up the traditional mountain food of dried apples, and certainly they didn't have time to do them at home because if you put them out in the sun, you've got to be there to turn them over, to keep the dogs out of them. That's the kind of ingenuity I admire. They still figured out a way to keep something of their tradition that was important to them in their lives. The other option would be to say, "Well, now that I'm working, I can afford to buy apples from the store. I don't need to do that anymore." It isn't fair for folks to expect us to still use the wash pot in the yard and that kind of thing. And people who do documentaries, movies, videos are particularly outrageous in that regard. (Rebecca Councill)

Now it isn't like back when I grew up. Now there's just as much difference as between day and night. What it is, they've got a-hold of money a lot easier, a lot of people have. And they give it to the younguns. They like to let the younguns go out on their own. See, that's what it's all about. People don't care for one another anymore.

But this stuff was gone until the young people took it up; it was gone. The tales and all were gone. Everything was gone down the drain 'til about fifteen or twenty years ago. Now then they're interested in it because a lot of them want to know what happened back in the old days. Everything had a purpose to it. They're looking for that. See, they've come from California, from everywhere, looking for this to get it up where it's gone.

Well, the only way, they'll have to go out and help people, if they ever find it. And to live that purpose. Hard work is going to bring a purpose back to people. What is done has been hard work; got a lot of propositions ahead of them, lot of expenses. We've got a lot of good young people yet. Your life and my life and all the young generation's life is just exactly what you make out of it. You can make a good life or you can make a bad one. *(Stanley Hicks)*

A lot of the older people, like my parents, liked the way they lived. Their children didn't like it. They wanted to do something about it. I think a lot of the people that are my dad's age would be just as happy no matter how they had to live. If he wanted to go to the outhouse—I mean if it were necessary—it wouldn't bother him. And my mother likes to cook on a wood stove. She doesn't want to give it up. She enjoys having that electric stove sitting there for her convenience when she doesn't feel like messing with it, but she still likes having her wood stove there. I think there's a lot of other people the same way. I don't think any of them have ever had any children that have had a home with a wood stove in it. *(Wanda Moss)*

Now we're having trouble keeping our own identity and to keep enough of our own property. The

Florida people are coming in here, which is good. A lot of them are fine. We don't want to sell too much. We don't want to give up our inheritance. One old man came up. He was a newspaper editor in Florida, and he was born and raised down there. He told me about how many of the natives there had sold the land. I said, "What becomes of the natives?" And he said, "They just push them back. These new people get all the good land, all the good property, and they [the natives] think they're getting a fortune."

When it comes down to it, a little money is a whole lot to us. We don't have too much money. We sell our places lots of times for what seems to be a big thing, and then we're pushed out. Most of our land here is from one generation to the other. I own land up above here that belonged to my mother and my forefathers. I don't plan to sell that. *(Carrie Burnette)*

Here we are. We're going through a period of change, and there's no direction to it, no real direction to it. I don't know where we're going to go, and I don't think anybody else does. I don't think we have a lot of time to make a decision. The time is coming in this county, and I don't think it's far away, when we are not going to control our destiny because the Floridians and the Georgians and the "outsiders" are going to outnumber us. *(Jim Ryan)*

The most disturbing things happen and there is nothing you can do about it. Both my sister and I had to really go away to make a living when we grew up. There was nothing here. So, you can't turn up your nose at industry coming in. You've got to have something, and you want to have something that will keep young people in this area, very much. But we are very disturbed at the lack of control. *(Freda Siler)*

In trying to get it done, there are so many people, both native and those who have come in, who want to do what they want to do. Between the developers and the old farmers who say, "It is mine and I want to do with it what I want to," it is diffi-cult. "The land has been inherited and handed down from all these generations, and it's mine and nobody can tell me what to do with it." That, plus the ones who come in. Thank heavens the state held out for getting the law passed forbidding the high rises on the mountain ridges. *(Margaret Siler D'Onofrio)*

The whole thing is that they raise the taxes on the people. They're cash poor, but they're land rich. And that land's been passed from generation to generation. They can't afford to pay the taxes. So they have to sell it, and that land is more valuable to them than money or anything else. But the taxes and stuff are raised to the point where they have to sell it. It's robbing the people of their history and their rights. There's still the thing of clans of people passing things on from generation to generation, passing land and houses all the way through, the first son and so forth. Usually the youngest child, the daughter or son, gets the house; the home is left to the youngest. And it was for years and years done that way. (Mike Phillips)

People were proud to be mountain men, or mountain people. For a long time people lived up all the little creeks and all the little hollows, and they don't do that anymore. They have all either moved down next to the highways, or they have moved in closer to Sylva and to Bryson City. Where they lived has totally changed. They had their own little homestead. It's all kind of moved in. That's probably the biggest change that I have seen in my lifetime. Of course, the way they lived then was so much simpler than the way it is now, and I wonder how much farther it is going to go the other way. *(Reg Moody)*

One-room school house, Ledge, Mitchell County

The Beech [Mountain] was the cleanest. It was really superior—or was before the timber was cut and before it was messed up with the ski resort. Now it's not city. It's not mountain. It's not level country. It's not like anything that I would expect to find anywhere. It's just ruined. It's the most ruined place that I've ever seen in my life. Condominiums and houses, all roads and cut up, ski slopes, just messed up. You don't know where you are. You don't see anything. And what beauty there was there just couldn't take it. What little fern you see there is kind of sickly, what's left that you can see between places.

That's another thing about the mountains. There was a freshness in the air there that it just made you want to go on and on. You got the best fresh air on the Beech Mountain. You could just drink it in and inhale it and fly off somewhere, it was so fresh. It just had a freshness there that you don't find anywhere else. Now occasionally, on top of the Grandfather and Blowing Rock, up there around in some of those places, you can get a little air that will imitate it. *(Raymond Presnell)*

One of the professors here does a lot of writing, and he's from Texas. I remember he thought he would bring us some culture. And then he discovered that the mountains had a culture of their own. I think that's a point that a lot of people don't understand when they speak of mountain people as "mountain people." They think of them as hillbilly, the shiftless man in his overalls and corncob pipe. They think of people who were so alienated, and they were, and isolated, but that they didn't know anything. It took a lot of ingenuity [to survive] in some cases, and a lot of endurance. (Rose Marie Feimster)

I've never been a very orthodox banker. I used to lend little ol' ten- and-twelve-year old kids fifty dollars to put out a bed of strawberries with. Never lost a dime at it. And I'd let them have enough to go buy a dairy calf from down in the Piedmont; and they could run it for two years and sell it back as a producing cow. I let two boys, one of them was nine, one fourteen, have 600 dollars to put out an acre of strawberries; and they sold 3,600 dollars worth of strawberries. I used to lend boys over at the industrial arts department 25,000 dollars to build a house with and not charge them any interest. They'd sell the house and pay me. I've done all sorts of things like that. The bank didn't make any money off those kinds of things, but it was building friendship and building customers. You're not running a bank for next week or the next month. You're running it for way out there. I don't think they'd let you do that anymore. *(Alfred Adams)*

AN INDEPENDENT SPIRIT

Boyd Payne

We come alive as a community only when something crystallizes us. You'd never think there was a sense of community around at all, but there'll be some cataclysm that will awaken all this spirit of helping our brother that has been a part of us all the time.

The converse of our strong individualism is that we do not cooperate easily. You can't say we don't cooperate absolutely because that wouldn't be true, but we do not cooperate easily to achieve a common goal. *(Cratis Williams)*

Mountain people are strong, hardworking, and fiercely dedicated to their beliefs. But the other side of this is that it is almost impossible to get a whole bunch of people together to do something. And we've been trodden on politically and economically simply because no two of us will get together and say, "Now, here's what we ought to do." One of us is bound to say, "Maybe that's what you're going to do, but I'm gonna do just like I want to." So we have this thing to overcome. It's real hard to get people to pull together—to organize is very hard. *(Mr. Jan Davidson)*

Another thing that bothers mountain folks is when outsiders come in and they want to change the community. They want to do this and that, that's never been done, and it takes a little while for the mountain folks to accept some of these things. They come in here and tell us what to do, you know, and it ain't none of their business. This is our community! We had a real problem around here. They organized the fire department. It wasn't that the native people were against the fire department. It's that those fellows were trying to push something down our throats. That's the problem. If it could have been handled differently, and a few of the natives got to talk this thing over, it'd gone over twice as smooth. There's a little bit of that independent streak in these old mountaineers that says, "You don't come in here and tell me what to do!" Whether it'd be good or not, you still don't tell me, you know. *(Jonah Parker)*

Each wants his first. And when he gets his, then he's perfectly willing to help keep the other fellow under control. It's all right to move into this mountain and tear it all to pieces and provide a place for me to build a 250,000 dollar home. I've had my eye on this nice stretch of woodland that I can see from my patio that I consider a part of the value of my place. I don't own that, though. I just own about thirty feet on up the hill. Now when I learn that somebody's going to go up there and tear down all those trees and pile rocks over the side of the hill down to my line and then ignore that and build him a place up there that'll cost a little more than mine so he can stand in his backyard and pee on me, I'm not going to have that. I'm going to exert every bit of influence I have to keep him from doing that. I've already done mine. And we're like that. *(Cratis Williams)*

One of the things that gets us in trouble is this fierce independence and this belief in our own ability to manage our own lives. It causes problems. One of the best examples that I've seen of that in the last year, I guess, is the problem with the Ridge Law and the structure up on Little Sugar because most mountain people don't want the buildings there. Well, they don't want condominiums anywhere, but they sure don't want them on top of their mountains. There were a lot of public meetings sponsored by one group or another, and the thing that came through so loud and clear was the conflict in the mountain person between having a government force at whatever level tell you what you could build on your land if you owned it and what was obviously better for the common good. Most mountain people believe that if you own it, you ought to be able to do whatever you want to with it. There were some real conflicts between mountain people's values. (Rebecca Councill)

Some people think, "It's really not the government's business to tell me what I can grow on my land." I don't believe there's the social stigma connected with it that you would find most places, because many of those people have grandfathers, fathers, and uncles who spent time in the federal penitentiary in Atlanta because of moonshine. And they don't get that upset if their sons get caught,

you know, with an acre or two of pot. They just don't think the same. They think, there again, "It's really my land. I can grow whatever I want to on it." *(Rebecca Councill)*

Last year, within half a mile of my house, there was a marijuana field spotted and cut down. My husband went and watched them cut it down, and he brought some leaves up to show me what they looked like. I didn't know. This was a million or more dollar crop. So we got a lot of publicity, but we don't like that kind of publicity. *(Faye Dancy)*

There is an independent nature in these mountain people. In the natives there's an inbred independence that's still there. I don't know whether their independence is a type of pride that's getting in the way. I don't know how to put it, but it's a type of pride that says, "Even though I might be wrong, you've got to care." *(Jonah Parker)*

I think it's important that in every generation they've taken advantage of what opportunities, education, and otherwise were offered to them. And I think if you look at the mountain culture, people don't quit learning. They don't say, "Well, I've got this education. Now I'm ready to go out and make my living with it and not learn any more." They keep an open mind. *(Ted White)*

Elsie and Harold Bennett were long-time friends of my family and have known me since I was born. Both Elsie and Harold had grown up in Asheville and provided interesting insights into the area and its history. I'll never forget sitting around their dining-room table one evening. There were just the three of us. Elsie had prepared a wonderful dinner as usual, and the table was bathed in candlelight. I watched Harold's expressions in the soft illumination as he spoke of Thomas Wolfe and his

(Opposite) Lilly Wykle

Coat and rocker waiting by the river

return to Asheville after writing You Can't Go Home Again. *Earlier he had described a little bit of Tom's growing up in his hometown and his working as the local newspaper delivery boy. Some local people had been upset by their portrayals in* Look Homeward, Angel. *Tears began to well up in Harold's eyes as he described Tom's statement that he had found that he really could come home again. This made the description glisten with emotion but, at the same time, reflected the bonds of kinship that are so strongly felt among these mountain people no matter what stream of life they find themselves following.* (W.M.)

I think that one of the best books that Thomas Wolfe wrote was *Of Time and the River*. But *You Can't Go Home Again*, to me was an unusual story

because he had so many incidents in the book about people I knew. For example, he would combine two people into one character. He combined Judge Phillip Cocke with the blind judge of the police court called Judge Sam Cathey. And he wrote stories that were so identifiable. The people in them were so identifiable by people who had known Asheville people that everybody was just very irritated at Tom because he had written about them. *Look Homeward, Angel* was the first book, *Of Time and the River* was the second, and *You Can't Go Home Again* came later. I thought *Look Homeward, Angel* was a great book. It was so full of poetry, pure poetry.

Mr. Wolfe was a monument carver/maker. And that's where the *Look Homeward, Angel* came from. He didn't carve it, but he had bought it from someone, and it was a thing that sat out in front of his monument works in Asheville, not far from where the present Jackson Building is. Tom Wolfe left Asheville under a great cloud after he wrote *Look*

Homeward, Angel because he mentioned names; not the actual names, but he described people whom everyone could recognize. People in Asheville knew the people he was referring to by unusual names. Tom was told by one Ashevillian that "you'd better not come back here or I'll kill you" because Tom had implied that this man had a child in the hospital and that he was afraid the child would be black. And Tom said, "If I ever come back to Asheville, you can kill me." So Tom felt estranged from Asheville.

But in 1936, I think it was '36 because I was taking the bar [exam] that year, Tom did come back. And he came back as an invited guest with Carl Snavely, who was the University of North Carolina football coach. They were both guests at an alumni party and dinner out at the old Asheville Country Club. Tom had delivered papers to my mother and father when we lived on Bank Street in Asheville. That was on his paper route. I met him at that dinner party of the alumni association. At the dinner when Tom was introduced, he got up and made a very touching speech. He said, "I wrote a book called *You Can't Go Home Again,* but I was wrong. I am home again." And tears were in his eyes when he said it. So he found he could come home again. *(Harold Bennett)*

Mrs. Wolfe kept wanting her children to be somebody and to do something. That was the drive that she had and, of course, she was brought up of this old mountain stock that could meet almost any situation. I always say that Tom really inherited the genius from his father, because old Mr. Wolfe really had a great appreciation for literature and was a very knowledgeable man. He was really an artist, but he became an alcoholic. Of course, he and the old lady, they just became at dagger points almost for the last year. They both had separate houses; and Tom just went, he just migrated from his father's house to his mother's house. One of the sisters took care of the father and lived with the father. I think it was Mabel that looked after the father. That house stood there for years. I used to go by it every day when I was in school. When I was in school in Asheville, Mrs. Wolfe was still running the old boarding house, and she had it up to the very end. If Mrs. Wolfe were to come back today and pass by the Dixieland, she would think it was the Vanderbilt Estate. It's been fixed up so much that she wouldn't know it.

Tom said he wanted to stay over here (Nu–Wray Inn); he really would have liked to have come and stayed over here and just gotten a little place where he could write. Of course, he went to Asheville then, and then people began to get very much interested in him. He took a little cabin out somewhere in Chunns Cove, I think it was, but he said he never got anything accomplished because there was always somebody knocking on the door or somebody there. And he was very gracious; he was very humble in what he had done. I remember this statement; he said, "I think some day I'll write something that will be worthwhile, but as yet I don't think I've reached my Mecca or my peace." Because he felt that it still was to come, that he was building up to something. *(Rush Wray)*

FINDING NEW PURPOSES

The tourist trade will be here as long as there's a Parkway. And the Parkway was an asset to the people of the mountains. You can take any place—I don't care how isolated it is—and build a good road, and you'll find out by building good roads and good schools, it brings up the economy. It brings up the culture. It brings up the way of life. It has always done that. And if you'll put a good church in that community, or two, it'll bring up the spiritual side. *(B. Hensley)*

For a while it was cut this down, move this out, tear this mountain down, do all kinds of stuff. I think it's changing. We're using the things that are already here. In this area you've got so much more to offer. You've got the mountains and you've got skiing; you've got fishing and boating and crafts. There's always a crafts fair going on just about all year around. *(Cynthia White)*

Handicrafts are a recent development coming out. They had the art festival out here in the square this summer where people took a lot of the things that they had been making to sell. That's just new, I guess, about ten or fifteen years old. We have a little pottery store here now, what they call a gift shop. They make their own pottery here. *(Lula Wise)*

When I was teaching school out in the county, I always took my students to visit what I call the "strip" there where the factories were, because if you learn arithmetic, you might be the foreman someday. Their future was a foreman. Their future was not to go to college. They weren't going to be lawyers and doctors. They were going to be the foreman of that factory and raise a good family and be a regular Baptist. They're the backbone of this county, and you can depend on them. The most workable thing that's in Wilkes County is that Holly Farms chicken business because they hire our

people. Our people are law-abiding, good people. They're really our backbone. We are fortunate to have them. These people that hire them tell you that. The young girls make excellent secretaries, and they're quick in their math. They're good at computers. And we have a work force born in them. *(Annie Winkler)*

I don't think you will see the changes in the next twenty years that you've seen in the past twenty years. I think you will see the areas changing because of the people coming into the area. Twenty years ago most everybody here was local. I think you are going to see a trend where it is going to be fifty-fifty before long, and then I think that you are going to see, especially in the Sylva area, it is going to be hard in the next fifty years to find somebody that is totally native, where both parents are native. I really believe that. It is becoming increasingly harder as a business person to deal with it because of the differences of opinions, different backgrounds. You will have to prove yourself to them because they will not know you that well.
(Reg Moody)

The reason we like to live here is because life is good. The reason people like to come see us is because of that, and if we just go for the quick dollar, it would be destroying the very thing that sustains us. It's important that a person who comes in understands our system that they are dealing with. When we look to the future of what's going to happen in the mountains, we realize that this period we're in right now is important. We are now faced with irreversible decisions that must be made —in cultural affairs and in environmental affairs. Like everything else in the world, technology's speeded up the amount of time we have to make decisions. You make quick decisions that are going to affect everything forever. It's just an awesome responsibility. *(Mr. Jan Davidson)* patch of cane, maybe a row or two of broom corn to make you a few brooms. Well, when you got that planted and got it hoed three times, then you didn't have anything to do 'til gathering time. When you got it gathered in and put up for the winter, you had nothing to do all winter except get a little wood to keep warm: Eat, drink, be merry, and keep warm. Now you've got to work to pay your electric bill; you've got to work to pay a phone bill; you've got to work to pay a gas bill each month; and you've got to work to pay insurance. And if you're making enough right now to pay your insurance and taxes, you do pretty well. You've got to work to get the money to pay it. Back then you had nothing like that to pay. It is a known fact, the more you have, the more you have to work. *(Edd Presnell)*

Junior Johnson

We're having to work more now than we did back in the thirties and forties. You see, back then, come spring of the year you could get your horses up and plow you up three or four acres and plant it in corn. Plant you a couple of bushels of potatoes and a little patch of cabbage, a few beans, maybe a little

I think they'll find new purposes, but I think they'll lose the human values. The thing that's always intrigued me, and I've always hoped was wrong, but it's progress that destroys what we all really stand for, when you get right down to it. You can look at it a thousand different ways, and progress is what destroys your values of life. If somebody comes out and gives you two or three big cars and a lot of money and stuff, you lose the value of what you really stand for. If you had gone out and worked for it and got it through the process of your brain power, manpower, sweat, blood, however you got it, you would appreciate it. But by it being totally given to you, you don't appreciate it. You accept it, and that's it. I don't agree with it, but I see it happening.
(Junior Johnson)

They go out and do their basic thing all day long and run in at suppertime, and if supper ain't on the table, they'll run down the street and get them a Hardee's hamburger, or McDonald's, or something of that nature. And that's pretty tough to take back to my way of a young boy growing up. You went in and if supper wasn't on the table, you either went and got in wood or milked the cows or fed the horses or mules or whatever you were doing to cultivate the land with. You went and did something that was adding to the structure of your livelihood until supper got ready. You didn't just go in and flop down in a chair and sit there and "rear back on your morals" and wait for somebody to bring you something. You went to work, and you found something to do that was an additive to the family. *(Junior Johnson)*

The more you get, the more work you've got to do. And I reckon they call it progress, but everything's just going downhill. What we're into right now, they came through the Stone Age; they passed on through the Iron Age; then they passed on into the Machine Age; come on down to the Atomic Age; and what we're in right now is the Computer/Money Age. That's what we're in right now. Everything's on computer, and we're living in a money-mad world. You can't talk to anybody now very long about what you've done without, "Did you earn any money?" (Edd Presnell)

See, we have a substitute for heat—wood. Of course, I usually get my own wood, but last year the fire department knew I was sick and they came in and cut my wood; and, I've got enough to last me for another year. But what I'm saying is I came up all the time, and I've had to cut my own wood and just use the central heat for backup heat, but never

used it just all the time because it costs you to heat a house year-round if you just use that furnace. I can't see how people make it that work on the job and live out of the store. It's hard to make it. Still hard, but I've always worked hard and made a garden, and we've always canned. We always had plenty of good food. We've got cornmeal in there. We don't buy anything more than we have to. We used to keep pigs. Last year was the first year that I haven't had one. We always get a calf and fatten it out every other year. Last year was the year for me to do it, and I never got one. *(Clifford Casey)*

Holy Trinity Church in Glendale Springs is serving tourists and large groups of tourists who come by tour bus, or people who are driving on the Parkway who stop off to see the beautiful frescos. They are drawn there by that. The very impact that you get is a religious experience. It's a religious home away from home. It's just simply magnificent what Faulton Hodge is doing. But his mission to tourists and to travelers and to people who come in now to see the frescos is a new mission. It's a new legend. It's reaching out to people in urban areas who only feel the impact of the economy, but they go away touched by this experience.

So now we have rural—but I cannot really call it rural—America because I don't think my section of Glendale Springs is dependent upon the grains and forage. I'm not up there enough really to know, but I do not believe that they are dependent upon the agricultural organizations for their life. I think that they have made sort of a small-town atmosphere for their lives because so many of the people who live there are not mountaineers. They are not farmers. There are very few farmers left up there. Those that are there are farming beans for the big market. They are farming Christmas trees. But this is not the old-time farm life. It is definitely not backwoods any longer in that area. When I was a girl growing up, nobody thought about going up to Appalachian to college, and now I am extremely interested that Greensboro has discovered Appalachian State University. Many of our young people are going up there because they get a splen-

Mountain homestead, Alleghany County

did education at Appalachian. Boone is drawing a number of our people. Not only did they discover it because of the skiing, but with transportation being what it is and people being drawn to the mountains and being able to get to the mountains to have the view available to them on the Parkway, they've discovered the schools. The school itself, of course, got its beginning from men who wanted to bring a good, solid education to mountain people. Mr. Dougherty did simply a marvelous job. Now our young people down here in the lowlands are beating a fast track up to Appalachian.
(Emma Sharpe Jeffress)

The mountain universities have gone through different periods of different kinds of attitudes about their own history. The universities have gotten to the point now where they realize that part of the reason they exist here in the mountains is to not only be close to a group of students who may not be able to afford to go far, but also we have a duty to give the people who live here a part of their self-image that they can't get otherwise. At our best, we can help provide some of that sense of who you are. *(Mr. Jan Davidson)*

In our three counties, we justifiably deserve some of being stereotyped, but in trying to bring in industry and create a financial status for our area, knowing the way things are changing today, a technical institute was something that we needed. Before you could offer industry an incentive to come in, you had to train the people that could operate the equipment, the technical aspect of it. No one of our three counties [Mitchell, Avery, or Yancey] was able to do it. So we decided if we could get the county commissioners from the three counties to agree to support it one-third each, we could go with it. And we were able to do that. The technical school is Mayland Technical College, and we get the name from Mitchell, Avery, and Yancey, the first three letters: M-A-Y, Mayland. And we're already out of room. *(Bill Wilkins)*

LASTING VALUES

Clouds over the mountain

One of the things I regret, when I first went to teach in this little school, I was correcting every bit of the colloquialisms. I had red ink all over the papers I would hand back, and I wish that a lot of them I had never corrected. There was a beauty in the native tongue of these people who had been isolated for so long.
(Louise Morgan Rodda)

No part of this nation is too distinct from any other part, really. Because of the television and the magazines and the newspapers and highways and automobiles and the railroads and the airplanes, no longer is one part of the country too different from another part. That's happened, certainly in this section, since the coming of the railroad about the time I was born. There's a lingering feeling of independence, a certain underlying drive on the part of the individual. But the people read the same newspapers and watch the same TV programs, go to the same places and listen to the same radio. All that sameness. I think in a way it's unfortunate. It doesn't leave local color very much. People are too much alike anymore to be interesting. The change in that respect has been so dramatic that it's one of the things that has created such tension in our lives. People don't adjust as fast as science has asked us to adjust. Human beings take a long time to change their nature. We need to maintain certain standards that are as good as they ever were. Certainly in the field of our relations to other people, and morality, there isn't any change. There are still some things that are true and some things that are false. There are some things that are right and some that are wrong, no matter what the circumstances are. *(Bob Phillips)*

People were very intelligent, but had not had the advantages of education and cultural contacts because of the lack of roads in the area. There was not contact with the rest of the world. Of course, I think television is a great evil. It has done a lot to standardize and to give wrong values to people. It seems to me that there is sort of a lack of regard. *(Louise Morgan Rodda)*

I think the radio and TV, plus the influx of—as we used to call them "outsiders" or "foreigners," all have a tendency to make people more uniform. In other words, even in the most remote sections they have TV and radio. So they know what's going on in San Francisco, New York, London, and everyplace else. Their own language tends to change. It becomes more universal. In the early days down on the east coast of North Carolina, and in the mountains, people used a lot of the Old English words and expressions. Gradually it is disappearing because the language becomes more uniform as time goes on. *(Dan Moore)*

We used to build a fire at the top of the hill and sleigh-ride off the side of the mountain. There wouldn't be a car pass for weeks 'cause there was snow on the ground. We'd sleigh-ride every night, build a big fire, 'til your mother or daddy came out to run you home. They weren't bad to do that, though. They knew where you were. The parents would help keep the fire, make coffee, hot choco-late, maybe a little moonshine on the side. It was no different than it is today, only we made a fun thing out of things we had to do, where kids today make it drudgery. Everything we did we'd kind of make a game out of it, even putting up hay, whatever we did. There wasn't any money for anybody to worry about. So I think that was the main difference from what it is today. Everything's money, money today, and back then it wasn't. *(Frank Norris)*

It's a complex world that we live in, a fast pace. There's so many more things to deal with. Life used to be simple. There wasn't near the personal, emotional problems. When I was growing up, we weren't exposed to much that could really mess up your life. We weren't exposed to drugs. Pornography was unheard of. Alcohol, there was some around. Now kids grow up, and they've got to deal with all of this. Whether they get involved or not, they've still got to deal with it. They've got to make decisions, and I really feel for them. (Jonah Parker)

I like this part of the country. I kind of believe that people have gotten away from the basics and the fundamentals of living. Modern society has pretty well enveloped us to where we forget where we started from basically, and from the ground up. I doubt seriously that many of us now could go back to the old ways. We'd probably be dead in six months or a year. We couldn't get acclimated to the fact that we had to cut a living out of the soil and make our own tools and just harden ourselves to live like that. Society has softened us to a point that I think it's almost to a danger point. We need to go back and look at ourselves and see where we came from. In other words, we just need to stop and smell the roses occasionally and be thankful for our heritage. *(Jack Brinkley)*

There are things you've got to give up to accomplish things you want to do and be successful. That's where the mountain people have an advantage over the people in the cities. They do put their spare time and their efforts into what they're doing to accomplish or accumulate. When you learn to make do with what you've got, then you don't rely on a modernized piece of machinery as something to do all your thinking for you and all your work for you. We've certainly lost that in today's lifestyle. *(Junior Johnson)*

The old people are gone. The old breed is gone. There aren't many left. Go look at the tombstones. Even the names were harsh. But the old breed has died out. (Lewis Green)

Bea Sennewald, Bo Bryan, Greg Katz, and Bob Bradley in Smoky Mountains, Swain County

The values, I think, are worth more to us in this particular area. You did things from the heart, not for personal gain. The mountain people are not looking for the almighty dollar. They've learned to survive without it, and they're perfectly happy without it. They don't want to have some of the stuff that the city life offers, and all that people have that comes along with that almighty dollar. So they're willing to sacrifice the dollar for happiness, you might say. It will continue in certain areas. I can see a big change in the younger generation in this area here. We lose a lot of our young people in

my area here now to the city life, Detroit's industry-type city. We're already losing a lot of them to that kind of atmosphere. The only way, I think, we'll be able to save them and keep them in our area is for the industrial-type things to come in to supply jobs. Progress has always been a destroying factor in humanity. Anything you have to sacrifice is a disaster of the future. Once you start destroying things for progress, there's no end to your destiny. *(Junior Johnson)*

My father was the youngest of thirteen children. His father had a leg shot off at Gettysburg when he was in Pickett's Charge during the Civil War. Every one of those children got out of the mountains of Fines Creek in Haywood County. They became lawyers, they became doctors, and they became ministers. And they really did something that in that day indicates that people had to get ahead. Had to go forward and make something out of themselves. I'll say one thing I know about Western North Carolina people. They have a tremendous sense of humor. It's something that's brought them through a lot of problems and travail in their quest for survival. They've lived a very hard life. *(Harold Bennett)*

I was visiting my brother's family in Washington, D.C., one summer. There was a National Folk Festival being held on the mall. A colleague of my brother thought I might be interested in going, as half of it was devoted to the Southern Appalachian Mountains. Friends told me that a moonshiner had been written up in the Washington Post *and that I should go and meet him to try to set up an interview. That Saturday, we decided to go over and wander around. The first thing we did was try to find the moonshine exhibit. It took a while, but we finally spotted the copper still. Lo and behold, there was R. O. Wilson! We were old friends. He asked where I had been and what happened to me, as they hadn't seen me for a while. My brother and niece were amazed. R. O. and I had my niece, Alice, step inside the ropes to pose with him beside the still. Other people "captured the moment" with their cameras, too. My family soon realized that this had become "old home week" as we came upon the Cherokee Exhibit and I ran into Betty Dupree. She is an expert in Cherokee crafts and has been very helpful to me, although we have never yet been able to find the right time to set up a proper interview. We were glad to see each other and exchanged all kinds of news. My family and friends caught the feeling. They asked, "How do you know all of these people?" After having met a few of them themselves, they realized why I had been so happy to work on this for so many years.* (W.M.)

My theory is that you were born to live and not to make a living. Making a living comes secondary. Anybody can make a living. Not everybody can live. And your monetary value doesn't have anything to do with that. (B. Hensley)

The mountains—we possess just a little speck of them. There are people that talk about what they can own and what they can make. You can't make anything. You can take you, me or anybody else and give us all the machines there are in the world, and we can't produce a thing without some of God's given resources. And we can't change that. *(Edd Presnell)*

These mountains have produced a lot of intelligent people. Their success, I believe, has probably been tempered at least, maybe prompted, by the values they learned growing up in these mountains. A day's work for a dollar. A day's work for a day's pay, and be loyal to whoever you're working for or with. Be loyal to your family. I'd love to see people like that who've taken something away from here bring it back. You can't go home again, but if somehow some of those values could be reinstituted. . . (Jim Ryan)

I had a strong temptation one time to move to Greensboro. I was offered a partnership in the old firm of Brooks, McLendon, and Holderness when those three were still there. I went down there. They made me a very good proposition. And I came back, and I looked at Table Rock, and I called up Major McLendon, and I said, "Major, if I had moved when you did, at that age I could have done it, but I just can't leave these mountains. The highest thing I saw in Greensboro was the Jefferson Standard Building, and it's not nearly as pretty as Table Rock." I said, "Besides that, I've been a pall-bearer at funerals at every little churchyard around here, and I just couldn't move." So I stayed. And I guess if I hadn't, I'd probably never have gone to the Senate. I don't know. The North Carolina people have been awfully good to me.

So many people I knew, the good Lord's called them aloft. I was in Washington for twenty years, and I was serving on the State Supreme Court six years before then. So the people that I knew, the old lawyers are gone and the old politicians are

303

gone, which makes you a little sad because . . . this Mississippi writer, [Walker] Percy, wrote in *Lanterns On The Levy*. He speaks of the fact that the graves of our friends thicken along the way if we stay around a long time. And that's happened to me.

I think the young people are better educated now. They're far better educated, and I guess, they've got a good deal of independence, but probably not as much. Public schools tend to make people guilty of conformity. I got my law license in 1919, and I started practicing about three years later. I went back to law school. Most of the lawyers that were then practicing were sort of self-educated, and they were quite individuals. Now, of course, they all go through the same law schools, the same colleges, and they're not as individualistic as they used to be. They were rare characters in those days.

I think this area is continuing to advance, and I think we are doing well economically. One thing, so many of these people came out of the mountains and went into places like Gastonia to work in the textile plants. That's one reason why labor's never been able to organize them very much, because they're too individualistic to be organized and given orders. *(Sam Ervin)*

I think North Carolina's going to do all right. North Carolina's mountains have got the best people on earth, as I found out. **(Sam Ervin)**

Now Jack, he gets into a lot of ways. But the last time I saw him, he was doing fine. *(Ray Hicks)*

Mountain Profiles

The following information should provide a fuller view of all of the voices that have intertwined to form this book. It includes biographical information and photographs of most of the people who participated. Because of space limitations, a few of those listed here have not been quoted directly in the text; however, their contributions toward this project have made all of those listed an integral part of it. The information provided for each individual consists of a date of birth (and when appropriate, date of death); a birthplace and, occasionally, those places where the person was raised and currently lives; and a self-description of what each does (or has done in the past). All locations mentioned are found in North Carolina unless otherwise specified.

ALFRED T. ADAMS
Born 1911; Cove Creek area, Watauga Co., banker.

ANNIE and JOHN AGER
Annie: Born 1950; Fairview; homemaker. **John:** Born 1949; Atlanta, GA; operator, dairy farm; Director, McClure Foundation. **Children:** Eric, born 1974; Kevin, born 1975; Jamie, born 1977; Douglas, born 1980. All live in Fairview, Buncombe Co.

ELSIE and HAROLD K. BENNETT
Elsie: Born 1918–died 1989; Asheville; mother, jack of all trades, "cheap hired help." **Harold:** Born 1914; Mooresville, grew up in Asheville; attorney.

LANEY and LARRY BIXBY
Laney: Born 1937; Savannah, GA; teacher. **Larry:** Born 1931; Chattanooga, TN; Associate Director of the CAP Center, Western Carolina Univ.; President of the North Carolina State Beekeepers Assoc. Both live in Cullowhee.

MOLLIE BLANKENSHIP
Born 1919; Cherokee Reservation; Realty Officer for Bureau of Indian Affairs, Cherokee Indian Reservation; former member of Tribal Council.

MODEEN and ROSCOE BRADLEY
Modeen: Born 1906; Gerton Village, Henderson Co.; school teacher, homemaker. **Roscoe:** Born 1905–died 1989; McDowell Co.; carpenter.

BEN BRIDGERS
Born 1939; McAllister, OK, raised in Fort Smith, AK; attorney, tribal attorney for Eastern Band of Cherokee Indians; lives in Sylva.

JACK BRINKLEY
Born 1929; Haw Creek, Buncombe Co.; Inspector, meat and poultry Inspection Service, NC Dept. of Agriculture; now lives in Asheville.

JESS BROWN
Born 1906–died 1989; Little Canada, Jackson Co.; country store owner: was "trying to put the chain stores out of business."

WADE BROWN
Born 1907; Blowing Rock, Watauga Co., attorney in Boone.

CARRIE and LONNIE BURNETTE
Carrie: Born 1908; Mitchell Co.; Assistant Manager of Inn (The Chalet) Little Switzerland; mother and wife.
Lonnie: Born 1905–died 1987; Mitchell Co.; mining superintendent and farmer.

RUTH and NELSON CABE
Ruth: Born 1926; White Co., GA; former teacher, housewife, factory worker, lunchroom manager. **Nelson:** Born 1918; Macon Co.; farmer, logger, mill worker, and truck driver; retired.

PIERCY CARTER
Born 1900; Democrat, Buncombe Co.; retired attorney; Asheville.

CLIFFORD CASEY
Born 1921–died 1985; Cullowhee; Maintenance Supervisor, Western Carolina Univ.; farrier (blacksmith—shoeing horses).
ANNIE FRANCES CASEY
Born 1928; McDowell Co.; domestic worker.

MARY and GOINGBACK CHILTOSKEY
Mary: Born 1907; Marengo Co., AL; teacher, librarian.
Goingback: Born 1907, Cherokee; teacher, modelmaker, designer and carver, jewelry maker.

LYDA and MARION COFFEY
Lyda: Born 1899; Watauga Co.; farmer's wife and quilter.
Marion: Born 1896; Aho, Watauga Co.; farmer.

MAX COGBURN
Born 1927; Canton; attorney.

HORTON COOPER
Born 1893 (in log cabin)–died 1986; Mitchell Co., between Frank and Minneapolis; teacher, historian, folklorist.

JOHN COOPER
Born 1910; Cranberry, Avery Co.; construction, forestry, maintenance, Grandfather Mountain.

REBECCA COUNCILL
Born 1933; Boone, Watauga Co.; mother, grandmother, civic volunteer worker.

FAYE DANCY
Born 1923; Ashe Co.; Manager, Northwest Trading Post, Glendale Springs.

JOHN ALLEN "JAN" DAVIDSON
Born 1948; Murphy, Cherokee Co.; folklorist, museum curator Mountain Heritage Center, Western Carolina Univ., Cullowhee, musician.

MARGARET SILER D'ONOFRIO (DAISY)
Born 1905; Franklin; food services management and catering (sister of Freda Siler).

JAMES E. DOOLEY
Born 1930; Chattanooga, TN; Vice Chancellor, Western Carolina Univ., Cullowhee.

LOUISA D. DULS
Born 1905; Charlotte (now lives in Rock Hill, SC); teacher, English professor, Winthrop College; author; spent summers from 1911 on in Little Switzerland.

HARRIET "GRANNY" ECHOLS
Born 1896; Murphy, Cherokee Co. (now lives near Otto, Macon Co.); quilter, craftswoman, homemaker.

NELL (left) and WALTER F. EDMISTEN (center)
Nell: Born 1912; Watauga Co.; homemaker.
Walter: Born 1909; Watauga Co.; Wildlife Reserve
Commissioner. **RUBY MICHAEL (right)** Born 1915;
Middlefork Community, Watauga Co.; teacher.

MABEL and HERMAN ESTES
Mabel: Born 1905; Pinola, Avery Co.; mother, homemaker, woodworker.
Herman: Born 1897; Lee Co., KY; woodworker; furniture and cabinet-making instructor; fifth-generation
direct descendant of Daniel Boone. Both reside in
Brasstown, Clay Co.

SAM J. ERVIN, JR.
Born 1896–died 1985; Mor-
ganton; attorney, judge, U. S.
congressman; North Carolina
Supreme Court Justice;
United States senator.

ROSE MARIE FEIMSTER
Born 1932; Statesville;
English instructor, Appa-
lachian State Univ., Boone.

LOLA PAGE and FRANK D. FERGUSON, JR.
Lola: Born 1923; Waynesville; homemaker.
Frank: Born 1908; Waynesville, Haywood Co.;
attorney. Both live in Ox Ear Cove, Haywood Co.

**ORA and WADE
(not pictured) GASS**
Ora: Born 1905–died 1987;
Greens Creek, Jackson Co.;
homemaker. **Wade:** Born
1908; Stoney, Swain Co.;
raised in Whittier; schoolteacher and principal. Their
home is now in Bryson
City; Swain Co.

ELINOR GORHAM
Born 1910; Asheville; grew
up in Atlanta, GA; spent
summers (May–Oct.) in Flat
Rock; homemaker.

REBECCA GRANT
Born 1917–died 1988; Cherokee Indian Reservation
(Qualla Indian Boundary);
craftswoman, basketweaver,
wildcrafter.

LEWIS W. GREEN
Born 1932; Haywood Co.;
writer.

LOTTIE E. GREEN
Born 1905; Watauga Co.;
now resides in Boone;
homemaker.

MAMIE HALL
Born 1884–died 1984;
Buffalo Cove on Elk Creek,
Wilkes Co.; Postmistress of
Gilreath for over 30 years.

B. HENSLEY
Born 1919; Flag Pond, on
Higgins Creek, TN; black-
smith and ornamental
ironworker; Lives in Spruce
Pine at Gillespie Gap.
Living Treasure of N.C.
award recipient 1990.

MIKE HENSLEY
Born 1947; Spruce Pine;
blacksmith.

LETHA HICKS
Born 1913; Big Bend,
Haywood Co.; quilter,
gardener, "piddler" (raises
apples, chickens, dogs and
keeps bees), ginseng
hunter.

RAY and ROSA HICKS
Rosa: Born 1931; Matney (above Valle Crucis),
Watauga Co.; homemaker, grows and sells flowers and
wildflowers. **Ray:** Born 1922; Rominger (on Beech
Mountain), Watauga Co.; farmer, wildcrafter, storyteller, jack-of-all-trades, National Award: Master Traditional Artist, National Heritage Fellowship, 1983 (storytelling).

STANLEY HICKS
Born 1911–died 1989; Rom-
inger, Watauga Co.; farming,
instrument maker (banjos
and dulcimers); National
Award: Master Traditional
Artist; National Heritage
Fellowship, 1983 (craftsman-
ship); Foxfire, September 1983.

**LILLIAN and DOYLE
HOOPER**
Lillian: Born 1915; Patton
Community near Franklin,
Macon Co.; homemaker.
Doyle: Born 1915; Glen-
ville, Jackson.; farmer, main-
tenance worker, High
Hampton Inn.

RUTH and MYRON HOUSTON
Ruth: Born 1914; Spear, Avery Co. **Myron:** Born 1907;
Spear, Avery Co.; country store owners and operators,
Spruce Pine.

**EMMA SHARPE AVERY
JEFFRESS**
Born 1919; Greensboro;
Civic volunteer, wife and
mother.

CARRIE MILLER JOHNSON
Born 1887; Allegheny Co.; homemaker, mother.

JUNIOR JOHNSON
Born 1931; Ingle Hollow, Wilkes Co.; Winston Cup Racing.

LEON JOHNSON
Born 1937; Windy Gap, Wilkes Co.; motel operator; former moonshiner.

LOIS JONES
Born 1906; Langdale, AL; raised in LaGrange, GA; now resides in Franklin; teacher (dramatics and speech); clerk in husband's law office, civic worker, mother.

ETHEL and HAROLD KEENER
Ethel: Born 1947; Cullowhee; homemaker.
Harold: Born 1935; Franklin; drilling and blasting. Both live on Cullowhee Mountain.

CARL LAMBERT
Born 1911–died 1989; Tomotla, Cherokee Indian Reservation; historian Eastern Band of Cherokees.

MONROE LEDFORD
Born 1909–died 1985; Union Community, Macon Co.; farmer, construction worker, crafts man, broommaker.

CAROLYN and JOHNNY R. LEWIS
Carolyn: Born 1941; Montieth Branch, Jackson Co.; home maker and teacher's assistant. **Johnny:** Born 1939; Little Savannah Community, Jackson Co.; farmer and building maintenance.

DANNY R. LEWIS
Born 1963; Sylva, Jackson Co.; married to Caroline Moss; building maintenance.

JOHN LOOKABILL(right)
Born 1918; Grassy Creek, Watauga Co.; farmer.
BRENT WINEBARGER
(left) Born 1976; "in a hospital" in Boone; self-described as being "sixth-generation"; Walter Winebarger's grandson.

310

HETTIE LOVEN (center)
Born 1899; Montezuma; homemaker.
PEARL and GAYTON MARSHALL
Pearl: Born 1904; Montezuma, Avery Co.; school-teacher, homemaker. **Gayton:** Born 1914; Alexander Co. near Taylorsville; construction worker, heavy equipment operator, and road builder. Both live in Montezuma, formerly called Bull Scrape.

BERTHA LOWE
Born 1901; Wilkes Co.; homemaker, mother, gardener, homesteader, orchard and farm owner.

ZORA and EVERETT LYLE
Zora: Born 1900; Wilkes Co.; homemaker.
Everett: Born 1893–died 1983; Ashe Co.; mechanic and store owner.

ANNE and HOWARD MAST, SR.
Anne: Born 1899–died 1987; Valle Crucis; post mistress. **Howard:** Born 1903–died 1982; Valle Crucis; postmaster. Country store owners and operators.

DAN McCOY
Born 1943; Birdtown Community, Cherokee Indian Reservation; self-employed businessman; former member and chairman of the Tribal Council.

MYRTLE (not pictured) and BOB MERRELL
Myrtle: Born 1914; Buncombe Co., lives in Henderson Co.; homemaker, needleworker, quilter.
Bob: Born 1897–died 1984; Gerton Village, Henderson Co.; farmer, carpenter, stonemason.

PHELPS MERRELL
Born 1918; Gerton Village, Henderson Co.; lives in West Palm Beach, FL; art gallery work.

DONAV MESSER
Born 1943; Glenville; teacher (Lillian and Doyle Hooper's daughter).

CHARLES B. MICHAEL
Born 1938; Boone, Watauga Co.; raised in Cool Springs near Beech Mountain; Lieutenant Colonel, U. S. Army.

OLA MILLER
Born 1897–died 1983; Mast, Cove Creek; homemaker, mother, grandmother, great-grandmother.

REGINALD E. MOODY (Reg)
Born 1935; Sylva, Jackson Co., raised in Bryson City, Swain Co.; funeral director and businessman; vice-mayor, town of Dillsboro.

JEANELLE and DAN MOORE
Jeanelle: Born 1911; Pikeville, TN; homemaker, civic worker, former First Lady of North Carolina; presently chairwoman of Keep North Carolina Beautiful.
Dan: Born 1906–died 1986; Asheville, raised in Webster; attorney, former governor of North Carolina, North Carolina Supreme Court justice.

JIM MORTON
Born 1951; Wilmington, now lives in Watauga Co.; photographer, writer, trail designer and blazer, Grandfather Mountain.

CAROLINE A. MOSS
Born 1965; Cullowhee, Jackson Co.; married to Danny Lewis; pharmacist.

GRANNY (IDA E.) MOSS
Born 1901; Erastus (Hamburg Township), Jackson Co.; general store owner and operator in Cullowhee.

JOHN MOSS
Born 1930; Cullowhee; country store operator, teacher (son of Granny Moss).

WANDA and JIMMY MOSS
Wanda: Born 1939; Greens Creek, Jackson Co.; restaurant owner and operator (daughter of Delia and Grady Reed). **Jimmy:** Born 1936; Cullowhee; building contractor (son of Granny Moss).

SUZANNE MOSS
Born 1966; Sylva; Cullowhee, Jackson Co.; college student.

FRANK NORRIS
Born 1922; Boone, Watauga Co.; restaurant and store owner.

HATTIE and HAL OATES
Hattie: Born 1897–died 1989; Liberty, Henderson Co.; homemaker. **Hal:** Born 1897–died 1985; Bat Cave, Henderson Co.; North Carolina State Highway Commission.

SUE OATES
Born 1888–died 1984;
Gerton, Henderson Co.;
homemaker.

THOMAS LEMUEL OATES
Born 1902–died 1983; Bat
Cave (Bear Wallow),
Henderson Co.; native
craftsman.

J.B. and LULA MAE OWENBY
J.B.: Born 1928; Buncombe Co.; self-employed.
Lula Mae: Born 1940; Henderson Co.; homemaker.
Children: Brenda, born 1965; Norma, born 1967; Paula,
born 1969, Missy, born 1970; Ralph, born 1971.

DOUG and JEANNA MOSS PARKER
Jeanna: Born 1962; Cullowhee, Jackson Co.; homemaker
and student. **Doug:** Born 1962; Sylva, Cullowhee area;
Jackson Co.; construction.

**HELEN and JONAH
PARKER**
Helen: Born 1932; Brushy
Mountain, Wilkes Co.; home-
maker. **Jonah:** Born 1927;
Brushy Mountain, Wilkes
Co.; Baptist minister, fruit
grower, orchard owner.

INIS and BOYD PAYNE
Inis: Born 1929; Lower Big
Pine, Madison Co.; home-
maker, farmer's wife.
Boyd: Born 1922; Sodom,
Madison Co.; farmer.

JIM PHILLIPS
Died 1987; Little Canada,
Jackson Co.; country store
owner and operator.

RUTH and BOB PHILLIPS
Ruth: Born 1924; Mitchell Co.; homemaker.
Bob: Born 1902; Bakersville; school administrator,
retired farmer and orchardist.

NETTIE and EDWARD (EDD) PRESNELL
Nettie: Born 1918; Rominger, Watauga Co.; crafts-woman, wood-worker. **Edd:** Born 1916; Rominger, Watauga Co.; craftsman, instrument maker

RAYMOND PRESNELL
Born 1911; Watauga Co., beekeeper.

JACKSON BLAINE RAMSEY, JR. (Jacky)
Born 1970; Buncombe Co. (lives in Madison Co.); grandson of Posey Wilde, Jr.

DELIA and GRADY REED
Delia: Born 1912; Savannah Community, Jackson Co.; homemaker, Sunday School teacher, church worker, gardener. **Grady:** Born 1908; Greens Creek, Jackson Co.; farmer, butcher, coon hunter, hunting dog breeder.

CINDY and LYNDON REED
Cindy: Born 1953; Cullasaja, near Franklin, Macon Co.; salesclerk. **Lyndon:** Born 1946; Greens Creek, Jackson Co.; brick mason. **Children:** Justin, 1983; entertains grand-father Grady Reed. All live in Greens Creek.

CARMA REED
Born 1885–died 1987; Tathums Creek, Jackson Co.; lived in Greens Creek; one-room-schoolteacher, dollmaker (cornhusk dolls) and crafter.

BENNIE REESE
Born 1905; Franklin, Macon Co.; super salesman.

JEAN and LANDON ROBERTS
Jean: Born 1929; Gaston Co.; mother, grandmother. **Landon:** Born 1921; Marshall, Madison Co.; lawyer. Both live in Asheville.

LOUISE MORGAN RODDA
Born 1910; Laurinburg, grew up in western North Carolina, lives in Webster; teacher, high school.

HELEN and DELMER ROSE
Helen: Born 1913; Ashe Co. **Delmer:** Born 1908; Ashe Co. Retired country store owners and operators, Glendale Springs.

JAMES C. RYAN
Born 1929; Sylva, now lives in Glenville, Jackson Co.; park ranger, management assistant for the Blue Ridge Parkway.

RUTH and CLINARD SETTLES
Ruth: Born 1912; McDowell Co., 6 miles west of Old Fort; homemaker and four-leaf-clover collector. **Clinard:** Born 1908–died 1987; Fairview, Buncombe Co.; farmer.

MARY SHELL
Born 1913; Cherokee Reservation, Swain and Jackson Co.; expert in Cherokee Indian finger weaving. Demonstrates this art at the Oconaluftee Indian Village and teaches classes in the off season.

EULALA SHULAR
Born 1930; Caney Fork, Jackson Co.; homemaker, seamstress, quilter, craftswoman in needlework (daughter of Vena and Winton Shular).

VENA and WINTON SHULAR
Vena: Born 1903; Tuckasegee, Jackson Co.; homemaker, quilter, needleworker. **Winton:** Born 1899; Chastains Creek, Caney Fork, Jackson Co.; farmer, logger, woodcutting business.

LENA SHULL
Born 1896; Watauga Co.; homemaker.

FREDA SILER
Born 1908; Franklin; office worker in both government and private industry; craftswoman, specialist in handloom weaving (sister of Margaret Siler D'Onofrio).

315

CYNTHIA SMATHERS and TED WHITE
Cynthia: Born 1951; Dutch Cove, Haywood Co.; banker, bass player, "old-time" mountain musician (Quay Smathers' daughter). **Ted:** Born 1956; Spartanburg, SC; bluegrass musician (bass player), entertainment agent. Both live in Asheville.

QUAY SMATHERS
Born 1913; Dutch Cove, Haywood Co.; builder and carpenter, shaped-note leader, "old-time" mountain musician (guitar).

MAE SMITH
Born 1934; Heaton, Avery Co.; teaching assistant in special education.

ANNIE DEE LEATHERMAN (right) and WALTON R. SMITH (left)
Annie Dee: Born 1916; Franklin, Macon Co.; homemaker. **Walton:** Born 1910; Charlotte; forestry.

DEANNE WINIARSKI (center) Born 1939; New Orleans, LA; raised mainly in Asheville; CPA, Assistant Professor of Accounting, Western Carolina Univ., Cullowhee, (Annie Dee and Walton Smith's daughter).

MABEL BELL and THURMOND SPARKS
Mabel Bell: Born 1917; Wilkes Co.; homemaker, dairy operator, farmer. **Thurmond:** Born 1911; Wilkes Co.; farmer.

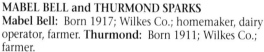

NANNY SUTTLES
Born 1912; Henderson Co.; housekeeper and gardener.

RACHEL and HAROLD SUTTON
Rachel: Born 1940; Greens Creek, Jackson Co.; food service manager for nursing home. **Harold:** Born 1935; Barkers Creek, Jackson Co.; meat market manager. They live in Bryson City, Swain Co.

IVOR VANCE
Born 1902–died 1988; Plum Tree, Avery Co. (was Mitchell Co. then); President of Tarheel Mica Company.

VIRGIE and CAS WALLIN
Virgie: Born 1916–died 1990; Sodum Laurel, Madison Co.; wife. **Cas:** Born 1903; Sodum Laurel, Madison Co.; ballad singer and farmer.

ORA and WILLARD WATSON
Ora: Born 1908; Deep Gap, Watauga Co.; quilter, home maker. **Willard:** Born 1905; Deep Gap, Watauga Co.; woodworker, farmer.

TEXIE WATSON
Born 1910; Stoney Fork, near Deep Gap, Watauga Co.; owner and operator of a produce and fruit (apples) market.

POSEY (JUNIOR) WILDE, JR.
Born 1927; Madison Co.; rock mason and farmer.

KAY and BILL WILKINS
Kay: Born 1920; Plumtree, Avery Co.; teacher and basketball coach, Appalachian square dance choreographer.
Bill: Born 1917; Spruce Pine; V.P. and General Manager (Sales), Deneen Mica Co., now retired. They both live in Plumtree.

CRATIS WILLIAMS
Born 1911–died 1985; Blaine, KY; grew up in Lawrence Co.; educator; Dean of Graduate School, Professor of English, Special Assistant to the Chancellor, Appalachian State Univ., Boone; folklorist.

FLORENCE WILSON
Born 1903–died 1987; Newland; seamstress.

RUTH and R. O. WILSON
Ruth: Born 1934; Cullowhee Mt., Jackson County; home maker, good cook and baker. **R. O.:** Born 1933; Speedwell, Cullowhee; shingle riving (splitting), logging, crafting, demonstrates the art of moonshine making.

WALTER WINEBARGER
Born 1918; Meat Camp
Creek, Watauga Co.; gristmill owner and operator,
farmer.

ANNIE F. WINKLER
Born 1913; Wilkes Co.;
teacher

LULA LOVE WISE
Born 1900–died 1983;
Newland, Avery Co.;
teacher, clothing store
owner and operator.

RUSH WRAY
Born 1911–died 1985;
Wray Villa, Cane River;
grew up in Burnsville,
Yancey Co.; Owner and
Manager, NuWray Inn.

HESTER MARIE WYKLE
Born 1946; Mack Town,
Jackson Co.; helper and
housekeeper.

LILLY WYKLE
Born 1907; Mack Town,
Jackson Co.; mother,
homemaker.

NOT PICTURED

MIKE PHILLIPS
Born 1950; Cow Camp, near
Newland, Avery Co.; designer/
contractor, custom homes.

MICHAEL WHITE
Born 1953; Tryon, Polk Co.,
raised in Cashiers, Jackson
Co.; Assistant to President,
The Cherokees Manufac-
turing Co., and former
teacher.

Acknowledgments

As I sit here looking out over profiles of buildings that form the New York skyline, terraces are coming into bloom with bright flowers and the lush green of plants. Large trees sometimes decorate the tops of buildings and shade roof gardens. The majestic and rhythmical flow of these buildings often reminds me of a mountain landscape. These are urban mountains filled with individuals. The natural ones harbor interesting stories, too; but they are spread out, less densely, over larger territory. This brings to mind all of the wonderful people whom I have met and who have helped me during the evolution of this book. This is a very personal book because it involves people and images, all of which enrich our lives with colorful detail. I am very fortunate to have had so many strong friends who helped and encouraged me throughout this entire project. Because of space limitations, I will only be able to name a few of them. However, they all know who they are, and I hope that they will consider this a thank-you to them as well as to those mentioned here.

First of all, I would like to thank my family: my parents, Rene and Beverly Moore; my brother, Beverly; his wife, Dee; and my two nieces, Caroline and Alice. All were tremendously supportive.

In the mountains, Sandy and Steve Forrest, Jimmy Morton, John and Marie Wright, and Bo Bryan put me up and helped me search out interesting contacts. Jean and Landon Roberts and Elsie and Harold Bennett acted as surrogate parents to me. They were family friends, but they encouraged me because they believed in the value of this undertaking themselves. Wanda and Jimmy Moss have made me feel a part of their family and have always offered any help needed. Many people have become treasured friends and have been so generous. Thank you Jane Franklin Galloway, David Shomaker, Doris Oates, Jim Clarke, Elspie Clarke, Annie and John Ager, Tom and Emma Wertenberger, and Sally Miller.

Ann Hagerty, Dorothy Chapman, Anne Harris, Dianne McConnell, Elizabeth Sloan, Renee Ring and Paul Zofnass, Cece and Lee Black, Russ MacAusland, Ken Davis, Nancy Moore, Ellen and Robert Worth, Sigmund Tannenbaum, Mary and David Eggleston, Winkie and Tim Harr, and Penny and Bruns Grayson constantly lent support and excellent suggestions. Margo and George Miars and Dr. Frank and Margurite Reynolds gave me their love and the use of their beach cottage when I needed it. They and other close friends in Wilmington know that Wrightsville Beach is a second home to me. Large parts of the book were composed there. Oscie and Evan Thomas, Mary Pope and Will Osborne, Jim Fitzgerald, Ray Roberts, Bill Strachen, Fred Chappell, Lewis Green, Linda Smith, Chris Yoahn, and my agent, Fecilia Abadessa, offered invaluable editorial advice and guidance during the course of my work. Marilyn Haft provided wise counsel and enthusiastic impetus throughout the various stages of getting this book published. All of these people have acted as great friends, and I thank them.

In compiling the vast amount of information gathered in a book such as this, the people who work with the nuts and bolts are extremely important. Many typists worked on this. All interviews had to be transcribed, and many drafts of copy were typed. Martha Patterson and Patti Wooten did most of the typing and should be applauded. Particular thanks go to Martha, who helped me organize the material in the very difficult early stages of editing. She even brought her own typewriter and set to work at my dining-room table to get things done. She also encouraged me to stick to the original premise of the book. Both she and Patti had grown to know all of the people from typing the transcripts. They could recognize their voices and had fallen in love with them as I had. I would also like to thank the people at Universal Printing in Greensboro, particularly Frank and Reggie, who made countless copies of transcripts, compiled manuscripts, and painstaking copies of cut and paste versions. Thanks also go to Carolina Camera Center and Camera World in Greensboro. Jonathan Keens at Chromex (Greensboro) deserves a special thank-you for his help.

I would particularly like to thank my editors, Sally McMillan and Leslie Daisey. They both have followed this book over the course of many years, and I will always be indebted to them. They believed in the value of this book and have held my hand in seeing it through. Their comments and editorial help were sensitive and taught me great lessons. Sally has pushed this project through and has been a great support all along as a friend as well as an editor. She deserves a great vote of thanks for her persistence and zest in helping me get this accomplished as well as for her wonderful editorial skills.

My students and their families in Greensboro and New York have been my backbone during this period of research, writing, and the agonies of book publishing. They deserve a great big thank-you, too. In working with my students, my own writing and editorial skills have been enriched and refined. Often many of their comments about copy, chapter titles, and such have been just as astute or even more so than those of many of the "grown-ups" whom I have consulted. I would like to thank Carolyn McNary, my elementary school principal. When I saw her on my return to Greensboro, I was amazed that she recognized me after so many years. She asked if I were still writing poetry as I had when I attended Irving Park Elementary School. I had almost forgotten about that, but she hadn't.

My greatest debt, of course, belongs to all of the wonderful people of the Southern Appalachian Mountains who shared their lives with me and cared enough to offer their interviews, advice on issues that they felt should be addressed in the book, and suggestions of interesting subjects to capture in photographs. They even helped me in the final stages with corrections and clarifications. I hope that they will be pleased with the outcome of our joint efforts. It is also my hope that my book will present a true picture of the area as they see it and serve as a legacy in which they can take pride.

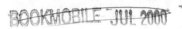